THE
AMERICAN FOUNDING
EXPERIENCE

CHARLES S. HYNEMAN

THE
AMERICAN FOUNDING
EXPERIENCE

*Political Community
and Republican Government*

EDITED BY
CHARLES E. GILBERT

UNIVERSITY OF ILLINOIS PRESS
Urbana and Chicago

Publication of this book was supported by a grant from the Earhart Foundation.

This book is printed on acid-free paper.

Library of Congress Cataloging-in-Publication Data

Hyneman, Charles Shang, 1900–1985
    The American founding experience : political community and
republican government / Charles S. Hyneman ; edited by Charles E.
Gilbert.
        p.   cm.
    Includes bibliographical references and index.
    ISBN 0-252-02053-7 (acid-free paper).—ISBN 0-252-06348-1 (pbk.
: acid-free paper)
    1. United States—Politics and government.   2. Political
participation—United States.   3. Political culture—United States.
4. Citizenship—United States.   I. Gilbert, Charles E., 1927–
II. Title.
JK1726.H96   1994
320.973—dc20   93-4095
                                                      CIP

Contents

Editor's Introduction

CHARLES E. GILBERT

THE CHIEF WORK of Charles Hyneman's last twenty years was the study of the American national founding experience. Of Hyneman's myriad commitments to teaching, research, writing, lecturing, collegiality, and friendship, none but the first (and that just officially) was diminished by his "retirement" at Indiana University in 1970, at age seventy. The study of the founding remained his central research concern. Its first major product was the two-volume *American Political Writing during the Founding Era, 1760–1805,* coedited with Donald S. Lutz and published in 1983.[1] An account of Hyneman's pursuit of the political literature of the founding era appears in the preface to that edition. A few selections from that literature (and from early congressional debates) are printed as appendixes to the present volume to illustrate some aspects of its argument.

American Political Writing was an attempt to "put into print a collection of the best writings of the founding era on the conception and establishment of republican government in America."[2] Building on that project, the present work represents Hyneman's own inquiry into these matters. It extends in new directions his career-long preoccupation with the fundamentals of republican government in America, using the founding experience to identify and illuminate certain issues in self-government both then and now. Hyneman was still working on the manuscript at the time of his death in January 1985. He had by then nearly completed the whole of what was evidently planned, though he may have envisioned a short concluding chapter. Sometime later I undertook to edit the manuscript.

The primary function of this introduction is to connect the book to Hyneman's previous work—to help define it as both a culmination and a departure. Four characterizing comments on the book deserve priority, however. First, since preparation of the manuscript for print pretty much coincided with the celebration of the Republic's bicentennial, which focused on the Constitution, I should declare that this is not another study of the writing or the meaning of the Constitution. It is instead an exploration of certain issues in the building of an American national polity from 1775 to 1800—issues that were raised, pursued, and defined or resolved for the most part by opinion and policy in many places but *not* primarily in the national charter. On the whole, this book has more to do with the national character than with the national charter.

Second, this is an exploration of certain issues and was not intended as a comprehensive account of the founding. Here, as so often in Hyneman's best work, his probing of issues tends to redefine them, and his identification of topics for consideration tends to amend presumptively settled perspectives. Much of the book's originality lies in the author's selection of topics for exploration and in the fresh perspectives that dictated it.

Third, this book was not written for specialists or scholars exclusively, or even primarily. Certainly Charles Hyneman intended it as a contribution to scholarship; and certainly it takes distinctive positions on some disputed issues. But Hyneman also evidently meant it to do so as an extended essay accessible to the general reader. I have added to it more of the usual scholarly apparatus than Hyneman probably planned (more on this later), but the essay can be read with minimal attention to that, reserving it as a source of suggestions for further reading on particular topics.

Finally, this is a political scientist's study, not a historian's, insofar as the fields are distinguishable here. True, it uses history, and it pursues historical investigations through original sources. Its purpose, however, is not so much to tell the story or to settle the record as it is to adumbrate, to illuminate, and most basically to locate on the continuing agenda of American politics certain problems that Charles Hyneman had come to regard as bedrock problems of American politics, beginning with the founding and continuing into today and tomorrow. Readers familiar with Hyneman's intellectual progress will recognize those problems as they appear in this book. For other readers they can best be identified in the light of Hyneman's earlier work.

The central concern of Charles Hyneman's work in political science was popular government—that is, the conditions of effective self-government, or what Hyneman commonly called popular control of government. This was the interest that largely motivated his principal works on American governing institutions, most notably on Congress and the president in relation to the bureaucracy and on the Supreme Court in relation to the elected branches.[3] It had to do not only with democratic theory or with republican forms but also with the modes and reality of popular control and sometimes with the popularness of government—with something like the pervasion of government by popular interests (which was not, however, to endorse an unconsidered or merely tropic response of government to these). Democracy for him, Hyneman wrote in 1968, is

> a political system in which the people have effective means for expressing expectations and preferences and for inducing compliance with their demands. . . . So . . . I shall [sometimes] speak of popular control of government when I am uncertain as to how many people exert influence and when the influence I refer to is either more than control or less than control. People suggest courses of action that their officials might pursue, they induce their officials to move one way rather than another, they press restraints on officials, and they deal out rewards and punishments. Perhaps at most points in this book when I speak of popular control of government I have in mind more of direction-setting than of coercing, rewarding, and punishing.[4]

This concern was populistic in a sense, though it paid little attention to such common doctrinal components of populism as majority-rule theory and the "organizational" or "responsible-party-government" versions of democracy. Some readers therefore thought the approach eccentric or inconsistent, while others simply attributed more usual populist views to Hyneman. Both responses tended to miss what Hyneman was driving at. Insofar as Hyneman's interests were populistic, they were so in his own intellectual way, which was deeply skeptical of, and seemingly immune to, systems, doctrines, and ideologies. In reading Hyneman it is not unusual to be surprised by turns in his argument that seem not to jibe with the system one imagined was motivating it. Typically in such cases Hyneman just was not subject to the system imputed to him and had a less conventional point to make, which a less projective reading would have discovered.

The popularness that was for Hyneman central in democracy is perhaps best expressed in Abraham Lincoln's of, by, and for. It was for Hyneman a highly valued possibility to be explored but not hypostatized or rationalized. As Hyneman's thought evolved, the political character of the populace, by extension from popular control of government, became increasingly a focus of his concern. We can think of this focus as the "political culture," if we leave it free of any particular psychological constructions. And we need to see how it came to play the large part that it does in this book.

In 1968, as he was digging into the project on the founding period, Hyneman published *Popular Government in America,* a discursive consideration of issues in the democratic theory of American politics and a revision and amplification of some of his earlier writings. There he sketched two democratic models, or "demand-response systems," which he termed the group-competition and the equalization-of-influence, or pluralist and populist, conceptions, indicating that for him the latter conception was of central democratic import. Still, as the analysis progressed, there were several concessions to the importance of the pluralist mode of politics—for its function, inter alia, of reflecting tested and substantial (if partial and not necessarily popular) claims or concerns to government. Here Hyneman was dealing with competing perspectives that, as of the time he wrote, dominated American political science; characteristically, he discerned benefits and difficulties in each perspective that partisans of its competitor commonly did not.

Elsewhere in that book he wrote of "the citizen's role" and the various forms it might take, suggesting that while the contributions of a free people to their own governance can be structured "from above" to some extent, they are ultimately diverse, voluntaristic, and pervasive—at least in this nation. The character of the populace, or the political culture, thus became an increasingly critical concern for Hyneman—one heightened by some tendencies he remarked in modern American life.

Hyneman saw clearly enough a central problem of "republicanism": however much government in America is an affair of the people, ideally or really or both, the people will disagree among themselves (not merely with "elites") about the directions government should take. Perhaps democratic politics begins with such disagreement, or perhaps it begins with the more inclusive aspiration for popular control of government. Much of American political science takes popular control as a given and is occupied with the terms of competition over policy. For Hyneman, "popular control" was too important to be taken for granted and was necessarily a matter of degree. He was not uninterested in the terms of competition over policy, but he was more interested in the related question of the *extent* to which what government does is subject to popular influence and informed by popular concerns.

Still, the question of divisions over governmental conduct and policy kept cropping up in *Popular Government in America*. The difficulty for Hyneman was partly, I believe, that popular divisions *might* work at cross-purposes with popular control or with the underlying conditions of popular control. Contests over who gets what might detract from concern for the responsiveness of government in general or from the balance or ballast of shared values and understandings that makes a population a people or a community, thus modulating and enabling the competition of liberal-democratic politics.

Various resolutions of this problem are imaginable. One is an elite leadership, or "elite pluralism," or a sort of managed disagreement at some insulated distance from popular intervention—and such seemed to be the implication of a major tendency within American political science in the 1960s. Another, related, possibility is greater reliance on bureaucracy and judiciary in governing. Clearly, neither of these resolutions was attractive to Charles Hyneman, who leaned toward two others. One of those was "limited government," perhaps especially at the national level—government limited in scope not so much by constitutional provision as by popular and official restraint, thus controlling political overload. Closely related to such restraint, the popular ethos or political culture, along with the structure of society, would have to meet some tests of democratic character, among which mutual respect, political understanding, toleration, and capacity for compromise were prominent in Hyneman's mind.[5]

In one view, this is a bootstrap resolution of the problem of political dissension and overload. In Hyneman's view, people get the kind of government they deserve, and they may well learn to deserve better—or come to deserve worse. To put this view more explicitly, given an appropriate history, what we make of it is a matter not of providence but of responsibility. In the end the people, leaders and others, make the polity.

As Hyneman saw it, the people, leaders and others, can do so in part by appropriate attention to the social requisites of democracy, which he identified broadly as autonomy, equality, and commonalty (or commonality). These, too, are not merely bequests of providence; they can be affected by public policy and by civic—let's say republican—concern and leadership. Writing in 1968, Hyneman saw these three requisites as closely interrelated, each affecting the others. He saw the *autonomy* of interests and persons, the pluralist element, as quite secure in American life, notwithstanding some then-current concerns about its status in a postindustrial world. He saw *equality* in appropriate degree as somewhat more problematic. He was especially concerned then for the success of black Americans' struggle for political equality, and he was also concerned about the implications for commonality of actions on both sides of this struggle.

But it was want of *commonality* that troubled Hyneman most in the American society of the late 1960s. Predictably so in that turbulent period, one might say; but Hyneman was not so topical as that in his diagnosis, nor was he one to be troubled by social turbulence or by trepidations over the future. He was, however, concerned about a longer course of changes in residential patterns, mass communications, and social attitudes that he believed were adverse to commonality and on which he commented at the end of the 1968 book. Most of all, perhaps, he was concerned about disregard and something like contempt for the ordinary person, and for the ordinary person's morality, on the part of intellectual, communicating elites, and about "middle America's" reciprocal attitudes about elites.[6]

This, in outline, is where Charles Hyneman's thinking on the foundations of American democratic government stood in 1968. The focus of his thought was shifting then from the constitutional and institutional conditions of popular government to the social requisites of popular government. While the present work is in part an extension of the 1968 work, it takes a new direction. As Ronald M. Peters (like the editor, a Hyneman student) puts it, Hyneman in the present volume

> moved from the question that had occupied him primarily . . . popular government in America—to a topic that was implicit in it but different from it: what are we as a people? I have no doubt based upon my conversations with him that his concern in the last years of his life was with the problem of virtue, of culture, of a new kind of America that he saw emerging and of which he knew he would not be a part. . . . This book is his way of approaching [this] problem of the American polity through the prism of the founding.[7]

We have here, then, an essay intended less as a contribution to historical knowledge per se than as a selective account of the founding viewed as a particularly instructive stage of a perpetual condition—the (re)making of the American democratic, or republican, polity, considered implicitly in the light of our condition today.

Part 1 of the book deals chiefly with the makeup of the political community that emerged from the founding—that is, with the founding as a set of decisions, deliberate or incidental, about membership of that community and the conditions of full citizenship. Some inhabitants of this land were accorded such citizenship implicitly, others subject to particular and contested policies, still others not at all—either by law or by practice. Certain criteria to qualify citizenship were proposed, reflecting conceptions of political community and personal responsibility in a new nation; but there were also at work the regrettable effects of prejudice and cupidity, together with calculations of "internal security" and electoral politics. While capacity for something like republican or civic *virtue* figured prominently among these criteria, declensions from that standard among the majority tended to motivate certain denials of citizenship and of its reasonable prospect.

The final chapter of Part 1 considers the social dimensions of commonality that prevailed by the last decade of the founding period. Here the argument is that in such matters as common language, literacy, and direct experience of (limited) self-government, the American population in 1790, more nearly than the people of any other Western nation, was a political community appropriate to self-government. Beyond such common capacities and practices, Hyneman suggests, something like common understandings of republican character, or virtue, may well have been requisite to the success of full-fledged self-government. The focus of discussion thus begins to shift from issues of the composition of the political community in Part 1 to issues in the central, theoretical tenets of republicanism in Part 2.

With this shift in focus goes a change in the nature of the historical evidence. More of the discussion is based on documents or statements from the political actors of the time: the early constitutions; the legislative debates; and, especially pertaining to central concerns of republicanism, the political literature that Hyneman had identified in working on *American Political Writing*. The nature of these primary materials is basic to the analysis. As Hyneman notes, he is dealing by and large with the products of leaders—of elites; and the extent to which this was representative of opinion in general is necessarily uncertain. Moreover, much of the individual writing that figures in the discussion was selected by Hyneman for the quality of its thought about self-government; and evidence of some sophisticated concern for institutional and civic responsibility could have figured in his selection of it. Late in the founding period, as party divisions deepen, these concerns from Federalist New England sometimes seem tendentious and conservative, but it helps when we can read them within the broader traditions of Puritan and republican political analysis.

The three central elements of republican political theory for Hyneman were liberty, equality, and virtue (compare Hyneman's earlier autonomy, equality, and commonality). One dimension of the inquiry of Part 2 concerns the meanings of these terms at the time—that is, their prevalent meanings, since there certainly was variation. Hyneman provides some new perspectives and interpretations, especially with respect to virtue. A second dimension concerns certain tensions and divisions in the new federal Republic between putative republican rights to organized dissent, protest, and resistance, on the one hand, and the claims of republican order, law, and common good, on the other. One sees in Hyneman's account that these tensions and divisions sometimes implicated different understandings of liberty and equality. Hyneman's primary focus, however, is on the republican hope that virtue could mitigate factional divisions—that conceptions of liberty and equality would usefully be tempered by common understandings of virtue. For Hyneman the regard for virtue was at least provisionally critical, sustaining the civic enterprise as a balance of autonomy and commonality and contributing substance to commonality or community as well as personal discipline to liberty or autonomy. The underlying concerns of Part 1 with responsible citizenship and political community thus continue in Part 2, though in somewhat different terms.

The argument in general needs no further exegesis here, except for comment on one unusual aspect of it in Part 2: Hyneman's consideration of the Alien and Sedition Laws, which extends an analysis he had published earlier.[8] Here the noteworthy feature is not so much the departure from received interpretations of this episode as the attention given to the episode's setting in the problems of a decade-old polity not yet used to the practices of organized electoral competition/opposition, facing arguably just such external and factional dangers as had been invoked forensically to support adoption of the new national Constitution and, as to the legislation itself, deeply divided over understandings of its common-law and constitutional status. Did the policies of the government resolve the claims of liberty and those of community in a new polity prudently? Has history evaluated both the policies and the actions of their opponents with due contextual sensitivity? Certainly Hyneman's view of these events is a minority view today; but arguably, by the republican standards of the founding period, if the policy of the government was in part repressive, the conduct of the opposition was also at times irresponsible. In probable fact, the republican standards of the day were ambivalent regarding the claims of liberty and community. The claims of virtue lost out to those of partisanship, perhaps on both sides of the issue.

In part, as has already been suggested, Hyneman was looking for clues to the future of American popular government in the conditions of the founding. In particular, he was looking for clues to attributes of political culture and community that would help support self-government. He appears to have looked to the founding period as a somewhat simpler time than ours. It is simplified at least in our perception by its distance from today, and it was certainly simpler in the functional tasks of government and in the range of political interests attending these. It was not, however, necessarily simpler in the task of establishing and sustaining public authority or "domestic Tranquility." Contemplating that period now, we can see that certain perdurable tensions in American politics were probably shaped by particular beliefs and disagreements then over ends and means of political association. For instance, the particular rhetoric of commitments to individual liberty and popular sovereignty, established in the revolutionary era, may still intensify perennial tensions of liberty and authority in American life—perhaps the more so without the moderating contributions that were expected of virtue in the founding period. Moreover, Hyneman came to believe that the founding emphasis on virtue, which largely "lost its virtue" in later years, was well conceived for the preservation and improvement of self-government, though he did not suppose that the founding virtue could simply be rehabilitated.

Hyneman certainly was not reverting to presumptive eternal verities in revisiting the founding. Instead, and characteristically, he was challenging received interpretations and opening new lines of inquiry; and he was doing so as much through his selection of certain topics and issues for consideration as by the substance of the considerations. His argument in this book is thus largely an agenda for the attention of others—citizens, political leaders, and scholars—as a different perspective on both the founding two centuries ago and the improvement of popular American politics today.

The manuscript of this book was complete in its substance at the time of Charles Hyneman's death. My subsequent editing of it entailed four principal tasks:

1. I expanded the conventional scholarly apparatus. Hyneman's citations were minimal, probably in keeping with his essayistic intent, though he might have meant to extend them later. I thought readers were likely to want more documentation of controversial statements, as well as contex

tual references. It was Charles Hyneman's way to work things out for himself, from the ground up, and this book is built far more on the primary sources of its period and on specialized secondary literatures than its citations may now suggest. Hyneman would have organized the reference material more authentically than I have been able to do.

2. I provided the kind of final editing of advanced draft that the manuscript seemed to need. Mainly, this meant getting inside the argument and reaching back to its origins to refine the work's organization editorially. I fixed the structure of the present table of contents, most of which was implicitly there, did the kinds of marginal moving around of statements within that structure, and made the kinds of decisions for or against redundancy that must normally be done in the late stages of composing a book. I gave particular attention to the beginnings and ends of chapters, augmenting these in general to try to structure the argument more strongly.

3. I wrote a concluding chapter to consolidate the message of the book.

4. A few sections of the manuscript were less advanced than the bulk of it was. I thought some of these called for more or less substantial revision. I provided this chiefly in the introductory chapter (to amplify somewhat the manuscript's historical prelude) and in chapters 7–9, where it seemed appropriate to elaborate the analysis. From these efforts there arises some risk of divergence from Hyneman's intent, but I think it is accurate to say that in extending and deepening arguments and adducing new material to support them, I have not added or eliminated any distinct arguments or dimensions of argument. There is, however, almost certainly some compromise of Hyneman's prose style; I did not labor to emulate it closely, for I have always thought it strictly inimitable. I *did* think I knew pretty well how Charles Hyneman would have augmented his arguments in substance if he had concluded, as I did, that this would improve the book.

Nevertheless, I also supposed that I might here and there have drifted too far off line from Hyneman's original intentions and message. So I asked three political scientists who, like me, were students and friends of Hyneman to review my revision against the manuscript Hyneman left, both in general and with special attention to the issue of fidelity. Lawrence J. R. Herson of Ohio State University, Ross Lence of the University of Houston, and Ronald M. Peters, Jr., of the University of Oklahoma performed this office thoroughly and thoughtfully. In every sense of the word, they have had a critical part in the production of this book. Because I have not adopted all their advice (and they disagreed in some of it), they are in this formal and usual prefatory sense relieved of editorial responsibility, but I am deeply grateful to them, and the book is immensely the better for their efforts. I am also indebted to George Carey of Georgetown University and Howard Penniman of the American Enterprise Institute for counsel, encouragement, and practical assistance and to David G. Smith of Swarthmore College and an anonymous reader for the University of Illinois Press for critical comment that helped a lot. Finally, editing at the University of Illinois Press by Jane Mohraz improved the work (my work in particular) greatly and set me at the end an example of strictly excellent editing.

These things gladly said, this remains Charles Hyneman's book. If (in the language of hi-fi) it has taken on a little alien coloration in some passages, it still approximates, I think, the energy and sensitivity its author would have given it had he lived to revise it further, and it has all the information of the original.

Notes

1. Charles S. Hyneman and Donald S. Lutz, eds., *American Political Writing during the Founding Era, 1760–1805* (Indianapolis: Liberty Press, 1983).

2. Ibid., pp. xii-xiii.

3. Charles S. Hyneman, *Bureaucracy in a Democracy* (New York: Harper and Row, 1950); Charles S. Hyneman, *The Supreme Court on Trial* (New York: Atherton Press, 1963).

4. Charles S. Hyneman, with the collaboration of Charles E. Gilbert, *Popular Government in America* (New York: Atherton Press, 1968), pp. 4–5.

5. Ibid., esp. chaps. 1, 17.

6. Ibid., chap. 17.

7. Ronald M. Peters to the editor, 9 January 1987.

8. Hyneman, *Popular Government in America*, chap. 13. See also Charles S. Hyneman, "Free Speech: At What Price?," *American Political Science Review* 56 (1962): 847–52.

THE
AMERICAN FOUNDING
EXPERIENCE

1

The Challenge of Self-government

THERE IS NORMALLY no distinct beginning in the flux of events that
produce a nation and fashion its basic institutions. There are, however,
critical eras in national histories—conjunctures when change runs at a
rapid pace, when problematic tendencies become prevalent and disparate
tendencies come together, when contrasts between what was and what is
become remarkable and stand apart in memory. Of such times we say that
history took a turn, that a new era dawned—or that a revolution occurred,
whether or not the civil and social orders were drastically disrupted.

Such was the state of affairs in North America late in the eighteenth
century. This was a time of both national beginning and institutional
creation. A scattered population—one almost exploding in growth while
both expanding and consolidating in location; one tolerably similar, if still
diverse, in European provenance but territorially disparate in culture and
economy—was launched on a path to nationhood. That departure entailed
defining a polity, redesigning governmental institutions, and learning to
make them work. True, there could be applied to these tasks the long and
largely autonomous civil experience of the North Americans, as well as
English principles of public law and republican government no less old, if
then conspicuously less continuous than American traditions. The tasks of
that time were immense, however, and that time has appropriately been
termed the founding period.

To bound this founding period precisely by dates may be to invite error
and misunderstanding. But there will be occasions in this book for charac-
terization of the period as a whole, so it should be said that the founding
experience contemplated here occurred in the quarter-century 1775–1800

or 1776–1801. Some other commensurate span of years, such as 1763–88, may better suit students of the American Revolution, especially when it is studied as a problem in British imperial or federal relations, or students of the Constitution, especially when it is construed as resolving that federal problem. Dealing in quarter-centuries is not essential, but in this case that interval comprehends the critical structuring decisions of self-government and nationhood and also the human maturities of many critical participants in those decisions. It is the establishment of full-scale self-government in the American states and nation with which this inquiry is concerned— transcending, even if partly reflecting, the practice of local or community self-government in the regions where that prevailed. If this founding experience has no distinct beginning or end, there is nevertheless a strong case for considering it when the basic lines of governmental institutions were laid down and when establishment of the national institutions was confirmed in decision, in administration, and in successful transitions between organized contenders for control of these.

The Colonial Tradition of Self-government

The founding period is etched in our minds as a time of separation from empire and creation of a new kind of government. By the end of the eighteenth century America, though its new Constitution had been tested for only a decade, furnished the Old World a generic, even generative, exhibit of republican government—one characterized in crisis some seventy-five years later as government of the people, by the people, and for the people. The political handiwork of 1776–89, moreover, gave lasting form to a particular American conception of the structure of republican government. Yet the North Americans had not imagined or mastered self-government in just a dozen years or even in a quarter-century of devising and constructing new institutions. Government by electorally responsible people, if not by *the* people, was a reality or a close approximation to reality for most (white) men in most colonies, and perhaps especially in their localities, long before the break with Britain.

New Englanders, with their town meetings, broadly elected legislative assemblies, and variously encumbered governors, may, within the social composition and political conventions of that day, have lived under regimes more effectively popular than those of their local descendants two centuries later. Neither New Yorkers nor southern colonists could look to a like diffusion of rule in contemplating independence. Nor could many southerners claim after ten or twenty years of statehood, considering the dominance of vestry, planter families, and county court in public affairs, that they had attained a level of popular control over government, especially local government, that New Englanders had known for at least half a century. Still, the best evidence now available indicates that in most, perhaps all the colonies, majorities of adult males—bare majorities in some and much larger ones in some others—were eligible to elect their legislatures well before the Revolution and the founding period. While the revolutionary state constitutions liberalized these arrangements a little here and there, they mainly continued or marginally extended colonial provisions for voting.[1] In this particular respect the experience of self-government was inherited by everyone alive in the founding period from one or more previous generations.

Yet voting alone, in open elections, is hardly the whole of self-government. If we are to make sense of the founding as a seminal exercise in self-government, we have to try to understand the status of self-government in America as that exercise began. Understanding where the American practice of popular government stood on the eve of the founding—and pretty much throughout the eighteenth century—helps us to know how far the work of the founding period established self-government in the states and nation, as distinct from confirming and more particularly structuring self-government.[2] We therefore need to notice five other aspects of American self-government in the eighteenth century: (1) home rule, (2) participation, (3) representation, (4) the societal context, and (5) political consciousness and doctrine.

Insofar as self-government means *home rule,* or the substantial reality of collective self-determination, there is ample evidence for such a "colonial" reality long before the irritations and tensions, beginning about 1763, that precipitated a declaration of independence. Most politically conscious colonials continued to value their British connection both tangibly and traditionally, yet they experienced colonial home rule progressively as colonial governments pursued it aggressively. Such rule was more than normally unobtrusive tutelage and taxation from London; it was the usually effective disposition by colonial legislatures and local governing institutions of the public business that most concerned most people. However much this state of affairs was challenged and changed by London after 1763, and whether or not the colonial reaction was excessive, something close to home rule, or to responsible government in the full meaning of that term, had nevertheless become increasingly the common expectation of Americans.[3] This we can conclude notwithstanding that royal governors retained a rough parity of strength with most colonial legislatures and that certain kinds of colonial legislation were regularly rejected in England.

Who, then, was self-governing, and how was this process organized? The "who," we may say, has to do with participation, and the "how" with representation. As for *participation* in elections to the colonial legislatures, the historian Bernard Bailyn tells us that

> it seems safe to say that fifty to seventy-five per cent of the adult male white population was entitled to vote—far more than could do so in England, and far more too, it appears, than wished to do so in the colonies themselves. Apathy in elections was common, in part because of the physical difficulty of travel to polling places; in part because of the lack of real alternatives in a society dominated by the sense that the natural leaders of society should be the political leaders; in part because of the lack, in certain periods and places, of issues that seemed properly determinable at the polls. But however neglected, the wide-open franchise was potentially a powerful weapon, certain to work against the ability of executives to control elections. . . .[4]

It was not uncommon for remote civil divisions to let their legislative representation go by default rather than bear the cost and inconvenience of it. This was another face of the apportionment issue that figured in the politics of some colonies. On the other hand, it appears that suffrage restrictions were frequently unenforced by sheriffs or other election officials, thus effectively enlarging the electorate—for the property qualification was chiefly considered a test of responsibility in the sense of personal autonomy, which might in many communities be recognized more substantively and individually than it was by the metric of property. And we also know that although electoral apathy was a common, perhaps the normal, condition, electoral activity was intense and electoral turnout heavy on occasion.[5] These generalizations apply to the colonial legislatures. As for participation in *local* self-government, practices varied widely from one colony to another.

Beyond basic electoral opportunity, it is hard to say how, in general, legislative *representation* functioned in eighteenth-century America—how far in its effects it rendered colonial government either responsively popular or periodically accountable. Several relevant points now seem pretty well established, however. Representation was expected to comprehend particular constituencies and even concrete interests instead of the ideal and "virtual" concerns that figured in more conservative British traditions. During the eighteenth century, moreover, there was a notable growth of political factions and contending interests in legislative life—though this emergent political pluralism was not then generally considered either beneficent or even wholly legitimate. In any case it apparently did not lead to much organized "lobbying" or regular two-way communication between legislators and constituents during legislative sessions. Accountability and consent were registered in elections, and constituencies (local governing units) sometimes issued specific instructions to their colonial legislators at election time. Elections were often sufficiently competitive, or at least contingently so, to lend a sanction to electoral accountability. This competition sometimes engaged family, social, or economic factions and tendencies; but these were rarely organized or extensive enough to qualify as "parties," which were not regarded as appropriate anyway. Finally, colonial legislatures were strong enough in the operative eighteenth-century structure of colonial politics to render representation effective.[6]

Conceivably, however, and regardless of the extent of popular participation, the *social context* of colonial politics was too traditionally deferential, too aristocratic or otherwise stratified, for self-government to amount to more than a remotely accountable oligarchy most of the time.[7] It has been argued that this social context became in some nontraditional respects more stratified and interest-aligned during the generation or so before the founding period, reflecting both urbanization and growing scarcities of agricultural land in some localities, perhaps compounded by the pattern of imperial regulation after 1763; and that "the colonial aristocracy, as it took form during the Eighteenth Century, owed a good deal to close association with government," through the evolution and articulation of political families.[8]

We can readily concede that American society was more traditionally aristocratic, by and large, in the first three-quarters of the eighteenth century than in most of the founding period and the nineteenth century, and even that it was tending in some respects away from equality during the former period. Yet it must also be conceded that this society was one of *comparative* simplicity and parity straight through the eighteenth century, according to European standards of the day; that its growing social complexity was associated with some secularization and pluralization of politics beside engendering serious democratic counterpressures; and that "without the rise of . . . a colonial aristocracy there could have been no successful movement against England."9 Still, I believe one would go too far in conceding that the rather stratified structure and culture of eighteenth-century American politics effectively restricted the experience of self-government to an aristocratic few or meant that self-government simply did not arrive for most Americans before the founding period. This is so even if we understand the American Revolution as more than colonial—as part of a secular shift in the structure of society and public authority pretty much throughout the Western world in the latter half of the eighteenth century.10

Finally, in the American experience of self-government, there is the aspect of *political consciousness and doctrine*—of people's conceptions of authority, consent, and obligation; of their understandings of what self-government promised and how it should be practiced. Our modern historical knowledge runs to the effect that such conceptions and understandings began to alter epochally over the dozen years of serious imperial discord before the Revolution (or even perhaps as early as midcentury), most notably as the founding period began, and continued to alter throughout the founding period.11 As historians have increasingly discovered during the last quarter-century, basic conceptions and expectations of self-government were subject to drastic change, beginning shortly before the founding period and continuing throughout it. For the most part, these changes apparently stemmed from the imperial controversy over the limits of colonial self-government and colonial rights to parliamentary representation that issued ultimately in revolution. They probably also stemmed to some extent from cumulative social changes in the latter half of the eighteenth century: economic (especially commercial) development, stimulated by the French and Indian War; rapid (natural) population growth and movement, together with new streams of immigration, most notably from northern Britain; and the liberalization and individualization of religious outlooks that came with the Great Awakening. All these trends made for greater social and economic differentiation, uncertainty, and (probably) domestic as well as imperial tension.

Through some three-quarters of the eighteenth century the colonists' practice and understanding of their somewhat circumscribed self-government was largely Whiggish—more accepting of established leadership and traditional collective interests than radically democratic.12 The Revolution and its preliminaries marked a watershed in political understanding. One aspect of it was a rapid American reception of English "Old Whig" political thinking based in seventeenth-century, civil-war republicanism. Much of the language and outlook of this "left" republicanism was shared with a larger, longer republican tradition, which figures in chapter 9 of this book. The Old Whig tradition, however, was especially libertarian and chronically oppositionist; in opposing the liberties of "the people" to the probable corruptions of government, its language, at least, was populistic.

A second, more general aspect of the shift in political vision was that the legitimacy of government and the agency of self-government came to be regarded in a new light. Increasingly government was to be justified by what it contributed to human well-being, beyond the basic maintenance of order. Consent began to mean more than agreement on the outlines of a political regime (or the mere forbearance from revolution) and more than periodic election of legislators or magistrates; it extended not only to the administrations of the day but sometimes, through petitions and instructions, to particulars of their policies and conduct. These perspectives probably gained ground gradually in eighteenth-century America through the dynamics of colonial self-government and later influence of Radical and Utilitarian literature from England and Scotland. Still later the Revolution was a critical impetus to their acceptance.[13]

Finally, in the course of the founding period, and out of the practical experience of augmented self-government in the new states, the reality of popular politics began to be regarded as inevitably or even appropriately pluralistic and "interested," not simply a matter of the people versus the rulers or of government as guarantor of an undifferentiated liberty and public good. The founding period then became a time for working out institutional conditions and practical implications of a politics more "modern" in conception than the politics of colonial America. In this sense, as in the preceding two, the founding period was a time of transition to a new age. James Madison's statement of the problems and prospects of popular politics in his well-known *Federalist No. 10* appears to straddle a divide, looking both backward and forward in political understanding.

Sometimes this interpretation makes it appear that contest and interest had almost no place in colonial politics, though this probably was not so. Sometimes it appears that basic understandings of politics altered radically overnight around 1776—that is, within a decade or less, though this seems an improbably drastic conversion to have occurred to numerous experienced practitioners of politics. Perhaps the magnitude, pace, and distribution of change in political understandings throughout the founding period cannot be established historiographically. It makes sense to suppose that such change was deeply influenced by the course of extraordinary events and institutional development: the altercation with England; the Declaration of Independence; the Revolutionary War; the experience of full political responsibility in the states; and the management of a new national polity. It is pretty clear that the founding period *was* a time in which the implications of new understandings of politics were worked out in practice and elaborated in theory—sometimes self-consciously so: *novus ordo seclorum*. Yet conceivably the extent of the conceptual break with the past has been somewhat overstated lately.

I have been arguing that American self-government was not per se a product of the founding period—that the constitution-writing and related basic policy departures of that period probably presupposed a considerable prior experience of self-government; that the decisions and initiatives of the founding gave a peculiar and durable American form to self-government but did not strictly establish it. The more abrupt the break with colonial politics, the more the work of the founding may rightly be held to have *established* popular government. I think the mutation of political consciousness and doctrine can hardly have been so sudden and so complete as to occlude all that went before. But I am also persuaded that perceptions and understandings of politics were shifting with special rapidity on the eve of and throughout the founding period. I believe this must have been a special and threatening challenge for the founding, for it meant that in possibly fundamental respects the terms of political legitimacy were shifting and unsettled. I suppose it was a special help in such circumstances that a pragmatic legacy of experience in self-government was generally available, though this was not clearly, and perhaps not nearly, enough to warrant the success or survival of self-government in America after the Revolution. And this was at the least no less evident to many responsible Americans then than it is now.

Full-scale Self-government:
New Regimes and a National Community

There remained much to be learned and determined in the founding period. Independence and full-fledged nationhood must have made a large difference and raised basic issues—issues not evident earlier under the British imperial umbrella and in the absence of ultimate local responsibility. With independence, questions about the constituents of nationhood and the conditions of self-government became unavoidable. This was especially so after national consolidation under the Constitution raised the stakes and complicated the issues of politics. These questions were partly addressed and resolved in the course of the constitution-writing for the states and nation that was itself a notable American contribution to the theory and practice of self-government.[14] Not all such relevant questions were so disposed of, however. Some critical aspects of defining a polity and fixing conditions of workable popular government were settled by regular legislation, either prior to the constitutions or, in part, as matters of constitutional interpretation. Still others—issues of theory and policy not necessarily appropriate for legislation—are to be found in the political literature and debates of the time, not in the constitutions or statute books.

There were, then, still fundamental tasks to be accomplished as colonial status was transformed into nationhood, notwithstanding stubborn progress by the colonists toward control of their governments. First, there was an apparent need for an authenticating statement about where the power to govern lay within the polity and within the population. Second, various unsatisfactory colonial relationships, and new postcolonial lacunae, among departments of government and between officeholders and citizens needed correction and fresh disposition. Indeed, as we can see now (though it was not so apparent then), some new understandings of governmental structure were needed. Third, it must have been obvious to nearly everyone that separation from a mother country was a propitious moment for making pronouncements about the proper exercise of governmental power and the rights of individuals, and the movement toward independence had contributed a strong impetus to do so. Fourth, after the first wave of state constitution-writing and in a growing void left by the Revolution, a movement toward a second, revisionary essay at defining and ordering a national (or federal) polity developed.

These issues were mostly confronted and in various measure resolved in an unprecedented endeavor to produce written constitutions during the years 1776–89. Almost certainly, the constitution-writing experience in itself contributed to the character of American politics over the long run—perhaps especially to a perception that popular sovereignty and fundamental law go together pragmatically, whatever their alleged theoretical inconsistencies. In retrospect, the experience dominates the first half of the founding period, and it figures prominently in the following pages—but chiefly as the setting of certain issues and decisions rather than in its plenary structuring function.[15] The story of the constitution-writing experience has been told and analyzed many times.[16] The closely related concerns to be explored here—those about defining the polity and adapting self-government to new democratic pressures—have had much less attention, though they are of similar foundational significance.

Anterior to the constitution-writing, and by 1775 perhaps as prevalent as the ambition for self-government, was a growing sense of American identity.[17] Conceptions of a common America were well advanced before the colonies declared themselves independent of England and fought a grueling war to prove it—though the war did strengthen American identity. Indeed, the opening sentence of the Declaration of Independence informed everyone that the rebellious North Americans were one people bent on winning for themselves the separate and equal station that attends full membership in the world's family of nations.[18] The notion that union and nationhood already existed, subject only to recognition by others, was, however, probably wishful thinking as well as a bid for assistance from others in the prospective war with England. Nevertheless, more than a century's colonial experience had by then revealed sufficient evidence of common character and purpose to justify Abraham Lincoln's statement some eighty-five years later that the Union is older than the states—though not enough evidence to relieve this assertion of controversy.[19]

During most of the colonial period, and for a full century before the Revolution, British colonial policy, rudimentary as it was, had treated the American possessions (including those in Canada and the West Indies) as a single overseas empire. This policy provided for broadly similar governing institutions in all the colonies, especially in those beside the four proprietary colonies, and for metropolitan review and contingent veto of American governmental practices. It also emphasized primary economic differences among the colonies as complementary elements of an integral program for national enrichment. Yet British oversight of American governmental action was poorly enforced and perhaps impossible to enforce effectively across the Atlantic. The economic policies were undermined in turn by the refractory self-governing aspect of colonial institutions—all the more so as Britain pursued a more centralized, imperial policy after 1763. When colonial delegates had met at Albany in 1754 to consider a plan of limited union, largely for mutual defense, neither the colonial governments nor the British government found such a plan acceptable; but at least Benjamin Franklin, its principal author, and some other leaders could perceive the long-run logic of colonial federation.[20]

Twenty years later, after a decade of wrangling with England over colonial policy, the movement for a Continental Congress began as if by spontaneous combustion. Sam Adams had suggested such an organization late in 1773. We do not know whether he managed to inspire the call for a congress by Virginia's defiant burgesses early in June 1774, in response to news of Britain's closing the Port of Boston after the Tea Party there. We do know that both the Massachusetts and Connecticut legislatures conceived the same suggestion almost simultaneously and that within three months all American colonies except Georgia—the youngest, most remote, and least populous—had answered Virginia's correspondence with delegates to the First Continental Congress that convened on 5 September. News of Concord and Lexington the following spring overturned the royal order in Georgia, which was represented in the Second Continental Congress when it convened in the fall of 1775.

It is hard to say how much these developments reflected aspirations for nationhood and how much they stemmed from recognition that the punishment or oppression planned for Massachusetts threatened the interests of all the separate colonies. Probably the fervor of the common response to the Intolerable Acts, following a decade of recurrent acrimony and crisis, is evidence of the community of sentiment as well as the commonality of interest. Perhaps by midcentury, and almost certainly by 1763, perceptions of both a common interest and a national identity were strong enough, particularly among "elites," to prevail over colonial divisions, once they were crystallized by the differences with Britain that began in 1763. Within a decade after that, Englishmen acquainted with the colonies were warning their government that the Boston Port Bill and the subsequent Intolerable Acts might well result in colonial concert against them. They had no pressing reason, however, to estimate whether this concert could long sustain a nation-state.

Moreover, nationhood in the sense of geographical identity, with the hope of its fuller recognition within the British empire, was one thing, but independence was another. The Declaration of 1776 was certainly not inevitable in the summer of 1774. If political thinking in the colonies had altered remarkably in the decade up to 1774, it still had, by and large, to contemplate in practical terms the novel problems and uncertain prospects of autonomous nationhood.

Probably more Americans at that time had mooted something like what we now know as dominion status than had seriously considered independence. How, then, could separation occur within two years? For many Americans it did not, at least not irrevocably and immediately. For a majority of the Third Continental Congress—at first a bare, then a large, and finally a lopsided majority—it did though. The majority included most of those members acting with authorization or even instruction from their state legislatures or revolutionary conventions. Explanations of this change of perspective are in the Declaration of Independence itself. Perhaps the movement toward the Declaration is best explained by the failure of what colonial leaders believed was the constitutional process of petition for the restoration of rights and by the effects of more than a year of bitter warfare.[21] Yet it seems significant that, in several states, leaders of the movement for independence questioned the right of anyone to adopt a constitution or to declare colonial transformation into statehood until specifically authorized to do so by the Congress acting for the colony-states altogether.[22]

Successive sessions of the Continental Congress sat in Philadelphia for fifteen years (except when forced by exigencies of war to meet elsewhere), produced and proclaimed the Declaration of Independence, financed and directed the war for separation, concluded a treaty of peace with England, drafted the Articles of Confederation that gave prospectively stable form to the national polity, and at last secured their adoption. The final significant acts of this continuing and evolving representative assembly included a call for the convention that met in Philadelphia during the summer of 1787; submission of the document produced by that convention to the thirteen state legislatures, with a recommendation that each of them submit it in turn to state conventions of elected delegates; and an ultimate resolution declaring the new Constitution duly adopted and fixing specific dates and provisions for the new constitutional process of electing a president.

Establishing the Power to Govern

Predictably in this time and context, the regulation and disposition of land was a major concern of the Congress, both directly and as incidental to nearly everything it did. Ratification of the Articles of Confederation was long delayed by conflicts among the states over claims to the western lands, which in the end passed to the national government. States' obligations for financial support of this national government were based on their acreage of improved lands. Probably Congress's most important domestic acts were the formulation of policies for surveying and settling the western lands and transforming those lands and their populations into states eventually.

Lands and populations are rudimentary elements of states and nations, giving rise to issues of territorial configuration and the makeup of political community. The fixed relationships, ways of doing things, realizable expectations, and habituated behaviors we call government are inseparable from the domain(s) of government—meaning the persons or peoples, creatures, objects, and territory over which government has authority. Government and its domain, connected and considered as a system, constitutes a polity. So we shall say here, though usage has not attached consistent meanings to either *domain* or *polity*. We can see that *authority* is often problematical as to living things, which perhaps will not acknowledge it or cannot even conceive it. The human race, awarded dominion over all the rest when the world began, may not today accord legitimacy to pure subject status for human beings—that is, to the identification of certain classes of men and women as mere domain, lacking opportunity to participate in self-government; where such circumstances obtain, the polity may be compromised or corrupted, in theory or in operation or in both.

In the founding period, however, it was far from clear that all the population on the land belonged to the political community at the base of the polity. Would some people, then, amount merely to "domain," or at any rate to less than full citizens? The appropriate conditions of citizenship would follow from conceptions of political community. If community implied not only common understanding but also significant obligations, then citizenship implicated attitudes and capacities perhaps not to be presumed of everyone, at least not without some probation or preparation. The eligibility for citizenship of some people, whether living in discrete pales or intermingled with the population at large, thus became a founding problem—one to be pursued in subsequent chapters for what it has to tell us about conceptions of political community at this time.

Severance of legal ties with England, signaling that the Americans were now on their own politically, quickened a realization that many questions relating to territorial jurisdiction and the subjection of certain categories of persons to political authority had not been settled explicitly during the years of colonial status. The resolve to draw up written charters for government impelled political thinkers and leaders to face up to these dangling problems of "domain."

One deeply complicating problem was that geographic boundaries of the colonies, or states, were in dispute from uppermost New England to both Carolinas and Georgia. Charters issued in London and authorizing the establishment of colonies were often vague or mutually inconsistent about territorial boundaries. Connecticut's claim to a portion of the Susquehanna River valley entirely within the boundaries of Pennsylvania disturbed relations between the two colony-states until 1786 and led to armed skirmishes. Maryland's insistence on *national* jurisdiction over a vast acreage claimed by Virginia (and partly by private investors resident in Maryland) held up adoption of the Articles of Confederation for four years—for the Articles as drafted and submitted for ratification said nothing about western boundaries of the states. In the ensuing competition between those states with large western claims and those without, cession to Congress of the trans-Appalachian claims became a condition for Maryland's ratification of the Articles, and Maryland's geographical position then seemed strictly critical to union. Eventually, leaders in Virginia set an example of national concern by recommending cession, and the other "landed" states followed.

This settlement of the territorial disputes established two principles of the highest importance. First, every state, save for outlying islands separated from the mainland by open water, was confined to contiguous territory. Second, every state was the supreme and sole political authority over the territory within its own boundaries, except where the national government was accorded jurisdiction over the military posts, parks and monuments, Indian reservations, forests, and other acreages to which it held title of ownership. While the second of these principles was probably implicit in the Articles of Confederation, the first one was not—nor is there any record of its conscious adoption. Together, these principles meant that the several states would be indistinguishable in scope of political authority within their respective boundaries. Moreover, the settlement of the western land claims left the states much more nearly equal territorially and otherwise than they might have been if, say, Virginia had extended to the Great Lakes and the Mississippi; and there *was* some conscious attention to this issue.[23]

The issue of interstate equality was no less troublesome in the construction of a national government, right from the first day of the First Continental Congress. John Adams reports two days of lively discussion of three alternatives: equality of voting power among the twelve delegations; allocation of votes according to state populations; or allocation of votes "by interests."[24] Two days were sufficient to illuminate these positions and the concerns of certain delegations and to show that the Congress could hardly afford the further time required for settling so complex a question.

The minutes for the second day record that not having at hand the materials requisite to determining the importance of each colony, it concluded that "each Colony or Province shall have one vote."[25]

The drafting of the Articles of Confederation began a year and a half later in the Second Continental Congress and stretched out over eighteen months. This should have been time enough for rough estimates of the relative importance of the several states (if still not nearly enough for congressional agreement on these and on their implications), but Congress could not in any case devote full time to this question. Whether from conviction or from resignation, twelve states voted on 15 November 1777, Virginia alone opposed, to continue the rule of one vote per colony.[26] As the Declaration of Independence had asserted that the new nation would assume equal station within the family of nations, so the Articles of Confederation accorded equality to this nation's member states.

The rule of one state, one vote in composition of the national government was abandoned for the House of Representatives and the Electoral College in the Constitution of 1788.[27] The twin founding principles of state contiguity and commensurate public authority in the several states have remained in effect, however, probably with fruitful results. Surely the contiguity principle has helped obviate conflict, sparing Americans some recurring animosities and hostilities that have plagued other parts of the world—for Americans there have been no Prussia split in two parts across a Danzig Corridor, no East and West Pakistan with a thousand miles of India thrust between them, no Austria and Hungary towering in constitutional powers and status over a half-dozen other elements of an Austro-Hungarian federal union. Disputes about boundaries between adjoining American states still arise for judicial disposition under the federal Constitution, and we can assume that they will for so long as the earth's surface alters in geological time; but the principle of contiguity is still intact, and beneficially so.

The benefits of the companion principle of commensurate, and plenary, public authority in the American states have been no less considerable. That "sovereignty" in the new American system was no longer necessarily singular or indivisible—that it could be distributed federally—has commonly been considered an American invention, coupled with and ultimately grounded in the revolutionary attribution of sovereignty to the people.[28] "Sovereignty" in this revolutionary resolution continued, however. The struggle of civil rulers against ecclesiastical and feudal rulers that so disrupted continental Europe for centuries had been settled more easily in

England in favor of civil authority some generations before the first plantations were chartered in North America—though certain ecclesiastical residues, such as benefit of clergy (no longer strictly a *clerical* privilege), persisted on both sides of the Atlantic, and the ecclesiastical settlement still seemed fresh enough in seventeenth- and eighteenth-century America to need watchful protection. Within the boundaries of the British state and later American states, then, civil authority was in principle complete; exceptions to this rule were the consequences of concession or chargeable to necessity, as in diplomatic immunities or the vagaries of ferae naturae. Moreover, in the "republican" doctrine that eighteenth-century Americans inherited from seventeenth-century England, civil authority was full and unrivaled within its legitimate sphere of service to the "public" well-being.

Responsible government within the new United States of America thus began substantially free of the feudal, ecclesiastical, and communal hang-ups that have troubled the origins and progress of many modern polities. Territorial integrity and the physical reach of public authority were not for long problematic. "The power to govern men and things," as Chief Justice Roger Taney years later characterized the police power, was generally applicable in the states, unencumbered by prescriptive reservations, parochial private governance, or ascriptive privileges.[29] Nor were there pronounced differences among the several states in these respects. Those provisions of the Articles of Confederation according privileges and immunities mutually among the states to citizens and full faith and credit reciprocally to the acts of governments—provisions then customary in international law—would not have to deal with many embarrassing interstate disparities. While various special perplexities about the structure of public authority and representative institutions attended the writing of the state constitutions, these arose within a common political tradition and reflected a practical need to replace British governing arrangements based in royalty and aristocracy more than any sense of fundamental dissatisfaction with colonial public institutions and their English constitutional origins.

Notwithstanding these firm underpinnings of the power to govern, several uncertainties and controversies over the application of authority to certain classes of persons troubled political leaders of the new American states at the time of the break with Britain. Some of these issues related to status, broadly conceived, as in the cases of Indians and of Europeans newly arrived in America. Others arose over standing in respect to particular rights and privileges, most prominently regarding the conditions of

Negroes not in slavery and of adherents to religions tolerated but still dishonored by dominant parts of state populations. A little later another problem emerged, equally painful—that of reincorporating into the body politic those Americans who had resisted independence or had assisted the British.

Altogether, these issues had to do with the terms of inclusion in the political community, or with the conditions of eligibility for citizenship—especially for *full* citizenship. They are the subject of Part 1 of this book, which deals with the position of the American Indian, the free Negro, the European immigrant, and the postindependence Loyalist in, or in relation to, the American states and nation.

The civil position of religious minorities and dissenters need not be considered here, since the momentum for removal of civil disabilities based on religion was strong and broadly effective by the end of the War of Independence.[30] Some contributions of religious diversity to early American national development are considered in chapter 5.

Finally, notwithstanding the strength of republican traditions in America —in habits of political thought and in limited political practice—and the adoption of republican constitutions, the break with Britain meant that Americans had to learn to make republican institutions work under the pressures of full responsibility, subject to a continuing need for national comity. These challenges soon led Americans to new constitutional arrangements and further national amalgamation. Then *these* new dispositions had be tested in action. All this rearranging, merging, and legislating in a short span of time tested severely the political values that had sustained the cause of independence as well as the sinews of political community.

Summary

By the founding period, Americans in many walks of life could take for granted a direct electoral role in self-government. To sustain the full-fledged republican governments that emerged in the founding, there could have been no substitute for this heritage of several generations. If it is true that the radical republican doctrine of popular sovereignty took root almost overnight in the mid-1770s, then the settled experience of self-government must have helped speed adaptation of American political institutions and practices to the pressures prompted by this doctrine. The adaptation was not inevitable, however, and it was often difficult.

The evolution of some sense of nationhood by 1775 surely helped sustain new national institutions—which were tested and stressed repeatedly throughout the founding period. It must also have been helpful that the component states of this new nation, notwithstanding numerous interstate rivalries and the familiar constitutional issues between large states and small, were alike in territorial integrity and plenary civil authority. These attributes pretty much ruled out various jurisdictional rivalries that were prevalent on the European continent, and they facilitated popular sovereignty. In these respects, potential sources of both interstate and intrastate conflict, while still plentiful as classically catalogued in *The Federalist*, were significantly diminished.

None of this is meant to suggest a litmus test or pH range of democratic viability. We cannot add up and net out the conditions just mentioned; we cannot confidently identify one or more of them as strictly critical. I have meant to indicate that Americans entered the founding period with important democratic advantages but that in reducing still-divergent doctrines of free government and earlier experiences of self-government to functioning full-scale state and national republican politics, they also faced extraordinary difficulties—extraordinary in that, outside a classic, largely abstract literature, no one had charted these seas save the Americans themselves, and they had done so only for vessels of lesser draft. The founding was therefore far from unproblematic, and no one could know at all precisely how problematic it was. Predictably, people disagreed in their diagnoses and evaluations of this.

In these circumstances we can see three potentially critical challenges to Americans in the founding period.

1. Who were to be the American people for purposes of popular sovereignty? How much and what should members of the political community have in common? What should be the tests for community membership, or the conditions of citizenship?

2. What would and should the practice of politics be like in the new American order? Would the free play of interests be tolerable, and what sorts of interests were predictable, permissible? Or was some common civic dedication essential to a democratic (republican) survival? How far might more or less fundamental dissent be carried legitimately in the new regime?

3. How would the principal ideals of republican or democratic politics play out in practice, and in what balance—if in sufficient balance? I have in mind here balance between liberty and equality but also something to govern the citizen's political engagement, to measure the citizen's political

obligations, or even perhaps to stand for community values—in the political lexicon of that time, the requirement of virtue, private or public, individual or civic, as an element of citizenship and a regulator of political action.

These challenges can be seen to overlap and interweave, but I am not prepared to simplify or reduce them, beyond having sorted and numbered them as above for summary introduction. Many Americans in the founding period perceived these challenges, and this book is about how they faced them. It is chiefly about the first and the third challenges, but elements of the second will figure inevitably in the narrative and analysis. Part 1 is about the first challenge, and Part 2 is about the third, in close association with the second.

I have just referred to narrative and analysis. Part 1 is largely narrative and description, much condensed. What matters most for my mission here is to record as best I can what happened—what policies American politics arrived at, sometimes implicitly, sometimes explicitly, about the constitution of the political community. Part 2, dealing with political arguments and issues, analyzes what was being said and evaluates its implications for the practice of democratic politics. The balance between narrative and analysis is thus quite different in Part 1 and Part 2.

Throughout, however, in seeking to understand the founding, I have to acknowledge that conditions of democratic success or survival, or understandings of what these would mean, are unlikely to be timeless in anything like precise terms—if indeed they can ever be rendered in precise terms. On the other hand, the founding was not final; it continues today—in altered circumstances, to be sure. The values we Americans attach to community, political obligation, personal and civic virtue, liberty, and equality still shape the American polity and its prospects.

Notes

1. Voting qualifications in preconstitutional America were once supposed to have been much more restrictive. Probably the most convenient modern summary on this matter is in Chilton Williamson, *American Suffrage from Property to Democracy 1760–1860* (Princeton, N.J.: Princeton University Press, 1968), chaps. 1–3. See also J. R. Pole, *Political Representation in England and the Origins of the American Republic* (London: St. Martin's Press, 1966); Elisha P. Douglass, *Rebels and Democrats* (Chapel Hill: University of North Carolina Press, 1955); Robert E. Brown, *Middle Class Democracy and the Revolution in*

Massachusetts, 1691–1780 (Ithaca, N.Y.: Cornell University Press, 1955); Robert
E. Brown and Katherine Brown, *Virginia 1705–1786: Democracy or Aristocracy?*
(East Lansing: Michigan State University Press, 1964); and Gordon S. Wood,
The Creation of the American Republic, 1776–1787 (1969; New York: W. W.
Norton, 1972), chap. 5.

2. The basic issue here is whether the American Revolution brought about
a pronounced departure from the practices and conceptions of domestic
politics that had prevailed in earlier eighteenth-century America. Historical
perspectives on the issue have shifted more than once in this century, agreement on it is still lacking, and there remain some critical gaps in our knowledge
of the period that may never be filled. In brief, we pretty well know now that
structures of colonial government broadly based in public election and consent obtained generally in eighteenth-century America; but there is disagreement about how popular or democratic such government was in either aspiration
or operation, and there is some disagreement about the extent of British
tutelage. There is now considerable agreement that the course of late eighteenth-
century events that directly led to and ensued from the Revolution entailed
pronounced changes in political attitudes and understandings; but there remains
ample disagreement over the extent to which American society and opinion
were divided politically during the constitution-writing phase of the founding
period and over the extent to which the division was basically between
democratic and conservative forces. Compare, for example, the perspectives
of Bernard Bailyn, *The Ideological Origins of the American Revolution* (Cambridge,
Mass.: Harvard University Press, 1967), and Jackson Turner Main, *The Sovereign States, 1775–1783* (New York: New Viewpoints, 1973). See also, by way of
illustration, J. R. Pole, "Historians and the Problem of Early American Democracy," *American Historical Review* 67 (1962): 626–46; Richard Buel, Jr.,
"Democracy and the American Revolution: A Frame of Reference," *William
and Mary Quarterly,* 3d ser., 21 (1964): 165–90; and Gordon S. Wood,
"Rhetoric and Reality in the American Revolution," *William and Mary Quarterly,*
3d ser., 23 (1966): 3–32.

3. Charles M. Andrews, *The Colonial Background of the American Revolution* (New Haven, Conn.: Yale University Press, 1924); Edmund S. Morgan,
The Birth of the Republic 1763–89 (Chicago: University of Chicago Press, 1956),
chap. 1; R. R. Palmer, *The Age of the Democratic Revolution,* vol. 1 (Princeton,
N.J.: Princeton University Press, 1959), chaps. 6–7; John R. Alden, *A History
of the American Revolution* (New York: Alfred A. Knopf, 1975), chap. 3; J. R.
Pole, *The Gift of Government* (Athens: University of Georgia Press, 1983),
chap. 3.

4. Bernard Bailyn, *The Origins of American Politics* (New York: Random
House Vintage Books, 1967), pp. 87–88.

5. Ibid, pp. 80–88; Pole, *Political Representation,* pt. 2; Williamson, *American*

Suffrage, chaps. 3–4; Edmund S. Morgan, *The Challenge of the American Revolution* (New York: W. W. Norton, 1976), esp. pp. 54–57.

6. Bailyn, *Origins of American Politics*, chaps. 2–3, and *Ideological Origins*, chap. 5; Samuel Beer, "The Representation of Interests in British Government: Historical Background," *American Political Science Review* 51 (1957): 613–50; Pole, *Gift of Government*, esp. chaps. 5–6, and *Political Representation*, pt. 2; Jack P. Greene, *The Quest for Power* (Chapel Hill: University of North Carolina Press, 1963). Also, published since this chapter was drafted, Bruce C. Daniels, ed., *Power and Status: Officeholding in Colonial America* (Middletown, Conn.: Wesleyan University Press, 1986).

7. "[W]hile the property qualifications for voting did not in fact prove particularly restrictive—something that Thomas Hutchinson and George Bancroft had understood long before Robert Brown painstakingly reestablished the fact—local [New England] communities showed great deference to the leadership and opinions of the principal personages and families. What one had in effect was a political democracy manipulated by an elite." Richard B. Morris, *The American Revolution Reconsidered* (New York: Harper and Row, 1967), p. 57; see also ibid., chap. 2. "For the most part, and most of the time, it must be said that the mass of the people deferentially accepted their places in a world in which their primary task was to make a living. They needed the stability given by good government, with firm, experienced, and knowledgeable leadership." Pole, *Gift of Government*, p. 63. See also Daniels, *Power and Status*.

8. Palmer, *Age of the Democratic Revolution*, p. 194, and generally pp. 190–206. See also Morris, *American Revolution Reconsidered*.

9. Palmer, *Age of the Democratic Revolution*, p. 195. See also Morgan, *Challenge of the American Revolution*, chaps. 3–4; Buel, "Democracy and the American Revolution," p. 165; and Wood, "Rhetoric and Reality in the American Revolution," 3.

10. Palmer, *Age of the Democratic Revolution*; and esp. (published since this chapter was drafted) Gordon S. Wood, *The Radicalism of the American Revolution* (New York: Alfred A. Knopf, 1992).

11. Probably the landmarks of this revised understanding are Bailyn, *Ideological Origins*; and Wood, *Creation of the American Republic*. But compare Main, *Sovereign States*, which, in the "Progressive" tradition, places greater emphasis on an altered balance of opinion after 1775, with the departure of many loyalists and the stimulus of independence, and gives significantly less attention to an alleged "paradigm shift" in the foundations of political thought pretty much throughout American society.

12. See, e.g., Pole, "Historians and the Problem of Early American Democracy."

13. Pole, *Gift of Government*; Pole, *Political Representation*, esp. pt. 3, chap. 13; Bailyn, *Origins of American Politics*. See also Garry Wills, *Inventing America:*

Jefferson's Declaration of Independence (1978; New York: Random House Vintage Books, 1979).

14. On the American contribution in this respect, see Palmer, *Age of the Democratic Revolution*, chaps. 8–9; Bailyn, *Ideological Origins*, chap. 5; and J. R. Pole, *Foundations of American Independence: 1763–1815* (Indianapolis: Bobbs-Merrill, 1972), chap. 5.

15. This is perhaps especially true of the later phase of constitution-writing that began around 1780 with the second (or even third) Massachusetts Constitution, which was the first to be undertaken by a special convention and subjected to popular ratification.

16. See Palmer, *Age of the Democratic Revolution*; Wood, *Radicalism of the American Revolution*; Allan Nevins, *The American States during and after the Revolution, 1775–1789* (New York: Macmillan, 1924), chaps. 2–5; Main, *Sovereign States*, chaps. 5–6; and Willi Paul Adams, *The First American Constitutions* (Chapel Hill: University of North Carolina Press, 1980).

17. Max Savelle, *Seeds of Liberty* (New York: Alfred A. Knopf, 1948), esp. chap. 10; Richard L. Merritt, *Symbols of American Community, 1735–1775* (New Haven, Conn.: Yale University Press, 1966).

18. One people, but just dubiously one nation, or state. The sentence mentioned follows the more ambiguous title: "A Declaration by the United States of America in General Congress Assembled"; and the Declaration concludes (penultimate paragraph) "that these United colonies are and of right ought to be free and independent states. . . ."

19. First Inaugural Address, 4 March 1861; and esp. Message to Congress in Special Session, 4 July 1861.

20. See, e.g., Andrews, *Colonial Background*; S. E. Morison and H. S. Commager, *The Growth of the American Republic*, vol. 1 (New York: Oxford University Press, 1942), chaps. 4–7; and Jack P. Greene, "'A Posture of Hostility': A Reconsideration of Some Aspects of the Origins of the American Revolution," in Jack P. Greene and William G. McLaughlin, *Preachers and Politicians* (Worcester, Mass: American Antiquarian Society, 1977).

21. Colonial divisions, hesitations over independence, and (especially) adherence to the forms and traditions of petition for redress of grievances are emphasized in Wills, *Inventing America*. Compare Alden, *History of the American Revolution*, chap. 16; and Max Savelle, "Nationalism in the American Revolution," *American Historical Review* 67 (1962): 901–23, for the view that a full-fledged, independent American sense of nationalism did not exist before independence and had barely emerged by the end of the Revolution, "the product of a slow intellectual and emotional growth" (p. 923).

22. See, e.g., *The Adams Papers: Diary and Autobiography of John Adams*, vol. 3, ed. L. H. Butterfield (Cambridge, Mass.: Harvard University Press, 1961), pp. 351–59.

23. Thus Richard Henry Lee of Virginia suggested in 1778, in arguing for cession of his state's land claims to Congress, that a state as large as the area claimed might not be viable as a republic; the Virginia legislature opined in 1779 that perhaps the trans-Appalachian land should later be made into new states; and of course the "landless" states were deeply concerned about prospective disparities. See Alden, *History of the American Revolution*, pp. 344–47.

24. *Adams Papers*, vol. 2, pp. 123–24.

25. Ibid, p. 126; *Journals of the Continental Congress* 1 (1774): 25.

26. Voting power in Congress was not the only problem of relative state roles to arise. Obligation for financial support of the national government was another, in which later debates in the Philadelphia Constitutional Convention about the counting of slaves in the basis for national participation were anticipated. The question was finally resolved in the Articles by basing tax participation on ratios not of population but of improved land.

27. As for the Electoral College, however, actual practice has apparently exceeded the expectations of the framers, most of whom probably looked to the Electoral College mainly as a nominating device and to the House of Representatives (voting federally, by state delegations) for election of the president in the normal case. See, e.g., James Madison's comments in *Federalist No. 37*; and Max Farrand, *The Framing of the Constitution of the United States* (New Haven, Conn.: Yale University Press, 1913), chap. 11.

28. See, e.g., Bailyn, *Ideological Origins*, chap. 5, sec. 3. For a traditional British perspective on this, see A. V. Dicey, *Introduction to the Study of the Law of the Constitution*, 8th ed. (London: Macmillan, 1924), chap. 3.

29. The familiar Taney quotation is from the *License Cases*, 5 How. 504 (1847), 583.

30. See, e.g., William W. Sweet, *Religion in Colonial America* (New York: Charles Scribner's Sons, 1942), esp. p. 339, and *Religion in the Making of American Culture, 1765–1840* (New York: Charles Scribner's Sons, 1952), chaps. 1–3. See also Anson Phelps Stokes, *Church and State in the United States*, vol. 1 (New York: Harper and Brothers, 1950), esp. chap. 5.

PART ONE

Conditions of Citizenship:
Inclusion and Exclusion

2

The Native American and the Free African American

In the century and a half before the founding, European settlement created a legacy of race and status differences that complicated conceptions of the nation or the civic community at the base of popular government. Relations with the indigenous population were not entirely characterized by conflict, but conflict dominated as the European objective of conquest and proprietorship of the land overshadowed the European "civilizing" mission. The introduction of African slaves and the later manumission of some left broadly similar disparities of race and status to complicate decisions on admission to the political community.[1]

In both cases the complications were several and serious. There were tensions between the liberal, civilizing European ideal, on the one hand, and European economic interests and social prejudices, on the other. There were tensions between formal policy at state and national levels, on the one hand, and its popular observance and official enforcement, on the other—besides which, policy was often either unclear or inchoate. Finally, hindsight identifies for us some difficult questions about the appropriate requirements for full membership of the American (or state or local) political community—not only over the extent to which these should include personal autonomy and interpersonal equality, however these were to be defined, but also over whether some common attributes of civilization and virtue might be required for the salubrity of republican government. If so, how were *these* to be defined, and was their requirement well considered, or even justified, or simply prejudiced or (in lawyers' language) pretextual?

To say today how these issues of the founding were resolved and how the questions just posed were answered then is probably not entirely possible. Uncertainties and ambiguities abide in much of what we know. It will therefore be best to follow the story of what is known. Most of the conclusions we can reach are implicit in that story, which is not, from our standpoint today, a happy aspect of the founding.

European-Native Relations: The Colonial Pattern

The presence of the Indian throughout North America stood adamant as a challenge to the British dogma of sovereignty at the dawn of settlement. It remained so throughout the colonial period and, indeed, continued so when "sovereignty" passed to the new Americans. Eventual confrontation with the indigenous inhabitants was high in the consciousness of the king and his governmental household when the first authorizations for settlement were made. Especially in the sector to be known as New England, however, circumstances allowed this looming issue to be put aside for a time while a toehold was established. "We have been given certainly to knowe," said James I in the patent of 3 November 1620, issued to Sir Ferdinando Gorges and others,

> that within these late Yeares there hath by God's Visitation raigned a wonderfull Plague, together with horrible Slaughters, and Murthers, committed amoungst the Savages and brutish People there, heretofore inhabiting, in a Manner to the utter Destruction, Devastacion, and Depopulation of that whole Territorye . . . whereby we in our Judgment are persuaded and satisfied that the appointed Time is come in which Almighty God in his great Goodness and Bountie towards Us and our People, hath thought fitt and determined that those large and goodly Territoryes, deserted as it were by their naturall Inhabitants, should be possessed and enjoyed by such of our Subjects and People as heretofore have and hereafter shall by his Mercie and Favour, and by his powerful Arme, be directed and conducted thither.[2]

Probably before and certainly soon after the beginning of settlement in Virginia, broadly similar native depopulation from white microbes and warfare had helped pave the way of sovereignty there, as in other colonies later.[3]

The providential bounty that cleared a place for the king's loyal subjects in the New World included the foresight to leave scattered about a sufficient number of natives to teach the English how to survive in an inhospitable wilderness. This benefaction came at a price: nature stipulates some give as well as take when peoples of variant cultures mix in a limited space. However reluctantly, though sometimes with alacrity, the English had to adapt their customs and culture in some degree to the ways of the American aborigine. The tribal populations awaiting the settlers varied in size, and their initial postures and responses ranged from curiosity, hospitality, and propensity for trade to occasional bellicosity right from the start. The colonists' behavior varied as well from one place to another. Native reactions to the first settlements were also influenced by still earlier encounters, and reports of encounters, with European explorers and fishing expeditions. But everywhere, perhaps unavoidably as the colonial enterprise swiftly developed, warfare soon came to play an implicit and defining role between the races, based on competition over space and the resources and ways of life the land favored for each race. In general, less than a decade was required for the white settlers to conclude that neither assimilation of the two races nor a pacific existence as neighbors would be easy to achieve. Long before the settlements had enlarged and combined to form thirteen colonies, it had become apparent to Indians and whites alike that deep-seated incompatibilities of the two cultures portended the utter failure of any attempt to intermix or meld the races.[4]

The image of the bloody savage of the wilderness that came to dominate the minds of whites as the frontier moved westward is now in dispute among scholars. The revisions are not confined to questions of latent hostility and active warfare, to frequency and intensity of bloodletting on the frontier, or to estimates of treachery, explosiveness, and brutality. They extend as well to the claim that Indian character and culture commonly have been misunderstood or misrepresented since the writing of American history began, perhaps especially with respect to the level and prevalence of agriculture, the place of industry and ecology in hunting and fishing, and the breadth of variety of Indian civilization.[5]

The revisions themselves rest heavily and necessarily on reports from early English (and other) settlers. Yet for these settlers, observation and inference were often hobbled by competing preconceptions of or projections on the indigenous population. In an idyllic vision of the noble savage the American aborigine was imagined as an unspoiled and innocent exile from Eden, unfettered by deeply rooted attachments to rudimentary religious precepts, yet malleable in adapting to the allure of civilization and the diverse truths of Christian theology. Counterposed to this image of simplicity and magnanimity was a widely held conviction that the defining characteristic of the American savage was savagery itself, in the worst sense to which the word had evolved—if not as cannibalism or innate blood lust, at least as an addiction to warfare and pillage and a proclivity to torture. The failure of experience to authenticate either of these ideal-types and the inability of moderates to negotiate consensus on a perception verified by experience virtually guaranteed a regime of racial relations marked by confusion of goals, inconsistency of policies, and recurring abrasions at points of person-to-person contact. Such hope as may have been warranted that the Indians would accept instruction in the fundamentals of European civilization receded before accumulating evidence that Indians had decided they could not trust whites.[6]

Regardless of what may be the true measure of their errors in perception and imprudence in policy, the white settlers must not be charged with entire responsibility for the growing incompatibility of the two cultures (notwithstanding their pragmatic convergences on some points of technology). It can hardly be doubted that the changes in life-styles and revisions of ethical codes that incorporation into the white communities would have entailed worked a powerful dissuasion on any tribes that may have contemplated it. More than a few white men and women of talent, in New England especially, made cultural conquest or "improvement" of the Indian their vocation, but success would have been problematical even if their numbers had multiplied. Instead of multiplying, the ranks of cultural and religious missionaries diminished, at least proportionate to the growing white population. Moreover, it seems never to have left the consciousness of the seventeenth-century English settlers that their primary mission in America was "inlargement of the King's dominions" and the advancement of their own fortunes and that the "reducing of the savages to civil society" and conversion to Christianity, while listed first in the royal patent for occupation of New England, was in fact a secondary goal, to be pursued in service to those of dominion and prosperity.

So it came about in New England within a few decades that the indigenous population separated itself in the colonists' minds into three classes, differing in social condition and entailing different relationships with the whites' government: Indians living in the tribal state; Indians who were or who sought to be incorporated into the white society; and Indians living apart from both the tribe and the white community. The tribal state could be further classified into so-called tributary and independent tribes (the former defined by continued location within the acknowledged boundaries of European land). There were also discernible degrees of tribal independence with respect to the several seaboard colonies and a few cases of "dependent" tribes controlled by an independent tribe acting as agent of the English (e.g., the Iroquois conquest of the Delawares in Pennsylvania). Indians joining white society did so, or were welcome to do so, in varying degree; they might do so either as households or in distinct, somewhat self-governing settlements (such as the "plantations" of early Massachusetts).[7]

These distinctions obtained generally in New England and the middle colonies, but the status of each group, considered as a problem for conceptions of the civil state and for political sovereignty, evolved over time and varied from one colony to another. Indians living in a tribal status—the vast majority of Indians altogether and of those whose tribes were still extant—were commonly acknowledged by white officials to be immune from jurisdiction of the white community and from application of the whites' laws, save, as a rule, for cases resulting from offenses against Europeans.[8] Recognition of this tribal status was often specified in formal pacts, the more imposing ones denominated treaties. The controlling agreement might give the colony's officials right of entry to the Indian village, or to the reservation if boundaries were fixed, for such purposes as apprehension of whites wanted for crimes in the white settlements or even in some cases for trial and punishment of whites committing crimes against Indian law on Indian land. Intrusions of the whites' law and of white officers into the Indian tribal state were certainly exceptional, however. If an Indian unduly abused his mate, neglected the nurture of his children, or committed mayhem upon one of his peers—that was a matter to be settled by the Indians in their Indian way.[9]

Indians who attached themselves to the white settlements brought themselves under the legal and administrative authority of colonial government. This is not to say that in general they became first-class citizens as we tend to understand that term today. Rather, they may have been seen as in a state of tutelage—internees in training for future full citizenship. How fully they were incorporated into the political affairs of the community must have depended on the readiness of the white population to accept them, as would also have been the case for their roles in the social life of the community. Both, no doubt, depended heavily on previous local experience in relations between the races. It was probably good policy to include an Indian or two in the jury at the trial of an Indian or a suit to which an Indian was party, and it is certain this was not an infrequent occurrence in the northern and middle colonies. In many places Indians who proved they had embraced civilization did jury duty in cases between white persons only, just as they served in the militia or worked on the roads or voted on election day. It is difficult, however, to generalize about these matters, since we lack systematic accounts of them for most colonies.

It seems probable that discretion rather than law largely determined the status of the third group of native Americans mentioned above—those who had left or been expelled from tribal society but had not affiliated with the whites. Here too, however, we are pretty much reduced to speculation based on occasional reports. Some of these Indians may have settled on the outskirts of white villages, but they probably tended to live invisibly in the forests, swamps, or hills between the fertile valleys. Colonial authorities would have insisted that these lonely strays were entirely subject to the white man's government. Local officials, however, must have realized that the deeply rooted beliefs and traditions of the Indians were not amenable to the norms of civilization and justice transported from Europe. Ignorance being less threatening to bliss than knowledge is, it was folly to take notice of what transpired among these people until they threatened or disturbed the peace of white settlers and traders.

The southernmost colonies are excepted from the foregoing account of the claims of colonial governments to political authority over the aboriginal Americans. The available evidence indicates that colonies based on a plantation economy were considerably less willing than those of the North to welcome the savage, no matter how noble, into their midst and that they were also less generous in conceding autonomy to Indians who kept their distance. It seems probable that the plantation economy and the land policies by which its white settlers were recruited denied southern Indians most of the opportunities for employment and food supply afforded by civilization in the villages of the North. The commercial auspices and social sources of the southern colonies probably led also to harsher relations with the natives, as no doubt did slavery, including the active Indian slave trade of the Carolinas. In any case, Virginia from an early date pursued a policy of pushing Indians back from great stretches of land that Europeans had brought under cultivation or had plans to occupy. To enter these precincts, Indians were required by 1646 to obtain a "ticket" from a plantation owner specifying the purposes of the visit and the length of stay. Georgia and the Carolinas appear to have been no more receptive to such natives as may have wished to make a living in the tidewater plains and valleys.[10]

By the time migration had spotted the uplands of Virginia and the Carolinas with settlements—that is, after the middle of the eighteenth century—Indians of the South, like those of the North, had probably concluded there was much less benefit than some of their forebears had thought in subjecting their destinies to European civilization and jurisdiction. Diffused along this southern frontier were tribes admired by Europeans for their achievements in agronomy and civil organization. But there were also tribes, or branches of tribes, that depended heavily on foraging for their food supply and were intermittent if not persistent poachers. Moreover, Indian tradition in the South, as elsewhere, was often tolerant of free-wheeling by ambitious braves who still had reputations to establish. For European settlers in the southern Piedmont these Indian depredations were generally more impressive than Indian cultural accomplishments. As they saw it, exclusion of the aborigine had brought peace to the tidewater country. Removal of Indians from the up-country they occupied became a permanent objective as soon as independence and union created a national government that could take on that job.

Just as the whites' toleration of Indians and adjustment to aboriginal ways varied from one colony to another, so these changed as time and the frontier advanced. Underlying both the variation and the change, however, was the idea, also steadily advancing, that it was God's will that European civilization should either transform the savages into the whites' image (including prominently the tradition of individual land tenure) or push them aside so Europeans could take title to the lands they were determined to occupy and make fruitful, pursuant to the original plan for Eden. That the former outcome was both preferable and feasible was a fond hope of not a few colonials along the coast and no doubt of some who established the log-cabin outposts farthest west. By the time independence was won and union negotiated, however, it must have been recognized generally that the whites would possess the land—at least contiguous land—stage by stage. Probably few were more sensible of this destiny than many prescient Indian leaders. Similarly, among the national (and nationalist) white leaders there emerged an intermediate position, which was that a peaceable, orderly, consolidating advance of European culture would, by its implicit pressure on Indian gamelands and way of life, lead inexorably to Indian retreat (or civilization) and to the economical transfer of land.[11]

American National Indian Policy in the Founding Period

This, in rude approximation, was the situation when the Articles of Confederation came into effect in 1781. Three provisions of this first constitution of the United States bore on the authority of the individual states relating to the Indians. Arguably, these gave the new national government a larger and more nearly exclusive role in relations with the Indians than in almost any other sphere. First, the sovereignty of the several states within their respective geographic boundaries was confirmed: "Each state retains its sovereignty, freedom, and independence, and every power, jurisdiction, and right which is not by this confederation expressly delegated to the United States, in Congress assembled" (Article II). Second, "No state shall engage in any war without the consent of the United States, in Congress assembled, unless such state shall be actually invaded by Indians, or shall have received certain advice of a resolution being formed by some nation of Indians to invade such state, and the danger is so imminent as not to admit of a delay till the United States, in Congress assembled, can be consulted . . ." (Article VI). Third, "The United States, in Congress assembled, shall have the sole and exclusive right and power of . . . regulating the trade and managing all affairs with the Indians not members of any of the states, providing that the legislative right of any state within its own limits be not infringed or violated . . ." (Article IX).

These provisions were the outcome of compromise in 1777 between a "national" approach to Indian policy (with roots in the abortive Albany Congress of 1754 and the British imperial policy of 1763) in proposals drafted by Benjamin Franklin and John Dickinson for the Continental Congress and, on the other hand, the "states' rights" view that pretty much prevailed in their revision.[12] Though stated in language of admirable precision, they invited dispute over jurisdiction in one condition that existed then and was bound to recur as territory to the west formed into new states. Some areas occupied by Indians living under tribal rule lay wholly within the limits of a single state of the new Union. Did Article IX endow the new national government with exclusive power of "regulating the trade and managing all affairs" regarding these Indians? Whatever the most reasonable conclusion on this point, the national government was denied the right to infringe on the legislative right of the state within which the Indian reservation was located. Inasmuch as most if not all colonies had, by treaty or with basis in legislation, regulated trade with tribes located within their borders, did it not follow that the states retained a legislative right to continue such regulation under the Articles of Confederation?

These issues were debated in Congress, as occasioned by disparate state interests, for seven years without provoking a serious showdown or evoking a clear resolution. State encroachments on Indian lands reserved by national treaties or breakdowns of trade with tribes inside the states could threaten the nation's peace and economic welfare, invoking the nation's war power *nolens volens.* Under such a threat from state actions and inactions in Georgia and North Carolina a special investigating committee, reporting in the last days of the Continental Congress (August 1787), sought to resolve doubts about the placement of authority in favor of the national government: "The laws of the State can have no effect upon a tribe of Indians or their lands within the limits of the state so long as that tribe is independent, and not a member of the state, yet the laws of the state may be executed upon debtors, criminals, and other proper objects of the laws in all parts of it, and therefore the union may make stipulations with any such tribe, secure it in the enjoyment of all parts of its lands, without infringing upon the legislative right in question."[13] In this case, the committee recommended that the states in question pursue peace with the Indians, cede Indian territories to the nation for its management of Indian affairs, and accept the nation as sole manager of trade with the Creek and Cherokee tribes. It also recommended that the Congress inquire further into the causes of the current hostility, with the understanding that it would levy war (only) "on tribes which make unjust and unprovoked attacks on any part of the United States." The committee's motions, however, failed to carry in the Congress.

The considerations that inspired the long sentence just quoted shaped national policy relating to Indians throughout the founding period. Especially after 1787, the national government assumed authority to regulate trade with the Indians and other troublesome aspects of Indian affairs wherever the Indians might be located—on tribal reservations within a member state of the Union or in more remote territorial holdings of the United States or beyond, whether congregated in tribal organization or living unattached in the woods and on the prairies. The policy continued indefinitely even though the language fixing federal authority in the new Constitution seems in some respects less generous than that in the Articles. In Article I, Section 8, the Constitution says, "The Congress shall have Power . . . to regulate commerce . . . with the Indian tribes." The reference in the Articles to managing "all affairs" was left out of the succeeding Constitution, but so were the qualifying clauses of the Articles.[14]

The principal issues and difficulties of national Indian policy in the founding period bear significantly on our conception of *domain*. We know little about those Indians who had chosen life among the whites or in their vicinity. Perhaps we should assume their full citizenship, but they were in any case not subjects of *national* policy. The issues of domain—of inclusion/exclusion in political jurisdiction and community—posed in policy toward the tribal Indians resulted, we may infer, from four chief factors: (1) the contrasting cultures and economies of Indians and Europeans; (2) the swiftly changing power positions of Indians and whites through the course of the founding period; (3) the sometimes confusing ultimate assumptions and the operational ambiguity of American national policy; and (4) the limitations of national policy in the beginnings of a federal state. No complete delineation of the course of Indian policy is appropriate here, but enough can be said about the tribal Indian's prospects of inclusion/exclusion, or of separate "sovereignty," in postcolonial America to illustrate the foregoing policy issues and influences.

The founding period was crucial for the substance of American public policy toward the tribal Indians—though not so much for broadly philosophic or jurisprudential reasons as because the pressure of events in this period pretty much settled the Indians' destiny without reference to national policy. England's Proclamation Line of 1763 had, after all, just tenuously fended off the pressures of an advancing frontier; and in doing so, it had helped fuel sentiments that led to independence. The Revolution disposed of that obstacle, and the new American governments were unable to effectuate anything like the Proclamation Line, though they tried to. Most of the Indian tribes, moreover, had in the end allied themselves with the British in the Revolution, and, as a result of some of the more savage actions of that war, tribes north of the Mason-Dixon line were much reduced in numbers and territory in New York and Pennsylvania. South of the Mason-Dixon line, however, there were larger tribal numbers and lands within state boundaries from Virginia through Georgia (though partly, in Virginia especially, because state land claims west to the Mississippi had not been ceded south of the Ohio).

The settlement with England left relations with the Indians unsettled. By European standards of warfare they required to be settled; and the new nation, as had the old, needed to determine its domain. Relations with various of the tribes were therefore settled by treaties, premised according to the Americans on the conquest of the tribes. These treaties were unstable: the tribes did not accept their premise of surrender; and more than a few whites, frequently with support from their state governments, were not ready to accept their territorial premises. In the first decade or longer, however, under both the Confederation and the Constitution, the paramount objective of national policy was to make peace as a condition of economic recovery and development. The new nation could not afford serious warfare with the Indians. Yet the national policy lacked support from the full national government. Under the Confederation the "national" objective just mentioned was represented most consistently by the secretary for war, Henry Knox, and much more problematically in the Continental Congress. Pursuant to this objective, right at the end of the Confederation the principal postrevolutionary Indian treaties were rewritten. In preference to warfare the nation paid for the land it had gained in the earlier treaties, and it thereby abandoned the conquest rationale.

Under the Constitution the same economic concern (and substantially the same administration in the person of Henry Knox) obtained for sometime. Now, however, there was an executive branch and an elected president to stand for a national Indian policy, and in general all administrations from Washington's through John Quincy Adams's stood for the same policy, which had begun under the Confederation. Besides the desirability of peace with the Indians, it emphasized explicitly justice, humanity, and integrity in dealing with them, not only for instrumental reasons but as exemplary republicanism. "If our modes of population and War destroy the tribes, the disinterested part of mankind and posterity will be apt to class our conduct with that of the Spaniards in Mexico and Peru," Henry Knox wrote to Anthony Wayne.[15] This policy also had a national security aspect, in which friendly tribes on the frontiers would serve as buffers against the British, French, or Spanish. From these interests and concerns it followed that Indian policy had to be *national* policy, under national administration, based on the war-making and treaty-making powers and including both plenary management of the critical function of trade with the Indian tribes and full control of the frontier regions.[16]

This policy, however, was also a land-and-population policy, the basic tenets of which have already been mentioned. It assumed that the advance of European civilization would lead inexorably to the Indians' retreat—conceivably, even probably on the then-available evidence, to the tribes' eventual extinction or at least to their attenuation and demoralization as pressure on gamelands from the East constrained recession westward toward ever-tightening tribal competition in the diminishing remainder of tribal lands. This much was not so much a policy as a prediction. The policy lay, first, in rendering retreat an orderly, economical, peaceable process under federal management; and, second, in the conception of tempering the process through efforts to civilize the Indians and thus provide for their incorporation in the new American society.

In a policy looking to the welfare and development of a European, new-American nation, these several elements fit together logically and logistically in concept, though there were serious difficulties in implementation. Probably the chief challenge was federal: how to effectuate the national strategy in the face of recurrent local and commercial pressures on Indian lands and trade. Often, of course, these pressures found support in Congress. The federal problem surfaced in the separation of powers and, as a difference between national policy and local interests, with some frequency in the federal trial courts, which in western districts tended to mitigate federal law and regulations in consideration of white property claims. Finally, the pressure figured in the actions of quite a few federal Indian agents in the field, who had to contend with dominant local white opinion and pressure. Nor were the Indians, whose leaders perceived the land-policy element, always cooperative or coordinated in support of national controls. Episodic military actions thus marked the changing balance of power between the whites and the tribes, and the treaties by which land changed hands became, on the whole, increasingly severe and one-sided. The land-and-population policy took such priority that there was not time enough for the civilization-and-incorporation policy to work, assuming it was workable. By and large, the latter policy was delegated, with public subsidies, to religious denominations and missionary societies, since Christianity was broadly believed to be implicit in European civilization. This early exercise in applied anthropology met with little success; in the end, the land was cultivated and incorporated, but the Indians were not.[17]

In national Indian policy the competition between, in modern terms, "cosmopolitan" and "local" values lasted half a century. We have seen that by the year 1781, when the Articles of Confederation were adopted, the white inhabitants of Georgia and the Carolinas were concluding that the only solution for their unhappy relations with the Indians was to ship them out. By the end of James Monroe's presidency this view was official and forcible in the southeastern states, and—at least as a policy of voluntary removal—it was gaining ground in national administrations. A decade later, in his first annual message to Congress, Andrew Jackson recommended removal of the southern tribes from Georgia and Alabama, and in an act of 28 May 1830 Congress authorized the president to designate areas west of the Mississippi "for the reception of such tribes of Indians as may choose to . . . remove there."[18] The first removal had already occurred in 1827 when, in a showdown between Georgia and the Adams administration, the Creek Indians lost and were transplanted beyond the Mississippi. That year the Cherokees adopted a constitution and declared themselves an independent nation.

Then in 1829 the Georgia legislature enacted a statute citing the territory within its limits currently occupied by the Cherokee Indians, declaring null and void within those limits all laws and regulations of Indian origin, and announcing that thenceforth native rule was superseded by the civil and criminal laws of Georgia. The national undertakings of half a century afforded the Indians no protection. Under national law and their treaties with the nation, the Cherokees argued, Georgia's action was unconstitutional. The Supreme Court, however, held that national law and treaties conferred no standing in court according to the terms of the Constitution, for the Cherokees were, said Chief Justice John Marshall in a landmark decision, neither a member state of the Union nor a foreign nation but rather a "domestic dependent nation" under U.S. sovereignty.[19] Yet the national laws, Marshall determined a year later, "consider the several Indian nations as distinct political communities, having territorial boundaries, within which their authority is exclusive, and having a right to all lands within those boundaries, which is . . . guarantied by the United States."[20] The Cherokees, however, were pinned between Georgia's intransigence and the national administration's reluctance—even, one must say, its probable inability—to enforce federal law. The policy of Indian removal, on which President Jackson was bent, abandoned as unrealistic and ultimately unhelpful to the Indians the longstanding ambition for their civilization and incorporation. It recurred in its premises to the original plan for Eden: the land belonged by right to those who would cultivate it intensively. It also construed the history of Indian treaties as essentially the tactical, unilateral acts of a sovereign toward a subordinate people. The removal policy and its justifications were debated strenuously then and have been since by historians.[21] Eventually, however, the Cherokees ceded their lands and removed, or were removed, beyond the Mississippi.

It remains only to repeat that national policy in the founding period envisioned a kindly and patient preparation of the Indians for conversion to civilization, subject to a firm resolution that the Europeans would ultimately possess the land if the Indians could not prove themselves worthy of partnership. This was the predominant aspiration, it appears, of those we believe to have been notably influential in shaping republican institutions during the last quarter of the eighteenth century. True, there were practitioners of terrorism and advocates of extinction among the white traders and settlers on the frontier, and they too have to be counted among the founders of the republic. It also can be argued cogently that when the morality of immediate confrontation met up with the morality of distant contemplation, it was the reactions of those up close that won out.

If, however, we say that in the eyes of our generation the founders were those who met in conventions, sat in legislatures and held other high offices, led the armies, made the speeches, and wrote the pamphlets that have survived—that these were the originators of republican government on the North American continent—then it can also be said that they did in the main manifest a sincere humanity toward the native Americans, although they did not live next door to them. As prospective neighbors later on, the Indians were noble savages. They were amenable to civilization. Forgiven their etiquette of the woods, approached in charity, trained with patience, and disciplined by a firm paternalism, they would prove worthy of the whites' companionship and could expect to share in occupancy and exploitation of the land. Though the policy of removal, or exclusion, won out in the end, the goal of civilization and inclusion was an element of federal Indian policy until well after Washington, John Adams, and Jefferson had had their turns in the presidency.

The Place of the Free African American

The legal and social status of the enslaved Africans in North America is not likely to be fully understood by anyone, black or white, who did not share it. Grant that intimate accounts of abusive treatment, prolonged sorrow, and nobility displayed in suffering may be vivid in the minds of many slave descendants; still, the most trustworthy re-creations must provide a pale and dilute image not only of slave reality but of reciprocal conceptions in white society throughout the colonial and founding periods. Lacking sure knowledge of the status and condition of the enslaved population and the presumptions and convictions of the white population, we cannot confidently imagine the status and treatment accorded the free Negro during the period when the self-governing republic was under construction.

One component of the enigma can hardly be better summarized than it was by Anthony Benezet, writing in 1792: "The low contempt with which they are generally greeted by the white lead[s] children, from the first dawn of reason, to consider people with a black skin on a footing with domestic animals, formed to serve and obey . . . and when they attain the age of maturity, can scarce be brought to believe that creatures they have always looked upon [as] so vastly below themselves, can stand on the same footing in the sight of the Universal Father, or that justice requires the same conduct to them as to the whites. . . ."[22]

A second assurance of present uncertainty about the predicament and prospect for betterment of the eighteenth-century free Negro is rooted in the cultural result of that predicament. Poverty of imagination, of aspiration and will, and of know-how and a dearth of friendly encouragement were integral to the experience of generations born into slavery, carried over to the growing numbers who were loosed from bondage, and must have infected the limited number of light-skinned men and women with African blood who eluded slavery from birth. Personal experience and an overpowering environment deeply stamped on this unfortunate people a character that white people, with few exceptions, perceived as an endowment of nature.

A dismaying incapacity to cope with the challenges and burdens of freedom was all but universally acknowledged by those farsighted white men and women who led an emerging movement to encourage increased manumission and ultimate termination of slavery. Writing four years after Anthony Benezet filed his plea for elemental justice, Samuel Hopkins conceded that "a state of slavery has a mighty tendency to sink and contract the minds of men, and prevent their making improvements in useful knowledge of every kind. It sinks the mind down in darkness and despair."[23]

The minimum requirement of justice, as Hopkins saw it, was for all owners of slaves to free them forthwith. The evil of slavery lay in the ownership of human beings and the control of human lives. The remedy for the evil lay in the voluntary surrender of title and the release of the enslaved. The obligation to proceed to this end with dispatch lay squarely on those who had asserted ownership and assumed the role of master. It would be helpful if legislation and public funds eased blacks' passage from bondage to freedom, but want of support from the rest of the white population supplied no excuse for delay in emancipation by the immediate agents of slavery.[24]

The suggestion that slaveholders should bear all of the costs of releasing everybody to whom the law gave them title, "even though they should be obliged to maintain them all their days," must have appeared as fanciful to most of Hopkins's readers as history proved it to be in succeeding generations. More carefully reasoned argument favoring the abolition of slavery was under contemplation as Benezet and Hopkins were opening the debate. Not counting on a sudden capitulation to virtue and justice, later proposals looked to incentives for manumission and avoidance of a glut of free persons unprepared for self-maintenance. The time seemed ripe for a comprehensive, scheduled emancipation.[25]

In 1772 Virginia, then locus of nearly half the slaves in North America, petitioned the king to permit the colony to enact such laws as might effectively check the importation of slaves. Four years later the Continental Congress, considering regulations to govern the external trade of the colonies, resolved that "no slaves be moved into any of the United Colonies."[26] By 1787 the public controversy over slavery was furious enough to discourage any probing of the subject in the Philadelphia Convention, save for a provision in the new Constitution that the national government should not, for twenty years, prohibit the movement of slaves from state to state or interfere with their importation from abroad other than by imposing a nominal tax.

Proposals for a gradual, progressive freeing of slaves specified three courses of action. Capable of being pursued separately or in conjunction, all indicated routes of ultimate universal emancipation: return to Africa; dispersion throughout the United States, with preference for relocation in unsettled territory; and reemployment in present situations, thenceforth as wage earners or sharecroppers or small farmers instead of servants in bondage. Of these, the suggestion—long an organized movement—for "colonization" in Africa had the support of a number of founders and national leaders through at least the first third of the nineteenth century. It is a striking fact that the polemical literature on emancipation, argued with acumen and broad comprehension in newspapers and pamphlets throughout the last quarter of the eighteenth century, gave scant attention to the prospect that any successful conversion of a horde of slaves into an incipient citizenry would necessitate huge outlays of public funds. It is also a striking fact that even the strongest arguments for emancipation conveyed little or no optimism that the freed Negro would enjoy a hospitable reception in the white communities of the North or South.

There was ample evidence to support a pessimistic view of the reception liberated Negroes would receive if they set their minds on the rights and privileges commonly enjoyed by the least favored stratum of the white population, no matter where they settled down when their last owners gave up title. Their prospects were best in the northern colonies, but the reality was discouraging even there. It was only under exceptional circumstances that slaves had been found profitable in New England and the Middle Atlantic colonies. They were prized as house servants in the cities, and owners of businesses operating at a stable level of employment might be able to keep a half-dozen black hands busy. If, however, slave owners contracted to supply black workers for factories or construction projects, they could expect trouble with a free white working class competing for jobs. Farmers with sizable acreages of tillable land could recover their investments in slaves and their families, except in Delaware and Maryland, where it was an unusual farmer who had an operation large enough to make profitable use of a dozen adult males. As a consequence of these factors, there were few slaves north of the Potomac, and the manumission rate was high among the fraction of the white population that had invested in slave labor.[27]

Probably at least a third of the free citizens of color residing in North America at the outset of the Revolution were located in the seven colonies from Pennsylvania north to New Hampshire.[28] This provided, let it be emphasized, that one does not put too much meaning into the word *citizen*. At that time, *citizen* and *citizenship* were touched with more than a wisp of meaning, surely, else Thomas Jefferson would not have referred to "our fellow citizens" in the Declaration of Independence, and John Adams would not have allowed the words to remain there. As will appear in the following chapter, however, neither the privileges and obligations nor the bases of citizenship found clear definition in American public law until after the Civil War, especially respecting the status of the free Negro. Thus it was that appeals to the courts infrequently brought blacks relief from community oppression. This was so even though no one questioned their total exemption from the chains of slavery or even (in perhaps a majority of northern states) their claim to be "citizens."[29]

Regardless of the dilution of pigment due to the prominence of Caucasians in their ancestry, men and women of color who passed from slavery to the status of free Negro were soon to find out, if they did not know already, that the autonomy they were to enjoy was a pale shadow of that which the poorest of the whites could claim.[30] Williamsburg's great scholar, St. George Tucker, called it a state of "civil slavery." True, civil slavery was broadly distributed throughout the world, for, in Tucker's view, civil slavery prevails wherever natural liberty is restrained beyond what is "necessary and expedient for the general advantage . . . whenever there is an inequality of rights or privileges between the subjects of citizens of the same states, except such as necessarily result from the exercise of public office." Civil slavery, he asserted, existed everywhere in Europe before the French Revolution and in the American colonies before they became independent states, "and notwithstanding the maxims of equality which have been adopted in their several constitutions it exists in most if not all of them at this day in the persons of our free Negroes and mulattoes whose civil incapacities are almost as numerous as the civil rights of our free citizens."[31] Free white citizens, he should have said.

Tucker wrote his hundred-page booklet as George Washington was closing out the second term of his presidency. Although the prime objectives of his writing were to urge an early abolition of slavery and to recommend means of accomplishing this with minimum damage to the economy and minimal disruption of the white social structure, he found it important to disclose how the Negro who was not in bondage fared in a country where slavery was endemic. There can be no doubt that he was carefully informed on the state of the people about whom he wrote. Tucker's prominence in the public affairs of Virginia would have ensured him more than a casual acquaintance with the suppositions and prejudices of prominent whites in that state and very likely in the immediately adjoining states as well. From such persons he must have heard a considerable amount of reliable testimony about how the free Negroes below the Potomac made a living and otherwise conducted themselves. We have proof that Tucker took pains to inform himself on conditions beyond the reach of his prior contacts.[32]

The acts and the high resolve of the nation's founders would have been fresh in Tucker's mind as he developed his inquiry into the prospects for emancipation and the prospective reception that the white population would extend to the former slaves when their bonds were lifted. He would have found among the fifty-six men who signed the Declaration of Independence, or among the somewhat smaller number who attested to the fundamental truth of the first paragraph of the Virginia Bill of Rights, little support for a contention that the human beings of nonwhite racial stock fall within the categories of "all men" who are "created equal" or "are by nature equally free and independent." Indeed, he quotes generously from a section of Thomas Jefferson's *Notes on the State of Virginia* in which the principal author of the Declaration advances "as a suspicion only" the view that the Africans who were transported to North America were by original creation or afterthought of the Creator rendered observably "inferior to the whites both in the endowments of body and mind." Dubbing this opinion a suspicion was a hedge; careful reading of the paragraph in which the remark appears allows no doubt that as of the time he quitted the governorship of Virginia, Jefferson had concluded that the Africans he knew as slaves and as free blacks were by nature's design a cut below whites.[33]

Whatever may have been the plasticity or tenacity of Thomas Jefferson's perceptions, it is certain that the revolutionary doctrines that infused new state constitutions with declarations of personal rights sounded a death knell for slavery throughout the North and triggered the passage of several thousand Negroes from legal bondage to varying degrees of freedom by the end of the century. Massachusetts moved promptly and decisively; from the Revolution to the Civil War its policies were probably the most humanitarian on this subject. The state assembly resolved that human bondage was contrary to the principles of liberty that animated the ongoing struggle with Britain; town meetings here and there declared the few slaves in their jurisdictions henceforth to be free and put the aged, disabled, and otherwise helpless on public relief rolls; and by 1783 the state's highest court authoritatively ruled that any lingering inhibitions and disablements of slavery had been terminated by the state's new constitution of 1780. By 1800 slavery had been outlawed everywhere in New England and Pennsylvania and within another twenty years in New York and New Jersey as well, except for a few aged blacks waiting for death to free them.[34]

South of the Mason-Dixon line, however, slavery was not legally abolished in any state before the Civil War—though by the 1830s voluntary emancipation was attenuating the institution in Delaware and Maryland. Indeed, during the founding period, when revolutionary and Lockean doctrines were influential, manumission had made some progress in those states and at least a little in Virginia and North Carolina as well. Over the years from the first census (1790) to the Civil War, free Negroes lived in roughly equal numbers north of the Mason-Dixon line and in the states of the upper South (originally Delaware south through North Carolina; later including Kentucky, Tennessee, and Missouri). Comparatively few—never more than 10 percent—of all free Negroes lived in the lower South, where the total black population was always much closer in numbers to the white. While in 1800, at the close of the founding period, free Negroes outnumbered slaves in the North, they were less than 10 percent of all blacks in the then six states of the *upper* South—a percentage that remained approximately constant up to 1860.[35]

The rights, privileges, and immunities most optimistically anticipated on release from slavery may be viewed as of four kinds. First, the right to own, utilize, and dispose of property, real and personal; to maintain a home and be secure in it; and to carry on a trade or calling of one's own choice with one's own tools and instruments, on one's own premises or elsewhere. Second, the right to move about as one wishes, within one's own community or from state to state; do business in public markets; and attend and participate in public meetings. Third, the right to enjoy full protection of law and government and to participate in the process of popular self-government, including service on juries, military duty, the right to hold public office if one could win approval, and the right to participate in public elections. Fourth, the right to choose a mate, marry, and produce children by mutual agreement and without restraints relating to race or other conditions not applicable to white persons.

It would be unrealistic to suggest that whatever state or condition was accorded white persons ought to have been conferred forthwith on the freed blacks. Women were rarely allowed to vote in those days, and there were many restrictions on their capacity to hold and dispose of property. Catholics, Jews, and Quakers were only the most prominent of the religious groups that suffered certain civil disabilities, chiefly in disqualification from public officeholding, though such disabilities were rapidly disappearing.[36] There was recurring contention that Europeans who had not shared England's political and legal legacy ought to undergo a long internship before being invited onto the American jury, into the town meeting, or to vote for public officials. The Negroes whose entire previous experience had been slavery can hardly have believed that they were ready to assume every responsibility and prepared to enjoy every privilege currently being celebrated as the distinctive marks of the American conception of freedom.

John Adams may have thought the creation of a republic was completed when he handed the keys of the White House to Thomas Jefferson in 1801. The truth is that settlement of the terms of membership in the new polity was just getting under way. Nevertheless, in the first few postrevolutionary years the prospect for incorporating free blacks into the new order of justice and liberty proclaimed in the preamble of the Constitution looked pretty good. Everywhere north of Virginia (and in North

Carolina as well) free Negroes were admitted to the polls on the same terms as the whites under the constitutions that transformed the colonies into states. In all of those states, it appears, black men might be called for jury duty and, if they proved their merit (which might include meeting the usual property qualifications), be elected or appointed to public office. Nowhere within the new nation, however, was interracial marriage lawful—or, if in some states lawful, then socially countenanced—and, where cohabitation of black and white was not a crime, it was at least a good way to get two adults and their offspring into trouble.[37] Furthermore, it took a farsighted strategy to improve one's lot by moving around, for several states by then forbade immigration to black people who could not cite a previous connection with them or establish cause for thinking they would be assets if admitted.

These were promises and boundaries of freedom written down in the law. The facts of life were always less certain and usually less generous. Equally devastating to black people's dream of ultimate absorption into the society that was being fashioned by white people for white people were reversals of the strides toward freedom and equality that had been stepped off during the years of winning independence and establishing government by the people. The Revolution led to a much larger, darker free-Negro population as a result of military service, manumission, and escapes from slavery—which tended to counter liberal revolutionary attitudes, especially in the upper South but also in the North. An economic revival of slavery and apparently stronger prospects of slave insurrection both developed in the 1790s, tightening white racial attitudes throughout the South, and concern about free-Negro economic competition led to pressure for discriminatory public policies in both the North and South. Changing law and largely unchanged popular opinion thus combined to exclude black men from anything like full participation in civil society in both the South and North.

Consider in this regard the central right of suffrage. Delaware, Maryland, and North Carolina were the southernmost states that allowed the free black man to stand by the white man on election day. In 1792 Delaware withdrew the privilege, and Maryland followed suit in 1801, both by constitutional provision. Kentucky, which (like Tennessee) had entered the Union with no racial restriction on suffrage, added one in 1799; and the first Ohio constitution of 1802 also contained one. Indeed, of new states admitted between 1800 and the Civil War, only Maine permitted "free" Negroes to vote. Meantime, New Jersey, notwithstanding the broad suffrage provision in its constitution, limited voting legislatively to white males in 1807. Connecticut and Rhode Island, still under their old colonial charters, abolished black suffrage by statute in 1814 and 1822 respectively, each later confirming this step constitutionally. In 1821 New York's revised constitution imposed on Negroes stiff property qualifications for voting, while eliminating any such qualifications for whites. Tennessee in 1834, North Carolina in 1835, and Pennsylvania in 1838 all adopted constitutional bars to black voting—although social pressures and informal measures had already pretty well accomplished this, perhaps most notably in Pennsylvania.[38] On the eve of the Civil War, then, blacks were permitted to vote only in Maine, Vermont, New Hampshire, Massachusetts, and (if sufficiently rich) in New York—and even in those states informal practices frequently qualified this basic right.

Writing about developments in the South in the founding period—about the fading by 1800 of the promise that had appeared in 1776—the historian Ira Berlin says:

> By the beginning of the nineteenth century, the ambiguity that characterized the status of the free Negro during colonial days was gone and the equalitarian enthusiasm of the Revolutionary years had run its course. Whites had pushed free Negroes into a place of permanent legal inferiority. Like slaves, free Negroes were generally without political rights, were unable to move freely, were prohibited from testifying against whites, and were often punished with the lash. Indeed, the free Negro's only right that escaped unscathed was his ability to hold property—a striking commentary on the American idea of liberty.[39]

In this statement (but not elsewhere in his book) Berlin may have underestimated tactics that loosened blacks' hold on property to which they held clear title. The inability to testify against whites in court was only one of several inhibitions on blacks' ability to invoke judicial power to secure their control over property or the product of work. By 1810 this particular legal disability existed everywhere south of the state of Delaware, and those new northern states that were settled heavily from the South (i.e., Ohio, Indiana, Illinois, Iowa, and California) all applied the same restriction. In the northern states, as the nineteenth century wore on, Negroes were excluded from service on juries by law or by practice everywhere except in Massachusetts. This pattern largely reversed that of the early founding period, and it must have been universal in the South.

The crippling effect of these discriminatory provisions on judicial procedures and remedies depended on where free Negroes lived and where their property was located. A search through the statute law of Connecticut for the year 1796 turns up no evidence of intention to allow the freemen of one race less autonomy than was permitted to those of the other in occupancy of a home or control of property; and this may well have been the case generally in New England then, though it was at least somewhat less so south of there, and considerably less so south of the Potomac. In time, fear of free-Negro competition with white labor complicated matters even in New England, especially in lower New England. Probably central to Negro prospects of advancement or assimilation, Negro education, where available, was thoroughly segregated everywhere by the end of the founding period. In the nineteenth century most northern states followed the southern states in tightening restrictions on free Negroes' immigration, thus implicitly calling into question their citizenship under Article IV, Section 2, of the Constitution long before the *Dred Scott* decision—though such restrictions were far from systematically enforced in the North.[40]

As for citizenship, in all its ambiguity of provenance and privileges at that time, the leadership of the federal government was by and large discriminatory both in the founding period and later. For instance, in 1790 Congress restricted the naturalization of immigrants to whites alone (see chapter 3). In 1792 it limited militia enrollment to able-bodied white male citizens, and by early in the nineteenth century all *state* militias excluded blacks.[41] In 1800 the House of Representatives simply refused to entertain a petition from some free Philadelphia Negroes regarding the African slave trade, the Fugitive Slave Act, and the (gradual) abolition of slavery. As early as 1802 the postmaster general warned Congress of the dangers to national security should Negroes be employed in carrying the mail, and Congress accordingly regulated federal contracting for that function in 1810. In 1820 Congress reserved election to District of Columbia offices for whites and authorized the District to adopt a "black code."[42] That same year the tense debate over the admission of Missouri raised directly but did not nearly settle the issue of Negro citizenship, federal or state. The next year an opinion of the U.S. attorney general (William Wirt of Maryland) construed the Constitution to confer citizenship on no one "who has not the *full* rights of a citizen in the State of his residence."[43] Ten years later, in 1831, another U.S. attorney general from Maryland, Roger Taney, endorsed this view in an unpublished opinion for Congress, accepting state racial restrictions on interstate and foreign commerce as police-power measures of internal security and anticipating *Dred Scott* by a quarter-century.[44]

Southern attitudes and interests governed federal race relations policies during the founding period, because of their greater intensity, southern strategic agreement, and near-parity of southern congressional representation —which is also to say that these attitudes and interests (save in debatable degree for those concerning slavery) were widely shared in the North. Clearly the pattern of both legal and extralegal black disability was on the whole harsher the farther south one found it. Ultimately, however, in a pattern emerging if not yet necessarily established in states and nation by the close of the founding period, the regularity of denials of effective citizenship can be seen to have exceeded their regionalism by an appreciable margin.

Evidently most American opinion and most political leaders either placed low priority on providing civil rights to free men universally or doubted the Negro's readiness to assume and use full citizenship then if ever. That black people, through participation in American civil and military institutions, might come to combine for their own purposes, adverse to those of white society, was apparently a prominent concern.[45] That they lacked moral capacity for civic participation was another, not necessarily consistent (or inconsistent), concern. There was not in the leadership of the new American polity, it must be said, more than a small minority prepared to argue publicly (whatever their private views) for larger, more generous convictions against the foregoing concerns.

The Three Races in the United States[46]

It is a striking fact that the movement to bar the free Negro male from participating in elections and to hamper his resort to judicial protection was at its flood just as the liberating impulses of Jacksonian democracy became transcendent. Partly, the restrictions of Negro suffrage that set in by around 1820 were accommodations between longstanding concerns about Negro participation, on the one hand, and the movement toward popular democracy, on the other—for it was apparent that any general liberalization of suffrage eligibility would enlarge Negro participation disproportionally. The answer—and there was little lack of candor about it—was to restrict or eliminate black voting, which no doubt facilitated other discriminations as well.[47]

Partly, too, this second peaking of a determination to elevate the common man was tailored for the white man's benefit in a somewhat different sense—primarily for white men of English and Scottish stock, with special favor for those long resident or born here. It occurred in a time of emphasis on the creation of a nation, something more elemental than the cementing of a republic. An America rightly melded into nationhood would, it was hoped, develop and sustain consensus on matters of highest importance. Consensus, it was thought—and fervently believed by many— could be attained only if the society were dominated by an element of the population rooted in a common culture and made cohesive by a common genetic heritage.

This national aspiration or ethos or mood was one that made the times rough for Catholics, for Irish because they were Catholics though still more because they were Irish, and for recent arrivals from anywhere in Europe, especially if they grew up or acquired their names from territory east of Berlin and south of Munich. Hardest hit by the surging impulse to bring the nation under the hegemony of one harmonious constituency, however, were the native Americans and the black people. The former were unmistakably advised that they could be tolerated only if they removed themselves and their belongings to distant parts of the country or submerged their identity by assuming submissive roles that effectively stripped them of personal autonomy. Blacks, though they may not yet have fully realized their fate, were being served notice that they would for an indefinite period be pariahs in the Republic their labor had helped construct. Neither native Americans nor blacks would be admitted to partnership in the polity that would soon proclaim itself a secure haven of freedom and a friend of the oppressed for Europeans in general, no matter how far east or south.

At this Jacksonian juncture in the Republic's development, Alexis de Tocqueville and his friend, Gustave de Beaumont, were on hand to appraise the prospect of a bright future for the European majority of the American polity, by then sufficiently reconciled in religious sympathies and fundamentally infused with democratic ideology. These visitors' observations and recorded conversations on the lives of Indians and free Negroes in that polity, or on its fringes, rank among our most poignant and perceptive documents on how things stood in the multiracial American political domain half a century after its white inhabitants secured their independence of Europe.[48] When Tocqueville's *Democracy in America* was published, it was acclaimed perhaps most of all—at least in Europe—for its diagnoses of American democratic conformity, "tyranny of the majority," submission to popular opinion, and (projected) progressive deference to public authority. Probably less noticed, though no less notable, were its predictions—among the most pathetic, pessimistic, and prescient in our history—of both the Indians' unfortunate future and the unlikelihood that black and white Americans could make a viable society, given their heritage of slavery and racial alienation.[49]

Notes

1. A note about terminology, or proper nouns, seems appropriate here. In discussing races in this chapter, I have followed no particular conventions and have instead varied my terms with an intent to serve historical and particular contextual purposes and meanings primarily. I have thus referred to native Americans, Indians, and aborigines. Similarly, I have written about Negroes, blacks, ex-slaves, and African Americans and about whites and Europeans. I intend by my usage no comment at all on the appropriateness of the various terms for current use; still less do I intend disrespect by any of the terms employed for the three groups. There seems to be a minor issue of capitalization; I have proceeded in this respect according to what I take to be the most common practice.

2. William Macdonald, ed., *Select Charters and Other Documents Illustrative of American History, 1606–1775* (New York: Macmillan, 1899), p. 25. It followed an earlier patent of 1606 to Gorges and others—a group of entrepreneurs called the Council for New England. No permanent settlements ensued from either patent, but grants or charters from this council to others in turn figured in the founding of Plymouth and Massachusetts Bay colonies and in the separate establishment of Maine and New Hampshire. See, e.g., James Truslow Adams, *The Founding of New England* (Boston: Atlantic Monthly Press, 1921), chap. 3; and Charles Francis Adams, *Three Episodes of Massachusetts History*, vol. 1 (Boston: Houghton, Mifflin, 1892), chap. 7. The precolonial depopulation of New England is considered in, e.g., Frances Jennings, *The Invasion of America* (Chapel Hill: University of North Carolina Press, 1975), chap. 1; and Alden T. Vaughan, *The New England Frontier*, rev. ed. (New York: W. W. Norton, 1979), preface.

3. Bernard W. Sheehan, *Savagism and Civility* (Cambridge: Cambridge University Press, 1980), esp. pp. 141–43; Wesley Frank Craven, *White, Red, and Black* (Charlottesville: University Press of Virginia, 1971), esp. pp. 65–66; Wilcomb E. Washburn, *The Indian in America* (New York: Harper and Row, 1975), pp. 104ff; Gary B. Nash, *Red, White, and Black: The Peoples of Early America* (Englewood Cliffs, N.J.: Prentice-Hall, 1974), passim; Verner W. Crane, *The Southern Frontier, 1670–1732* (Durham, N.C.: Duke University Press, 1928), esp. chaps. 5–6.

4. Nash, *Red, White, and Black;* Washburn, *The Indian in America;* Karen Ordahl Kupperman, *Settling with the Indians* (Totowa, N.J.: Rowman and Littlefield, 1980). On cultural accommodation, see Nash, *Red, White, and Black,* which also nicely summarizes different English colonial practices in different places; James Axtell, *The European and the Indian* (New York: Oxford University Press, 1981); and James Axtell, *The Invasion Within* (New York: Oxford University Press, 1985).

5. A useful survey is Harold E. Driver, *Indians of North America,* 2d ed. (Chicago: University of Chicago Press, 1970). On the controversy, works already cited by Axtell, Jennings, and Nash should be mentioned.

6. On the contrasting European preconceptions, see Sheehan, *Savagism and Civility;* Robert F. Berkhofer, Jr., *The White Man's Indian* (New York: Alfred A. Knopf, 1978); and Roy Harvey Pearce, *The Savages of America* (Baltimore: Johns Hopkins University Press, 1953).

7. See Vaughan, *New England Frontier,* chap. 7, esp. pp. 189–91. See also Berkhofer, *The White Man's Indian,* part 4, esp. pp. 131–33; Wilcomb E. Washburn, *Red Man's Land/White Man's Law* (New York: Charles Scribner's Sons, 1971); and Yasu Kawashima, "Jurisdiction of the Colonial Courts over the Indians in Massachusetts, 1689–1763," *New England Quarterly* 42 (1969): 532–50.

.8. In general, however, Europeans were subject to trial in European courts for crimes against Indians, so the law was asymmetrical for criminal cases. Civil cases—largely those involving claims to land—were more commonly settled by diplomatic than by judicial process.

9. Vaughan, *New England Frontier;* Douglas Edward Leach, *The Northern Colonial Frontier, 1607–1763* (New York: Holt, Rinehart and Winston, 1966); Allen W. Trelease, *Indian Affairs in Colonial New York: The Seventeenth Century* (Ithaca, N.Y.: Cornell University Press, 1960), chap. 7.

10. See Craven, *White, Red, and Black;* Nash, *Red, White, and Black;* Crane, *The Southern Frontier, 1670–1732;* and W. Stitt Robinson, *The Southern Colonial Frontier, 1607–1763* (Albuquerque: University of New Mexico Press, 1979).

11. On the views of this circle—most notably Philip Schuyler, George Washington, Henry Knox, Patrick Henry, and John Marshall—see Walter H. Mohr, *Federal Indian Relations, 1774–1788* (Philadelphia: University of Pennsylvania Press, 1933), chaps. 3, 5; and Reginald Horsman, *Expansion and American Indian Policy, 1783–1812* (East Lansing: Michigan State University Press, 1967), chap. 1.

12. Mohr, *Federal Indian Relations,* chap. 5; Merrill Jensen, *The Articles of Confederation* (Madison: University of Wisconsin Press, 1940), chap. 6; Francis Prucha, *American Indian Policy in the Formative Years* (Cambridge, Mass.: Harvard University Press, 1962), chap. 2.

13. *Journals of the Continental Congress* 33 (1787): 458–59.

14. This statement in the "commerce clause" is the Constitution's only reference to Indians, and the records of the Constitutional Convention show scant consideration of Indian matters. In our constitutional law the language of John Marshall for the Supreme Court in *Worcester v. Georgia*, 6 Pet. 515 (1832), declaring unconstitutional an attempt to extend Georgia law to a missionary on the Cherokee reservation in that state, is often cited. Considering the issues arising from the language of the ninth article in the Articles of Confederation and the committee report to Congress quoted above, Marshall said, "The correct exposition of this article is rendered unnecessary by the adoption of our present constitution. That instrument confers on Congress the powers of war and peace; of making treaties, and of regulating commerce . . . *with the Indian tribes.* These powers comprehend all that is required for the regulation of our intercourse with the Indians. They are not limited to any restrictions on their free actions. The shackles imposed on this power, in the confederation, are discarded." Quoted here from Wilcomb E. Washburn, [ed.], *The American Indian and the United States: A Documentary History*, vol. 4 (New York: Random House, 1973), p. 2621.

15. Quoted in Horsman, *Expansion and American Indian Policy*, p. 61. Other useful secondary sources on the course of policy in the founding period and up to the time of "removal" under Andrew Jackson include George D. Harmon, *Sixty Years of Indian Policy: 1789–1850* (Chapel Hill: University of North Carolina Press, 1924); Prucha, *American Indian Policy in the Formative Years*; Bernard W. Sheehan, *Seeds of Extinction* (Chapel Hill: University of North Carolina Press, 1973); Robert F. Berkhofer, *Salvation and the Savage* (Lexington: University of Kentucky Press, 1965; Westport, Conn.: Greenwood Press, 1977); and Ronald N. Satz, *American Indian Policy in the Jacksonian Era* (Lincoln: University of Nebraska Press, 1975).

16. Trade, it should be noted, was integral and strictly critical to Indian policy from the first settlements, as a condition of peace and, in time if not in the beginning, of Indian dependence. Beside trade, there was gift-giving, to the same ends. Thus Georgia in the 1780s, notwithstanding its chronic role in undermining national Indian policy then and thereafter, still favored national responsibility for trade and, especially, for regular presents to the tribes, which Georgia found it difficult to afford. On the federal government's Indian-trade policy in the founding period, see especially Prucha, *American Indian Policy in the Formative Years*.

17. Thus Henry Knox wrote as early as 1789:

It is . . . painful to consider, that all the Indian tribes, once existing in those States now the best cultivated and most populous, have become extinct. If the same causes continue, the same effects will happen; and, in a short period, the idea of an Indian on this side of the Mississippi will be found only on the page of the historian.

How different would be the sensation of a philosophic mind to reflect, that, instead of exterminating a part of the human race by our modes of population, we had persevered, through all difficulties, and at last had imparted our knowledge of cultivation and the arts to the aboriginals of the country. . . . But it has been considered to be impracticable to civilize the Indians of North America. This opinion is probably more convenient than just.

That the civilization of the Indians would be an operation of complicated difficulty; that it would require the highest knowledge of human character, and a steady perseverance in a wise system for a series of years, cannot be doubted. But . . . [while] it is contended that the object is practicable, under a proper system, it is admitted, in the fullest force, to be impracticable according to the ordinary course of things, and that it could not be effected in a short period.

Report of July 7, 1789, *American State Papers: Indian Affairs,* vol. 1 (Washington, D.C.: Gales and Seaton, 1832), quoted in Berkhofer, *The White Man's Indian,* p. 144.

18. The Removal Act is printed in Washburn, *The American Indian and the United States,* vol. 3, pp. 2169–71; quote on p. 2169. See also Satz, *American Indian Policy in the Jacksonian Era,* chaps. 1–2; and Prucha, *American Indian Policy in the Formative Years.*

19. *Cherokee Nation v. Georgia,* 5 Pet. 1 (1831). Marshall appears to have doubted soon afterward that he should have construed the Cherokees' status so narrowly. See Satz, *American Indian Policy in the Jacksonian Era,* pp. 45–46.

20. *Worcester v. Georgia,* 6 Pet. 515 (1832), quoting from Washburn, *The American Indian and the United States,* vol. 4, p. 2619.

21. Compare Prucha, *American Indian Policy in the Formative Years,* chaps. 9–10 and epilogue, and *The Great Father,* vol. 1 (Lincoln: University of Nebraska Press), pt. 2, with Satz, *American Indian Policy in the Jacksonian Era.* See also for a thoughtful account, Robert V. Remini, *Andrew Jackson and the Course of American Freedom, 1822–1832,* vol. 2 (New York: Harper and Row, 1981), chap. 15, esp. pp. 263–66, 275–79.

22. Anthony Benezet, *Mite Cast into the Treasury: Or Observations on Slave-Keeping* (Philadelphia: n.p., 1792), p. iii. Noah Webster asserted in a pamphlet of 1793: "I have heard elderly people remark that in the early part of their lives it never occurred to them that it was unjust and iniquitous to enslave Africans. It is within a few years only that the question has been generally discussed." He credits Anthony Benezet, spokesman for Philadelphia's Quakers, with having

instituted public remonstrances against slavery about forty years earlier. Noah Webster, *Effects of Slavery on Morals and Industry* (Hartford: Hudson and Goodwin, 1793), pp. 33–34.

23. Samuel Hopkins, *A Dialogue concerning the Slavery of the Africans* (1776; New York: Arno Press, 1969), p. 51.

24. Hopkins's argument takes on special significance because of its endorsement by a New York Society for Promoting the Manumission of Slaves, organized in 1776 with John Jay as president. The society may have sponsored or expressed approval of the pamphlet in its original issue; in any event, it ordered the printing of two thousand copies in the reissue in 1785.

25. Useful accounts include Ira Berlin, *Slaves without Masters: The Free Negro in the Antebellum South* (New York: Pantheon Books, 1974), chap. 2; Winthrop P. Jordan, *White over Black* (Chapel Hill: University of North Carolina Press, 1968), chap. 7; Philip S. Foner, *History of Black Americans* (Westport, Conn.: Greenwood Press, 1975), chaps. 11–12; and John Hope Franklin, *From Slavery to Freedom,* 3d ed. (New York: Alfred A. Knopf, 1967), chap. 10.

26. *Journals of the Continental Congress* 4 (1776): 258.

27. See, e.g., Foner, *History of Black Americans,* chaps. 15–17; Franklin, *From Slavery to Freedom,* chaps. 10–12, 14; Jordan, *White over Black,* chaps. 4–5; and Leon Litwack, *North of Slavery: The Negro in the Free States, 1790–1860* (Chicago: University of Chicago Press, 1961), chap. 3.

28. This is necessarily a rude estimate. We know better how things stood circa 1790, at the time of the first Census, when a larger proportion of free Negroes were to be found in the North. Carter C. Woodson, *The Negro in Our History,* 6th ed. (Washington, D.C.: Associated Publishers, 1931), p. 243; Ulrich B. Phillips, *American Negro Slavery* (New York: Appleton, 1918); more generally, E. Franklin Frazier, *The Negro in the United States* (New York: Macmillan, 1957), pp. 59–67.

29. On citizenship, see James H. Kettner, *The Development of American Citizenship, 1608–1870* (Chapel Hill: University of North Carolina Press, 1978), esp. chap. 10. Perhaps the standard surveys of the civil condition of free blacks, North and South, are Litwack, *North of Slavery,* chap. 2; Berlin, *Slaves without Masters;* and Jordan, *White over Black.*

30. Prior to the revolutionary era, freed slaves were commonly mulattoes, of lighter color. Berlin, *Slaves without Masters,* prologue and chap. 1.

31. St. George Tucker, *A Dissertation on Slavery: With a Proposal for the Gradual Abolition of It in the State of Virginia* (Philadelphia: Printed for Mathew Carey, 1796), pp. 18–19.

32. In January 1795 St. George Tucker wrote to Jeremy Belknap in Boston, submitting eleven questions about the history of slavery in Massachusetts, past and present conditions, and the problems confronting free Negroes who

maintained residence in that state. Belknap, a Congregational minister of wide repute for opposition to slavery, distributed Tucker's letter among some forty persons thought most likely to assist with relevant information and subsequently responded to Tucker's eleven questions in a highly informative letter of approximately eight thousand words. The questions and answers (the latter spill over into other New England states) are in *Collections of the Massachusetts Historical Society, Year 1795* (Boston: Joseph Belknap, 1795), pp. 191–211.

33. Quoted by Tucker, *Dissertation on Slavery*, pp. 86–88; from Thomas Jefferson's *Notes on the State of Virginia* (New York: Harper and Row, 1964), p. 138. Jefferson did not, however, except Negroes from entitlement to natural rights, as to which "all men" were created equal.

34. Foner, *History of Black Americans*, chap. 15. See also David Brion Davis, *The Problem of Slavery in an Age of Revolution* (Ithaca, N.Y.: Cornell University Press, 1975), chaps. 6–7.

35. Berlin, *Slaves without Masters*, chaps. 1–3, tables on pp. 46–47, and appendix 1.

36. See, e.g., Anson Phelps Stokes, *Church and State in the United States*, vol. 1 (New York: Harper and Bros., 1950), esp. chap. 5.

37. Interracial marriage was outlawed universally in the South, but in the North the legal situation was less uniform, notwithstanding general social condemnation. Jordan, *White over Black*, pp. 469–75; Litwack, *North of Slavery*, p. 65.

38. Emil Olbrich, *The Development of Sentiment on Negro Suffrage to 1800* (Madison: University of Wisconsin Press, 1912; New York: Negro Universities Press, 1969); Marion T. Wright, "Negro Suffrage in New Jersey, 1775–1875," *Journal of Negro History* 33 (1948): 168–72; James T. Adams, "Disfranchisement of Negroes in New England," *American Historical Review* 30 (1925): 543–47; Litwack, *North of Slavery*, pp. 74ff.; and Berlin, *Slaves without Masters*, passim.

39. Berlin, *Slaves without Masters*, p. 97.

40. On this paragraph, ibid, p. 96; and Litwack, *North of Slavery*, pp. 92–94, 71–74.

41. Litwack, *North of Slavery*, pp. 31ff.; Jordan, *White over Black*, p. 411.

42. Litwack, *North of Slavery*, chap. 2.

43. Kettner, *Development of American Citizenship*, p. 321.

44. Litwack, *North of Slavery*, pp. 52ff.

45. When Congress declined to entertain the Philadelphia Negroes' petition in 1800, Representative Harrison Gray Otis of Massachusetts argued that it "would teach them the art of assembling together, debating, and the like, and would soon . . . extend from one end of the Union to the other." *Annals of Congress*, 1st session, pp. 229–45, quoted in Litwack, *North of Slavery*, p. 34. Attorney General William Wirt's opinion of 1821 maintained that "if nativity, residence, and allegiance combined, (without the rights and privileges of a

white man,) are sufficient to make [a free Negro] a 'citizen of the United States' in the sense of the constitution, then free negroes and mulattoes are eligible to those high offices, *and may command the purse and sword of the nation.*" Quoted in Kettner, *Development of American Citizenship*, p. 321 (emphasis added here). On militia and military service, see Litwack, *North of Slavery*, chap. 2, passim; and Jordan, *White over Black*, pp. 411ff.

46. From Alexis de Tocqueville's *Democracy in America*, ed. Phillips Bradley and Henry Reeve (New York: Vintage Books, 1945, reprinted from the original edition). This is the abbreviated title of chap. 23 that appears as a page header. The full title is "The Present and Probable Future Condition of the Three Races that Inhabit the Territory of the United States."

47. Litwack, *North of Slavery*, pp. 74ff.

48. Alexis de Tocqueville, *Journey to America*, ed. J. P. Mayer (1959; New Haven, Conn.: Yale University Press, 1960); George Wilson Pierson, *Tocqueville and Beaumont in America* (New York: Oxford University Press, 1938).

49. Tocqueville, *Democracy in America*, chap. 18.

3

The Newcomer to the Land:
Immigration and the Evolution
of American Citizenship

THE AMBIGUITY that marked the legal status of the free Negro for a full two centuries derived in good measure from failure to arrive at a mature conception of citizenship. Unwillingness to give free blacks a voice in the selection of public officials need not have inhibited precise definition of the rights and privileges of citizens, since the prescriptions of nature would have barred infants and children from the polls and there was virtually no question that women (citizens) were without voting rights. Still, the history of citizenship, as it had developed in Greece, Rome, England, and no doubt all major European countries as well, had extended the cloak of citizenship to infants, youths, females, and the masses of adult males who were widely denied any rights of political participation. Had the rights and privileges entailed by citizenship been sharply etched in the minds of early American lawyers, then either legislative enactments and judicial rulings would have assured the free black man a status identical with that of the white man on matters of fundamental importance, or they would have pronounced him not to be a citizen, thus precluding much of the contention about his rights that is reported in the preceding chapter.

Citizenship in the Colonies and Confederation

As far back as 1368 it was established that the monarch of England acquires a new subject every time a child is born within the realm. Within another hundred years it had become a practice to acquire additional subjects by act of Parliament or exercise of the monarch's prerogative. Differentiated and formalized, these processes of adoption were known, respectively, as naturalization and denization. Whether issuing from Parliament or Crown, the act of adoption exacted an oath of allegiance to the monarch and a promise of compliance with the law of the land. Acts of denization often, if not usually, prescribed a special status for new subjects, containing stipulations limiting their place of residence, pursuit of occupation, and range of free choice in respect to this and that. Naturalization in contrast, effected by administrative or judicial office under provision of statute at large, conferred en bloc the privileges and immunities and imposed the duties and responsibilities that at the time were understood to distinguish the status of the free-born English from that of aliens residing in the monarch's realm.[1]

What the rights of homegrown English were when settlements were first planted in Virginia and New England and what they were a century later was nowhere to be found in codified form. English law, when it came to be searched out by lawyers and pronounced by judges, differentiated the Scotch and Welsh from the English, imposed restrictions on Catholics that were not applicable to Protestants, and preserved for persons of English nativity some grounds for believing that they were first-class citizens in a land that also harbored second- and third-class citizens.

This is how matters stood in England when the first colonists came to America, and this is how they stood in America when the thirteen colonies announced their conversion to independence. Bitter controversy over natural rights, inalienable rights, rights of the English, and the giving and withholding of consent to be governed that swept up and down the Atlantic Coast after 1760 would seethe for a quarter-century because lawyers could not say with confidence what one's rights were as an English subject and whether an allegiance acknowledged to the monarch brought one under the rule of England's Parliament.

The foundations of a law of citizenship developed faster in the thirteen colonies than in the homeland, however. This was so because the main business of the English in America, beyond wringing out a living for those on hand, was opening up the land, pushing back the Indians, and attracting new settlers from the British Isles and continental Europe. Many of the continent's fugitives from hard times, political oppression, and religious intolerance made their way to the New World and had the forethought to become British subjects on the way by denization or naturalization. They were welcomed as citizens of any British colony in which they settled.

These acts of adoption in London, however, came at a high cost in fees; and naturalization, which conferred the fullest claims to citizenship, was not available to classes of people identified by previous enactments as offering too slim a prospect of contributing to the welfare of the empire. Catholics and non-Christians generally were excluded from naturalization, though they might be admitted to some highly desirable rights and privileges if the crown was prepared to issue orders of denization.

In consequence of the costs, delays, restrictions, and uncertainties of beneficence in London, a steady stream of continentals poured into North American ports, prepared to take a chance on being accorded an honorable condition in what they supposed to be a hospitable society and a land of opportunity. The white population that had preceded them offered the newcomers a fuller protection of the laws than settlement in England would have afforded and opened doors to participation in the political system that would have been closed to nearly all of them in England. Variance among the colonies and over time in naturalization and denization practices was too complex for rehearsal here. These summary statements, derived from thorough research, may be regarded as authoritative:

> In fact, the American colonists had not waited for Parliament's formal delegation of authority, but had adopted aliens as fellow subjects almost from the beginnings of settlement. . . . Although the legal authority of the colonial governments to admit foreigners to the status of English subjects was questionable, the colonies quickly began to exercise this power, receiving no challenge from London until the late seventeenth century. Methods varied from colony to colony, but generally bore some resemblance to the English practices of executive denization and legislative naturalization and reflected some familiarity with established principles of allegiance and subjectship.[2]

General naturalization laws of colonial origin, fixing requirements for admission to citizenship and procedures for determining compliance with requirements, were rare and commonly ephemeral. In the main, naturalization and denization were accomplished by special acts, sometimes by the governor based on legislative authorization, sometimes by the citation of names and the conditions of admission in the statute itself. By such provision, lone individuals might cross the line from alien to subject; frequently the induction encompassed a group (e.g., a shipload of Lutheran refugees from Salzburg en route to Georgia in 1733), occasionally a class of persons (e.g., resident foreigners professing Christianity who subscribed an oath of allegiance in New York in 1683).

As the colonials must have anticipated, this medley of policies for converting foreigners into subjects of the monarch excited serious concern in England. There was a theory, if not a rule of law, that a person who was a subject in any part of the kingdom was a royal subject in all parts of the kingdom and outside the realm as well. Without a doubt, as London many times made clear, the colonials were promising royal protection and bene-faction to innumerable persons whose petitions the monarch would have rejected. In consequence, increasing numbers who bore an American imprint of citizenship found their status and claims to rights and privileges disputed when they did business with British merchants or traveled to the British Isles. At long last Parliament accomplished enactment of a general provision for naturalization proceedings in the colonies. An act of 1740 required applicants for naturalization to have resided in one or another of the American colonies for seven years uninterrupted by more than sixty con-secutive days of absence, to take a prescribed oath of allegiance, and to give proof of attachment to the Christian faith by having taken the Sacrament within the preceding three months. Quakers and Jews were excepted from the religious requirements; Catholics were not acceptable on any terms.[3]

If top management of the British empire expected the specification of tests of eligibility and a seven-year probationary period to displace colonial exercise of discretion about who would make useful citizens, they were fated for disillusionment. There was a steady admission of individuals who met London's requirements, but for another thirty years colonial legislatures persisted in acknowledging special circumstances and bestowing citizenship on attractive newcomers who were both then and prospectively ineligible under the tests proclaimed by act of Parliament. By 1773 London authorities had had enough. In November of that year an order in council instructed the colonial governors to cease assenting to acts of denization and naturalization designed to evade the tests of eligibility or shortcut the time requirements fixed by the act of 1740. Thus was another flammable log tossed on the pile that was already alight. Three years later, in the Declaration of Independence, Thomas Jefferson put high up on a list of injuries and usurpations that moved the Americans to strike for indepen-dence: "He [the king] has endeavored to prevent the population of these States; for that purpose obstructing the Laws of Naturalization of Foreigners; refusing to pass others to encourage their migration hither, and resisting the conditions of New Appropriations of Lands."

Necessarily, the term *citizenship* is used loosely in the foregoing paragraphs. Throughout the period of colonization there was not, in England or in North America, a single definable status acknowledged as common to all British subjects. Individuals who had been born in England or of English parents while living abroad enjoyed a status more favorable to freedom than that accorded persons of French, German, or other foreign stock who had become British subjects by naturalization; and the naturalized acquired rights, privileges, and immunities not conferred by the process of denization. In America operative differences between naturalization and denization rapidly disappeared, but ascriptions of status based on place of birth or previous residence appeared and persisted. The early emergence and continuing development of popular participation in church, government, and other community affairs forced a realization that life was easier if those who ran things and those who could jeopardize harmony by dragging their feet shared a common heritage of English law, English views about status and deference, and English ways of doing things generally—but not necessarily common "exemptions and impunities."

Accordingly, settlers of British origin were preferred and, in some colonies (but not others), assumed higher legal status as well—principally with respect to rights of political participation. But time and the course of intercolonial competition for settlers worked against these distinctions, progressively leveling them. At bottom, in most colonies, the competition for settlers was a race to elevate land values and to maintain military security. Something like citizenship was legally prerequisite to the assumption of free and indefeasible land titles; something like *full* citizenship must have seemed politically assimilable or essential to military obligation. In general, then, the conditions of colonial development assured potentially productive newcomers from outer Britain and the European continent, not just the English, a warm welcome. Increasingly, the price offered to recruits was a package of political liberty, religious tolerance (within limits, as a rule), immediate progress to ownership of land, and early admission to civic participation. A practically founded democratization of American life was thus well under way before events in the 1760s and 1770s led to colonial talk of liberty and independence.

This is not to say, however, that such civil parities relieved colonial life of social disparities or that shared "English" rights removed divisions among religious and ethnic communities. The differences, and even animosities, were among the elemental conditions of colonial development. Legal progress toward conditions of common citizenship was unlikely to transcend them or even, perhaps, to do much to end them. On the other hand, "English" government in London was unlikely to understand the contrariness of Americans in so freely admitting foreigners to the body politic.

The public declaration of a new regime of independence set off a wave of constitution-writing that by 1784 provided eleven of the associated states with new frames of government—plus one for Vermont, which would wait fourteen more years for admission to the Union. Four of the new constitutions made some provision for incorporating the oncoming waves of Europeans into the body politic. New York was most forthright and businesslike about it. The final paragraph of its constitution (1777) read as follows:

> And this convention doth further, in the name and by the authority of the good people of this State, ordain, determine, and declare that it shall be in the discretion of the legislature to naturalize all such persons, and in such manner, as they shall think proper: Provided, All such of the persons so to be by them naturalized, as being born in parts beyond sea, and out of the United States of America, shall come to settle in and become subjects of this State, shall take an oath of allegiance to this State, and abjure and renounce all allegiance and subjection to all and every foreign king, prince, potentate, and State in all matters, ecclesiastical as well as civil.

Pennsylvania and Vermont were more specific about the terms of taking in the migrants expected to knock on their doors:

> Every foreigner of good character who comes to settle in this state, having first taken an oath or affirmation of allegiance to the same, may purchase, or by other just means acquire, hold, and transfer land or other real estate; and after one year's residence, shall be deemed a free denizen thereof, and entitled to all the rights of a natural born subject of this state, except that he shall not be capable of being elected a representative until after two years residence. (Sec. 42 of the Frame of Government, Pennsylvania, 1776; Chap. 2, sec. 38, Vermont, 1777.)

North Carolina brought the same provision to a close by asserting that having arrived, settled, and sworn allegiance, the erstwhile foreigner "shall be deemed a free citizen" (Sec. 40 of the Form of Government, 1776).

References to "citizen" and "citizenship" were no more frequent in the new constitutions than were references to naturalization and denization. Only Massachusetts, New Hampshire, and North Carolina found a need for either of those words in their fundamental documents. In view of John Adams's well-earned reputation for precise language, it is surprising that he appears to have chosen at random when to insert the word *citizen* in his draft of the Massachusetts Constitution of 1780. The body politic, he wrote, is formed by a social compact "in which the whole people covenants with each citizen and each citizen with the whole people" (Preamble). "It is the right of every citizen" to be tried by free, impartial, and independent judges; therefore, "for the security of the rights of the people, and of every citizen," it is desirable that judges hold their offices for as long as they behave themselves well. Elsewhere in the draft he wrote that "in order to provide for a representation of the citizens of this commonwealth, founded upon the principle of equality," districts for the election of members of the House of Representatives shall be as hereafter specified. And, finally, in order to assure "the citizens of this commonwealth" that the public treasury is their property, no man may serve as treasurer more than five years successively.

Adams cannot have thought these were the only concerns peculiar to citizens: "The people of this commonwealth have the sole and exclusive right of governing themselves"; "all the inhabitants of this commonwealth, having such qualifications [as shall be established] have an equal right to elect officers, and to be elected"; "each individual of the society has a right to be protected by it"; "every subject of the commonwealth ought to find a certain remedy . . . for all injuries or wrongs which he may receive." One concludes that Adams intended no precise meaning for the word *citizen*, and his loose usage is consistent with the promiscuous use of the words *citizen, people, inhabitants, freeholders,* and *freemen* that occurs throughout the constitutions of all the states.

The changes in state of mind that raised the term *citizen* to ascendancy over the term *subject* are obscure. There is nothing hazy in the evidence that *citizen* and *citizenship* had become the accepted terminology by the end of the decade of the Declaration of Independence, the War of Independence, and government under the Articles of Confederation. Before the Congress created by the new Constitution could act, all of the thirteen states plus Vermont had reasserted the authority to convert aliens into subjects that the 1773 order in council had effectively snuffed out. Moreover, in the announcements of policy and decrees of admission, *citizen* and *citizenship* were the preferred words. The Articles, viewed as the initial national constitution, lent no aid to this development and may actually have hampered it. The Continental or Confederation Congress was not endowed with a power to create citizens, and while many of its official acts were highly determinative of the rights and privileges of persons claiming to be subjects of one or another member state, the Congress made no attempt to define a national citizenship or to identify classes of persons who could lay claim to such a status. The hindrance to clear thinking on this subject, if it was such, that the Articles imposed lay in their privileges and immunities clause: "the free inhabitants of each of these states, paupers, vagabonds and fugitives from justice excepted, shall be entitled to all privileges and immunities of citizens in the several states" (Article IV).

The Maryland legislators who held up ratification of the Articles for a full four years to win a point about the western boundaries of member states might have been forgiven for stalling still longer in protest against the careless language of Article IV. The intent of the reference to "citizens in the several states" is dubious at best, considering the utter improbability that anyone supposed the benefits of citizenship to be identical in all the member states.

Far more troublesome, it turned out, was the implication that "free inhabitants" (with the exceptions mentioned) of any state could claim the privileges and immunities of a citizen by the simple expedient of moving across a state line. Certain it is that every delegate to the Second Continental Congress knew that his own state harbored many a "free inhabitant" who could make no claim to citizenship and yet was no pauper, no vagabond, and fugitive from no justice, save that of a European power. Later references in Article IV to "the people of each state," to "any person," and twice to "inhabitants" justifies a surmise that the same random choice that seemed to determine John Adams's selection of words for the Massachusetts Constitution ruled the committee that fixed the language of the Articles of Confederation two years earlier. The term *citizen* did not have a distinctive meaning in the 1770s, and putting the word *free* in front of it can hardly have furthered understanding, implying as it must have that some citizens were not free.

One necessary implication, then, of the existing vagaries of citizenship, on the one hand, and the language of Article IV, on the other, was that any state's admission of someone (say, an alien) to simple residence in effect conferred upon that person citizenship of all the other states. So James Madison remarked in *Federalist No. 42.* Another implication, perhaps less certain and almost certainly unintended, was that an American *national* citizenship had thereby been created.

Citizenship under the Constitution

The adoption of a new Constitution put an end to much of the ambiguity that had encumbered thinking about citizenship for generations, though it left to inference some decisions that might better have been stated explicitly. Something, if not everything, in the experience of waging the struggle for independence taught Americans that they suffered from lack of a common national citizenship as surely as they were handicapped by want of an effective national government. The delegates who assembled at Philadelphia appear to have come into the convention agreed that all persons who, as of then, were acknowledged to be citizens of one of the member states should thenceforth be recognized as citizens of the United States and that any revised or new constitution should give the national government authority to extend national citizenship to additional persons by acts of naturalization.

Admission of foreigners to citizenship in the new Republic by act of the national Congress was established distinctly by the new Constitution: "The Congress shall have power ... to establish an uniform rule of naturalization, and uniform laws on the subject of bankruptcies, throughout the United States."[4] By "uniform rule" the framers seem to have meant not a single rule for all persons seeking admission to citizenship but rather a set of rules, which, taken together, would constitute a policy having common application in all parts of the country. This we infer from the fact that Madison reports no opposition to his statement in the Philadelphia Convention that "the Natl. Legislre. is to have the right of regulating naturalization, and can by virtue thereof fix different periods of residence as conditions of enjoying different privileges of Citizenship."[5]

It may be seen as remarkable that the Philadelphia Convention should write "We the People of the United States ... do ordain and establish this Constitution" yet withhold from their draft any assertion that the duly acknowledged citizens of the several states should thereafter be citizens of the United States. No such declaration is in the document. The institution of a national citizenship was accomplished by inference. To serve in the U.S. House of Representatives, one must have been "seven years a citizen of the United States"; to serve in the Senate, "nine years a citizen of the United States" at the time the Constitution was adopted. Read by a stickler for logic, these were qualifications impossible to meet. George Washington could prove himself to be a natural-born citizen of Virginia beyond any likelihood of dispute. If he or anybody else was a citizen of the United States prior to the adoption of the new Constitution, the blessing must have been bestowed retroactively, conferred by an inference from the fact that nine states ratified a document containing these words. To qualify Oliver Ellsworth and twenty-five others to sit in the first session of the Senate, the retroactive effect had to reach back to 1780.

The endowing of Congress with the power to make uniform rules ("establish an uniform rule") of naturalization did not specify that Congress was to have the exclusive authority to admit aliens to citizenship; that thenceforth one national act of naturalization would convert aliens into citizens of the United States and of the state in which they were domiciled; or that citizenship of a state could no longer be acquired independently of national citizenship. Neither the language of the first federal naturalization law (1790) nor the debate in Congress that preceded it indicates that members of the First Congress understood that such a unification or integration of citizenship had been established, and for a short time several if not all of the states did continue to issue certificates granting citizenship. In a debate in the House of Representatives in 1798 William Craik of Maryland said that "many" individuals had been "naturalized under the State laws" since the federal act of 1790. Earlier that day Albert Gallatin of Pennsylvania estimated that there were some seven to eight thousand persons of this description in the state of Pennsylvania alone.[6] Whatever the number of states continuing the practice, they received official notice to drop that line of business in 1795. Effective 29 January 1795 a new naturalization law replaced the act of 1790; its opening sentence declared "that any alien, being a free white person, may be admitted to become a citizen of the United States, or any of them, on the following conditions, and not otherwise."[7]

Somewhere along the continuum of transpiring events it was fixed in the minds of American political leaders and constitutional lawyers that the act of converting aliens into citizens of the United States also made them citizens of the state in which they were domiciled and assured them that if they later moved about they would pick up citizenship in any state where they established permanent residence. Realization that under the new constitutional regime everyone with a valid claim to citizenship had been stamped with dual citizenship and that thenceforth only the national government could impress that double stamp on aliens excited no controversy. To legitimate dual citizenship, however, was not to resolve all questions about the priority of the claims of state and nation to the loyalty and allegiance of citizens. Here was a gap in common understanding and constitutional provision capacious enough to harbor the spawn of conflicting interests that came to be known as the states' rights controversy.

Competing claims to the citizen's loyalty may have been aggravated by uncertainties that lurked in the language of privileges and immunities referred to earlier. The confusing reference to both citizens and inhabitants in the Articles of Confederation was removed in drafting the Constitution of the United States. Article IV, Section 2, read, "The citizens of each State shall be entitled to all privileges and immunities of citizens in the several states." Still, a measure of equivocation remained; to say "privileges and immunities of citizens in the several States" is not precisely the same as saying "privileges and immunities that an individual may rightfully claim in the state that recognizes him as its citizen." Judicial efforts to bring precise meaning to this aspect of Article IV, Section 2, at best enjoyed only modest success. The barrier to clarification lay in the ambiguous status of former slaves claiming freedom or acknowledged to be free. Released from slavery, had they entered into citizenship or were they only in a civil purgatory indulging in a dream that they had passed into the precincts of an unqualified citizenship reserved for white people?

The full depth of the gulf between eminent constitutional thinkers in their understanding of this issue became evident only generations later, in two epochal events. One of these was the congressional debate in 1820–21 on admission of Missouri as a state; the other was the irreconcilable opinions by members of the Supreme Court in the *Dred Scott* case of 1857. The constitutional subtleties of the issue can be left to history, since the issue as a whole was settled by the ensuing Civil War. That is, the Civil War produced the conditions for its settlement by the victors on the only terms we could find acceptable today. In the Civil Rights Act of 1866 Congress (without the seceded states of the South) thus declared "all persons born in the United States . . . excluding Indians not taxed" to be "citizens of the United States," adding that "such citizens, of every race and color" should share alike in a broad range of rights. There were constitutional doubts about this, too; and in large part to cure these the Thirty-ninth Congress a few months later passed the Fourteenth Amendment and later made its ratification a condition of readmission for the defeated states, thus assuring its passage. The amendment, which became effective 28 July 1868, opens with this sentence: "All persons born or naturalized in the United States, and subject to the jurisdiction thereof, are citizens of the United States and of the State wherein they reside." This language, it is generally acknowledged, provided at last a national definition of citizenship, one in which *national* citizenship took primacy in determining state citizenship.[8] By the terms of the sentence Negroes became citizens of both nation and state; but the phrase about U.S. jurisdiction was presumably included to exempt most tribal Indians from such status, though it has been subject to some dispute and litigation.[9]

Since 1868 we seem not to have been much troubled by doubt about who should be regarded as a person, what constitutes birth, or how naturalization is accomplished. More baffling for differentiating the privileges and immunities of citizens from those of aliens residing in this country is the sentence of the Fourteenth Amendment immediately following: "No State shall make or enforce any law which shall abridge the privileges or immunities of citizens of the United States; nor shall any State deprive any person of life, liberty, or property, without due process of law; nor deny to any person within its jurisdiction the equal protection of the laws." The most inclusive embrace of this language extends to "persons." Due process and equal protection of the laws are made the just claim of all persons, at least all persons within the state's jurisdiction; these are not promises of a preferred status for citizens. The initial clause referring to privileges and immunities of citizens suggests that citizens may assert some claims that cannot be sustained by aliens living next door—but what these may be is as uncertain today as it was when the members of Congress were enlarging their understanding in the first great debate on citizenship in February 1790. In general, and there *are* some exceptions—most notably election to federal office and congressional restrictions of federal benefits, but also some others possibly subject to judicial decision—the legal protections of citizenship can be claimed by all "persons" today under the rubrics of due process or equal protection, especially with respect to *state* regulations.[10]

Citizenship and Immigration in the Founding Period: Three Basic Issues

Since the particular blessings of citizenship remain at least a little uncertain some two hundred years after the Constitution was adopted, we should not be surprised to learn that members of the First Congress were thrown for a loss in their initial attempt to extend the dimensions of the polity by providing for naturalization of aliens.

Creating the government ordained by the Constitution and providing for its revenues and its power to govern were workload enough for the first session of Congress. A naturalization bill was the first important matter before the House in its second session. Debate on a bill prepared by a committee of three opened in the House on 3 February, continued through the following day, and culminated in resubmission of the bill to a committee of ten. Further debate several days later on a substitute bill is not reported in the *Annals of Congress*. We cannot be certain of the considerations that determined the final language of the first naturalization law, but the first two days of debate in the House may inform us sufficiently.[11]

The proposal that the House took up for consideration in February pressed three challenges on its members: (1) racial exclusion; (2) personal qualifications; and (3) rights, privileges, and immunities conferred with citizenship. The first thing to notice about the bill is that it provided for the naturalization of free white persons only. Clearly, the intention was not to accept new immigrant persons of color into the citizenry of the United States. No one who participated in the debate called attention to the exclusion of black persons; no one said anything to indicate that he might have preferred to extend the opportunity of citizenship to black people coming from Africa or the West Indies. The report of debates in the *Annals of Congress* is not verbatim, and it must be assumed that not everything said on the floor seemed to the reporters important enough to take down; however, it is a good guess, considering what they did take down, that the *Annals* would tell us if anybody had made a plea to open up the naturalization process to non-Caucasians.

The second challenge confronting Congress posed the staggering question of who, among Europe's millions of whites, should be welcomed into the polity that must prove to a doubting world that self-government could provide just government for an extensive and scattered population. The committee's bill proposed a year of residence in the United States and the convincing of a judge that the applicant intended to continue residence in America. Satisfied on these two points and that the applicant was free and white, the judge would administer an oath of allegiance. There was no provision for finding applicants to be of good moral character or for inquiring into what they had contributed to society during their year or more of residence in America. The debate on this bare-bones formula for enlarging the citizenry illuminates then-ruling conceptions of the desirable citizen and indicates why America's political leaders wished to draw on Europe for a steady supply of them. "The reason of admitting foreigners to the rights of citizenship among us is the encouragement of emigration, as we have a large tract of country to people," declared John Lawrence of New York. The need for settlers is so urgent, thought Thomas Tudor Tucker of South Carolina, that the newcomers ought not be held up so much as one year in their purchase of land. Since he supposed that under the proposed law citizenship would be a prerequisite for gaining title to land, he could not agree to make citizenship wait on twelve months of lingering somewhere in America. For others, the need for importing labor was not so desperate. Theodore Sedgwick of Massachusetts thought (as New Englanders had long believed) that the policy of settling the vacant territory by immigration "is of a doubtful nature" and that the population might be multiplied "by a more eligible and convenient mode."[12]

The urgency of attracting Europeans to America and the possibly deterrent effect of a probationary year before citizenship were evidently not preeminent concerns of the First Congress, however. What bothered members most about the required year of residence, not necessarily confined to a single community, was the insufficient opportunity it would offer neighbors of good judgment and civic concern for appraising immigrants' characters and advising on their fitness for American citizenship. Virginia's James Madison reminded his auditors that we were not seeking incomers simply to increase the population count: "No, sir, it is to increase the wealth and strength of the community." He would be extremely sorry if our naturalization policy "excluded a single person of good fame who really meant to incorporate himself into our society; on the other hand, I do not wish any man to acquire that privilege but such as would be a real addition to the wealth or strength of the United States." For James Jackson of Georgia there was a great deal more to be thought about than his Virginia colleague had mentioned. The terms of the bill before the House were, in his mind, much too easy for the interests of the people of America:

> I think before a man is to enjoy the high and inestimable privileges of a citizen of America, that something more than a mere residence among us is necessary. I think he ought to pass some time in a state of probation, and, at the end of the term, be able to bring testimonials of a proper and decent behaviour ... if bad men [for example, vagrants, paupers, and other outcasts of Europe] should be dissatisfied on this account and should decline to emigrate the regulation

will have a beneficial effect, for we had better keep such out of this country than admit them into it.[13]

Need for national settlers and artisans of advanced skills and the desirability of winnowing out the riffraff figured prominently in the debate as reported so far. There was another consideration in some minds, but it got little mention. This was a recognition that naturalized male citizens sooner or later would be voters and a concern that prospective voters must understand the fundamental character of republican government, be devoted to it, and be able and willing to contribute to the success of America's experiment in popular self-government. Michael Jenifer Stone of Maryland spoke most directly to this point:

> I would let the term of residence be long enough to accomplish two objects before I would consent to admit a foreigner to have anything to with the politics of the country. First, that he should have an opportunity of knowing the circumstances of our Government, and in consequence thereof, shall have admitted the truth of the principles we hold. Second, that he shall have acquired a taste for this kind of Government. And in order that both of these things may take place in such a full manner as to make him worthy of admission into our society, I think a term of four to seven years ought to be required.[14]

Thus was projected into policy a perception that augmenting the white population to raze the forests, drain the swamps, and repel the Indians was not enough. Beyond this objective, immigration and naturalization should preserve or enrich the moral quality and productive capacity of the nation as well as the republican character to which the new nation was committed. It cannot be doubted that 3 and 4 February 1790 were days of expanding consciousness for several members of the first Congress elected by the American people. It is equally certain that for most if not all of the men who participated in the debate, these were days of a dawning realization that the new adventure into federalism they were launching would greatly complicate any strategy for nursing union into nationhood. The problem of how to fit a national policy on citizenship into the distribution of authority between nation and states was the most baffling of the three challenges Congress faced in its first attempt to fashion a "uniform rule of naturalization."

The bill under debate in 1790 reflected a presumption that a given body of rights, privileges, immunities, and obligations inhered in citizen-

ship and would bedeck the new, naturalized citizen *ex necessitate rei* unless
specific reservations were written into the law. One such reservation was
in the bill. The requirement of a year's residence as a prerequisite for
admission to citizenship was followed by the statement that the applicant
"shall be entitled to all the rights of citizenship, except being capable of
holding an office under the State or General Government, which capacity
they are to acquire after a residence of two years more." Tucker of South
Carolina, who ought to have known better, assumed that citizenship was a
precondition to acquiring title to land and moved to strike out the requirement of a year's residence. It was the object of his motion, he said, "to let
aliens come in, take the oath, and hold lands without any residence at all."
As Tucker supposed that the right to acquire real estate inhered in
citizenship, so others jumped to a conclusion that citizenship conferred a
right to vote in elections and hold public office. They were determined not
to let this happen until a period of residence, before or after completing
naturalization, had prepared the immigrant for a role in republican
government.[15]

A cloud of misapprehension thus blew in to befog the debate. Alexander White of Virginia made an admirable attempt to clear the air. As he
saw it, the power of Congress "extends to nothing more than making a
uniform rule of naturalization. After a person has once become a citizen,
the power of Congress ceases to operate upon him; the rights and privileges of citizens in the several states belong to those states . . . all, therefore,
that the House have to do on this subject is to confine themselves to a
uniform rule of naturalization, and not to a general definition of what
constitutes the rights of citizenship in the several States." One may quibble
that the Virginia congressman should have mentioned the authority of
Congress to prescribe rights and duties in those sectors of affairs that had
been listed in its delegated powers, but clearly he was on the right track. It
was not until well into the second day of discussion, however, that the
disjunction of a naturalization process and the law governing the rights
and duties of citizens won general recognition in the House. Theodore
Sedgwick called for time out for more thinking. The *Annals of Congress*
reported:

> He did not recollect an instance wherein gentlemen's ideas had been
> so various as on this occasion; motions and observations were piled
> on the back of one another, and [the congressmen] from the want of
> understanding the subject had involved themselves in a wilderness

of matter out of which he saw no way to extricate themselves but by the rising of [the Committee of the Whole]. . . . He conceived himself as much in fault as any member because he had not yet turned his attention so seriously to the subject as he ought.

To which William Smith of South Carolina added that he wished to take his share of the blame for not understanding the subject.[16]

Within a month of this two-day experience in self-education, both houses of Congress had agreed to a naturalization act that stemmed from an entirely new bill. The act, effective 26 March 1790, made no reference to the rights accruing to citizens or the duties and obligations that any arm of government could exact from them. The residence requirement was raised to two years, doubling the period specified in the bill that had been scuttled. Furthermore, twelve consecutive months of the required twenty-four must have been spent within a single state, and it was in that state that the applicant would stand before the judge for a determination on fitness for citizenship. Several other provisions not found in the first bill were included, relating mainly to the effect of naturalization of parents on the citizenship of their children.[17]

Step by step, members of the First Congress groped their way to reconciliation of the potentially clashing objectives uppermost in their minds as they fashioned a national policy for incorporating foreigners into the American body politic. The first naturalization law (1790) was an enactment of one paragraph and less than three hundred words; it was replaced in 1795 by an act more than three times as long; this in turn gave way in 1798 to a statute of some two thousand words; and finally what proved to be the enduring statement of naturalization policy came in 1802 in a slightly longer law. These four basic acts, supplemented and modified by occasional amendments, fleshed out a policy on extending citizenship to immigrants that was to maintain its essential character until after the Civil War.

The restriction of naturalization to "free white persons," specified in the act of 1790, was reiterated in the act of 1795, incorporated by implication in the law of 1798, and again made explicit in 1802 by reiterating the opening words of the acts of 1790 and 1795: "That any alien, being a free white person, may be admitted to become a citizen of the United States. . . ." Indians who were born into a tribal society and remained under tribal rule were deemed, even after adoption of the Fourteenth Amendment, not to have been born subject to the jurisdiction of the United States and so were not citizens of the United States. Not being white, they could not, by leaving the tribe and putting themselves under the jurisdiction of the United States, clothe themselves with American citizenship by process of individual naturalization. Whole tribes or fragments of tribes did from time to time weary of their separate nationhood and became citizens of the United States en masse by special act of Congress, and special legislation or treaties made provision for individual Indians and families to renounce their tribal allegiance, remove themselves from their tribal society, and invoke a status of citizenship putting them on a par with white persons born in the United States.[18]

Black persons and persons of mixed blood continued to be denied citizenship by naturalization until Reconstruction days. A motion in Congress to terminate this exclusion at any time prior to the Civil War would only have excited invective, deepened the abrasions that frustrated accommodation and agreement, and endangered legislation on other subjects that were crying for attention. In July 1870, two years after the Fourteenth Amendment became effective, and with the eleven former member states of the Confederacy again represented, Congress wrote into the statutes that "the naturalization laws are hereby extended to aliens of African nativity and to persons of African descent." American Indians remained in the limbo described above, and Asians who could not justify classification as Caucasians continued to be excluded from naturalization proceedings.

Of the three critical issues with which the national naturalization debate began, then, the *first* was effectively settled for eighty years in 1790 and then resettled by civil war. The *third*—the issue of the particular privileges and immunities of citizenship—was left to the states by Congress in 1790 and, as a national matter, to the implications of Article IV, Section 2, in decisions of the federal courts.[19] If the Civil War and the Fourteenth Amendment seemed to settle this issue by reconstructing federalism, the *Slaughterhouse Cases* in 1873 nullified that settlement almost immediately. Since then, however, much of the substance of national citizenship has been inferred by the Supreme Court from the Fourteenth Amendment's due process and equal protection clauses, and it seems fair to say that the Court has outweighed Congress by far in dispositions of this issue.

Finally, there was the *second* issue—the appropriate personal qualifications for citizenship in a republican society. This issue was the one of the three that preoccupied Congress throughout the founding period, but political developments imposed new perspectives on it after the 1790 legislation. These were to some degree perspectives of partisan advantage. Party alignments were taking shape in Congress and its elections by then; and it turned out that immigrants were voting Republican preponderantly, giving Federalists reason to try to restrict immigration or (more feasibly) to delay conferring citizenship on immigrants, insofar as federal legislation alone could do so.[20] There was, however, some tendency for those political leaders later prone to "Federalism" to have been, in 1790 and before, relatively conservative in their concerns about the social and personal qualifications of immigrants for republican (*lower*-case) citizenship; and it was apparent in the congressional debates that most members shared such concerns in some shape or form. The issue did not simply reflect party interests but helped determine party divisions; and in doing so it reflected conflicting perspectives on, inter alia, the French Revolution, the virtues of social homogeneity, the conditions of national security, and the nature of republican government. The alignments and arguments over subsequent legislation on citizenship and immigration were thus complex and are worth following further.

Regulating Citizenship: Community and Security, Partisanship and Republicanism

Debate on the bill that produced the naturalization law of 1802 was not reported in the *Annals of Congress;* the great fight over the organization of the federal courts and a few other salient issues pushed the business of making citizens to the back of the public mind. Debate on the bills before Congress in 1795 and 1798 was reported in sufficient detail to indicate the members' principal concerns. Perhaps most striking is the absence of much evidence in those years that they wished to expedite the settlement of vacant lands. There was occasional notice of this concern but not a lot—not much more than the occasional acknowledgment of concern about partisan naturalizations of new voters in certain states. The initiatives in the legislation of 1795 and 1798 were taken by those apparently endeavoring to temper the entrepreneurial quest for new Americans and to determine more carefully the qualifications of immigrants for republican citizenship and useful employment.[21] By 1798 Federalist concerns about national security were also apparent, for armed conflict with France seemed probable by then and the activities of radical aliens were arguably dangerous. The naturalization law of 1798 has thus been seen by some historians as a first phase of the alien and sedition legislation that came later that year.[22]

One hundred sixty individuals were sitting in the House of Representatives when one or both of the naturalization laws of 1795 and 1798 were under consideration, and almost exactly one-third of them are shown by the *Annals of Congress* to have taken the floor during the debate on these two measures and another one designed to impose a sizable tax on certificates of naturalization. Under the best of circumstances, there is considerable risk in attributing a dominant mood to so many persons. The risk rises when it is recognized that remarks are reported in the third person and abbreviated, summarized, or suppressed altogether according to the reporter's notion of what readers wanted to read. Even so, and conceding the implicit partisan aspect of the debates, it appears that members of Congress were nearly united in the opinion that admissions to citizenship under the first naturalization law had been too generous. There was little evidence of dissent on either occasion, 1794–95 and 1797–98, from the sentiment that America should serve as a haven for refugees from Europe's political and religious despotisms. There was, however, a counterbalancing concern: reception of the foreign born into American society, no matter what their personal appeals for deliverance, must not be permitted to impair the republican principles and institutional fabric that made the United States a land of promise for people in despair. William Vans Murray of Maryland revealed the dilemma on the second day of debate in December 1794. According to the *Annals of Congress*, Murray "was quite indifferent if not fifty emigrants came into this Continent in a year's time. It would be unjust to hinder them, but impolitic to encourage them. He was afraid that, coming from a quarter of the world so full of disorder and corruption, they might contaminate the purity and simplicity of the American character."[23]

It was the democratic excesses of the French Revolution that excited Congressman Murray's apprehension; it was the success of the revolutionary crusade and the stubbornness of the resistance it encountered that a week later impelled William Giles of Virginia to move a provision that before admission to citizenship any person who "shall have borne any title or order of nobility in any Kingdom or State from whence he may come . . . must renounce all pretensions to his title" before the court in which his petition for citizenship is heard and that his renunciation must be entered on the records of the court. Representative Samuel Dexter of Massachusetts chose to view this demand for repudiation of European attachments as a rebuke to a faction or party, now called Federalists, which had lately been advertising its hostility to the hordes of French then pouring into America and available to whip up sympathy and support for the revolutionary cause in France. Dexter countered Giles with a motion to attach to the language requiring renunciation of titles of nobility a further requirement that if a petitioner for citizenship "shall, at the time of his application, hold any person in slavery, he shall in the same manner renounce all right and claim to hold such person in slavery." The House voted 63 to 28 not to require slave owners to renounce their claims to their slaves and then voted 59 to 32 to accept Giles's motion to require members of any European nobility to renounce their titles. Five members of the House voted to impose both requirements; nine voted to impose neither. There was a core of the then-nascent partisanship in the voting, but there were also many votes independent of it.[24]

The debate on renunciation of titles and slaveholding took up three of the nine days devoted to the naturalization bill. The reporters who provided copy for the *Annals* thought the free-for-all generated by Giles (a slaveholder, though he lamented it) and Dexter (clean as a whistle on that count) worth as much attention as all other pending issues on naturalization and citizenship. Their emphasis may have been provoked by the flagrant display of partisanship and sectionalism, but a moderate disposition to credit the protagonists with concern for the nation's well-being suggests that the dominant concern in the House was to fix standards and procedures for admission to citizenship that would tend to sustain enlightened self-government and assist national development. Pursuant to this concern, differences of opinion appeared frequently within, as well as between, each of the emerging parties.

John Page, a third-term (Republican) congressman from Virginia in 1794, spoke first on an omnibus motion to revise the original naturalization law of 1790. He sympathized with the goal of the motion: to increase assurance that only persons of good character, goodwill, and productive capacity would be added to the roster of American citizens. It was reported in the *Annals* that "he thought nothing more desirable than to see good order, public virtue, and true morality constituting the character of citizens of the United States; for without morality, and indeed a general sense of religion, a republican government cannot flourish, nay cannot long exist since without these disorders will arise which the strong arm of powerful government can alone correct or retrieve." He would vote against the proposed changes, however, because he thought the provision that two witnesses attest to such character would be an unwarranted impediment to good applicants and no impediment to bad ones, who could easily find supporters to swear for them, and because the suggested procedures depended too heavily on oaths, which he found repugnant. He said his Virginia colleague, James Madison, agreed with him.[25]

If there had been a motion to endorse John Page's dictum that public virtue and true morality are indispensable for the survival of republican government, it is unlikely it would have stirred a single dissenting vote. But a further resolution that victims of oppression who had caught a vision of free institutions and developed a lavish admiration for the American political system could, without an extended internship in an American community, be counted on to contribute significantly to the success of republican government probably would have lost by a sizable majority in 1795. Theodore Sedgwick (proto-Federalist) of Massachusetts, for instance, "had pride, and he gloried in it, believing his countrymen more wise and virtuous than any other people on earth; hence he believed them better qualified [than any other people] to administer and support a republican government." He would not turn away "such virtuous individuals as might fly here as an asylum against oppression," but he rejected the rash theory that such people, brought up under despotic, monarchical, and aristocratical governments, "are, as soon as they set foot on American ground, qualified to participate in administering the sovereignty of our country." The character that he attributed to his country with such pride "was the result of early education, aided indeed by the discipline of the Revolution."[26]

These were themes on which a dozen congressmen dilated. Thomas Fitzsimons from Pennsylvania (himself an Irish immigrant and fledgling Federalist) thought that a ten-year residence requirement, which had been proposed, was much too long a time for an alien to have to wait for citizenship; it would turn fugitives from despotism into enemies of our own government. Samuel Smith of Maryland (Republican), on the other hand, was for making them wait for the longest stretch of time that anyone was likely to propose, so that prejudices the aliens had acquired in the lands of their birth might be effaced "and that they might by communication and observance of our laws and government have just ideas of our Constitution and the excellence of its institutions before they were admitted to the rights of a citizen." Not even this precaution was quite sufficient for James Hillhouse (Federalist) of Connecticut. If the sponsor of the motion before the House would amend it with a view to "incapacitating all foreigners whatever from holding, upon any account, a civil office in

America [he, Mr. Hillhouse] would agree with him because he did not want to see any of them in such offices, and conceived that Americans could legislate much better for themselves without any such assistance."[27]

Fisher Ames, staunch Federalist and supporter of the Alien and Sedition Acts four years later, may have been the most sanguine and prescient among the congressmen sitting in the House in 1794–95. The question immediately before the House, he said, when the proposal to require renunciation of titles of nobility was under consideration, is the relation of that provision to the objective of the naturalization bill in its entirety. The basic objective, he asserted, is "to make a rule of naturalization for the admission of aliens to become citizens on such terms as may consist with our tranquility and safety." It would not be safe or proper to admit aliens to citizenship indiscriminately, he said,

> yet a scrutiny into their political orthodoxy might be carried to a very absurd extreme. . . . Now, said he, do we think of refusing this privilege to all heretics in respect to political doctrines? Even that strictness would not hasten the millennium. For our own citizens freely propagate a great variety of opinions hostile to each other, and, therefore, many of them deviate widely from the intended standard of right thinking; good and bad, fools and wise men, the philosopher and the dupes of prejudice, we find could live very peaceably together, because there was a sufficient coincidence of common interest. If we depend on this strong tie, if we oblige foreigners to wait seven years, till they have formed it, till their habits as well as interests become assimilated with our own, we may leave them to cherish or to renounce their imported prejudices and follies as they may choose. The danger of their diffusing them among our own citizens, is to be prevented by public opinion, if we may leave error and prejudice to stand or fall before truth and freedom of inquiry.[28]

The first naturalization law, enacted by the First Congress in 1790, had required applicants for citizenship to appear in court in a state where they had dwelt for twelve months and supply evidence that they had completed two years of residence somewhere in the United States. On 8 January 1795 the House of Representatives approved the language that replaced the law of 1790. As under the original act, candidates for citizenship had to petition for it in a state where they had lived for a year; now, however, the petition had to document their residence somewhere in the United States for at least *five* years and their having filed with a court of record at least *three* years earlier a declaration of intent to sever ties with all sovereigns that might claim them as subject and to become a citizen of the United States. The first naturalization law had asked for nothing from applicants other than a specified residence, a promise to support the Constitution, and a good impression on a judge. The Third Congress, impressed as we have seen with the importance of preserving "the purity and simplicity of the American character," called for them to make the renunciation of allegiance to any foreign power that they had promised to make at least three years earlier; to renounce all hereditary titles and any attachments to an order of nobility that they might previously have borne; and to swear to support the Constitution of the United States. Finally, satisfied on these specifics, the court must find—"it shall further appear to their satisfaction"—that throughout his residence in the United States the applicant "has behaved as a man of good moral character, attached to the principles of the Constitution of the United States, and well disposed to the good order and happiness of the same."[29]

This was the best balance Congress could fashion then between a policy generous in its welcome to immigrants seeking the protection of a republican government and a naturalization procedure intended to screen out those of counterfeit or indifferent commitment to such a government. The act of 1795 was not two years old when a strong contingent in Congress reached the conclusion that counterfeits had become a menace. In major American cities there were too many newcomers fresh from Europe who proved by their conduct that the search for a good life in a new land was secondary to a wish to embroil Americans in Europe's rivalries; if they were not so numerous as they seemed, this was because they were so busy and so noisy. In June 1798 Congress sent to the president for signature a measure requiring all aliens to report periodically to a designated court or official their location in the United States, increasing from three years to five the time of advance notice of intention to file for naturalization, and extending from five years to fourteen the length of residence required before conferral of citizenship.

This was the Congress that enacted the ill-famed Alien and Sedition Laws—a further response to the concerns that sparked the alien registration provisions of the new Naturalization Act. Probably the majority that passed the Naturalization Act would have written it differently if they had believed they could do so constitutionally. Almost certainly they would have ordered the deportation of aliens who, in proper proceedings, were adjudged dangerous to the peace and safety of the United States; and they did empower the president to do this in a bill that became law a week after the Naturalization Act took effect. But they might well have let stand the five-year period of prior residence and three-year notice of intention to apply for citizenship in the Naturalization Act of 1794 and have written instead an exclusionary immigration law. Such an approach assumed high priority in discussions of that day about how to deal with the problem of "internal security." Exclusionary legislation would probably have provided for the selective granting of entry permits in European cities and seaports and, after immigrants' arrival on our shores, for further inquiry into their characters and previous conduct as well as their plans for employment in the New World. Such legislation might or might not have succeeded in Congress if proposed, but it was beyond the constitutional authority of Congress and was not proposed. Determined to avoid controversy over the further importation of slaves until a new Constitution was agreed upon, the Philadelphia Convention had provided that Congress could not before 1808 prohibit "the migration or importation of such persons as any of the states now existing shall think proper to admit." So Congress in 1798, unable to deny entry to high-risk foreigners, denied them instead any chance for citizenship until they had lived at least fourteen years under American jurisdiction.

The decision of a bare majority (forty-one of the eighty-one who voted in the House) to raise the residence requirement to fourteen years drew some of its support from a growing sentiment that admission to citizenship ought not carry with it the right to hold public office or vote in the election of public officials. Back in 1795, in the debate on the second Naturalization Act, James Hillhouse of Connecticut had suggested that immigrants be barred from voting or election to office for the remainder of their days. Three years later Hillhouse was in the Senate, but there was still some support for his position in the House. Robert Goodloe Harper of South Carolina was part of it. It was high time, he argued, to recover from the mistake of 1790, when the decision was made to admit foreigners to citizenship. According to the *Annals,* "he believed the time was now come when it would be proper to declare that nothing but birth should entitle a man to citizenship in this country." He therefore proposed a substitute to the motion before the House: "that provision ought to be made by law for preventing any person becoming entitled to the rights of a citizen of the United States, except by birth."[30]

Harper was a man of vigorous convictions, yet this proposal may have been a bit drastic, even for him. Still, when Harrison Gray Otis of Massachusetts proposed that "no alien born, who is not at present a citizen of the United States, shall hereafter be capable of holding any office of honor, trust, or profit, under the United States," Harper declared himself willing to support the motion if it was extended to bar such persons from voting in the election of members of Congress and the several state legislatures. Congressmen who may have been sympathetic with this view had no special call to say so, since the question was not before the House as an amendment. Moreover, regulation of the right to vote on any elective office, including the House of Representatives, was, Harper conceded, beyond the constitutional powers of Congress.[31]

Robert Goodloe Harper and Harrison Gray Otis should not be offered in evidence as representative of the views of their time on the augmentation of America's citizenry through immigration. High Federalists in the first rank of uncompromising support for the 1798 Sedition Act, they held minority positions on many public issues of their generation. On the record of the First, Third, and Fifth Congress, however, we cannot easily assume that opposition, say, to the Alien and Sedition Acts bespoke support for a citizenship policy conferring rights of suffrage and officeholding on immigrants who lacked any prior experience of republican political life. There had persisted during the decade of government under the Constitution a conviction that probably had a considerable acceptance even before the end of the colonial period. Thomas Jefferson voiced it in responding to a set of questions from the French consul in Philadelphia. Jefferson's reply, later published as *Notes on the State of Virginia,* was penned in the summer of 1781, soon after the Articles of Confederation went into effect.

One of the French consul's queries concerned the number of people living in Virginia. Jefferson extended his reply to the rate of population growth and the consequences of a continuing inflow of migrants for civil life in America as a whole as well as Virginia in particular. Acknowledging the need for further import of "useful artificers," he turned thumbs down on proposals to keep up a rapid influx of foreigners. He had written in 1776 the immortal statement about people's right to organize their government in such way as seems to them most likely to effect their safety and happiness. Now, just five years later, he added for the benefit of the French consul, "It is for the happiness of those united in society to harmonize as much as possible in matters which they must of necessity transact together." The measure of harmony essential to an acceptable minimum of happiness is not compatible with the rate of in-migration currently favored, in Jefferson's view:

> Civil government being the sole object of forming societies, its adminis-tration must be conducted by common consent. Every species of government has its specific principles. Ours perhaps are more pecu-liar than those of any other in the universe. It is a composition of the freest principles of the English constitution, with others derived from natural right and natural reason. To these nothing can be more opposed than the maxims of absolute monarchies. Yet from such we are to expect the greatest number of emigrants. They will bring with them the principles of the governments they leave, imbibed in their early youth; or, if able to throw them off, it will be in exchange for an unbounded licentiousness, passing, as is usual, from one extreme to another. It would be a miracle were they to stop precisely at the point of temperate liberty. These principles, with their language, they will transmit to their children. In proportion to their numbers, they will share with us the legislation. They will infuse into it their spirit, warp and bias its directions, and render it a heterogeneous, incoherent, dis-tracted mass. I may appeal to experience, during the present contest, for a verification of these conjectures. But, if they be not certain in event, are they not possible, are they not probable? Is it not safer to wait with patience [two or three decades] longer, for the attainment of any degree of population desired or expected? May not our govern-ment be more homogeneous, more peaceable, more durable?[32]

In time, the high Federalist sponsors of the Naturalization Law of 1798 and the Thomas Jefferson of 1781 were overruled by their peers. In 1802, almost four years after the residence requirement for naturalization was raised to fourteen years, Congress reduced it to five years, where it had been fixed in the second Naturalization Law of 1795. Five years was to remain the waiting period from 1802 until the present day.

Citizenship and Political Community

Colonies and later the American states welcomed and generally encour-aged immigration from all sectors of Europe. Support for this approach to American settlement was not unanimous though, and from late colonial times onward there were concerns about impairment of common culture and political competence by diverse streams of immigration. Such views seem to have been most frequent in New England, where communal traditions were strongest and economic incentives to bid for immigrants were weakest. By and large, however, American policies and practices concerning immigration from the European continent were, chiefly for economic reasons, far from exclusive.

The Constitution handed Congress responsibility, or at least authority, for a national policy on citizenship (a "uniform rule of naturalization")—though *not* for regulating immigration in the founding period. De facto, whatever the constitutional expectation, authority over citizenship, or naturalization, was not Congress's alone, for states continued to naturalize their own immigrants and to confer rights of political participation independently during the founding period. Nevertheless, the formulation of a national policy on citizenship became one of the first priorities of the First Congress, once certain essential tasks of establishing an operational government were completed.

As Congress assumed this responsibility, questions of appropriate qualification for republican citizenship, and of an adequate basis in political community for republican government, quickly became paramount. The uniform rule was written three times in the 1790s, and the conditions of citizenship were tightened each time. As party alignments took shape in Congress, differences of opinion concerning citizenship—especially about how soon to confer it—came to figure in those alignments, both for reasons of party electoral advantage and because genuine differences of perspective on this issue tended to divide and to shape the nascent parties. In time these partisan differences were assimilated to others, chiefly concerning reactions to the French Revolution and perceptions of threat to national security. Under constitutional limits, revising the rule of naturalization became the only feasible way of regulating immigration for those who wished to do so. In reviewing the reports of debates in the House of Representatives on revisions of naturalization law in the 1790s, one's attention is likely to be drawn to progressive disagreement and partisanship. One might therefore miss, in a casual reading of these debates, the evidence of substantial agreement among members on the critical place of enlightened, responsible citizenship in a viable republican government. For most members, apparently, this also implied a consentient society—one able to sustain common civic attitudes and practices, grounded in common moral norms. There was disagreement, to be sure, about the gains and losses for these objectives to be expected from the particular criteria and procedures proposed for inclusion in the law, but there was no evident disagreement about the appropriateness or priority of these objectives for public policy.

The thread that runs most prominently through congressional debates on the naturalization acts is a concern to promote responsible citizenship, based on personal character and adequate experience of (or at least exposure to) republican institutions. There was no certain way of doing this, and Congress simply did the best it could, relying heavily on character witnesses and applicants' asseverations of commitment and also looking at the length of opportunity for acculturation and accumulation of civic experience. (In 1794 Giles of Virginia proposed to amend the naturalization bill to include, as a test, evidence that the applicant for citizenship was "attached to the Republican form of government." Some members doubted that this test was sufficiently definite to be administrable; others opined that it could be too easily satisfied pro forma. James Madison, for instance, thought the term *Republican* was adequately understood, yet there were signs in the consideration of this issue, and certainly elsewhere in the proceedings, that a serious definitional effort might occasion protracted partisan debate. In the end, after an interesting discussion, the proposal was withdrawn.)[33]

A secondary, closely associated thread in the legislation was a concern for fostering political community, premised on cultural similarity and, for some, on social homogeneity, as a source of the common moral norms considered essential for effective self-government. In the face of diverse migrations to America, past and present, this concern was almost bound to generate disagreement over the sort and degree of homogeneity to be promoted; and so it did. The disagreement contributed to party differences and, from the revolutionary international context of the time, tended to merge with the national security issue. Since immigration could not be limited constitutionally, the attention of those most concerned about homogeneity and security then turned to regulation of the terms of citizenship and, in a time of international tension, to the regulation of aliens.

These concerns are likely to seem parochial today—not that they have been rare in modern times but rather that they are so often reprobated as illiberal. In the founding period, too, there were liberal doubts—for instance, those of James Madison and John Page—of a procedural nature about the propriety in the naturalization process of certain inquiries or requirements bearing on personal character and belief. There is no evidence of doubt about the desirability of what Page, following closely the language of the legislation of 1795, called "good order, public virtue, and true morality of character" as objectives of a naturalization law.[34] The disagreements in the founding period about the value of privacy and integrity of personal beliefs, interpretations of the French Revolution, the degree of foreign danger confronting the nation, the appropriateness of various measures to safeguard internal security, and the legitimacy of various tactics of political demonstration and opposition appear not to have been much different from disagreements we have known in our own time. Agreement on the importance of responsible citizenship, in an accordant political order, was evidently greater then, though.

As party differences deepened in Congress, the interests and impulses of partisanship per se probably pulled the positions of Jeffersonians and Federalists further apart, as did the association of citizenship issues with other interparty differences of opinion. On both sides, by the end of the decade, there were some extreme partisans with extreme opinions on citizenship and its associated issues, as I argue in chapter 7. In this episode the contributions of a common civic virtue to self-government may have come to seem chimerical, at least temporarily, but the Naturalization Act of 1802, passed by a Republican Congress, clearly reflects the civic and citizenship concerns of the founding period's earlier legislation.

Notes

1. James H. Kettner, *The Development of American Citizenship, 1608–1870* (Chapel Hill: University of North Carolina Press, 1978), chap. 1, esp. p. 13. Most of the history in this section is drawn from Kettner's book, which provides much more detail.

2. Ibid., pp. 78, 83.

3. Ibid., chap. 4.

4. U.S. Constitution, Article I, Section 8 (4).

5. Max Farrand, ed., *The Records of the Federal Convention of 1787*, vol. 2 (1911; New Haven, Conn.: Yale University Press, 1937), p. 235.

6. *Annals of Congress* 8 (1798–99): 1775–80.

7. *Statutes at Large of the United States of America*, vol. 1 (Boston: Charles C. Little and James Brown, 1845), pp. 103, 414.

8. See, e.g., the well-known discussion by Justice Samuel Miller for the Supreme Court in *Slaughterhouse Cases*, 16 Wall. 36; 83 U.S. 36 (1873).

9. Kettner, *Development of American Citizenship*, chap. 10.

10. See, e.g., the summary account in Gerald Gunther, *Constitutional Law*, 11th ed. (Mineola, N.Y.: Foundation Press, 1985), pp. 670ff. For another account of exceptions by a commentator not given to accepting exceptions to

due process and equal protection rights, see Laurence H. Tribe, *American Constitutional Law* (Mineola, N.Y.: Foundation Press, 1978), sec. 16–22.

11. *Annals of Congress* 1 (1789–90): 1147–64. The Senate did not admit reporters to its proceedings in the early sessions of Congress, but Pennsylvania's Senator William Maclay provides us with a substantial record of what was said in that body on the naturalization measure that the House considered. William Maclay, *The Journal of William Maclay, United States Senator from Pennsylvania, 1789–1791* (New York: A. C. Boni, 1927), pp. 203–14.

12. *Annals of Congress* 1 (1789–90): 1155.

13. Ibid., pp. 1150, 1154–55.

14. Ibid., p. 1157.

15. Ibid., p. 1147; see also pp. 1154–55.

16. Ibid., pp. 1152, 1164.

17. *Statutes at Large*, vol. 1, p. 103.

18. Kettner, *Development of American Citizenship*, chap. 10.

19. The case with which decisions of the federal courts in this field begin is *Corfield v. Coryell*, 4 Wash.C.C. 371, 6 F.Cas. 546 (C.C.E.D.Pa.1823). The best-known and probably most consequential cases are those closely akin to cases under the "commerce clause" involving state attempts to protect their own commercial interests, e.g., *Toomer v. Witsell*, 334 U.S. 385 (1948); and *United Building and Construction Trades v. Camden*, 465 U.S. 208 (1984).

20. On the evolution and extent of party in Congress in this period, see Joseph Charles, *Origins of the American Party System* (Williamsburg, Va.: Institute of Early American Studies, 1956). Charles classifies members of Congress as Federalist, Republican, and Neutral. For 1795 he identifies 45 Federalists, 38 Republicans, and 20 Neutrals; for 1798 he finds 51 Federalists, 48 Republicans, and 6 Neutrals (p. 94). See also Rudolph Bell, *Party and Faction in American Politics* (Westport, Conn.: Greenwood Press, 1973). There were, however, limits to what could be accomplished by federal legislation to limit immigrant voting, for *states* continued to naturalize immigrants and, in their discretion, to permit them to vote. James Morton Smith, *Freedom's Fetters: The Alien and Sedition Laws and American Civil Liberties* (Ithaca, N.Y.: Cornell University Press, 1956), chap. 2.

21. *Annals of Congress* 8 (1798–90): 1567–82 passim.

22. See, e.g., Manning J. Dauer, *The Adams Federalists* (Baltimore: Johns Hopkins University Press, 1953), p. 165; and Smith, *Freedom's Fetters*, chap. 2.

23. Smith, *Freedom's Fetters; Annals of Congress* 4 (1793–95): 1021–64 passim, 1023 (Murray).

24. *Annals of Congress* 4 (1793–95): 1034 (Giles), 1041 (Dexter).

25. Ibid., pp. 1004–5.

26. Ibid., pp. 1005–9.

27. Ibid., pp. 1065–66 (Fitzsimons, Smith), 1045–46 (Hillhouse).

28. Ibid., pp. 1047–49.

29. *Statutes at Large*, vol. 1, pp. 414–15.

30. *Annals of Congress* 8 (1798–90): 1566–82, 1567–68 (Harper).

31. Ibid., p. 1567.

32. *Notes on the State of Virginia* in *The Writings of Thomas Jefferson*, vol. 2 (Washington, D.C.: Thomas Jefferson Memorial Association, 1905), pp. 120–21.

33. *Annals of Congress* 4 (1793–95): 1021–23. Some of its flavor appears in the following remarks. Mr. Dexter (Federalist, Mass.): "The word Republican implied so much that nobody could tell where to limit it.... Why use so hackneyed a word? Many call themselves Republican, who, by this word, mean pulling down every establishment: Anarchist would be a better term." Later, Mr. Dayton (Federalist, N.J.): "With all the ambition of [Mr. Giles] to be called a Democrat, both he [Dayton] and Mr. Dexter would more properly be called Republicans." Still later, Mr. Madison said he thought "the word was well enough understood to signify a free Representative Government, deriving its authority from the people, and calculated for their benefit"; but Madison was for other reasons opposed to the entire amendment to which his Virginia colleague, Giles, proposed to attach this Republican test.

34. *Annals of Congress* 4 (1793–95): 1004.

4

True Faith and Allegiance: The Loyalists and the New Polity

THE PRIMARY CONSTITUENTS of the new American polity were the white population living in the several colonies that audaciously proclaimed themselves independent of England. They vastly outnumbered the Indians, the free Negroes, and the few Europeans who arrived while the War of Independence was in progress. They had the powerful advantage of taking it for granted that the country belonged to them whether they were successful or defeated in the effort to sever their bonds with Britain. No question more deeply disturbed the leaders of the rebellion than this: How many of the colonials scattered between the Canadian and Spanish borders would support the effort they had launched? Later the question would arise: Should any of those who opposed it be accepted for membership in the new American polity?

The Social Sources of Loyalism

William H. Nelson, one of the most careful contemporary students of the distribution of support for breaking the ties with the homeland, remarks, "An old and symmetrical guess that a third of Americans were revolutionists, another third Loyalists, and a third neutral, has long been accepted by historians as reasonable." He concludes, however, "During the Revolutionary War perhaps half as many Americans were in arms for the King, at one time or another, as fought on the side of Congress. . . . Perhaps the best guess one could now make is that the Loyalists were a third and the revolutionists two-thirds of the politically active population in the colonies."[1]

Sure knowledge of the numbers opting for the new regime, the old regime, or neither is hardly crucial to assessing the moods and passions that later determined who would be welcomed to the fold when independence was won. Other questions are of more lasting concern to students of the founding of a new nation. What manner of people found themselves, from personal attachments, moral principles, or political conviction, unwilling to disavow England or incapable of urging their compatriots to risk a struggle so likely to prove disastrous? What circumstances of residence and immediate environment, economic condition and business interest, proximity of British military forces or revolutionary activities regulated their readiness to disclose and exploit a sincere conviction that attachment to England offered a brighter or righter future for Americans than a resolution to go it alone—assuming without any assurance of that result, that the rebellion would prosper and England would release its hold on the New World? Finally—of critical concern for this study—on what terms would that sizable constituency of the king's loyal subjects who survived the war and remained in America be admitted to the new republic established by a successful rebellion?

Few generalizations can safely be made about the various attributes that distinguished Loyalists from Patriots.[2] No doubt the latest arrivals in the new land were hesitant to join in the clamor for a redress of grievances they might not have experienced. Refugees from continental Europe probably preferred to stay out of the quarrel, and the evidence at hand indicates that most of them endeavored to do so. Some lacked facility enough in English to comprehend the causes of the conflict. Those who chose consciously between the old establishment and the new claimants to authority may well have drifted to the side they thought most likely to win or, less happily, to the side they thought they had better align with if their main consideration was security amid their immediate neighbors.

Undoubtedly similar considerations controlled the side-taking of many colonists of English, Scottish, or Irish extraction who had been born in North America or had left their homeland decades ago. Moreover, the belief that English government was the best in Europe and that the rights of the English were widely envied elsewhere was for more than a few an article of faith akin to those of the established Church. It was therefore expectable that numerous British colonists would assume that the current troubles would blow over if all parties to the quarrel would cultivate patience and moderation. Families of Scottish and of Irish origin seem to have reacted mainly in this fashion; English stock, for reasons not sufficiently understood, were notably more ready to opt for independence. But readiness to join in the rebellion or stand up for the king and his empire must have turned for all classes of people largely on a contest between personal spunk and estimations of sentiment dominating the surrounding community. If attachment to principle ruled in a family living in Tory territory, it might well declare its preference for negotiation and temporization; another family, less staunch for principle, more likely would refrain from argument and try going about its business as usual. If surrounded by a rebellious and irate environment, persons of steadfast principle might announce their neutrality and resolve to pray nightly for the king; the timid of heart might assert their commitment to separation but lag in their support of the Continental Congress as much as their judgment told them they safely could under the circumstances. As the struggle for independence advanced, estimating the final outcome was less difficult, and this no doubt figured in decisions by the uncommitted.

Proximity of British military forces would also have much to do with how one resolved the contending impulses to stand on principle or play it safe. Every port the British occupied was a special case, but Boston was signally so. There was the birthplace and early nursing site of the Revolution. Rebels so dominated the Massachusetts capital and its surrounding countryside that British commanders could do little for the safety of the king's supporters other than give them a free ride to England or other hospitable soil. New York stood in sharp contrast. There the high incidence of loyalism within the city and on Long Island combined with extensions of British military control of territory far beyond the city's limits to signal opponents of independence throughout New Jersey and well up into Connecticut that they might safely fit their behavior to their convictions. Therein lay a message for the weak of heart as well, regardless of their convictions or taste for straddling fences. British troops and seamen supplied a rich market for provender grown on the farms where most Americans lived, and the farmers who met the market's call must have included some who conceived that the terms of a sale would be improved by a false avowal of affection for British rule. Something of the same effect seems to have ensued from the British capture of Charleston, but the occupation of that city came late in the war and was cut short by Yankee victories elsewhere.

Such appear to have been the contending inducements to the ordinary person to line up for or against independence. Admittedly, the foregoing paragraphs reach beyond proof, but the sketch of attractions and deterrents supplied here is meant to accord with the judgments of historians of that critical period. Hypotheses that *most* of the choices between rebellion and continuation of colonial status could be accounted for by religious commitments, occupation or broader economic interests, or regional location have fallen in the face of inconclusive or contrary evidence. William H. Nelson's highly regarded effort to identify the elements of British support concluded:

> Of all the approaches that might be used in an attempt to separate intelligibly the Loyalists from their Patriot kinsmen, that of occupation or social class seems the least fruitful. . . . When an Act of Banishment was passed against some three hundred Loyalists in Massachusetts in 1778, they were listed by trade or profession. About a third were merchants, professional men, and gentlemen; another third were farmers, and the rest were artisans or labourers with a sprinkling of small shop keepers. . . . The social heterogeneity of the New York Tories is evident in the list of people arrested there in June 1776 on suspicion of plotting to assassinate George Washington. These people included the mayor of New York, some other officials and gentlemen, some farmers, several tavernkeepers, a shoemaker, two doctors, several apprentices and labourers, two tanners, a silversmith, a saddler, two gunsmiths, a tallow chandler, a miller, a schoolmaster, a former schoolmaster, a former constable, a pensioner with one arm, and one unfortunate man described only as "a damned rascal."[3]

There is some evidence of a regional bias, according to the same writer:

> The main centers of Tory [Loyalist] strength fall into two distinct regions: The first was along the thinly settled western frontier, from Georgia and District Ninety-Six in South Carolina, through the Regulator country of North Carolina and the mountain settlements of Virginia, Pennsylvania, and New York, to the newly-occupied Vermont lands. The other [center of loyalism] was the maritime region of the Middle Colonies, including western Long Island and the counties of the lower Hudson Valley, southern New Jersey, the three old counties of Pennsylvania, and the peninsula between Delaware and Chesapeake Bay. There were also locally important concentrations of Tories elsewhere along the Atlantic seaboard: at Charleston, around Wilmington and Norfolk, and around Newport and Portsmouth in New England.[4]

Geographic location is only a clue to the circumstances and the reasons that led individuals and families to line up as they did on the issue of independence. Loyalists and neutralists, Nelson concludes, "may have formed a majority of the population" in the strips and patches of territory where they were in greatest concentration; however, they all had neighbors, and may have been outnumbered by neighbors, who supported rebellion in varying degrees of aggressiveness.

So it was with people who took their religion seriously. Catholics and Jews are thought to have supported independence generally. Congregationalists were heavily Patriot. If the latter had been cool or lukewarm to severing British ties, there would have been no American independence, for all New England was heavily Congregationalist, New England was the nesting ground and birthplace of resistance to British policy, and Massachusetts and Connecticut were persistent providers of fighting men and monetary resources, from the rifle fire at Lexington to the cannonade at Yorktown. Nevertheless, not a few Congregational ministers, merchants, and prominent lawyers enlisted in the opposition to separation, and the names of Congregationalists, rich and poor, are to be found in modest numbers on the lists of Loyalist refugees who put out from New England's ports. Adherents to the Church of England tended strongly to favor retention of the political ties to England, but again the exceptions were numerous. Virginia and Maryland were the main strongholds of Anglicism. After painstaking research Wallace Brown, a cautious historian, concludes that of the more than a hundred Anglican clergymen in Virginia, about one third came out for independence, leaving twice as many others to spread out on a continuum, from keeping still about their preferences to belligerently advocating on behalf of England. In Maryland the Church of England had established some forty livings. The best guess Brown would risk is that "most of the Episcopal clergy seems to have remained loyal [to England]."[5] The division of other religious denominations into the three camps—Patriot, Loyalist, and uncommitted—was enough like that of the Congregationalists and Anglicans to render comment on the experience of Baptists, Presbyterians, Methods, and Quakers unnecessary.[6]

There were, then, personal and family tendencies toward loyalty to Crown and empire, or toward independence, that are traceable today to social traditions and environments of the time. For some people, and perhaps for many, such tendencies were enough, without serious, searching thought. For many, however, the decision was so difficult socially, emotionally, or intellectually as to be unreachable without recourse to principles and analysis. If in retrospect we endow the decision with personal responsibility or endeavor to understand why opponents might find it unforgivable, then we should probably assume that it was taken deliberately, based on the political arguments of the day. For both sides, those arguments might later bear on whether those who lost the conflict could continue to live in this land, along with the winners.

Loyalty and the Legitimacy of Rebellion

Not unless present judgments are revised by trusted historians will we have credible grounds for believing that more than an occasional Loyalist of revolutionary America differed in the least from Patriots on the first-order propositions of the Declaration of July 1776: that all men are endowed by their Creator with certain inalienable rights; that governments derive their just powers from the consent of the governed; and that whenever any form of government ignores or denies those rights ("becomes destructive of those ends"), it is the right of the people to alter or abolish it and to institute a new government that in their judgment offers more promise of effecting their safety and happiness.

Thoughtful people in the British homeland who adhered to this position in the last half of the eighteenth century could rightfully call themselves Whigs, and Whiggism (or Whiggery) dominated political thinking among Americans, notably those who traced their origins to the British Isles but also those of Continental ancestry if they had experienced a few generations of Americanization. Persons who denied that just governments derived their powers from the consent of the governed or rejected a right of the people to resist abuse of power reeked of Toryism in the lexicon of the times. If anybody in America notable for leadership or prominent in political thought espoused this extreme of Toryism at any time from the initial stages of protest until the treaty of peace, history has consigned him or her to obscurity.

This is not to say, however, that true Whigs could find no fault in the Declaration of Independence. It is probable that virtually everybody who publicly accused Britain of abuse of power could accept Jefferson's statement of a supporting principle: "But when a long train of abuses and usurpations, pursuing invariably the same object evinces a design to reduce them under absolute Despotism, it is their right, it is their duty, to throw off such Government and to provide new Guards for their future security." But here many a Whig must have hesitated, and some would have stopped. From this point on, the Declaration became for many not a statement of Whig principles but an expostulation of radical dogma, ignoring options for remedial action and resting partially on misconceptions and exaggerations of fact. "Such," continued the Declaration, "has been the patient sufferance of these Colonies; and such is now the necessity which constrains them to alter their former systems of Government. The history of the present King of Great Britain is a history of repeated injuries and usurpations, all having in direct object the establishment of an absolute Tyranny over these States."

The history at issue here was one of some sixteen years. However one might interpret it though, Whigs who had denounced taxation without representation and recommended force of arms to reopen the port of Boston could insist without impeaching their honesty and consistency that neither the king nor his ministers had absolute tyranny in mind and that even if they did, they were not beyond revising their intentions when confronted with an unyielding resistance far less drastic than severing the bonds of empire.

Jefferson wrote that the purpose of the Declaration of Independence was to explain to the world why Americans were disconnecting themselves from their parent country. Its immediate, distinct impact was to divide the population into two camps of individuals equally concerned for the well-being of the inhabitants of the thirteen colonies. Tom Paine's *Common Sense* beat Jefferson's statement to press by six months. Paine's mission was to convince his readers that the structure of England's government made tyranny inevitable—that constitutional defects, not just the current regime of corruption, barred the way to effective reforms toward a tolerable existence for colonies under British control. Paine's blend of fact, historical interpretation, and outrageous fabrication was indeed convincing, but there was conviction on both sides of the issue. Well before the Declaration was in draft, it was reasonably clear (or is now, in retrospect) that leaders of political thought and action in colonial America would not be united in resort to force, no matter how bright the prospect that it would redress current grievances and root government durably in the consent of the governed—whether through British imperial reform or American independence.

Incompatibilities springing from differences in goals and estimates of feasibility were exacerbated by the precarious conditions of legitimacy attributed to revolutionary governments. This must have been especially disconcerting to revolutionary leaders who had been careful to maximize proofs of popular consent at each step in the creation of new offices for governance and the transfer of authority from the Old World to the New World. The Continental Congress not only instituted a national deliberative process but also provided an authentic voice for communication with both persecutors and well-wishers abroad. No rival source of opinion or pronouncement could pretend to represent thirteen colonial governments or the people who inhabited those political jurisdictions.

The first-priority business of this new national assembly was the adoption of policies toward England, the relief of colonies or ports under British military pressure, and the creation of a national consensus on either accommodation or separation, as circumstances, judgment, and persuasion might dictate. Formidable as these challenges were, they could not obscure concern about what should be done at the provincial and local levels to fortify public authority against current interruption of communication with London and the conceivable abrogation of British authority altogether.

The Second Continental Congress had barely seated its members when it received a plea from the Massachusetts General Court for "the most explicit advice, respecting the taking up and exercising the powers of civil government."[7] It is a cause for wonder that the Bay Colony's political leaders should be calling for advice on how to make the break from foreign rule; the Adams family alone, months earlier, had established a favorable balance of trade in the export of revolutionary ideas. What the General Court of Massachusetts wanted was not a packet of advice but a label of legitimacy. The question of how to fashion a relocation of authority would arouse a lingering debate; the question of who had authority to design and decree a new authority structure needed to be settled at once and publicized throughout the incipient American nation.

A certification of legitimacy is what the Continental Congress accorded. Eleven months after receiving the Massachusetts appeal, the Congress resolved that "it be recommended to the respective assemblies and conventions of the United colonies, where no government sufficient to the exigencies of their affairs have been hitherto established, to adopt such government as shall, in the opinion of the representatives of the people, best conduce to the happiness and safety of their constituents in particular, and America in general."[8]

America's Loyalists who aspired to put their opposition to independence on a foundation of reasoned political thought might well have derided these verbal maneuvers as political antics, pure and simple. The fact appears to be, however, that the blessing the Continental Congress conferred on the replacement of London-issued charters by locally adopted constitutions served effectively to convert cautious rebels into resolute Patriots and almost totally wrecked the main talking point of the king's friends. Furthermore, the onrushing course of events must have eroded rapidly any thoughtful person's confidence that much would be gained by taunts of illegitimacy. As determination to repulse aggression and teach London a lesson evolved into aspirations for independence, those pledged to found government on consent of the governed must have seen increasingly that the search for more inclusive consensus would have to wait until those bent on reconstituting the polity had organized themselves for power. This compulsion of circumstances must have been as apparent to thoughtful Loyalists as it was to those in the forefront of Patriot leadership. Charges of illegitimacy disturbed the atmosphere, no doubt, every time a state legislature enacted a measure regulating or penalizing Loyalists, but public reaction to such measures probably depended much more on their substantive justification and their severity than on resentment of rule by usurpers.

The legitimacy the Continental Congress bestowed on the state governments it created extended also to courts and local governments, even if these received no mention in the new state constitutions. Issues of legitimacy were frequently and rightfully raised, however, in connection with the acts of local revolutionary committees. Such organizations, initially referred to as Committees of Correspondence, were sanctioned from their beginning by colonial legislatures and local governing authorities and later were not only recognized but also encouraged by the Continental Congress. Throughout New England their claims to legitimacy could hardly be assailed, since ordinarily their existence and instructions for action derived from the local town meetings. Elsewhere, perhaps in all states from New York south, there were lapses in the authority structure that left communities with no forum for accusations and debate and thus left officials without clear authorization to impose quiescence on a neighborhood or to compel self-appointed investigators and executioners to moderate their behavior. Many were the occasions when a Loyalist family, confronted by a high-handed committee, had every reason to plead "Show us your credentials! Who gave you this assignment? By what authority are we required to answer your questions or answer to your command?"

The Condition of Loyalists during the Revolution

Time has doubtless clouded forever any confident assessment of the behavior of these local patrols of moral and political obligation, the rectitude of their manners, the harshness of their castigations, or the justifiability of their demands. We do know from the records available that many inquiries and confrontations were conducted with exemplary sobriety and disposed of with a discriminating charity, but we have perhaps as many reports of callous rudeness, brutish intimidation, and arbitrary decision.[9]

Our knowledge about official *state* policy on the treatment of Loyalists is fuller and more reliable than our knowledge about local treatment because legislative enactments were printed and have been preserved. By the end of 1777 every one of the newly created state governments was firmly in the hands of men committed to a tenacious and protracted war, with independence the paramount goal, and confident that there was a better than even chance of winning it. Everywhere the incumbents of public office assumed that the state governments had, within their borders, full power to do all "acts and things which Independent States may of right do." Certainly to command all residents of the state to obey the state's laws and refrain from making war against it was what Thomas Jefferson and other members of the Continental Congress had in mind when they wrote these words into the Declaration of Independence.

Pennsylvania moved first to tag the Loyalists, define their status, and circumscribe their movements in an enactment by the convention that drafted its constitution in 1776. This first effort to define treason and punish seditious utterances was quickly replaced by a series of statutes collectively aimed at requiring opponents of independence to affirm their position publicly and defining and fixing penalties for specified acts of treason, for attempting by speech or action to discourage or inhibit military and other measures against Great Britain, or for giving aid and comfort to an enemy of Pennsylvania or the confederated states. Penalties ranged from fines and imprisonment to forfeiture of estates and death by hanging. This was, in general, the intent and mood of legislation in each of the twelve other colonies in transition to statehood.

Massachusetts, in its 1777 act establishing an oath of fidelity and allegiance, authorized and required justices of the peace to call before them any resident of Massachusetts cited in a written statement asserting that there is, in the opinion of the signer, "just and sufficient reason to suspect" that the person named "is inimical to the *United States.*" Such a proceeding could be instituted by, among others, any civil or military officer of a town or county or "any two substantial freeholders." The statute did not instruct justices to hear witnesses or otherwise inquire into the conduct of the accused. They were directed only to administer an oath by which the accused, if they complied, swore or affirmed that they would "bear true faith and allegiance" to the state of Massachusetts, would "faithfully support and maintain and defend the same against the King of Great Britain, his abettors, and all other enemies and opposers whatsoever," and would "discover all plots and conspiracies" against Massachusetts or any other of the United States of America. If the accused should refuse to commit themselves to this state of mind and course of conduct ("So help me God!"), they were allowed forty days, operating from within the county jail, to collect money owed them, pay their debts, dispose of their estate, and attend to any other business they might find time for before being "sent off by order of the Council of this State [at their own expense if their estate was sufficient] to some port in the dominions of the King of Great Britain." Finally (and final it would be), "if any person or persons so sent off from this state as aforesaid shall voluntarily return into that state again, unless leave be obtained from the General Court for that purpose, he or she being duly convicted thereof (in a court of appropriate jurisdiction) shall suffer the pains of death without benefit of clergy."[10] These two statutes were not strictly typical of what thirteen different state legislatures did to discourage, contain, proscribe, and punish Loyalist activity and those who abetted it. We can say, however, that the actions of Pennsylvania and Massachusetts represented in general the mood and strategy of legislative policies in all of them.[11]

As the war continued, it became increasingly clear that the colonials were not the pushovers London had supposed. It also became more apparent to Americans, both Patriots and Loyalists, that Britain was not going to mobilize its full potential to crush the rebellion. These growing certainties induced more than a few families who were most stubborn in their convictions, or well enough off to finance their exile, to abandon America for a more hospitable site and probably stimulated a good many more who favored the king to announce a change of heart and to pledge fealty to the new state governments. One surely would not be far wrong in fixing twenty-five thousand as the maximum number who vacated the thirteen colonies before the defeat of Cornwallis at Yorktown in 1781—a figure that comprehends both involuntary and voluntary exiles and includes whatever extended households chose or were selected to go along. The greater exodus took place after 1781, when the loss at Yorktown shattered the last hopes of ultimate victory, and peaked after 1783, when the terms of the peace treaty stirred to a boiling point the vindictive mood that had been fired for close to a decade.

The decisive victory at Yorktown effectively settled the issue of continuance in the British Empire or independence; the Treaty of Paris three years later formally acknowledged admission of the most Europeanized segment of the New World into the family of nations. It is believed that, when the great exodus had run its course, the number of refugees from America living in Canada, Europe, and the Caribbean islands may have run as high as 100,000 and that there remained on American soil at least twice that number who by their own admission or impact of law were classified as Loyalists. These estimates, like the previous ones, are speculative. Wallace Brown, who made an imaginative and systematic effort to refine the estimates, concluded that "the difficulty of discovering and even defining the Tories means that no accurate count can ever be made, and it may well be that the precise number is comparatively unimportant."[12]

The importance of this division of the American people at the beginning of their career as a sovereign nation can hardly be exaggerated, if indeed fully appreciated. Viewed as an episode in history—a civil war waged on scattered and shifting fronts in varying degrees of tenacity and intensity and pursued simultaneously with the conduct of hostilities against a foreign adversary—the Revolutionary War is full of lessons for promotion and preservation of frontline and homefront morale; stimulation and maintenance of military supply; strategy in the choice of military objectives and planning of campaigns; the uses of guerrilla warfare; and the pursuit of tactics both oblivious and sensitive to the depletion of productive facilities and of the reservoirs of sentiment that transform a population into a people.

Studied for its contributions to political theory and statecraft, the American Revolution is no less prolific in the lessons it propounds. Startling challenges for political theory flash from the Declaration of Independence, a flamboyant pronouncement that its truths are self-evident notwithstanding. It is the right of a people to alter, abolish, and replace their government when it has ceased to secure their inalienable rights and (or?) no longer commands the consent of the governed. But what defines or circumscribes a population that may rightly be called a people? What showing of agreement is sufficient proof that the altered government, or a successor government, has captured and promises to retain the consent of the people?

When has enough become enough? The injuries and usurpations spelled out in the Declaration of Independence are laid at the feet of King George III—if they were not entirely his own doing, he had a hand in the planning or execution. His misdeeds are labeled a long train of abuses; in explicit language, their purpose is said to be the establishment of absolute tyranny over the American colonies. How long have these intolerable acts been going on? This will indeed be a point of great importance in the debate if there is doubt about whether the time has come to issue ultimatums, institute a reign of terror, or announce a state of belligerency. No less relevant for making the irrevocable decision will be the state of opinion about the persistence of ill will and the consistency and regularity of abuses of power on the part of the ruling regime.

These are considerations that go to sufficiency of cause for rebellion against or replacement of a government. The answers they provoke do not force conclusions about the timeliness of resistance or the feasibility of rebellion. What is the promise that the tyranny of the past will be suffered in the future unless drastic preventive measures are adopted? How much of the population that is necessary for effectuating a remedy is of common mind on this prognosis? How many whose minds are prepared for rebellion will stand up after the shooting starts? If rebellion is judged feasible, is there any hope that an alternative remedy, less costly in blood and wealth, may yet be discovered?

How many should be how certain on so many things? Did the Virginia constitutional convention of 1776 help nail down a self-evident truth in its assertion that whenever any government is found to be inadequate for or contrary to the purposes for which it was formed, regardless of whether it is tending to absolute tyranny, "a majority of the community hath an indubitable, unalienable and indefeasible right to reform, alter or abolish it, in such manner as shall be judged most conducive to the public weal" (Paragraph 3 of the Declaration of Rights)? Even if it be agreed that "majority" means 50 percent plus one of those counted, adult men and women or males only, is not a finding that so slight a margin withholds consent or favors a decision to abolish and replace a government a certain signal that it is the worst of all times to design a new one? If so narrow a division of conviction and prejudice does not ensure civil war, surely it forebodes compromises so pervasive and so profound that common sense dictates a waiting period until the minimum numbers required by "consent" have been augmented by a considerable advance toward consensus.

These and a host of other questions hounded the generation that achieved independence and founded a republic. They may have seemed of small moment to most of those who hastily chose sides, for knee-jerk Tories must have been encountered as frequently in 1776 as their counterparts among liberals and conservatives were two hundred years later. Regardless of the motivation among the least thoughtful and the most impulsive of their contemporaries, it is certain that the division between the proponents of independence and those who clung to the British Empire forced every meditative and conscientious man and woman, separatist and king's friend alike, to search out the meaning of Jefferson's words and sentences and ponder the wisdom of the little group who advised him and the larger number who signed the Declaration of Independence.

The Loyalists in the Revolutionary Settlement

If 1775 and 1776 were times that tried men's souls, 1782 and the decade immediately after were years that tested their adherence to intellectual convictions and moral principles. In the conviction that individuals have souls and that there is an Almighty God who scrutinizes their conduct, it must have been judged wholly honorable in 1776 to favor continuance within the British system, to speak in favor of patience and compromise, and to expend one's influence and resources in behalf of the British cause. But between 1776 and the spring of 1783, when Congress gave provisional approval to the final draft of the peace treaty, standards for judging the character and the prospective behavior of individuals and families changed.

With American independence acknowledged and British military forces withdrawing, the generation in charge faced the challenge of redefining the American people and specifying the parameters of a new nation. Honest conviction that continued membership in the British Empire promised a brighter future than an independent America trying to go it alone could not be viewed as ground for exclusion from full membership in the new state and nation, unless the thought had fathered conduct too offensive to be forgiven or regarded as compatible with allegiance to the new order. So also for a wrong guess in foretelling the outcome of a struggle that tough-minded observers thought might go either way. More arguable would have been the case of opponents of separation and abettors of Britain, whose aggressive behavior generated enough resentment to guarantee ill will within their communities for decades to come. Reiterated proof that an outspoken Loyalist harbored contempt for the new political institutions and their leadership might well have been considered sufficient cause for proscribing such persons without waiting for evidence of change of mind. Judgments like these could not be passed over or simply left to the ministrations of time.

The Americans negotiating at Paris in the last months of 1782—John Adams, Benjamin Franklin, and John Jay—were fully aware that the United States was no longer the underdog. Not only had the former colonials won the war, but the wartime ministry was out of power in London, and there was talk too serious to dismiss as frivolous that George III would be wise to abdicate. Relinquishment of British authority in the thirteen former colonies was a precondition of convening at the treaty table, and the choice of words to consummate that result excited no contention. The treaty opened, "His Britannic Majesty acknowledges the said United States, viz., New Hampshire, Massachusetts [and on in order of location to Georgia] to be free, sovereign, and independent States; that he treats with them as such," and from there you are into the business for which the meeting was called.[13]

This designation of the party that joined with his majesty in stating the terms that settled a dispute and inaugurated a reign of peace between two countries of equal station must have been most satisfying to the American negotiators. Throughout the treaty there are references to the United States and to the citizens of the United States, but nowhere (except one instance of great interest here) is there an explicit statement of right or obligation for which a *government* of the United States would be surrogate. This was so notwithstanding that the Articles of Confederation gave the Congress "sole and exclusive right and power" of determining on peace and war, entering into treaties and alliances, and performing specific other acts of international relations—all subject, however, to qualifications protecting the autonomy of the individual member states. The single instance in which the treaty pledged the central government to act preserved the principle that the several states were seats of sovereign power in America. Article V of the treaty made the Congress an agent to intercede with the legislatures of the several states in behalf of persons seeking redress for loss of property and other injuries sustained because of attachment to the parent country and opposition to the bid for independence.

The British government's quest for Loyalist restitution from the United States much complicated the treaty making. Before the American delegation assembled in Paris, Benjamin Franklin, chairman in title if not in role, had a letter from the American secretary of foreign affairs urging that the treaty be kept clear of references to Loyalists and their claims; less than a month later he heard the principal spokesman for the newly designated government in London make a plea to assign first priority in the negotiations to justice for those who had opposed rebellion and independence on principle. Franklin's response amounted to "Not a chance!" and with that the British government seemed to drop the subject.

It fell to the Americans to draw up an initial sketch of articles of settlement. Adams and Jay took on this assignment. For weeks, if not months, they had been assured that the government now speaking for Britain was strongly committed to resuming friendship and fashioning ties with the new American nation. Playing from strength, the American team resolved to ignore the interests of Loyalists and concentrate on expanding the boundaries of the United States and exacting guarantees of generous fishing rights in the North Atlantic. In principle, in the traditions of belligerency, in personal inclination, and considering the politics of American assent to a treaty, the commissioners had no time for the Loyalists. When they faced the British in serious discussion, however, they learned immediately that the other side had not abandoned the Loyalists.

For the British side of the table, the American Tories were the king's loyal subjects; they had acknowledged their obligations of citizenship and responded to the call of duty. They were not disloyal, seditious, or guilty of treasonous behavior, for there had been no legitimate authority in Philadelphia or the thirteen state capitals to command their allegiance and no body politic in North America with an obligation to enlist in a cause opposed to the king. Moreover, considering the domestic politics of British treaty approval, the Loyalist problem seemed critical to the future of the then British government.

Whether from the force of argument or the implacable stance of the three Americans, or both, the British negotiators eventually settled for a stipulation that the Congress of the Confederation would "earnestly recommend" to the several states that they undertake various remedial actions, including the enactment of legislation that dispossessed Tories could regard as tolerant if not truly benign. To this policy of passing the buck to the individual states, there was one important exception. Article VI of the treaty, if read to mean what it said, pledged the Congress as well as the thirteen separate states to make no further confiscations, exact no further charges deriving from past judgments, drop pending prosecutions and begin no new ones, and empty the jails of persons held on account of collaboration with the British in the war.

Adams, Franklin, and Jay, who participated in the treaty making from the start—and no doubt Henry Laurens, who appeared in time to sign—had a strong distaste for just about everything they promised concerning the future status and treatment of Loyalists.[14] But they left evidence sufficient to remove any doubt that they acted in good faith, however far the treaty terms varied from instructions Franklin had received from Philadelphia. They viewed their concessions to the sensibilities of the British government as a fair exchange for dissolution of British obstinacy on several points precious to the Americans, and they hoped that when the tradeoffs were fairly assessed, the world's newest nation would be judged to have bargained successfully.

There was in 1783 and has been since considerable disagreement about the perspicacity of the American negotiators and their skill in defending their initial bargaining position. Who deserved medals for his performance at Paris is, however, a side issue for this study. We are concerned with the admission and exclusion of the king's friends from the American polity then being redefined and with the effect of how this was handled on the later development of American nationhood, or political community. Acknowledging scholarly disagreement on this subject, we may hazard a few conclusions on these issues.

First, although the treaty of peace was formally ratified by the Congress of the Confederation, Article V and Article VI promising amelioration for American Loyalists were effectively nullified in practice. If anyone who participated in the Paris deliberations supposed there was a chance that Congress would "earnestly recommend" action of any character to the state governments, he must have been blissfully ignorant of the institutional debilitation on exhibit in Philadelphia, Princeton, Annapolis, or wherever a fragment of the Congress gathered while awaiting enough more delegates to satisfy the quorum requirement. In time, of course, a quorum did materialize, and a copy of the treaty went to all the state capitals. The records of the Congress, however, do not indicate that it was accompanied by any statement of obligation to comply with the treaty provisions or by any urging of the civic and economic benefits to be expected from a generous policy of readmission and rehabilitation.

Second, Article VI of the treaty stipulated that confiscations of property and other aggressions against American Loyalists and their families should cease forthwith. This injunction embraced the vacating of prison sentences and other disabilities that had not yet run their course. The American Congress, after 1781 at least, had authority to encumber opponents of rebellion with inhibitions of one kind or another and must have enacted some resolves with that end in view. Considering the cumulative effect of the security measures, harassments, and expropriations practiced by the states, Congress was a minor contributor to the debris that the treaty of peace sought to clean up.[15] References to indefensible mistreatment of Loyalists sanctioned by the American Congress are obscure, if indeed there are any to be found. However that may be, Congress was in no position to set models for alacrity for anybody on anything because of the all but total demoralization that characterized its proceedings in the months surrounding the exchange of ratifications in the spring of 1784.

Third, policies of vindictiveness or charity, rejection or acceptance, general amnesty or selective rehabilitation varied from one state to another. Despite assiduous explorations by historians, the local circumstances that were critical to policy decisions have not been ascertained and clarified sufficiently to buttress common judgments two hundred years later. Just as conditions of fear and animosity, of persecution and expropriation varied from place to place throughout the years of warfare, so there were remarkable differences in states' readiness to allow refugees from revolutionary America to return to their former homes and reclaim such former holdings as had not been dissipated beyond hope of recapture.[16]

In agreeing to the terms of the treaty, England acknowledged that Americans would never permit the return of all Tories who were in exile and that the thirteen states would not adopt policies of compensation and restitution that approached uniformity. For relief from this bleak outlook, the British ministry pinned its hopes on one particular stipulation in Article V: all exiles who had not borne arms against the United States, regardless of their unacceptability as citizens of the new nation, should be granted an amnesty of twelve months in which to return to the United States and, "unmolested in their endeavors," do what they could to "obtain the restitution of such of their estates, rights, and properties as may have been confiscated."

It appears that none of the states accepted this article as an obligation, but the consequences of their rejecting it fell most unevenly on Americans who had left the country of their own accord. One or two years had been time enough for many refugees to find Canada's weather and forests unendurable or England's hospitality unresponsive to destitute colonials; time enough for many of them to decide that the worst they would have to put up with back home was better than what they had wandered into. Long before victory for the rebel cause was assured, a steady trickle of voluntary exiles had reversed their trek and headed back to the revolutionary scene they had sought to escape. They met with varying receptions; some were shipped out again, but many made avowals of change of mind and of intention to comply with local expectations sufficiently reassuring to win permission to stay. Few, perhaps, were fully restored to their former holdings and prospects for economic well-being, but probably none faced a future as forbidding as the settlers had when they first set foot on the American homeland. So it happened that well before 1783, when the terms of peace were under consideration by Congress, a few of the states had already assented to the refugees' return and made at least some amends for mistreatment to a sizable proportion of Loyalists.

Assent and amends were not typical, however. As the Patriots grew in confidence that they had won the war, they were freed from cautions that had previously restrained some of them in stripping Loyalists of their property and rights, especially in states that were in enemy hands at the close of hostilities. Writing at the beginning of this century, the eminent historian Claude Van Tyne said:

> In spite of the recommendation of Congress, which had been made in accordance with the terms of the treaty, little moderation could be seen in the legislation concerning the Tories. Confiscation still went on actively; governors of the states were urged to exchange lists of the proscribed persons, that no Tory might find a resting place in the United States; and in nearly every state they were disfranchised, while in many localities they were tarred and feathered, driven from town and warned never to return. In the South where the partizan warfare had been most bitter, the Tories fled for their lives, and a few of the bolder ones who attempted to return to their homes, were warned and then attacked; eight being murdered and the rest fleeing from the country.[17]

Van Tyne is thought to have been a reliable reporter, but the states of mind and behavior that he found prevalent in 1783 are now believed not to have lasted very long. A careful scholar of our own day, Wallace Brown, says, "The pace of readmission varied from state to state, but mostly it was remarkably quick (except for a few of the most hated Loyalists, some of whom could never have returned even if they should have wished to), and by 1790 anti-Loyalist legislation was largely a thing of the past everywhere."[18]

Mary Beth Norton, among the scholars more recently reporting, quotes observers of the American scene who were convinced that the peak of anti-Loyalist frenzy was timed to give a hot reception to the peace treaty, the terms of which made American newspapers early in March 1783. With the passing of little more than a year, it was becoming evident that a conciliatory mood was in the making. In the spring of 1785 Benjamin Franklin, a consistent Tory-hater throughout the war, felt confident enough to testify that the circumstances of the Loyalists in the United States were daily mending as memories of the burning of towns and the massacre of friends and neighbors began to cool.[19] The latest date Van Tyne reports in his tabulation of state statutes imposing disabilities on opponents of rebellion and independence is 10 February 1787.

The Course of Reconciliation

How did it happen on the American side that hatred, expropriation, and expatriation could be reduced so soon to some degree of acceptance, restoration, and rehabilitation? British policy must have made an important contribution, as it encountered Americans' concerns about the legitimacy—especially the international legitimacy—of their new nation. These two factors—the policy of the British government and the concerns of the American citizenry—need further exploration.

A critical step toward reconciliation, I believe, was the British government's decision to assume the burden of financial relief of those colonials who had suffered most for loyalty to the British cause. Well before the treaty negotiations had advanced to a final draft, the British ministry had concluded that most Americans in exile—plus perhaps as many more in America who had been conspicuous in lending aid to British forces and an undetermined number of other British sympathizers who had been especially offensive to American authorities—would never obtain redress from any American government. Accordingly, Parliament provided by law for redemption from the British treasury in all instances where rightful claims were proved to the satisfaction of a five-member commission. Some nine months before the ratifications of the treaty of peace were exchanged (May 1784) the commission had organized itself for business and had begun its investigations and hearings. Six years later the inquiries were completed, recommendations for granting awards were made, and a final report was filed. As a board of inquiry and adjudication, the commissioners appear to have performed exemplarily.[20]

In retrospect one may surmise that the British decision to indemnify the Loyalists worked effectively to undercut resistance of ordinary American opponents of reconciliation and played into the hands of American leaders who foresaw an urgent need to recruit every strong back, nimble mind, and source of capital that might usefully contribute to the national economy. If Britain had restricted its compensation to losses resulting from direct involvement in the British cause—say, for services rendered and supplies furnished to British forces—it could have been argued that this was constrained by superior American strategy at the bargaining table or by special sensitivities of the British government to justice—that principles of constitutional theory and international law had played no part in the decision. Such an inference, however, must have paled in the light of the statutory language including "all such persons who have suffered . . . during the late unhappy differences in America in consequence of their loyalty to His Majesty, and attachment of the British government."[21] The inference disappears entirely when one learns that the board of inquiry recommended and the appropriating authority approved payments from the British treasury for no better reason than that the claimant had refused to renounce fealty to the king and empire and had abandoned home and property in a flight for personal safety or had been enmeshed in some other fabric of circumstance negating any chance of later recovery from the states and national government.

The British compensation policy thus must have seemed to be the acceptance of an obligation existing under the British Constitution and international law. No official statement concedes as much, but none denies it, either, or asserts that considerations of charity or national interest alone, unsupported by legal obligation, induced His Majesty's government to afford numerous Loyalists the relief that law, reason, and natural right obliged the Americans, without effect, to afford.[22] Thus relieved of obligation—of legal necessity and economic expense—by the British, the Americans were much more open to reconciliation than they would have been otherwise.

In these proofs of capitulation and concession on the part of Britain's rulers—in the treaty, in the parliamentary act absorbing Loyalist losses, and in other events coincidental and interrelated—rest sufficient grounds for predicting the early dissolution of an ambivalence that had burdened American minds for almost a full decade. The most important effect of British policy was not, however, on American pocketbooks prospectively—for the Americans were not about to afford the Loyalists financial relief or, for the most part, restitution of property in any case. Instead, British relief of American legal obligation enhanced the legitimacy of the American states and nation—that is, their formal stature among other states and nations. In this regard British policy encountered, and relieved, a nagging concern that had burdened many American minds for a decade or more.

"These are the times that try men's souls," wrote Thomas Paine to open *The Crisis* (1776). The reference here was to mounting military difficulties and the hard prospect of a war for independence, but there was more to trouble souls than warfare alone. There were the questions of the rectitude of it all that were explored in earlier pages of this chapter—all those questions of withdrawing from the British Empire and going it alone or giving the king, his ministers, and the English people a few more years in which to come to their senses.

Grant that most of the population must have resolved these questions one way or the other or, short of that, ignored them. Still, many must have nursed a troubling array of doubts throughout the years of incipient and active civil war between protagonists of independence and those who continued in allegiance to Britain. This was the complex of uncertainty that seems to have dissipated as Americans perceived the policy of the new government in London. The first sentence of the treaty erased any reasons for doubt that the thirteen former colonies, viewed individually or as united to form a nation, were now disconnected from England and fully clothed with sovereignty. The parliamentary enactment, publicized in America before the treaty was ratified, plainly invited a conclusion that the new nation, having given the doubters a reasonable time in which to decide, had no obligation to harbor dissenters or to permit their return at a later date. By clear implication, it could be argued by one who needed such support for a shaky conscience, this was a British admission that the rebelling colonies had in truth absolved themselves from all allegiance to the British Crown, dissolved all connection between themselves and the British state, and assumed an equal station among the world's powers—all this marked fait accompli and formally promulgated in Philadelphia early in July 1776.

These conclusions rest on less than certain premises, evidence, and inferences, but I do not find that close students of the postrevolutionary experience offer a better explanation of how it came about that aggressions against former objectors to independence, violent to the point of bloodletting, suddenly went out of fashion instead of hanging on to taper off over decades, and that legal barriers to repatriation were ignored, overridden, or swiftly swept away. It may be of little importance to know with certainty why public attitudes and public policy underwent a rapid instead of gradual transformation. It is, however, of first importance for the objectives of this study to appreciate that, with the cessation of hostilities and the assurance of independence, there emerged promptly an opinion, nationwide in its appeal and constitutional in its significance, that late arrival at a decision to embrace republican principles and swear allegiance to the new regime would not, of itself, bar admission to the new American polity.

This consensual endorsement of repatriation did not, of course, reach out to all the former colonials who had dissociated themselves from the struggle for independence. Acceptance into the new American polity was selective. Thousands had been too emphatic in their expressions of disdain for popular government to be regarded as tolerable risks by those responsible for an experiment in republican government; others had figured too prominently in military combat and atrocities to be allowed a hearing on their subsequent state of mind. Among those thought fit for repatriation, readmission to the body politic did not in all cases entail restoration of all the rights and privileges of citizenship. For numerous applicants it carried the condition of ineligibility for public office for a specified or indefinite time; for a lesser but still substantial number of persons the price of readmission was exclusion from the polling place on election day. On the other hand, resumption of citizenship by oath of allegiance was not a sure sign that a sinner had come to repentance or that a monarchist was transmuted to a true believer in republican government.

It is a cause for wonder that the most probing investigations into this episode in American history bespeak a sharper interest in the subsequent careers of American Loyalists who continued in exile than in the adaptations to rapidly changing American ways of those who elected and were permitted to spend their remaining years in the United States. It appears that on the whole those who settled permanently in Canada or the Caribbean possessions of Great Britain, and apparently to a lesser extent in the British Isles, lived out their lives in honorable and productive employment. More than a few assumed positions of high distinction. We know less about the contributions to republican government of those former skeptics and dissenters who in time committed their postwar years to the building of a new nation in the West.

Guesswork rules, perforce, in speculation about how the repatriated Loyalists fit into the national endeavor to give a fair trial to their commitment to republican government. It will be surprising if, after further study, we learn that more than a very few of the former opponents of independence made much impress on the processes of popular self-government; if any did, they must have been the most youthful part of the Loyalist contingent, young enough in 1784 that time would revise memories as they established proof of their commitment to republican institutions. The way to influence in the political sector, save through judicial posts and practice before the courts, was by election to public office in the early decades of the Republic, and a reputation in the community of having actively opposed independence would have been a heavy yoke for anyone seeking support at the polls, regardless of age and personal talents.

Common sense tells us that the laggard converts to republican government would, in the main, endeavor to shake off the onus of their former resistance to separation through high achievement and exemplary conduct. Denied prospects for success in political forums, they would turn in unprecedented proportions to commerce and industry. Noteworthy contributions to the productive economy that burgeoned in the decades immediately following the return of peace to the land may have been seen by their contemporaries as having an importance equal to that of the most honored performers in political arenas. Whether this was so, and if so how successfully so, remains a subject for speculation. The paucity of scholarly concern about the postrevolutionary political experience of former Loyalists is matched by an indisposition to distinguish between former rebels and adherents to the empire in their contributions to early American economic development. It is as if the onset of reconciliation signaled the keepers of the records to close the books on a rift in sentiments and principles that threatened to hinder American coalescence into nationhood.

If the founding generation pursued a mistaken policy in choosing candidates for repatriation, it would almost certainly have erred on the side of overcaution—of drawing a line between acceptability and unfitness that excluded some Tories who were prepared to embrace the new Republic if allowed to demonstrate their loyalty to it. Wherever the line was drawn, there would have been wrong guesses; misjudgments and successful deceptions would have occurred. How many of the thousands who were exiled or were denied reentry would have made model citizens if given the opportunity is not knowable. But unwillingness to live in peace with neighbors and to cooperate in community affairs, refusals to fulfill obligations of citizenship, occasional convictions of complicity in antagonistic designs, and other evidences of hostility to American authorities or republican government surely would have been recorded for our notice if more than a very few persons of such disposition had been on the scene to stir up trouble during the half-century immediately following the close of the Revolution. Troublemaking there was, and enough of it to generate sleepless nights for more than one state governor and president of the United States, but neither contemporary chroniclers nor subsequent historians have attributed the instigation of such trouble to former opponents of independence.

Of those various past, then-present, and prospective inhabitants of America least likely to find full acceptance in American society, the Loyalists were by and large—except for those who had been most active in counterrevolutionary warfare—the least subject to exclusion, probation, and (probably) prejudice. Once the new Republic was on a secure legal footing, both in its own regard and before the rest of the world, those who were late in accepting it were nonetheless acceptable as citizens. We cannot be certain of the qualities, or presumptive qualities, that facilitated this acceptance, but we may surmise that the common roots of *most* Loyalists in English stock (notwithstanding the important roles of ethnic minorities in Loyalism), shared linguistic, legal, and religious-denominational traditions, and particular capacities for making their way economically were influential factors. When combined with basic acquiescence in the new political order, these were the terms of membership in the new political community—which thus exhibited substantial continuity with the old political community.

Notes

1. William H. Nelson, *The American Tory* (New York: Oxford University Press, 1961), p. 92. The "old and symmetrical guess" is generally attributed to John Adams.

2. For a particularly interesting reconstruction, see Wallace Brown, *The Good Americans* (New York: William Morrow, 1969), chaps. 3, 8. On the history of loyalism since the eighteenth century, see esp. Bernard Bailyn, *The Ordeal of Thomas Hutchinson* (Cambridge, Mass.: Harvard University Press, 1974), Appendix: "The Losers: Notes on the Historiography of Loyalism."

3. Nelson, *The American Tory,* pp. 85–86.

4. Ibid., p. 87.

5. Wallace Brown, *The King's Friends* (Providence, R.I.: Brown University Press, 1965), pp. 172, 188.

6. Nelson concludes, "Taking all the groups and factions, sects, classes, and inhabitants of regions that seem to have been Tory, they have but on[e] thing

in common: they represented conscious minorities, people that felt weak and threatened. The sense of weakness which is so marked a characteristic of the Tory leaders, is equally evident among the rank and file. Almost all the Loyalists were, in one way or another, more afraid of America than they were of Britain. Almost all of them had interests that they felt needed protection from an American majority." Nelson, *The American Tory,* p. 91.

7. *Journals of the Continental Congress* 2 (1775): 76.

8. *Journals of the Continental Congress* 4 (1776): 342. Much earlier—on May 9, 1775, a week after Massachusetts's request was received—the Congress responded "that in order to conform, as near as may be, to the spirit of the charter [of the colony], it be recommended to the provincial Convention to write letters to the . . . several places, which are intitled to representation in the Assembly, requesting them to chuse such representatives, and that the Assembly, when chosen, do elect counsellors; which assembly and council should exercise the powers of Government, until a Governor of his Majesty's appointment will consent to govern the colony according to its charter." *Journals of the Continental Congress* 2 (1775): 83–84.

9. See, in general, Nelson, *The American Tory;* Brown, *Good Americans;* and, as illustrative studies of particular states, Robert O. DeMond, *The Loyalists in North Carolina during the Revolution* (Durham, N.C.: Duke University Press, 1940); Adele Hast, *Loyalists in Revolutionary Virginia* (Ann Arbor, Mich.: UMI Research Press, 1979); and Harold B. Hancock, *The Loyalists of Revolutionary Delaware* (Newark: University of Delaware Press, 1977).

10. Massachusetts, *Session Laws* (Boston: Eades, 1778; American Antiquarian Society Microprints 15883, 15884), 1777, chap. 17, p. 160; 1778, chap. 13, p. 207.

11. The enactments of the several state legislatures directed against professions of loyalty to the monarch and Loyalist activities are summarized in Claude H. Van Tyne, *The Loyalists in the American Revolution* (1902; New York: Macmillan, 1959), pp. 318–41.

12. Brown, *The King's Friends,* pp. 252–53.

13. The story of how the Loyalists figured in the peace negotiations is outlined in Van Tyne, *Loyalists in the Revolution,* pp. 301ff.; and in various general accounts of the peace negotiations, including Richard B. Morris, *The Peacemakers* (New York: Harper and Row, 1965); Jonathan R. Dull, *A Diplomatic History of the American Revolution* (New Haven, Conn.: Yale University Press, 1985); Richard W. Van Alstyne, *Empire and Independence: The International History of the American Revolution* (New York: John Wiley and Sons, 1965).

14. See, e.g., their statements in Morris, *The Peacemakers,* pp. 368–69, 419. For Franklin's view as late as 1785, see Jared Sparks, ed., *The Works of Benjamin Franklin,* vol. 10 (Boston: Tappan and Whittemore, 1840), pp. 190–94.

15. More than a few, and perhaps most, of the states came to rely on sales of expropriated Loyalist property for financing the War of Independence—as a way of meeting the requisitions of Congress. In North Carolina, for instance, most of these sales occurred after the Revolution, in 1786–87. See DeMond, *Loyalists in North Carolina*, chap. 8; and, in general, Van Tyne, *Loyalists in the Revolution*, pp. 275ff.

16. For general accounts, see Van Tyne, *Loyalists in the Revolution*; Allen Nevins, *The American States during and after the Revolution, 1775–1789* (New York: Macmillan, 1927), pp. 645–56; and Merrill Jensen, *The New Nation* (New York: Alfred A. Knopf, 1958), pp. 265–81.

17. Van Tyne, *Loyalists in the Revolution*, p. 295.

18. Brown, *The King's Friends*, p. 251.

19. Mary Beth Norton, *The British Americans: The Loyalist Exiles in England, 1774–1789* (Boston: Little, Brown, 1972), pp. 242–49.

20. John Eardley-Wilmot, *Historical View of the Commission for Enquiring into the Losses, Service, and Claims of the American Loyalists, at the Close of the War between Great Britain and Her Colonies in 1783* (1815; Boston: Gregg Press, 1972); Charles R. Richeson, *Aftermath of Revolution: British Policy toward the United States, 1783–1795* (Dallas: Southern Methodist University Press, 1969), esp. pp. 55–56 and chap. 4.

21. *The Parliamentary History of England, from the Earliest Period to the Year 1803*, vol. 27 (London: T. C. Hansard, 1816), p. 610.

22. Eardley-Wilmot, *Historical View of Commission*, p. 43 and passim.

5

Aspirations for Nationhood

COLONIALS WHO BELIEVED that the king and his ministers needed a strong rebuke for abuse of authority but who considered immediate withdrawal from British rule too drastic a remedy could find a number of sentiments and assertions in the Declaration of Independence to dispute or reject out of hand. One presumption of the signers of the Declaration, surely worth careful scrutiny and analysis, seems to have encountered no challenge at all, however. This was the initial, simply implicit premise that the white inhabitants of the thirteen American colonies were sufficient in numbers, contiguity of location, and commonality of association, interests, and cultural norms to qualify as "one people" entitled to enter the family of nations whenever sufficient reasons for doing so presented themselves. The presumption was hardly unfounded.

Colonial Elements of Nationhood

The terms *a people* and *a nation* have no standard definition today, and the meanings attached to them were even less certain two hundred years ago. If one thought that common language, and therefore ease of communication, prepared a population for cohesion and identification as a people, then by this test the white inhabitants of the American colonies had a better claim to recognition as a distinct people than did any definable population living in equivalent propinquity on the European continent or its adjacent islands. As the eighteenth century closed, English was the language of everyday communication for an estimated 90 percent of the adult white inhabitants. At least 65 percent were of English ancestry and another 15 to 20 percent were Scotch, Irish, or Welsh, who at worst spoke a crude English. French and Scandinavian settlers, since there were only a few, could not avoid frequent contact with English-speaking communities and took up the speech of their neighbors as rapidly as their children could teach it to them.[1]

The Dutch and Germans were exceptional. The Dutch, who came early—first settling around the mouth of the Hudson in 1634—preempted the fertile farmland in what is now northern New Jersey, in wide strips on both sides of the Hudson River, and well out into the Mohawk Valley. This gave them room for an expanding population that could sustain its own churches, schools, and trading centers. The Dutch language was sufficient for their needs, and they clung to it for a full century after the English assumed dominion over their possessions in 1664. The Dutch were only 3.5 percent of the white population of America in 1790 but were 20 percent of the white population in New York and New Jersey. Continental troops moving up and down the Hudson and in the environs of New York City would have encountered numerous old people who could neither pray nor swear in English, but they would also have found throughout the region enough English-speaking Dutch to keep their compatriots abreast of developments in the English-speaking world.

The German element in colonial America resisted still more stubbornly the intrusion of English into their vocabulary and syntax. First to cross the Atlantic in significant numbers were refugees from hunger, whose lands in the Palatinate had been ravaged by warfare. In America they clung together, mainly along the western edge of the Pennsylvania frontier. Isolated in Appalachian valleys, the children had few opportunities to pick up the vernacular of American-born playmates. Feeling ill at ease in American courthouses, at public auctions, and in community gatherings, the Germans nurtured one another and preserved their native language. Within a couple of decades, a more copious German migration began, responding less to hunger than to religious oppression and more than occasional persecution. Distrusting government in any guise and apprehensive that the freedom of worship promised in the New World might prove to be fantasy, these immigrants clung together upon arrival in America, forming large enclaves on the frontiers of colonial settlement.

Germans became the largest colonial foreign-language minority—about 12 percent of the entire population in 1790 but as much as 33 percent in Pennsylvania. Many of these immigrants, shunning government altogether, refrained from voting, avoided entanglements with law and the courts by settling their own disputes, and ensured their exemption from jury duty by their linguistic inability to follow the proceedings. By political withdrawal they eluded a major inducement to learn the language of their surroundings, thus protecting the social insularity they had carefully practiced since arriving in the new land. Yet these zealous sectarians made a deep impress on American life, especially in agronomy, horticulture, and animal husbandry. They could do so simply through demonstration and the limited stock of English words they acquired for marketing their farm products.

The Scotch and the Irish, on the other hand, were anything but insular or reclusive, and they naturally found it expedient to knock the rough edges off their dialects. The Scotch and the Irish who had lived for a decade or so among American-born neighbors probably could have got about the streets of Boston, New York, or Philadelphia more easily than their cousins who came down to London, Bristol, or Liverpool from north of Solway Firth or west of the Irish Sea. So also for the Welsh, though they were not a numerous minority in the revolutionary period. For everyone, however—including the vast bulk of the population who came by English directly—the spoken and written language was far more uniform in North America than in the British Isles. New Englanders who traveled by sea or land from Boston to Charleston had no trouble at all communicating in any home or tavern they visited. If English novelists who have tried to reproduce their native tongue as it was spoken on the home soil at the time of the American Revolution approached the reality, little-traveled residents of Yorkshire would have encountered considerable difficulty in making their way about London, and Lancashire residents would have had just about as much trouble making themselves understood by both Londoners and natives of Yorkshire.[2]

Where a population is spread extensively, communication by writing or print acquires special importance. It follows that those who settled in North America and rolled back its forests had special cause for resort to written messages, for much of their business was with other colonials living too far away for face-to-face discussion, and many of them were pressed by family ties to keep in touch with at least a few people in the old country. These conditions, plus a firm determination of certain sects that someone in every family should be able to read the Bible, seem to account for the high levels of literacy in many parts of North America at the time of separation from England. Tapping Reeve, chief justice of Connecticut's Supreme Court of Errors for a term but best remembered as founder and head of eighteenth-century America's most highly regarded school for lawyers, once remarked that in all his years of law practice he had encountered but one native-born witness in court who could not write.[3] Reeve was born in 1744 and was no doubt commenting on literacy during the decades of the Revolutionary War and the adoption of the Constitution. Allowing that Connecticut may have held the North American record for literacy, there is persuasive testimony by observers, some of them reputed for caution, that Americans far outreached the Europeans of their day in ability to read and write. Fisher Ames of Massachusetts spoke eloquently to this point in the U.S. Congress in December 1796. He would allow those who knew the region better to assess the level of enlightenment in the southern states, but in the eastern states, with which he was particularly conversant, he "knew the people in them could generally read and write and were well informed as to public affairs." How sharp the contrast with Europe: "go through France, Germany, and most countries of Europe and it will be found that, out of fifty millions of people, not more than two or three millions had any pretensions to knowledge. . . . In France, which contains twenty-five millions of people, only one million was calculated to be in any respect enlightened. . . ."[4]

Pretensions of knowledge and claims to enlightenment presumably would have included a modest ability to read a printed page and write in the local idiom. Alexis de Tocqueville, taking his readings of the state of civilization in America in 1831–32, described a condition that could not have confronted him had literacy not been well advanced a half-century earlier, when the new nation was proclaiming its birth:

> The Americans are scarcely more virtuous than others; but they are infinitely more enlightened (I speak of the masses) than any other people I know; I do not only want to say that there are more people there who know how to read and write (a matter to which perhaps more importance is attached than is due), but the body of people who have understanding of public affairs, knowledge of the laws and of precedents, feeling for the well-understood interests of the nation and the faculty to understand them, is greater there than in any other place in the world.[5]

Ease of travel and transportation may rival common linguistic facility as a factor in developing a sense of nationhood. That the Atlantic coastline had a short hurricane season and weather favorable to sailing nearly year-round was an enticement to intercolony trade from an early date in

English settlement. Except in New England, rivers of sufficient year-round depth permitted cargo carriers of modest draft to reach deeply into most regions of settlement and cultivation, thus assuring a source of supply and a market for the products most favorably grown in one zone or another. There must have thus developed by the early eighteenth century a colonial appreciation of comparative advantage and mutual dependence. It also must have been the case by then that in a dozen coastal cities there was a sizable number of shipowners and sailors, fishermen, merchants, manufacturers, factors, and agents, who had a solid acquaintance with people they had done business with in half, if not every one, of the other seaport cities. England no doubt could match America in the nationalizing effect of travel and trade; so probably could The Netherlands and Portugal—all these of far less geographic sweep than England's colonies in America. For most regions of continental Europe, however, distance and mountain ranges would have imposed far more frustrations to development of the commonality that characterizes a population conscious of exhibiting a national character.

As for highways—cart roads and turnpikes—crisscrossing the populated territory of North America, speculation from limited knowledge becomes hazardous. Transport of farm produce and trade goods by canoe and log raft may have matched or exceeded movement by pack train, cart, and ox-drawn wagon. Whatever the means of conveyance and whatever the volume, moving produce and wares to distant markets would have been a primary contributor to the diffusion of customs, aspirations, and perceptions of common interest. This was a unifying and homogenizing factor that would have been observed in the Old World as well as the New World. Still, the ubiquity of traversable roads in isolated communities and at the edge of the American frontier astounded Tocqueville and his companion Gustave de Beaumont some forty years after the inauguration of Washington as president, and Tocqueville wrote in his diary:

> The roads, the canals and the mails play a prodigious part in the prosperity of the Union. . . . In France there are large and very concentrated populations through which winds no road, with the result that they are more separated from the rest of the nation than half the world formerly was. I don't doubt it would take longer and cost more to have ten sacks of wheat brought from certain *communes* in lower Brittany to Paris than to transport to the same spot all the sugar of

the new world colonies. In America one of the first things done in a
new State is to have the mail come. In the Michigan forests there is
not a cabin so isolated, not a valley so wild, that it does not receive
letters and newspapers at least once a week; we saw it ourselves.[6]

Religion is a unifying or a divisive force in a population according to the
distribution and intensity of convictions and loyalties. At the time of their
self-election to membership in the family of nations, Americans were
notably, perhaps singularly, free of sectarian animosities and belligerencies.
Arguably they were so largely because of the very diversity of their religious persuasions. Moreover, the diverse convictions of earlier generations
had been tempered and moderated, not only by time but also notably by
Arminian and Socinian—evangelical and deistic—developments, not to
mention the considerable spread of religious indifference during the second half of the eighteenth century. Jewish Americans were too few to
excite apprehensions; the first arrivals seem to have been received with
considerable cordiality, and their numbers remained small until decades
after events had determined the essential character of the new polity—
probably less than twenty thousand of some fourteen million white inhabitants as late as 1840.

Eight of the initial state constitutions restricted state public officeholding,
particularly in the legislature, to Christians or, more commonly, to Protestants. They did so through general statements on eligibility or by the
language of a stipulated oath of office. (Most of these same constitutions
also contained strong freedom of worship declarations, limited in some
cases to Christians.) The South Carolina Constitution of 1778 went further,
confining the legislative electorate to persons who believed in "a future
state of rewards and punishments." Five such constitutional provisions
had disappeared by the end of the founding period, but three continued
well into the nineteenth century.[7]

Decisions on the composition of a polity do not finally determine who
will be recognized as critical for the fabric of a nation. With the removal or
desuetude of constitutional, statutory, and common-law provisions bar-
ring them from officeholding, denying them the right to vote, and imposing restrictions on their enjoyment of rights and privileges accorded other
sects and denominations, Catholics and Jews would have had to acknowledge that they held full formal membership of the polity. If at the same
time, however, they could have supplied proof—as quite conceivably they
could have—that their religious-minority status put their political opin-

ions and participation at a discount, then they still fell short of parity membership in practice.[8]

If this account approximates the conditions that actually prevailed in the colonies on the eve of their break from British rule, then the reference to "a people" in the Declaration of Independence rested on solid ground, whether or not it was justified beyond question. Lacking, one might contend, is proof that the white population was suffused with an itch for unity, a consciousness of affinity and common interests, a bonding more potent than the political amalgamation proposed in 1777 and declared in effect as Articles of Confederation in 1781. But general conviction that a population constitutes one people, that it satisfies all the requirements for acceptance as a nation, promises something more than an invitation to associate themselves under one government. If they have amply a common culture, common interests, and a common understanding of their institutions, they will tend to respect authority and know how to move authority into compliance with their wishes and expectations. Even more important, they will by compatible conduct and concerted actions eschew abrasive situations, temper harsh demands, settle disputes voluntarily, and thus remove from the agenda of public policy and the forums of governmental decision much of the business that so frequently sets governments on a course of oppression. These are ground-level realities of political existence, and they were well known to political leaders of the generation that fashioned the new political structures erected in the decade that witnessed the withdrawal of British arms and final certification of American independence.

Nation-building in the Founding Period

Progression from complaint about arbitrary decisions in London, to resistance, to assertion of independence and preparation for war was accompanied by unfolding proof that fighting men, public leaders, and productive contributors to the economy were enough of one mind to assure that people of the thirteen colonies were going to hold together. By cautious steps, forward leaps, and a good deal of floundering, no doubt, a people growing in consciousness of need for social cohesion as well as for political union moved toward that end. This progression was witnessed by, for example, the rush of supplies to Massachusetts when London's edicts and blockades plugged the Bay Colony's seaports and by the early revelation that riflemen from Maine to Pennsylvania made thoroughly dependable foot soldiers while gentlemen from Virginia and the Carolinas made admirable officers, sagacious in decision and sensitive to human frailties in exercise of command.

The swaddling and nursing of nationalism that advanced apace with military campaigns seem to have culminated in the apotheosis of George Washington. Observable in the closing years of the Revolutionary War, the exaltation of the Virginia planter was to reach its crescendo during his years as first president of the new Republic. The achievements with which Washington was credited in myth and legend may be grounded in authentic accomplishments, but the character and qualities ascribed to the man have the epic, ultimately incredible cast of the exploits of Hercules. Granted that common cause in a war tends—universally it seems—to precipitate the creation of heroes; still, the extent of the enticements to adulation that lifted Washington above a generation of founding fathers to the role of father of his country could find few precedents in European history since the eclipse of Imperial Rome, and they preceded the nationalistic celebrations abroad of Napoléon and Wellington.

Why the erection of an icon so towering that his presence dwarfed the stature of all other claimants to a share of the national esteem? It cannot be that the victorious rebels lacked nominees for a roster of heroes. George Rogers Clark, Nathanael Green, John Paul Jones, and a dozen others supplied a nation with a plentitude of materials—men who begot victories when victories were scarce and anxiety bred dejection. It is an attractive hypothesis that the transcending hero was created because the nation, by and large, felt a need for a towering figure, a single personage who combined the roster of virtues they believed were requisite for the survival of a self-governing republic, who could sustain the charisma required for uniting in common cause a people scattered in residence and divided in their perceptions of a public good, who was marked by steadfastness of purpose and a sensitivity to statecraft that could foresee and surmount the entrapments spawned by scheming European powers. A supposition that contemporaries, gifted with perception and ambitious for leadership, were conscious of a purposeful process is not essential to this hypothesis.[9]

The continuing consolidation of an American character is concisely summarized by an American historian highly regarded for the thoroughness of his research and the caution suffused in his judgments. Noting that historians have endorsed a thesis that the War of 1812 marked a forward surge in American nationalism, Marcus Hansen suggests that it may have served only to accelerate a longer movement toward the unity and commonality that make a nation. The Louisiana Purchase figured in this longer trend as the source of a sense of manifest destiny. So did the coming of age of children of the revolutionary generation. So did the steep decline of immigration during the Napoleonic Wars, a decline that, Hansen thinks, hastened the Americanization of earlier, non-British immigrants.[10] Commenting on the final capitulation of the Dutch and the Germans to the realization that the first language of the children was destined to be English, Hansen tells us a bit about the terms of surrender:

> These folks [the Dutch of New Jersey and New York] took a reluctant part in the political movements that became the Revolution; but whether lukewarm, patriotic or silently pro-English, they could not escape the new order which it created . . . as the Hudson River developed into the great commercial artery toward the north, the sleepy villages on either side awoke to the new opportunities. No longer was Dutch all-sufficient. Old merchants struggled to master the strange English words: the young more easily adopted the new speech. English became the language of trade.
>
> But many a man of affairs who willingly employed English six days a week balked at its use in religious services. . . . Whatever the local variations, compromise paved the way to solution: first one sermon a month in the new tongue, then one sermon each Sunday. Gradually the proportion increased until Dutch was reserved for those special occasions when the elderly attended in full force. In the meantime English Bibles, English hymn books and English catechisms supplanted the old. The children breathed an entirely new ecclesiastical atmosphere, and by 1815, except in the remoter rural parts, the new basis had been attained. . . .
>
> The fate of German, which was spoken by about three times as many persons, varied with the circumstances that surrounded the main groups. The descendants of the Palatines who had remained in Ulster County and on the Mohawk Flats in New York were subjected to the same influences and underwent the same transformation as the Dutch. The action of the New York Ministerium of the Lutheran Church in 1800 in declaring that henceforth English should be the language of its deliberations and records gave the movement a decisive official impetus. With even greater facility the German colonies in the West and South, far distant from the main stem of their fellow countrymen in Pennsylvania and Maryland, adopted the new

institutions and speech. To prevent the younger generation from going over to the popular frontier denominations, the churches and ministries perforce fell into line. . . .[11]

The end of the War of Independence brought widespread recognition of an urgent agenda for nation-building. Two concerns pressed the political leadership and the articulate elite relentlessly: (1) the fashioning of a more perfect political union, and (2) the cultivation of a finer conception of virtue as a quality that could inspirit and regulate the public life of the nation. In these concerns American leaders looked not only to national opportunity but also to national vulnerability. Despite the ongoing debate and the compromises forged in the Congress of the Confederation and the sharing of danger and suffering by men in arms, there persisted a gnawing anxiety that contrarieties of interest would forestall the mitigations of state autonomy still required for a central government adequate to independence. There also remained a sticky suspicion that divergent community identifications would, when fended by distance, dissolve the cohesion that for a time had made Americans a nation.

American historians have succeeded admirably in chronicling our forebears' progress in realizing the first of these grand objectives—to devise a government for a people aspiring to a place of respect among world powers yet not prepared for the concentration of authority that had come to characterize the principal world powers. Historians have perhaps been laggard, however, in searching out and illuminating the founders' efforts to expand the conception and strengthen the fabric of national character. Of these two presumptively critical missions of a new political leadership—the institutional development of a new federal state and the inculcation of a sustaining political ethos—the second will therefore be emphasized in the rest of this chapter and indeed in the rest of this book.

As for the first mission, the ambivalence exposed with every proposal to transfer authority from the member states to the government of the states united repeatedly dampened, instead of quickening, the prospect of advance toward a more perfect political union. Every flare-up of opposition to consolidation of the ruling power sharpened public awareness of conflicts of interest that made foot-dragging not only inevitable but defensible. Yet at a rate rapid enough to challenge belief, this three-million-plus people who had come to be a polity made the journey from governmental embarrassment to a new form of confederation fitted to republican principles and fit for coexistence in the not so happy family of nations. We need not trace the forward steps; it is enough merely to mark off the mileposts:

Year 1, 1774	A national Congress that prescribed the terms of its own legitimization.
Year 3, 1777	Permanent Articles of Confederation agreed upon by the national Congress.
Year 7, 1781	Permanent Articles of Confederation approved by the several states and declared in effect.
Year 12, 1786	Recommendation by delegates of five states that each of the states appoint commissioners to consider the situation of the United States and "to devise such further provisions as shall to them seem necessary to render the constitution of the Foederal Government adequate to the exigencies of Union."[12]
Year 13, 1787	Convention of delegates representing twelve states drafts a new constitution, which it proposes become effective for such states as ratify when approved by conventions designated for that purpose in nine or more states.
Year 14, 1788	The new Constitution of the United States becomes effective by ratification of the ninth state.
Year 15, 1789	Government under the new Constitution instituted by electing and seating the president and Congress, with thirteen states participating.

I have contended that the white inhabitants of the thirteen English colonies could make a better case in 1776 for status as "a people" than any substantial population in Europe one might have marked out to examine for like character and identity. Surely the near-decade of warfare sharpened that sensibility of solidarity. Still, the contention can only be sustained by removing from the count of American citizenry both the estimated 4 percent who went into exile at the outset of the Revolution and the many remaining in the thirteen states whose commitment to Britain lasted at least until American victory was in sight. Some, or most, of the resident dissenters were sincere, as of 1783–84, in their declarations of readiness to give the new venture in self-government a fair trial. Who these best prospects for citizenship were, and how staunchly any of them would stand up under adversity, could only be guessed at, however. Many a proven patriot, worn to the bone from years of enlistments and military engagements, must have magnified into incipient treachery the murmured half-hopes of a few that England under new leadership might reform, repent, and restore Americans to a place in the empire. It must also be said that many American leaders were warily concerned about Toryism as a potential source of subversion for a decade or more after Yorktown and that residues of this concern surfaced in partisan conflicts for a decade or more after adoption of the Constitution.

Perhaps nothing discloses more clearly the contemporary sense of need to initiate a conciliatory course of instruction for the new nation than an essay published in Charleston in the fall of 1784. Prompted to write by the violent reaction of some partisans of independence to legislation they considered too charitable to Tories, the author proceeds from severe reminders that not all can have their way to incisive analysis of the moods and procedures that could guide a free people in fixing the bounds of their consent to be governed. This introductory lecture on citizenship appeared over the pen name Philodemus; the persuasiveness of its argument would have increased with currency of the rumor that its author was Thomas Tudor Tucker, a man unimpeachable for service to the cause of independence and with few peers in repute for intelligence and public stature in his state and community. A few sentences extracted from the thirty-page essay expose the mission and the earnestness of the writer:

> It is true indeed, that [in a government approaching democracy, the people] sometimes mistake the object they are in pursuit of, and still more frequently, the proper means of achieving it. . . . They are at all times intitled to demand an ample redress of grievances yet it is not by violent means that this is properly or effectually to be sought. Violence can only be justifiable where it is the only resource [recourse?]. This is commonly the case in countries where a standing force is kept up, which may hinder the peaceable deliberations of the people, and render it impossible for any matter to be quietly determined by a majority of voices. . . . Nor are secret combinations better authorized, or less dishonorable to the characters of the promoters. They are to be regarded in no other light than as insidious and treacherous attempts of a minority to rule a majority; which is the very definition of an aristocratical government, so loudly and so justly condemned. . . . An honest man, and a real lover of freedom, will fairly and openly declare what he has to propose, and leave to a majority to judge of it, to adopt or reject it. He is free to support his

opinion by every possible argument, but he must finally allow others the liberty of having an opinion too. It is a strange way that some men have of vindicating the cause of freedom, by denying others even the freedom of thinking. Whoever acts in this manner is a tyrant at heart, and should he, under the cloak of patriotism, gain influence with the people, he will be no longer their friend than whilst he stands in need of their countenance and support. Whenever he can securely do it, he will shew himself the bitter enemy of all who stand in the way of his ambition.[13]

The Bonds of Community and the Obligations of Citizenship

The Philodemus essay was written in the early stages of an emergent campaign to draw the nation together with stronger attachments of understanding and trust; to cultivate an awareness of common interest and interdependence; to infuse the population with ideals and expectations about the character and conduct of public officials, the distinguishing marks of good citizenship, and the rights and obligations of individuals under the new regime; and to persuade Americans that if they would stand fast in common purpose, zeal, and adherence to virtue, nothing could stay their march to the first rank of enlightened nations. This was not an undertaking preplanned and subject to central direction. It was, nonetheless, a concurrent and remarkably concordant effort, emanating from many population centers and small towns. Its protagonists compare favorably with the kind of national sample of political and opinion leaders likely to satisfy a pollster of our own day.[14]

One should keep in mind that the Philodemus essay made a late entrance into the course of instruction in citizenship that had been underway for more than a century in New England's churches—most notably, but not only, in election sermons. Emphasis had shifted, to be sure: first, proof from the Bible that civil rulers are ordained of God and charged to do good—that disobedience to their ordinances is an offense against religion; then, as allegiance was rubbed raw by grievances against England, that it is a right or a duty—equal to the obligation to obey just rulers—to resist civil authorities when they direct their conduct to tyrannical purposes and cease to exercise their powers for good alone; then on to the rights of English citizens that were being denied Americans and to more embracing questions of the meaning of liberty in a free society and how to secure it in a nation based on consent of the governed. Here we encounter Philodemus.

Prominent in this discourse at all stages was an earnest appeal to individuals, whatever their vocation and social station, to swathe themselves in the vestments of virtue. (The meanings and implications of virtue are explored in greater depth in chapter 9.) Also notable as the discourse evolved was the emergence and, in time, the primacy of a preoccupation with patriotism, close kin to virtue in republican tradition. "Love of country" was a phrase occasionally encountered in sermons and other addresses before the break with England; it was more often cited as a consequence of good government than as a prerequisite to good government. Americans were blessed with good rulers and good laws secured by the British Constitution; it was natural that they should love the country so endowed. When the rebels took to arms, "patriot" came to identify those who fought for independence, and "patriotism" identified the sentiments and proofs of their attachment to the cause. It did not take long for those competent at reading an audience to discover that references to bitter trials, indisputable successes, acknowledged heroes, and, above all, the humbling of the greatest power in Europe was a surefire tactic for capturing an audience, and regular occasions for patriotic exhortation were rapidly established.

Public gatherings memorializing victims of the Boston Massacre date back to the first anniversary of that bloody evening in 1770, but these stirrings of resentment against intrusion by foreigners and recitals of atrocities to be anathematized in memory were a local development. Orations celebrating the anniversary of the Declaration of Independence must have been common during the years of battle and bloodshed, but if so, few would have been preserved in print owing to scarcity of paper and pressure for space from more urgent events.[15] Not until a full decade after the Liberty Bell rang out in Philadelphia could it be said that pamphlet copies of the Fourth of July address had come to be expected in all parts of the Republic. In preparation for this book, I examined ninety-three orations celebrating the anniversary of independence. Seven were delivered prior to 1787; eighty-six were delivered between 1787 and 1803. Items with titles indicating they were sermons delivered in church were not included in the count.

As the passing of time altered judgments about what most needed to be stressed in preparing Americans for the burdens and opportunities of republican citizenship, conviction grew that coalescence of all thirteen state populations as a nation was essential for the survival of republican government. Sermons and orations during the Revolution and for some two decades afterward frequently and eloquently opened with reference to qualities of heroism and the exemplary doings of certified heroes. Patriotism figured largely in this rhetorical tactic. Love of country was thus linked to republican virtue and portrayed as a state of mind conducive to the development of virtue. Virtue in turn was a medley of attributes that were never entirely itemized, though for New England they might have been cataloged from more than a century of Congregational sermons. During the revolutionary period, the learned clergy pretty much took the lead in explication and exhortation toward public awareness that self-government necessarily depends on faith, belief, and conduct rooted in virtue. Political leaders joined in, and nearly half of the first round of state constitutions cited various specifications of the content of a virtuous life as "fundamental principles" (more on this in chapter 9).

With the end of the Revolution and the status of former Loyalists unsettled, a growing emphasis on patriotic celebration might well have been calculated to assist the cause of national unification. Certainly patriotism, or love of country, appeared as an indispensable virtue to some moral leaders. Consider the first election-day sermon under New Hampshire's new government in the spring of 1784. Rehearsing the virtues requisite to self-government, the Reverend Samuel MacClintock began with religion, then turned to love of country. The gist of the reasoning that supported this priority is compacted in the following paragraph:

> In absolute governments, where the power is lodged in the hands of one or a few, the constitution may be maintained tho' the people are grossly ignorant and corrupt, because they have no concern in the affairs of government. They are governed by brutal force, and are mere machines which move only as they are moved by an exterior power; but in free governments where all [power supplied] originates with the people and the authority delegated by them to their rulers, is revocable at their pleasure, it is essential to existence and to the public welfare, that people should be virtuous, and entertain just ideas of the relation and mutual obligations between them and their rulers, and the common interest they have in the good of their country.---It is of great importance they should be sensible that their country is not the land where they were born, or the soil they possess, but the great body of the people of which they are members, and the laws and constitution under which they live---that the people are *their* people---the laws *their* laws, which

they have consented to be govern'd by, and the rulers *their* rulers, to whom they have solemnly promised obedience and subjection, in the exercise of lawful authority; and that as in the natural, so in the political body, its prosperity and happiness depend on the wisdom of the head, the soundness of the vitals, and the activity and regular exercise of the members in their several places---such sentiments generally diffused among a people, will engage them to obey from a principle of duty, and will make them ready and cheerful in contributing their support to measures calculated to promote the public good---They will prefer the welfare of their country to their chief joy. It was this principle of public spirit and love of their country, which was cultivated with a religious care, from their earliest age in the citizens of Sparta, Athens and Rome, that produced such astonishing efforts of heroic virtue.[16]

Uncertainties and apprehensions about the future conduct of former Loyalists, especially those lately returned or expected to return from exile, may well have led this most candid of preachers to exaggerate his conviction that a patriotic zeal for the untried republic was sine qua non for its continued existence and for the deep-rooting of republican principles. If we think of this as a special circumstance, deviating from the expected or normal, it must be allowed that anxieties about divided loyalties continued to disturb thinking throughout the 1780s and for at least another fifteen years. Hardly had the once-hated opponents of independence taken the edge off uneasiness about their reconciliation with republican government than the eruption of the French Revolution challenged enlightened men and women of all nations to reexamine the precarious state of justice in the country of their own residence. By 1793 or 1794 the ideals summed up in "liberté, égalité, fraternité" led many Americans to believe that the French upheaval was nothing less than the legitimate issue of a revolution touched off at Lexington and Concord twenty years earlier. For many other Americans, however, friends of the French Revolution were Jacobins, and no Jacobin was a friend of republican government as it had been intended for the welfare of Americans.

This interlude of rancor, mistrust, and accusations of disloyalty probably peaked with the Alien and Sedition Acts of 1798, the gestures toward nullification by Kentucky and Virginia in response, and the subsequent election of Thomas Jefferson to the presidency. Regardless of waves of intensity, the recrimination was continuous for at least a full decade, providing ample reason to suppose that those who were quickest to put a blessing on patriotic zeal may have been subject to emotional tensions that led them to overstate their convictions. The truth of these matters we are not likely ever to know. It may be sufficient here to say that by the time the Fourth of July address had become institutionalized, the lay speaker was a stalwart ally of the cleric in affirming love of country among the virtues cited as of first priority. (Illustrative excerpts from three staunch declarations of faith and urgent calls for national cohesion appear in appendix 1.)

The Problem of Responsible Citizenship

The problem of responsible citizenship has been at the center of our concern in Part 1. It was, we have discovered, a recurrent concern of the founding. This was so because a regime of self-government, once it was established fully and independently, appeared to make special demands on, require special capacities of, its citizens. There was no standard list of the attributes of responsible citizenship, but a few desirable capacities were and are clearly inferable. Personal autonomy or nondependency was no doubt fundamental; beyond this, industry or the ability to make an economic contribution was important. As for politics, there was the classical republican virtue, a balanced regard for justice or the public good—the implication of *balance* here having to do not only with temperament but also with the preservation of personal autonomy, judgment, and effort, together with consultation of the common good. The place of patriotism, or love of country, has been emphasized: in the founding period the Revolution conditioned the significance of this virtue particularly. There was more, including a compliant response to the teachings and feelings of religion, but this list will suffice for our purposes, pending the discussion of virtue in chapter 9. Obviously, citizens, or prospective citizens, could not be evaluated on such capacities by formal examination; the virtues pertinent to citizenship were, rather, the presumptive products of common civilization, or community.

It appears in earlier chapters that eligibility for full citizenship was not at all readily accorded in cases of doubt—or categories of cases of doubt—about capacities to assume its obligations. Such cases or categories had chiefly to do with presumptive want of common civilization, or community commitments. The doubt may in some cases have reflected prevailing community perceptions, or prejudices, much more than evaluation of the case or category on its merits. But the very capacities in question militated this way. Acceptance for prospectively responsible citizenship required both autonomy and commonality, both individual (or family) self-sufficiency and evident participation in implicitly shared values. These requirements went together: without similarity of civilization the promise of autonomy was problematic, and so was the prospect of civic responsibility. In this light the different terms of civic inclusion/exclusion accorded the American Indian, the free Negro, the continental European immigrant, and the recanting Loyalist are perhaps rationally understandable, even if not, by our lights, entirely meritorious.

In our time, with the abolition of such general discriminations established as an object and preoccupation of public policy, the approach to the problem of responsible citizenship in the founding period is likely to seem unduly narrow and exclusive. On the other hand, the founding generations appear to have taken the problem of responsible citizenship more seriously than we do—seriously enough, that is, to be willing to make discriminations we tend to find offensive, raising for us the question whether a serious commitment to responsible citizenship requires not necessarily such discriminations but at least a commitment to certain civic or public virtues that may, in our day, be thought parochial or prejudicial or merely ethnocentric. Behind this question lies another for the student of politics today: whether the founding generation was mistaken analytically in its view of the requirements a republican polity entailed on its citizens—that is, that responsible citizenship, or the practice of civic virtue, was a condition of republican survival. There will be occasion in Part 2 to remark on the emergence late in the founding period of a different conception of republican politics—of a polity more nearly self-regulating or equilibrating through the checks and balances of political (perhaps even "factional") competition and thus arguably less dependent on community values and civic virtue. Systematic democratic theory today tends decidedly toward the latter conception, yet it is still not clear that the older republican model has been wholly invalidated, or even that the two conceptions are entirely antithetical. Emphasis on them seems rather to have alternated in American political history. To what extent and in what ways does the regulation of a politics of interests depend on elements of political community?

The chapters in Part 2 are chiefly concerned with the meanings and implications of liberty, equality, and virtue as central conceptions of republican government in the founding period. The focus shifts from citizenship and the political community to certain basic organizing principles of the political regime and thus to relations among the members of the community. Here we have to deal with competition among interests and values and thus with disagreements over the meanings and implications of the organizing principles. Such disagreements, primarily regarding liberty and the allowable boundaries of dissent, took shape increasingly in the first decade of the Republic as divisions sharpened symbolically and symptomatically between French and British colorations of republicanism. The emphasis on unity and patriotism mentioned at the end of the last section thus came to be the public concern of Federalists—who were for the most part in power and no doubt protective about it, but who were also offended intellectually by French-leaning ideologies—more than of Republicans, in the nomenclature conventionally linked to these divisions. Some regional differences in political culture may also have been involved, for the Congregational tradition of New England's (then largely Federalist) politics appears to have placed special emphasis on commonalities of political community and the indispensability of public virtue—notwithstanding examples of such concerns quoted above from Virginia. Probably, therefore, we cannot say that American political leadership was united throughout the founding period on particular values or valences of civic virtue, or perhaps even on the priority of patriotism.

These disagreements, however, receded after the founding period. The elements of political community and civic capacity that have been summarized in this chapter were conceivably sufficient to sustain both the nation and the practice of self-government for some sixty years, though they were progressively threatened by competing regional interests and constitutional ideologies. We cannot know for certain, however, that the adjurations to civic responsibility and the appeals to common experience delivered from pulpits and rostrums and in print during the founding period made a critical difference. We cannot even be sure that Americans' remarkable progress toward nationhood by the beginning of the founding period was later critical in enabling a polity newly national and not yet long independent to survive the divisions of its first decade. Perhaps the most we can know is that the adjurations and appeals were deliberate and purposeful acts of leadership and that the legacy of something like nationhood was real. We can also compare the experience of the United States in the founding period with that of both Britain and France contemporaneously— say, the Whisky Rebellion with Peterborough and the Vendée—to American advantage.

Whether necessarily so or not, then, the American Republic began with a strong emphasis on the values of political community and civic responsibility implied in then-prevailing conceptions of public virtue. Notwithstanding its prior colonial existence as separate states, the new nation was probably, among all sizable nations of that time, the one most endowed with attributes conducing to nationhood. Within the political leadership, enhancement of the conditions of political community and responsible citizenship were conscious concerns of high priority—especially, as time went on and the testing began, among those leaders most committed to national government, most concerned about public order, national security, and civic responsibility, and perhaps least confident of popular capacities. But such concerns were widely shared throughout the founding period, especially as the new national experiment began. This was so in large part because the creation overnight, from theretofore jealous jurisdictions, of an effective national regime of self-government, over a territory enormous in traditional republican terms, could be predicted to test the attributes of nationhood or national community, whatever their condition. It was so as well because successful self-government, at whatever scale, was believed to rest on the civic capacities of its participants, presupposing more than ordinary capacities. Thus it was that virtue, as well as liberty, seemed essential to self-government.

Notes

1. These estimates can be inferred from Louis B. Wright, *The Cultural Life of the American Colonies, 1607–1763* (New York: Harper and Brothers, 1957), chap. 3; Maldwyn A. Jones, *American Immigration* (Chicago: University of Chicago Press, 1960), chaps. 1–3; and American Historical Association, *Annual Report for the Year 1931* (Washington, D.C.: American Historical Association, 1932), p. 103ff. See also Bernard Bailyn, *The Peopling of British North America: An Introduction* (New York: Alfred A. Knopf, 1986), esp. p. 9 and chap. 3.

2. Daniel J. Boorstin, *The Americans: The Colonial Experience* (New York: Random House, 1958), chap. 41 and sources cited there. No general "melting-pot" interpretation is intended in the statements about language.

3. Samuel Church, "Litchfield County Historical Address," 1851, in Dwight C. Kilbourn, *The Bench and Bar of Litchfield County, Connecticut, 1709–1909* (Litchfield, Conn.: published by the author, 1909). See also Richard J. Purcell, *Connecticut in Transition , 1775–1818* (Washington, D.C.: American Historical Association, 1918), p. 302, n. 10.

4. *Annals of Congress* 6 (1796–97): 1642.

5. Alexis de Tocqueville, *Journey to America,* ed. J. P. Mayer (1959; New Haven, Conn.: Yale University Press, 1960), p. 258.

6. George Wilson Pierson, ed., *Tocqueville and Beaumont in America* (New York: Oxford University Press, 1938), pp. 589–90.

7. States *without* religious qualifications for officeholding in the founding period were Connecticut, Maryland, Massachusetts, New York, and Rhode Island. Two of these states wrote no constitution before the nineteenth century (the earlier in 1818); two maintained established churches well into the nineteenth century. See, in general, Anson Phelps Stokes, *Church and State in the United States,* vol. 1 (New York: Harper and Brothers, 1950), chap. 5; for the constitutional provisions, see Francis Newton Thorpe, ed., *The Federal and State Constitutions, Colonial Charters, and Other Organic Laws of the States, Territories, and Colonies Now or Heretofore Forming the United States of America* (Washington, D.C.: Government Printing Office, 1909).

8. Stokes, *Church and State,* chaps. 5–10.

9. The myth and legend of George Washington are sensitively limned and appraised by Marcus Cunliffe in his biography, *George Washington: Man and Monument* (Boston: Little, Brown, 1958), chap. 1. See also Daniel J. Boorstin, *The Americans: The National Experience* (New York: Random House, 1965), chap. 39 and sources cited on pp. 485–86.

10. Marcus Lee Hansen, *The Atlantic Migration, 1607–1880* (New York: Harper Torchbooks, 1961), pp. 72–73.

11. Ibid., pp. 73–74.

12. Report of the Annapolis Convention, in *Documents of American History,* vol. 1, 9th ed., ed. Henry Steele Commanger (Englewood Cliffs, N.J.: Prentice-Hall, 1973), 133–34.

13. [Thomas Tudor Tucker], *Conciliatory Hints, Attempting, by a Fair State of Matters, to Remove Party Prejudices* (Charleston: Printed for A. Timothy, 1784). Reprinted in Charles S. Hyneman and Donald S. Lutz, eds., *American Political Writing during the Founding Era, 1760–1805,* vol. 1 (Indianapolis: Liberty Press, 1983), pp. 606–30, quoted extracts on pp. 617–18.

14. This report on a campaign of instruction and exhortation derives from the reading of something over a hundred sermons, orations, discourses, and dissertations put into print between 1779 and 1804 and directed to the cultivation of virtue. More than half the items read struck me, on grounds of matters discussed, range of knowledge, and quality of thought, to be worthy of a place in the active library of political thought. In my judgment at least sixteen of the items—nos. 38, 39, 40, 42, 44, 45, 47, 54, 56, 63, 65, 66, 70, 72, 73, and 74—reproduced in Hyneman and Lutz, *American Political Writing,* fall in this category..

15. Philip F. Detweiler, "The Changing Reputation of the Declaration of Independence: The First Fifty Years," *William and Mary Quarterly,* 3d ser., 19

(1962): 557–74; Charles Warren, "Fourth of July Myths," *William and Mary Quarterly*, 3d ser., 2 (1945): 237–72.

16. Samuel MacClintock, *A Sermon Preached before the Honorable the Council and the Honorable the Senate and House of Representatives of the State of New Hampshire June 3, 1784, on Occasion of the Commencement of the New Constitution and Form of Government* (Portsmouth: Printed by Robert Gerrish, 1784), pp. 35–37.

PART TWO

Republican Government: Equality, Liberty, and Virtue

6

A People Capable of Self-government: Equality and Liberty

"THERE IS NO GOOD GOVERNMENT but what is republican," wrote John Adams in the spring of 1776, and "that form of government which is best contrived to secure an impartial and exact execution of the laws, is the best of republics." What contrivance promises best to secure this end? That was the question asked by colleagues in the Continental Congress who enticed Adams to put on paper his thoughts on government. "The foundation of every government," he wrote, "is some principle or passion in the minds of the people." Of every *good* government, he should have said, or of every free government or government not in the clutches of despotism. "The noblest principles and most generous affections of our nature, then, have the fairest chance to support the noblest principles and most generous models of government."[1]

There is not, in the little pamphlet titled *Thoughts on Government,* an explicit assertion that in a "good" government, or even in the most nearly perfect of republican governments, the people will maintain a continuing control over the exercise of political power. But the author's first prescription for a government soundly republican in character is the construction of an assembly truly representative of the people who are to be governed. "The first necessary step, then is to depute power from the many to a few of the most wise and good." In the selection of these few, greatest care should be taken to make the assembly "an exact portrait of the people at large. It should think, feel, reason, and act like them. . . . [E]qual interests among the people should have equal interests in it."

Implicit throughout the *Thoughts* is an expectation or presumption that the representative assembly will be the supreme, the determinative, authority in all matters involving affairs of state except those particular matters entrusted to specified officials. Left up in the air was the question, "By what rules shall you choose your representatives?" John Adams's oblique response to that question gives every reason to suppose that he took popular election for granted and that he saw nothing to be gained by offering his personal advice on who should be trusted to vote.

John Adams deserves this primacy in attention because, it will hardly be disputed among today's historians, he was foremost among American colonials in conviction and in depth of thought about the feasibility of providing for just government without the instrumentality of monarchs and orders of nobility. Members of the Continental Congress from at least three colonies other than his own urged him to put on paper the best advice he could give them for guidance in writing constitutions for their respective colony-states in case separation from England should come. In slightly varying versions, his response was composed and delivered two months before Richard Henry Lee introduced his resolution asserting that the American colonies were, and of right ought to be, free and independent states.

Four more years were to pass before the Massachusetts lawyer-statesman set forth for scrutiny and public debate the vision of republican government that had been hastily sketched while minds were moving toward independence. Adams was charged with drafting a constitution for Massachusetts in 1780, and he laid such a heavy hand on the content and the wording that for more than two centuries he has been credited with little less than sole authorship of the document.

The constitution, as drafted and adopted, opens with a declaration of rights expressed in thirty articles (thirty-five paragraphs). The Declaration of Rights serves two purposes: it promises that government in Massachusetts will be government of the people, by the people, and for the people; and it describes or defines many of the critical relationships that shall obtain between the people and the officialdom called government.

Without doubt, John Adams's deepest convictions were engaged as he wrote the statements locating the power to govern in the people.

> The people of this commonwealth have the sole and exclusive right of governing themselves.... All power residing originally in the people, and being derived from them, the several magistrates and officers of government ... are at all times accountable to them ... the people have a right at such periods and in such manner as they shall

establish ... to cause their public officers to return to private life; and to fill up vacant places by certain and regular elections and appointments. ... The people have a right, in a peaceable and orderly manner, to assemble to consult upon the common good; give instructions to their representatives, and to request ... redress of the wrongs done them, and of the grievances they suffer.[2]

This was his way of stating forthrightly, unequivocally, the ground-level principle of republican government. The remainder of the Declaration of Rights, preoccupied with limitations on government and rights of individuals to be respected by governors, must have seemed of secondary importance to him. He may even have written some of them with distaste, but in 1780 demands for restriction of government and personal guarantees were compelling in Massachusetts. Limitations on governments and guarantees of personal rights figured prominently in half the state constitutions then in effect, and objections to a previous proposal by the Massachusetts General Court had made it abundantly clear that a document lacking a substantial bill of rights would encounter hard going in the town meetings of 1780.

It seems all but certain that in the spring of 1776, when he was in the forefront of the drive for independence, John Adams saw little need for guarantees of personal rights. Rights were secured by law and a process of adjudication. If government was established on sound principles, the persons charged with governing would make secure the rights of the governed. Put the power of governing in the right hands and distribute authority among those chosen for offices in a fashion that will assure deliberation before action, a matching of boldness with caution, hurdles in the presence of ambition, and a moderation of the claims that are successfully advanced by competing interests. This was the advice reiterated to colleagues in the Continental Congress, and there is not a sentence or phrase in the *Thoughts on Government* that suggested a possible need for reliance on restraints on government or on guarantees of rights claimed by citizens. Nor have biographers and other students of his time mobilized proof that John Adams, by 1780, had revised his simple formula for assuring good government.

A political theory that made no provision for enforcing restraints on acts of government would seem grossly deficient to Americans in our day. John Adams may have revealed a shortage of wisdom in 1776, but he cannot justly be accused of a callous disregard for individuals, whatever their economic or social class. He may have been naive not to admit a fear of tyranny by majorities, but his defense would have been that governments patterned to his specifications nurtured a sense of responsibility that reduced to a minimum the likelihood of tyrannical acts. This is his expression of faith, as announced near the end of *Thoughts on Government*:

> A constitution founded on these principles introduces knowledge among the people, and inspires them with a conscious dignity becoming freemen; a general emulation takes place, which causes good humor, sociability, good manners, and good morals to be general. That elevation of sentiment inspired by such a government, makes the common people brave and enterprising. That ambition which is inspired by it makes them sober, industrious, and frugal. You will find among them some elegance, perhaps, but more solidity; a little pleasure, but a great deal of business; some politeness, but more civility. If you compare such a country with the regions of domination, whether monarchical or aristocratical, you will fancy yourself in Arcadia or Elysium.[3]

There seems no reason to doubt the sincerity of this peroration, though one may well be surprised by the exuberance of the supposedly stuffy little man from a Boston suburb. He was a churchgoer, firmly set in Christian faith, and accustomed to recurring counsel from the pulpit, increasingly frequent during the preceding fifteen years, that only a virtuous population could sustain just government and that the best instruction in virtue was to be found in the words of the Hebrew prophets and the life and teachings of Jesus. It was highly relevant, then, to insert in his recommendations for the design of free governments an expression of confidence that a regime of public virtue would be their finest fruit.

Government of the people, by the people, and for the people was cited above as the ground-level principle of republican government in the mind of John Adams. Implied in that goal is a supposition that the people will be worthy of self-government. Whether the expectation would prove to be the reality after independence was won was a matter of deep concern throughout the struggle with England; lack of conviction that republican government could be made to work in America was an important factor in the decision of many Loyalists to stick it out with England. Indeed, in later years as experience accrued, John Adams seems to have grown progressively skeptical about disinterested "republican" virtue, as distinct from Christian virtue, and looked increasingly to governmental checks and balances, as distinct from declarations of rights, to preserve liberty and a modicum of civic equality.[4]

As the experiment in full-scale self-government began, debate arose about the convictions and behavior that would have to prevail among the citizenry if self-government were to succeed. Equality, liberty, and virtue were the three concerns most deeply implicated in this debate. As time passed, and under the continuing influence of a revolution, these concerns became increasingly subject to popular consideration and reinterpretation. They are considered here, however, as concerns of the leadership, looking to what this leadership set forth in print, particularly in the first American constitutions, as its republican understanding of the conditions of successful self-government. The focus, then, is on political theory, not social history; it is on government and how government should relate to individuals, not on such growth of "social" equality and decline of "social control" as may have occurred over the course of the founding period.

Equality, liberty, and virtue have, moreover, remained focal points of emphasis and contention in American political life since that time, in one sense or another. Certainly insistence on more equality and less constraint is as strenuous today as it has ever been in American history. While moralism is nothing new in American politics, the rampant moralism of today and the high levels of concern about low levels of public morality and about decline of those traditional institutions believed to have fostered traditional morality may serve to remind us of preoccupations that prompted the founders' prescription of virtue. Perhaps significantly, however, while equality and liberty have remained at the center of serious theorizing about self-government in America, public virtue or morality has not held equivalent status in modern times.

Preparing his readers for his own traverse of the perturbations and the debate that agitated thoughtful minds during the early years of American nation making, Paul S. Conkin remarks, "The very phrases that are most familiar—'we the people,' 'a government of law,' 'the natural equality of all men,' and 'life, liberty and the pursuit of happiness'—are often the least clear because of all the present ambiguities of language."[5] With equally good reason he could have added that words and phrases of signal importance lacked clarity and precision among the audience to which they were addressed. They offered a key to a package of conditions or ideas that the author had in mind, but often neither author nor reader (speaker nor auditor) could identify specifically the contents of that package. Inevitably, speculation figures, and will continue to, in even the most careful, least tendentious investigations into the views of the founders on equality, liberty, and virtue.

Our own investigation begins in this chapter with *equality* and *liberty*. Some pragmatic problems of liberty will then occupy us in the next two chapters, after which it will be fitting, in chapter 9, to consider *virtue*.

Equality

The word *equality*, when used to characterize a relation among persons, is a glaring invitation to trouble. It is appropriate to require a miller to supply equal amounts of meal to all who are charged the same price. A bushel can be precisely defined as a specified number of cubic inches or a specified number of pounds and ounces, and attainment of the specified measure can be agreed on by all parties to the deal. Not so in the case of a provision that government shall provide equal protection of the laws. The components of a regime of protection may not have been agreed on, and we have not devised tests capable of establishing that the protection afforded by any law of impressive significance falls with equal impact or equal consequences on any two or any two hundred persons. Words that have long been used for approximation of a condition or as a tent to cover a universe of items known to exist but as yet unexplored can be endowed with precise meaning (one horsepower $=$ 550 foot-pounds per second) or by common usage can be restricted in reference to some particular of a former array of significations (UFOs do not include objects hurled about by hurricanes).

No such transmutation or modification took place in the history of the English word *equality*. *Equity* seems not to have been pressed as an alternative for *equality* in giving directions for creating governments and fixing standards for making public policy. Nor did *egalitarianism* ever catch on with the general public as a word suitable for its vocabulary. We are thus obliged to report that the founders wrote in three of the initial constitutions that "all men are born equally free and independent," without the slightest intention of suggesting that agreement could be reached on what constituted freedom or independence for newborn infants or that tests could be devised to detect a variance in the measures of freedom and independence they enjoyed after arrival at maturity.[6] Viewed as a gesture of defiance, as a declaration that in this new nation the relations of citizens to their officials would be strikingly different from those between monarchs and their subjects, this expression of sentiment and intention may have possessed great utility and entailed no harm.

It is a fact, beyond dispute I should think, that for several decades prior to independence Americans firmly believed life in their colonies was marked by smaller and fewer distinctions based on class than would be encountered in the British Isles or anywhere else in Europe. By *class distinctions* I mean to include privileges and immunities, advantages and amenities vested in individuals or families by birth or subsequently acquired by royal favor, purchase, or contrivance of whatever sort, including reward for distinguished public service. In this broad comparative view Americans were probably correct, but it must also be the case that their confidence was greatly enlarged by their resolve to go to war to make secure their way of life, by recurrent contention with Loyalists, and by prolonged argument around campfires and in taverns.

Given the preoccupations dominating public discourse at the time, a pronouncement that "all men are born equally free and independent," or "born free and equal," as Massachusetts put it, may have been a satisfactory way of saying that under the new governments of the New World birth would entail no endowment or privileges. It is notable that the words *equality, equal,* and *equalness* make very few appearances in the initial round of state constitutions written and adopted between 1776 and 1784. It appears that when the founders intended to promise equal treatment, they preferred a different style of expression. "Every man," in criminal prosecutions, has a right to be informed of the charges against him, to confront witnesses who offer evidence against him, to testify in his own behalf, and to be convicted only by the verdict of a unanimous jury. "No subject" ought, in any case or at any time, to be declared guilty of treason or felony by the legislature. These are affirmations of equality since they stipulate that all persons without exceptions shall have the same status or be treated in the same way. To the proofs of intent to erase lodgments of privilege and advantage in individuals and social classes, these guarantees add evidences of a commitment to equal protection of the law.

Confident as we may be that the rebelling Americans looked forward to a regime of wide-ranging equalness in the application of law to individuals, we must not jump to a conclusion that it was their purpose to broaden the range of affairs in which equivalent treatment of all should be the rule. I am aware of no study of the equalness of protection in the thirteen colonies on the eve of independence. Nor has anyone made a comparative study of extensions or retractions of equalness in the application of laws in the thirteen states during their first decades of statehood. Beyond these admissions of ignorance, it ought to be noticed that many of the promises of like treatment in the initial state constitutions were followed by modifying provisos. Thus (in Maryland) "all persons professing the Christian Religion" ought to enjoy equal rights and privileges in the state "unless, under color of religion, any man disturb the peace, the happiness or safety of society." And (also in Maryland) "no man ought to be compelled to give evidence against himself" in any court "but in such cases as have been usually practiced in this state, or may hereafter be directed by the Legislature."[7]

A careful reading of these initial constitutions that attaches plain meaning to plain words affords no support for a conclusion that in contemplation of law or acts of government all individuals and all classes of persons would be treated alike or viewed as equal one to another—equal in assessments of personal character, equal in entitlement to privileges and immunities, equal in enjoyment of opportunities to pursue their safety and happiness. A modern constitutional doctrine that can justify affirmative-action programs and generate dispute about deprivations of constitutional rights resulting from denials of equal opportunity or from inequalities of condition as a consequence of public policies or actions is wholly foreign to the conceptions of equal protection of the law imbedded in the state constitutions that gave Americans their authoritative introduction to republican government.

Over time and by steps that are in large part obscure, the nation arrived at a conception of required equalization that is pervasive in its perception of significant variance in condition and rigorous in its differentiation of classes of persons among which some variations in public policies are tolerable. Of prime importance in this national evolution was the implanting of a myth that all human beings, in the natural order of things, are equal one to another, that all persons were created equal by intent and act of God Almighty. The first plantings of this doctrine probably were made by proponents of the abolition of slavery. Finding no support for the main pillar of their intellectual attack in the original state constitutions, they turned to the Declaration of Independence for proof that this was how the founders understood it. "We hold these truths to be self-evident, that [first to be mentioned] all men are created equal. . . ." Not equal in all things of trivial importance, surely, but equal in the right to claim status, conditions, and treatment essential for the pursuit of safety and happiness.

I happen not to agree with this reading of the Declaration, but it is an interpretation of the meaning or intent of a half-sentence that has had the support of a long line of highly regarded students of the American Revolution. It is an issue that should not be ignored in this work, but it can appropriately be removed from the main discourse (see appendix 2 for my interpretation of the meaning of personal equality in the Declaration as well as an argument for the more generally accepted view). We ought now to observe what a broader sample of the founding generation thought to be the relation of a regime of equality to a society's capability for self-government.[8]

Examination of several hundred items discloses very little concern or apprehension about equality on the part of those who produced the pamphlet literature of the founding era. The infrequent appearance of the words *equal, equalness,* and *equality* in the initial state constitutions is paralleled in the pamphlets by a minimal preoccupation with equalness as an attribute of free societies or as an essential for the effectuation of government sustained by the consent of the governed. Eight of the constitutions of the first round were introduced by a declaration of rights, the word *equality* (or an equivalent) appearing in four of these compilations of principles for a grand total of nine times; the word *liberty* (or *liberties* or *freedom*) makes fifty-five appearances, ranging from five to eleven in the eight documents. These figures provide a rough measure of the proportionate attention given to conceptions of equality and liberty in the pamphlet literature. The significance of the great difference in attention is highly problematic. As noted earlier, numerous restrictions on the authority of public officials assured identical immunities to all citizens; it is also a fact that many constitutional guarantees of "rights," without alteration of intent or effect, could have been rendered as guarantees of "liberties." No less worthy of note is the additional fact that references to the indispensability of personal and public virtue are all but missing from a majority of these constitutions, yet the continuing pleas for cultivation of virtue in the pamphlet literature provide some of the finest exhibits of penetrating thought in the legacy of the founders.

Robert Coram, writing in 1791, made the most comprehensive attribution of natural or innate equalness of all individuals encountered in this search. Of necessity, he would have acknowledged that children possess less physical strength than adults and that the lame and the halt suffer in physical competition with the hale and the hearty. The first differentiation he would have dismissed as misleading, a sciolism perhaps; growth is nature's way, and in due time the child become adult will demonstrate his or her equalness in a community of adults. The incapacities ensuing from disability, even if inflicted at birth and impairing the intellect, may be viewed as accidents incidentally thwarting nature's aim for perfection. They are challenges for individuals and institutions to mitigate or erase the consequences of misfortune; they are not signals for sentiment or action based on a presumption that mischances of life and perversions of nature call for removal of the victims from the protection and the comforts afforded by constitutions, laws, and the impulses of charity.

There is risk in interpreting or even paraphrasing a writer as independent and aggressive as Coram. Let him speak briefly for himself (for more, see appendix 3).

> In all animals . . . there is an evident uniformity and equality through every species. Where this equality is not to be found in the human species it is to be attributed either to climate, habit, or education, or perhaps to all . . . although there are instances of men who by mere dint of unassisted genius have arose to excellence, while others have been so deficient in mental powers as not to be capable of improvement . . . yet when we enumerate all the idiots and sublime geniuses in the world, they will be found too few in number when compared with the rest of mankind to invalidate the general rule that all men are by nature equal . . . although a mathematical equality among men neither exists or is necessary, yet the generality of men educated under equal circumstances possess equal powers. This is the equality to be found in all the productions of nature, the equality and the only equality necessary to the happiness of man.[9]

Coram's thesis was in dispute before he was born. In 1760 John Adams wrote in his literary notebook that "although there is a moral and political and a natural Equality among Mankind, all being born free and equal, yet there are other inequalities which are equally natural. Such as Strength, Activity, Industry, Genius, Talents, Virtues, Benevolence."[10] These were tests to be applied in estimating the measure of equality prevailing in a community or society; twenty-seven years later he ran the list of indices to eighteen, without mention of four that were in his earlier list of seven. To prove his point that differences in circumstances or conditions assured lucky individuals a head start in the competitive pursuit of safety and happiness, Adams cited a wide range of advantages accruing from wealth and family connections.[11] Presumably Coram, writing four years after Adams's *Defence of the Constitutions of Government of the United States of America*, would have contended that these advantages would rapidly diminish or evaporate if law and government removed the hurdles that other individuals and government itself had erected to stall so many contenders in the competition, but he did not argue this in print.

None of his contemporaries seems to have written in direct refutation of Coram's argument. The possibility and the desirability of a regime of personal equality, of parity among individuals, was not given high priority in the polemics of the day; those who wrote the pieces that got out to the public lent Coram little if any support. It seems safe to surmise that those who chose to rationalize their views on the matter thought that just rewards for making worthy contributions to society and setting models for emulation by others warranted the deference, accumulation of wealth, and other compensations that were the obverse of equality. Fisher Ames, Jonathan Maxcy, and Noah Webster were three men of great ability who, a decade after Coram's pleas for expunging inequalities, wrote in defense of a mixture of equality and inequality.[12] The burden of their arguments turned on the inevitability of inequality and on the certainty of continuing propagation and public support for differences rather than equalness in status, condition, opportunity, or advantage. Missing from their pieces, acute as they were, was any studied contention that some extra leverage should be assured to those members of the society whose performance and prospects warranted a gift of unusual status and condition.

Rejection of arguments that the founders thought a state of equalness in the enjoyment of life's blessings to be attainable must not be allowed to obscure their conviction that a condition of near-perfect equality in certain matters ought to be guaranteed. The bounding of those matters defies precise and succinct definition. Perhaps no one has done better than Elias Boudinot, one of the most respected U.S. senators, speaking to the Society of Cincinnati in 1793. The gist of his formulation seems to be that the American people and their governments will support every American citizen in the claim of a right to hold on to and make use of resources lawfully acquired and will guarantee to all a chance to do the best they can for themselves within the rules laid down by the law:[13]

> The first great principle established and secured by our revolution, and which since seems to be pervading all the nations of the earth; and which should be most zealously and carefully improved and gloried in by us, *is the rational equality and rights of men, as men and citizens.*
>
> I do not mean to hold up the absurd idea charged upon us by the

enemies of this valuable principle, and which contains in it inevitable destruction of every government, "that all men are equal as to acquired or adventitious rights." Men must and continually do differ in their genius, knowledge, industry, integrity, and activity.

Their natural and moral characters—their virtues and vices—their abilities, natural and acquired—together with favorable opportunities for exertion, will always make men different among themselves, and of course, create a preeminency and superiority over one another. But the equality and rights of men here contemplated, are *natural, essential,* and *unalienable;* such as the security of *life, liberty,* and *property.* These should be the firm foundation of every good government, as they will apply to all nations at all times, and may properly be called a universal law. It is apparent that every man is born with the same right to improve the talent committed to him, for the use and benefit of society, and to be respected accordingly.

Boudinot's argument, like those of Adams, Ames, Maxcy, and Webster mentioned earlier, could be taken less as a representative statement of the time than as the joining of an issue, and thus as indicating the presence of a body of much more decidedly egalitarian perspectives to be addressed. Clearly a corpus of such thought did exist—though not clearly a "body" of it in the customary sense of a movement or concerted tendency. Quite conceivably the political literature of the time most notable for cogency and analytic penetration (as I have reviewed it) underrepresented extant commitments to equality of a more thoroughgoing degree than I have identified here. Surely the problem of representativeness raises serious and difficult issues of attribution (whose views are to count?) as well as of interpretation (what *were* their views, anyway?); and I must concede that it has been far less feasible to bring the former than the latter to the surface for readers' inspection.

Considering, however, the constitutions of the founding period altogether (those of the revolutionary decade as well as later ones) and such public discourse and systematic political thought as have come down to us, the founding did not in its fundamental public norms and literary discourse project an egalitarian standard for society. (Nor, for that matter, did it project a populist standard for politics, though in some states at some times this question was closer, as appears in chapter 8.) Equality took second place to liberty. It was not a negligible concern, though it was a concern difficult to characterize today because differently tinged in meaning then by considerations of liberty and commonality. In the ordinary politics of the states the founding period was by and large a time of legislative rescission of particular privileges and disabilities—of progress toward civil equality or parity of legal status of those eligible or potentially so for citizenship. Still, public policy tended not to look toward compensation for the effects of individual differences or general redistribution of social condition—what Elias Boudinot termed "adventitious rights." Equality as an operative norm seems to have been more civil than social, more particular than general. Insofar as it was general, it was general indeed. Thus Boudinot could instance abstract equality in citizenship and protection of life, liberty, and property; but we know that the republican ideal of a common citizenship under equal laws was most unevenly applicable and effectively qualified by other conceptions of political community.

Liberty

Clarity of thought about a condition referred to as equality may have suffered because the word invoked a promise of relations among persons that stood no chance of being realized according to other common understandings of the time. The word *liberty*, cited as a state of affairs to be achieved, invited perhaps even greater confusion because usage had attached the word to a variety of conditions that excited the admiration of many people and invoked contemptuous rejection by as many others. Further aggravation arose from the fact that whereas argument about equality could be anchored to a root meaning subject to general acceptance—a conception suggesting exact likeness or inability to differentiate—dispute about desirable states of liberty could find no point of departure or focus of understanding outside the vagaries of personal experience or the varieties of imagination.

Preoccupation with liberty or freedom had one of its roots in a widespread and deep-seated conviction that sin, unbelief, and false doctrine wrapped the human soul in chains of bondage from which one could be freed only by embracing whatever dogma passed for the true religion. Political freedom, or civil liberty, had clashed with and won indispensable support from religious creeds for centuries before European settlement of America. Creedal conviction and civil liberty were not necessarily opposites. Nevertheless, continuous intermixing of discourse about freeing the soul from Satan and freeing human activity from domination by public author-

ity must have stirred uncertainties and contradictions, puzzling youngsters
and simple-minded adults about the meaning of liberty and freedom.
Consider these three statements from sermons delivered on the eve of the
Revolution by Congregational ministers in eastern Massachusetts:[14]

> *Amos Adams (1768):* But yet the gospel breathes the spirit of reli-
> gious *liberty*—*liberty* from the guilt of sin, and the condemnation of the
> law. *Liberty* from the dominion of sin, the slavery of Satan—Liberty
> from the elements of the Jewish LAW, AND LIBERTY from impositions of
> men. . . . These are *glorious liberties of the sons of God.*

> *Nathaniel Niles (1774):* Civil liberty consists, not in any inclination of
> the members of a community; but in the being and due administra-
> tion of such a system of laws, as effectually tends to the greatest
> felicity of a state. Herein consists civil liberty, and to live under such
> a constitution, so administered, is to be the member of a free state;
> and he who is free from the censure of those laws, may fully enjoy all
> the pleasures of civil liberty, unless he is prevented by some defect,
> not in the constitution, but in himself.

> *Gad Hitchcock (1774):* The beneficial improvement both of our civil
> and religious rights depends on liberty. Matters that pertain to
> conscience, and the worship and service of God, and the prepara-
> tion of our Souls for another world, are the objects of religious
> liberty; and those things that relate to our present security and
> happiness in civil government, are the objects of civil liberty. In this
> manner civil and religious liberty, are usually distinguished; but as
> there is a connection between those blessings which tend to our
> present happiness, in civil government, and those which are neces-
> sary to lay the foundation of that which is future and eternal, and as
> conscience is really concerned with both; and men can no more,
> without offending God, and violating the laws of society, resign, or
> neglect the former, than the latter; these two senses of liberty seem
> so far to intermix, and in a sort to become one.

Even in their entirety, these three sermons hardly yield a full survey of
the questions at issue in the meanings and implications of liberty during
the founding period. They do illuminate the religion-centered view of
liberty as a right relationship to God, and they indicate two other important views of liberty during the years that brought the American nation to
birth. In the first of these *civil* liberty consists in the felicitous or virtuous

ordering of civil authority, chiefly through a fabric of fairly administered law; or it exists in the life that can only be lived in such an order. In the second, liberty is essential to personal decision and thus to the moral development of the individual; and it is therefore a critical element for civic virtue as well as for religious salvation. Missing in these sermons, however, is mention of what may properly be considered *the* salient gift of America to contemporary conceptions of political freedom—one announced in the Declaration of Independence as a self-evident truth. There the civilized world was informed that it was the right of all human beings in societies amounting to "a people" to cast off the chains of despotism and to establish a government that seemed most likely to effect their safety and happiness. For many who lent their voices to the shaping of public opinion, it was a truth invulnerable to refutation that a people were shown to be free when they erected a government of their choice. Loyalists, of course, could rejoin that it was untimely and unjustified for Americans to break the link with England and select a different route to safety and happiness, though it may be that the thoughtful ones, if provoked to argument, would have acknowledged the right of any people to replace their government with another when absolute despotism was a proven fact or an inescapable prospect.

Independence or disconnection from a foreign power and the acknowledgment of a people's undeniable right to create a government of their own design could be only a first step to freedom broadly conceived. The promise of liberty won by razing a despotism could be thwarted by shortage of wisdom or frailty of resolution in erecting a new regime. This point was not lost on Niles in the sermon quoted earlier. Neither the opportunity nor the basic capability of creating its own government assures a nation a regime of freedom; liberty is won when the government thus erected proves its capacity to govern well, when it actually administers a system of laws that effectively tend to the greatest felicity. John Adams, honored to this day as author of the most succinct design for such a government, put it this way: "The form of government which communicates . . . happiness to the greatest number of persons and in the greatest degree, is the best." The form of government that most surely achieves that result will do so by securing "an impartial and exact execution of the laws." In a government that extends this promise, the principal authority will be lodged in an assembly that is "an exact portrait of the people at large," one in which, ideally, "equal interests among the people should have equal interests in it."[15]

No one understood better than Adams, writing in 1776, that the

interests of people sharing a government are diverse. In an empire of laws
(his phrase) the rules guiding a society apply to all within it, and the
administration of those rules should apply in like manner to all who are
embraced by their provisions. Exemptions, distinctions, and differentia-
tions in the application of a law may be specified in its text; discretion in
the adjustment of penalties to offenses may be provided for. Freedom
from compliance with the law ought not, however, be a gift from prosecutor,
judge, or jury just because the noncomplier happens to believe that a rule
more fitting to the circumstances could have been written, or that circumstances made it highly inconvenient or costly for him to do what the law
required, or that a message direct from God commanded him to kill an
agent of the Devil who had assumed human form. This is what Nathaniel
Niles had in mind two years before Adams wrote when he said, "Civil
liberty consists, not in any inclinations of the members of the community,"
but rather in the due administration of a system of the laws.

Niles's introduction of the term *civil liberty* was not without significance.
The term was not his invention, but references to *civil liberty* increased as
debate about the nature of liberty or freedom increased in the revolutionary period. It may have been seized upon to distinguish its referent from
freedom of conscience, more precisely expressed as freedom of religious
conviction, which was thought to be an endowment of the Almighty and
to be superior to claims of the state. In time the word *civil* may also have
had some utility as a differentiation of claims that set the state or community in opposition to the individual and to claims that individuals (with or
without the support of law) could make against other persons. Thus the
right of a wife to appeal to a court for protection from an abusive husband
might have been cited as evidence of personal freedom but would not
have been mentioned in a descriptive account of civil liberty.

It is a fact of no little interest that expositions of civil liberty during the
founding period throw little light on the boundaries of the powers that
states and municipalities could exercise over the citizenry. As noted earlier,
eight of the state constitutions contained numerous assurances to the
newly recognized citizen, some of these expressed as rights the individual
could assert against encroachments of governmental authority, others as
boundaries within which governors must confine themselves or as limitations on the manner in which they might pursue objectives within the
bounds of their authority. While the later documents leaned heavily on
the language of the earlier ones, there was still enough difference in the
texts to suggest that none of the conventions or committees that drew up

the first constitutions had searched for language that, by combining general applicability with specification of particulars, would cover the full range of liberties they wished to make secure. Furthermore, as noted earlier, what appear to be faithful promises are mixed with provisos that the guarantee is to be viewed only as an assurance that the practice of colonial days will be continued—or even that the content of the guarantee and the duration of its validity are dependent on the will of the legislature. Finally, it should be said that many a paragraph in a declaration of rights turns out on close reading to be less an assurance of immunity from abuse of governmental power than a proffering of advice that the legislature had no obligation to accept. The 1784 recommendation of New Hampshire concerning cruel and unusual punishments is extreme, but it serves to illustrate the tendency to provide an admonition where a guarantee might have been more appropriate:

> All penalties ought to be proportioned to the nature of the offence. No wise legislature will affix the same punishment to the crimes of theft, forgery and the like, which they do to those of murder and treason, where the same undistinguishing severity is exerted against all offences; the people are led to forget the real distinction in the crimes themselves, and to commit the most flagrant with as little compunction as they do those of the lightest dye: For the same reason a multitude of sanguinary laws is both impolitic and unjust. The true design of all punishments being to reform, not to exterminate, mankind.[16]

Why the early writing that has been preserved for us was not more systematic in its elucidation of civil liberty and why the specification of guarantees in state constitutions was so spotty are accounted for by Oscar Handlin and Mary Handlin, two historians who bid for preeminence in the study of America's founding:

> The source and nature of those rights was by no means clear. American conditions which tended to destroy inherited institutions, habits, and customs generated frequent claims that the individual was himself competent to guide his own conduct and gave him the presumptive right to do so. The definition of rights therefore proceeded not through the logical development of theory but in response to evolving practices. Rights which were never invaded, never received explicit formulation; men simply acted as if they

existed. In other cases, the assertion of a right came in resistance to some challenge to it and was expressed in negative terms. The resistance to the challenge was itself evidence that a positive belief in the right had already developed. Whence? Still other rights were widely respected long before they were explicitly recognized in legal or constitutional documents and sometimes despite the fact they were never so recognized at all.[17]

Herein is a sufficient explanation of why it could happen that when the writing of state constitutions and big talk about all men being equal triggered a considerable relaxation of restrictions on free Negroes, there was little if indeed any impulse to even up the conditions distinguishing the status of white women from that of their brothers and husbands—at least not in constitutions, though such an impulse was reflected in the statutes of several states. Herein is also an explanation of why that grand old systematizer John Adams did not put in the Massachusetts Constitution (as Pennsylvania and Vermont had done in theirs) any recognition of a right to pack up one's family and goods and move out because nature had been miserly in bestowing its gifts or because one had had a bellyful of the neighbors' nosiness or of the community's life-style. Failure to guarantee a right to choose one's place of residence may appear ironic because for generations Massachusetts towns had had a harsh practice of requiring transients to resume their journey if a brief stay offered small promise of their being assets to the community. Perhaps some additional irony can be extracted from the fact that in our own day it is a scholar long resident in Massachusetts who best stands for the thesis that the taproot of American freedom lies in the ability and readiness of people to move out when they find a community oppressive and to resettle where they find a promise of more compatibility.[18]

Accepting the Handlins' judgment that we are forever denied a full comprisal of the claims for immunity from acts of government that were nesting in the minds of revolutionary America, we are excused from bare mention of the many that found expression in print. In general we have learned that liberty in the political thought of the founding period was, notwithstanding the central conceptual equation of free government and self-government, in its specifics and interrelations more an ad hoc than a systematic project intellectually.

Nevertheless, three issues concerning liberty in the founding period deserve further exploration—for three reasons, chiefly. Each has been controversial in our own time; in each, parties to the controversy have claimed constitutional legitimacy for their views as allegedly based in opinions or practices of the founding period; and each was at least potentially a critical, make-or-break issue for republican government in its fledgling American phase. These issues in liberty can, of course, be given statement either as constraints on civil authority or as zones of individual discretionary action—or, finally, as facets of tension between appropriate civil authority and rightful immunities of the citizen. Stated mainly as claims of discretion, the three issues are, first, freedom to choose one's religious faith and practices; second, freedom to express beliefs and recommendations in speech and in print that may be conceived to threaten civil authority or national security; and, third, claims of the right to join in organized protest against the conduct of government and to resist, by violation of laws and hindrance of their enforcement, the putative undue rule of government.

The first of these claims, indifferently referred to as freedom of conscience, freedom of religion, or freedom of worship, is best deferred to the discussion of virtue in chapter 9. Piety was a candidate for first place in listings of the elements of public and private virtue. Cultivation of piety, once childhood was passed, was universally recognized as mainly the responsibility of the church and its clergy. Measured against European levels of religious controversy, the American colonial experience was remarkably free of disputation over freedom of conscience and relations between church and state. If anything, the incidence of such issues diminished as American governments became sovereign, since the colonial inheritance of established religions was by then attenuating. In practice, then, the explosive potentiality of the compound issue of religious liberty was not fully realized in the founding period. Today's religious controversies as they relate to civil liberty have chiefly to do with judicial elaborations of the "establishment clause" of the Constitution and its extension to the states; they have generic parallels in the founding period, but the substance of dispute is on the whole remote from and marginal to the concerns of an earlier day.

The other two controversies, however—freedom of expression and freedom of organized protest, in their relation to civil authority and the public interest in it—have been no less serious or central in the politics of our own time than they were in the founding period. Arguably, organized protest and resistance have loomed larger in our age; certainly each period has witnessed critical episodes posing the issue of freedom of expression versus public order as the matrix of civil liberty. There is enough to be learned from these issues about the politics of the founding and about the legacy of the founding for liberty and authority in our time to justify separate chapters for each, beginning with the problem of freedom of expression as an apparent threat to the civil order.

Notes

1. John Adams, *Thoughts on Government*, in *American Political Writing during the Founding Era, 1760–1805*, vol. 1, ed. Charles S. Hyneman and Donald S. Lutz (Indianapolis: Liberty Press, 1983), p. 403.

2. Extracted from articles IV, V, VIII, and XIX of the Declaration of Rights of the Massachusetts Constitution as adopted in 1780 and in effect today.

3. Adams, *Thoughts on Government*, p. 408.

4. See, e.g., Charles Francis Adams, ed., *The Works of John Adams* (Boston: Little, Brown, 1854), vol. 9, pp. 602–4, vol. 10, pp. 377–79, 385–87; and John R. Howe, Jr., *The Changing Political Thought of John Adams* (Princeton, N.J.: Princeton University Press, 1966), chap. 6. Adams continued to think virtuous republics the "best possible governments to promote the interest, dignity, and happiness of man," but he came to regard the prospects of their realization or (especially) preservation in virtue as remote.

5. Paul S. Conkin, *Self-Evident Truths* (Bloomington: Indiana University Press, 1974), p. ii.

6. Pennsylvania, New Hampshire, and Vermont. The Massachusetts Constitution said, "All men are born free and equal."

7. Maryland Constitution of 1775, secs. 33, 20, in *The Federal and State Constitutions, Colonial Charters, and Other Organic Laws of the States, Territories, and Colonies Now or Heretofore Forming the United States of America*, vol. 3, ed. Francis Newton Thorpe (Washington, D.C.: Government Printing Office, 1909), pp. 1688–89. On these initial constitutions, see p. 220 below.

8. References to equality, liberty, and virtue in published correspondence are not cited hereafter because such correspondence did not then enjoy wide circulation or contribute directly to public debate. John Adams's *Defence of the Constitutions of Government of the United States of America* is treated here as if it were a pamphlet, though it was published in three volumes (London: Printed for Hall and Sellers, 1787).

9. From Robert Coram, *Political Inquiries* (1791), pp. 83–89, which is reprinted in full in *American Political Writing*, vol. 2, ed. Hyneman and Lutz, pp. 757–811; extracted here from pp. 797–801.

10. Quoted from an unpublished source in Howe, *Changing Political Thought*, p. 137.

11. *A Defence of the Constitutions of Government of the United States of America*, in *The Works of John Adams*, vol. 4, ed. Charles Francis Adams (Boston: Charles C. Little and James Brown, 1851), pp. 391–92.

12. Fisher Ames, "Equality" (1801), in *Works of Fisher Ames*, vol. 2, ed. Seth Ames (Boston: Little, Brown, 1854), pp. 207–28; Jonathan Maxcy, "An Oration," in *American Political Writing*, vol. 2, ed. Hyneman and Lutz, p. 1042; Noah Webster, "An Oration" (1802), in *American Political Writing*, vol. 2, ed. Hyneman and Lutz, p. 1220.

13. *An Oration Delivered at Elizabeth-town, New Jersey . . . [before] the State Society of Cincinnati, on the Fourth of July 1793* (Elizabeth-town, N.J.: Printed by Shepard Kollock, 1793), pp. 10–11.

14. Amos Adams, *Religious Liberty, an Invaluable Blessing* (Boston: Kneeland and Adams for Leverett, 1768), p. 7; Nathaniel Niles reprinted in *American Political Writing*, vol. 1, ed. Hyneman and Lutz, pp. 185ff.; Gad Hitchcock, *A Sermon Preached at Plymouth* (Boston: Edes and Gill, 1775), pp. 12–13.

15. Adams, *Thoughts on Government*, pp. 402–3.

16. Thorpe, *Federal and State Constitutions*, vol. 4, p. 2456.

17. Oscar Handlin and Mary Handlin, *The Dimensions of Liberty* (Cambridge, Mass.: Belknap Press, 1961), p. 59.

18. The thesis, developed by John P. Roche, is most fully and persuasively stated in his "American Liberty: An Examination of the 'Tradition' of Freedom," in *Aspects of Liberty: Essays Presented to Robert E. Cushman*, ed. Milton R. Konvitz and Clinton Rossiter (Ithaca, N.Y.: Cornell University Press, 1958), pp. 129–62.

7

The Limits of Liberty:
Freedom of Expression

IN ANY SOCIETY, only a little of what is said in the presence of others or is distributed in print excites enough concern about its consequences to result in suppression or punishment. In general, attempts to identify by organic law or statute the limits of freedom of communication turn out to be unproductive. In no country are the subjects of permissible address or the purposes of permissible comment particularized in a code. The limits of freedom of expression are discovered instead by feeling out the edges of the restrictions that will be imposed when authority is invoked. One's right to communicate becomes an issue in public discourse when restrictions to which the community is accustomed are attacked or when new restraints are perceived as threatening.

The first few generations of Europeans on American soil could not escape a continuing revision of economic, social, and political beliefs and preferences. The preponderance of an English heritage forced major adjustments in toleration, acceptance, and drift into tradition on the part of minority ethnic groups. Novelty of the environment and distance from the site of supreme legal authority gave the English cause and sufficient free rein to fashion laws more fitting to newly recognized needs. As for freedom to speak one's mind and publish one's thoughts on matters other than religion, including criticism of public authorities and their policies, these adjustments of law to New World needs and anxieties seem to have been accomplished during the first hundred years following the earliest settlements in Virginia and New England.[1]

Free Speech and Press in the Founding Constitutions

The Declaration of Independence was an audacious flaunting of sentiments ordinarily reprehensible to established authority. It was not, however,
an assertion of natural right to criticize rightful rulers or petition a sovereign to pursue a policy more just in the governance of subjects. The
signers at Philadelphia were placing their bets. If they lost, they could
anticipate hanging by their necks; if they won, they reserved a right to
stretch the necks of fellow Americans who favored the king or guessed
wrong on the outcome of a war. It would have seemed inopportune for
their emerging governments to elaborate rules differentiating permissible
from nonpermissible expressions of belief, preference, purpose, and so
forth. It would prove no embarrassment for those in power, however, to
put a muzzle on speech and writing about the unwisdom or untimeliness
of breaking away from the home country; and a nervous population might
be reassured by formal pledges that American governments after independence would preserve an environment favorable to independence of
mind and communication. Pennsylvania was first, and extreme, in attaching
the muzzle; Virginia led off with the reassurances.

Pennsylvania's action may be said to have come in response to the
Continental Congress. In August 1775 King George III by proclamation
called on his loyal subjects in America for assistance in suppressing rebellion and sedition. Much disturbed by the prospects this raised, Congress
in the fall of 1775 recommended that the provincial authorities and
committees of safety restrain persons "whose going at large may endanger
the safety of the colony, or the liberties of America." Seven months later it
recommended that the colonies terminate all royal authority, and, a month
later, that their legislatures enact punishments for those giving aid or
comfort to Britain or the enemies of America. In due course the colonies
complied—or followed their similar inclinations.[2] In September 1776,
while the provincial assembly was in recess, Pennsylvania's constitutional
convention enacted two statutes of this nature, defining and punishing
"high treason" and "seditious utterance." The second statute was drawn in
draconically broad terms and was soon repealed, following which a spate
of informal hearings, arrests, and indefinite imprisonments took place.[3]
Pennsylvania adopted a test oath and punished liberally for refusal to
execute it. Yet the constitution adopted by Pennsylvania's convention was,
in its declaration of rights, the world's first to include freedom of speech

along with freedom of the press; it was followed by only one other state constitution (Vermont's) in the founding period.[4]

Among the reassurances of individual liberties, Virginia's was the most renowned and probably the most influential. Advised that the Continental Congress soon would declare the colonies severed from England, Virginia's legislative assembly resolved to assume the task of writing a constitution suitable for a sovereign state. Two months before the proclamation of independence in Philadelphia, forty-five members of the Virginia House of Burgesses convened in Williamsburg and turned their attention first to formulating a declaration of rights. On 29 June 1776, seven days before the bells began to toll in Philadelphia, they voted to adopt an entire state constitution (a bill of rights and a frame of government).

The Virginia Declaration of Rights opens with a few statements that attempt comprehensively to identify the character and designate the purposes of governments designed for the rule of free men. Section 3 states that "when any government shall be found inadequate or contrary to these purposes [and fundamental characteristics], a majority of the community hath an indubitable, inalienable and indefeasible right to reform, alter, or abolish [their government] in such manner as shall be judged [by them] to be most conducive to the public weal." Later, looking toward the societal conditions that would fit a people for such autonomous behavior, section 12 declared that "the freedom of the press is one of the great bulwarks of liberty, and can never be restrained but by despotic governments."[5]

Duly noting that this declaration of principle failed to mention the dependence of liberty on a vigorous exercise of the vocal cords, we must infer that those who wrote the Virginia Constitution believed a free press would give them all the leverage they needed for thwarting evil intention and calamitous judgment on the part of governors selected and subject to removal by the people. The language they had chosen for a formal charter could be useful for fixing presumptions in favor of freedom to criticize, complain, condemn, and recommend when dissatisfaction was rife and passion was raging. Should the time come, however, to forbid saying certain things out loud—urging slaves to rebel and hide out in the swamps, for instance—it would be better not to have in print a presumption that despotic government was required for the protection of planters and their families.

The Virginia reading of the mood of colonials bent on separation from England fit the American scene from New England to Georgia. Connecticut and Rhode Island thought their colonial charters sufficient for a regime of self-government; New Jersey and New York adopted constitutions establishing elective government, but these said almost nothing about personal rights and boundaries of governmental authority. To Virginia's citation of freedom of the press as a bulwark of liberty, Pennsylvania and Vermont added that the people have also "a right to freedom of speech, and of writing." The seven states that contributed the remainder of the initial twelve constitutions (Vermont included) found it sufficient to say either that freedom of the press should not be restrained or that it should be inviolably preserved.

Probably none of these declarations on speech and press, however, carried anything like the extensive connotations generally given them today. They almost certainly accepted implicitly as traditional and legitimate the common-law position that government might punish severely after the fact for speech or publication that in effect defamed the government or its officials or that tended toward public disaffection from them. (More on this later.)

Scattered through the several constitutions are additional references to relationships between the individual and government, tending to reinforce the common understanding that, after independence, government would be lodged securely in the hands of the people. These statements also attest a lively realization that effective popular control can be expected only if there are open channels for the spread of information, a climate friendly to inquiry and investigation, and an audacity in the population that steels those with grievances and convictions to stand up against those of ability and power. Most prominent and probably most important of these assurances of an open society were the provisions for public assembly and petitioning the legislature. Pennsylvania gave constitutional status to these safety valves in the late summer of 1776, asserting that "the people have a right to assemble together, to consult for their common good, to instruct their representatives, and to apply to the legislature for redress of grievances, by address, petition, or remonstrance." That language satisfied four other states. In Massachusetts John Adams managed, by stretching the sentence out to half again its length, to get in a caution that in assembling, consulting, instructing, and applying, the people ought to proceed in a reasonable fashion.

If these events are cast as a drama, the next act is the replacement of the Articles of Confederation with a Constitution establishing a federal union. Since the debates at the Philadelphia Convention were not recorded verbatim, we are denied full knowledge of the judgments and the preferences that found expression at the drafting stage. We are reliably informed by the convention's journal that during the consideration of a proposed draft, Charles Pinckney of South Carolina recommended the inclusion of several guarantees, one of which was that "the liberty of the press shall be inviolably preserved," and it is evident from the meager reporting of debate that from that point on uneasiness about the absence of provisions appropriate to a bill of rights spread among the delegates and grew in intensity. George Mason, principal author of Virginia's Declaration of Rights, was prominent in the leadership of the disaffected group. When the time came to sign the proposed new constitution, he refused to put his name to it. Colonel Mason left Philadelphia in exceeding ill humor indeed, James Madison wrote to Thomas Jefferson: "He returned to Virginia with a fixed disposition to prevent the adoption of the plan if possible. He considers the want of a Bill of Rights as a fatal objection."[6]

How widely the Virginia planter's disaffection was spread in the membership of the convention or in the population at large can only be guessed, but it is a solid and a significant fact that at the stage of ratification seven of the thirteen state conventions recommended changes in the wording of the document. Six of the seven submitted a comprehensive declaration or bill of rights, four of which asserted that freedom of the press (or freedom of both speech and the press) is a bulwark of liberty that ought never to be violated.[7]

The First Congress of the new federal government proposed twelve amendments to the Constitution that had come into effect in the summer of 1788. Ten of the twelve that Congress submitted to the states were duly ratified. They are printed as amendments one to ten of the Constitution and are popularly known as the Bill of Rights. Two of the three clauses in the First Amendment recognize speech and press to be bulwarks of liberty and undertake to secure them. They proclaim that "Congress shall make no law . . . abridging the freedom of speech, or of the press; or the right of the people peaceably to assemble, and to petition the government for a redress of grievances."

James Madison introduced the resolution proposing the addition of several statements of principle—of rights not to be infringed and restrictions on how government might exercise its power. His notion at the time was that these should be inserted into the body of the Constitution, modifying or supplementing the text as might be required to preserve its character as an integrated document. The decision of Congress was to retain intact the exact language the states had initially ratified and to append all subsequent changes as numbered amendments.

The abbreviated report of debate in the House of Representatives—the Senate permitted no reporting—adds little in the way of solid evidence to what we have already surmised about the expectations that supported including declarations of rights in state constitutions. Facing an assembly sprinkled with men who thought it inappropriate to open the career of a constitution by changing it, who thought declarations of principles out of place in frames of government, or who thought other business ought to be attended to first—facing a front of opposition and indifference—James Madison, already a recognized leader of the House, offered on 8 June 1789 the fullest justification of the American innovation of constitutional guarantees of which we have any knowledge.

In recommending a series of provisions designed to guard against objectionable uses of governmental power, Madison directed his argument to two considerations. It was common knowledge, he said, that a sizable proportion of the American people found the new Constitution deficient for want of the citation of personal guarantees, and satisfaction on this point would bring them to support of the new government. Reason supported the judgment, he added, that including guarantees of rights and inhibitions of offensive uses of power would have a salutary effect. Madison did not then press a third point often made: support for adoption of the Constitution had been won in ratifying conventions by statements delegates had read as promises that sincere efforts would be made for immediate addition of personal guarantees by adopting amendments.

James Madison had completed his thirty-eighth year months before he made his appeal in Congress for a bill of rights. He brought to the subject superb preparation: long and attentive study of history, philosophy, and law; an active role in the Virginia convention that drew up both the Declaration of Rights and the frame of government, which together became the first American state constitution; service in the Continental Congress from 1780 to 1783 and from 1786 to its end; and, most notable of all, leadership in the Philadelphia Constitutional Convention, followed by authorship of more than a third of *The Federalist*. Note that Madison's address (see appendix 4 for extended excerpts) gave no special attention to freedom of expression and communication or to the right to assemble in groups convened to formulate complaints about the acts of governments. (Indeed, the entire debate on what became the First Amendment apparently made little mention of speech and press, focusing instead on proposals to add to "petition" the popular "instruction" of elected representatives—or so it appears in the reports.) Madison did assign high priority to freedom of the press and of religion (or, in his usual language, of conscience) and also to the right to trial by jury, conducted according to the long-established procedures of English and colonial courts. Indeed, he proposed, and the House at first adopted, guarantees of these rights against the states as well as against the national government. The relative importance of particular rights need not, however, be an urgent concern if one is confident that the whole list underwrites collectively a regime of justice for everyone in the society and that no rights individually have special implications for an enlarged understanding of the foundations of justice or of how security and happiness may by pursued most efficaciously.

Madison's speech may have been most remarkable of all, especially to modern readers, in two respects. One was his opinion that the likeliest source of such abuse as might tend to undermine liberty and justice was not the government but the people. The other was the absence of any direct suggestion that the Father of the Constitution foresaw the practice that we know today as judicial review—foresaw that the courts would read constitutions as evocations of law, honor constitutional provisions (including bills of rights) as the supreme law of their constituent jurisdiction, and give or refuse effect to the acts of legislatures and other governmental agencies according to judicial views of what the Constitution permits, requires, or forbids. These two points deserve further comment.

There was no hemming or hawing or search for middle ground in Madison's identification of the seat of the chief threat to freedom in the new Republic: "I confess that I do conceive [that in the government we have set up], the great danger [of abuse of liberties lies rather in] the community than in the legislative body. The prescriptions in favor of liberty ought to be levelled against that quarter where the greatest danger lies, namely that which possesses the highest prerogatives of power. But this is not found in either the Executive or Legislative Departments of Government, but in the body of the people, operating by the majority against the minority."[8] In these remarks in the House of Representatives, making the best case he could for a federal bill of rights, the Virginian expanded the argument he had made a year and a half earlier when *No. 10*, the first of his contributions to *The Federalist*, recommended thwarting tyranny by diluting the influence of faction in a larger polity.

How striking the contrast between James Madison's projection of a future marked by recurring or continuing contentiousness and the felicity

John Adams predicted for the world's first true republics if Americans could only cut themselves loose and establish governments all their own.[9] It is timely to inquire whether Madison, in 1788–89, thought that pursuit of an unrealizable vision of perfection had run its course, had reached a point where further pursuit could lead only to disillusionment and a reaction disfunctional for ideals that had invigorated the drive for independence. That inquiry will conclude my later discussion of the elevation of public virtue to highest priority as a requisite for republican government. Now, however, we must consider Madison's views on the enforcement of constitutional guarantees and restraints on governmental power.

As for judicial review, James Madison could lay no claim to idiosyncrasy because he did not foresee how America would outstrip Europe in using the judiciary to establish the "empire of laws," which John Adams said is "the very definition of a republic."[10] Many of the nation's lawyers probably assumed from their first careful study of the new Constitution that if a complaint properly filed averred that an act of Congress imposed a duty on an article exported from one of the states, the judge would inquire into the truth of the charge and, if convinced the Constitution had forbidden such an exaction, issue a decree forbidding collection of the tax. The Constitution contains various prohibitions cast in language that lawyers regularly encounter in court. These are not like the broad principles that George Mason championed so staunchly for inclusion in the Virginia Constitution. The Constitution's Bill of Rights is, to be sure, more incisively prohibitive than the Virginia Bill of Rights. Moreover, Madison did count on the courts especially for protection of rights "expressly stipulated for in the Constitution."[11] Yet nothing we encounter in his writings leads us to conclude that James Madison, pleading for more explicit constraints on the central government in 1789, would have dissented from Alexander Hamilton's dismissal of fears of judicial aggrandizement in *Federalist No. 81:*[12]

It may in the last place be observed that the supposed danger of judiciary encroachments on the legislative authority, which has been upon many occasions reiterated, is in reality a phantom. Particular misconstructions and contraventions of the will of the legislature may now and then happen; but they can never be so extensive as to amount to an inconvenience, or in any sensible degree to affect the order of the political system. This may be inferred with certainty from the general nature of the judicial power; from the objects to which it relates; from the manner in which it is exercised; from its comparative weakness, and from its total incapacity to support its usurpations by force. And the inference is greatly fortified by the consideration of the important constitutional check, which the power of instituting impeachments, in one part of the legislative body, and of determining upon them in the other, would give to that body upon the members of the judicial department. This is alone a complete security. There never can be danger that the judges, by a series of deliberate usurpations on the authority of the legislature, would hazard the united resentment of the body entrusted within, while this body was possessed of the means of punishing their presumption by degrading them from their stations. While this ought to remove all apprehensions on the subject, it affords at the same time a cogent argument for constituting the senate a court for the trial of impeachments.

Only a Nostradamus could in the time of John Adams, George Mason, and James Madison have foreseen the redoubt of constitutional prohibitions and imperatives that now confronts all arms of government, all corporations and individuals engaged by public agencies or favored with public funds, and all majorities or minorities that may trench on a terrain known today as civil rights. Only the arrogation of supremacy to courts' interpretations of the Constitution in the context of cases before them (or some equivalent not yet seriously considered) could have lent the aspirations of George Mason the force of law they enjoy today.[13]

James Madison's role in the Philadelphia Convention and his contributions to *The Federalist* account primarily for his title, Father of the Constitution. His sponsorship of the amendments known as the Bill of Rights and the deference accorded his judgment by congressional colleagues during that episode render his claim to the title no less warranted than that of Washington to national paternity. One may therefore regret that only a decade after the Constitution was declared operative, he suffered what he might well have regarded as the greatest embarrassment of his political career—his joinder with Thomas Jefferson in certain constitutional fulminations, the Kentucky and Virginia Resolutions, that betokened the later, destructive doctrine of nullification.

The Alien and Sedition Acts

The Kentucky and Virginia Resolutions had their source in the storm over the Alien and Sedition Acts that blew up during the presidency of John Adams, with waves of emotion that still disturb historical understanding of the episode. Though there is no space here for another full-dress attempt at such understanding, we must nevertheless consider the episode of the Alien and Sedition Acts in outline, for it was, in the founding period, the formative national controversy over the constitutional issues we have just been reviewing. It was the first serious national test of the limits of liberty of communication; the first serious suggestion that the Constitution forbade the national government to regulate communication at all, without reference to limits; and—as Leonard Levy has shown—the first serious public discussion of the meaning of the First Amendment at all, not excluding the course of its adoption.[14] It was an early and hasty experiment with certain cumbersome institutional methods of vacating laws alleged to be unconstitutional. It was also an early trial of the question whether, in conditions of severe dissensus and in a nation committed to liberty, regulation of communication would conduce to moderation and healing or exacerbate matters, acting as a medicine worse than the disease.

The significance of this first venture of the national government into the policing of speech and publication and the restraint of public agitation can be appreciated only within its complex historical setting. Summarily, that setting included the long-standing rule in England and the colonies that public officials were immune from adverse criticism, even when it was grounded in fact and directed toward the public well-being; a long-running but largely unsuccessful campaign to have prosecution and punishment of libels against public officials removed from the agents of government who preferred the charges and lodged instead with courts and juries empowered to determine both the truth of the allegations and the rules of law applicable to the circumstances of the case; the strong belief of many of those opposed to the Alien and Sedition Laws that the Constitution gave the national government no authority to pass such legislation, thus stirring anew the distaste for the whole Philadelphia contrivance that had made constitutional ratification so problematical a decade earlier; public perturbation over animosities and aggressions directed toward the United States from the Old World and public concern over prospects of war; and the partisan acrimony that split the population into contending camps of often uncritical, sometimes fanatical apologists for Britain and France.

The point about partisanship bears further emphasis, for just as we need to remind ourselves that the common-law tradition bearing on freedom of communication then fell far short of modern understandings, so we may find it hard to appreciate how threatening and even illicit the partisanship we take for granted today seemed to both sides—to government and opposition alike—when it was still novel in practice, without familiar justification in political theory, and apparently colored by alien connections. In this context Federalists could readily believe, and did, that security, order, and therefore freedom were in jeopardy; Republicans could believe, and did, that the Federalist national security legislation was meant to put them out of business electorally and put the nation on the road to monarchy. Two central tenets of modern liberal democracy—electoral competition and open communication—thus became entangled before their functions and affinities were understood well.

The following remarks, delivered to a grand jury six weeks before enactment of the Alien and Sedition Laws by Chief Justice Thomas McKean of the Pennsylvania Supreme Court (a Jeffersonian), give us a reliable clue to the intemperance that was fueling partisanship in almost every community large enough to call itself a city:

> Every one who has in him the sentiments of either a Christian or gentleman, cannot but be highly offended at the envenomed scurrility that has raged in pamphlets and newspapers, printed in Philadelphia for several years past, insomuch that libelling has become a kind of national crime, and distinguishes us not only from all the states around us, but from the whole civilized world. Our satire has been nothing but ribaldry and Billingsgate: the contest has been, who could call names in the greatest variety of phrases, who could mangle the greatest number of characters, or who could excel in the magnitude and virulence of their lies. Hence the honor of families has been stained; the highest posts rendered cheap and vile in the sight of the people, and the greatest services and virtues blasted.[15]

Such expressions of anxiety, distrust, rage, and alarm were in historical perspective—and especially in the context of a political regime just concluding its first decade—plausibly cause, I believe, for those holding responsibility to legislate as restrictively as percipient diagnosis and judgment suggested would tend to subdue the commotion. (Their calculations, ideally, would have included some risk of counterproductivity—of deepening division and a helical progress of incitements and attempted repressions.) This interpretation, and the particular regard for political probabilities and responsibilities on which it rests, must number me in the distinct minority of American scholars who have written about the Sedition Act of 1798 in the twentieth century. Perhaps the following interpretation of the act is too confident to be cited as typical, but it is far from atypical of historical judgments today: "Moreover, the Sedition Act was an implied acknowledgement by the Federalists that force and coercion rather than reason and argument were to be the ultimate arbiters of political controversy in the United States. Differences of opinion were to be erased and the American mind was to be forced into an intellectual straightjacket fashioned by Harrison Gray Otis and company."[16]

This is not, I am sorry to say, the occasion for an extended review of the evidence and argument that have led me to question the prevalent view of this legislation. My presumptions now are pretty much identical with those I discussed at some length twenty years ago.[17] I did, however, discover soon after publishing those apparently perverse views that long ago the illustrious Supreme Court Justice Joseph Story and more recently the esteemed American historian Samuel E. Morison had reached conclusions similar to my own. On 27 December 1817 Justice Story wrote to Harrison Gray Otis, newly elected to the U.S. Senate:

> At the time when I first turned my thoughts to political subjects in the ardour of very early youth, I well remember that the sedition law was my great aversion. With the impetuosity and desire of independence so common to zealous young men, I believed it to be unconstitutional. I have now grown wiser in this, and I hope in many other respects: and for many years have entertained no more doubt of the constitutional power of Congress to enact that law, than any other in the Statute book. My present opinion has been forced upon me by reflection, by legal analogy, and by calm deliberation. You may smile at my confession, which I hope you will not call, as Mr. Randolph on another occasion did, "a precious confession."[18]

Following the quotation from Story's letter, and closing his own account of Otis's support of the Alien and Sedition Laws, Morison remarks:

> Abominable though these acts seemed at the time, to very many Americans they seem insignificant after two world wars, a cold war

and sundry legislative attempts to cope with communism. To call the Alien and Sedition Acts a "Reign of Terror," as the Republicans did at the time and as many historians have done since, is a gross perversion of the truth. Nobody was hanged, nobody went before a firing squad, nobody was tortured; the rule of law operated, public discussion remained free, and the writ of habeas corpus ran. A few persons obnoxious to the Federalists were imprisoned for short periods; that is all.[19]

Two statutes concerning the political activities of aliens on American soil and one concerning the conduct of American citizens were enacted by Congress in June and July 1798. The first two laws authorized the president in his discretion to restrain or deport citizens of countries with whom the United States was at war or facing the threat of war and citizens of any foreign country when the president determined that their further unfettered presence endangered the peace and safety of the United States. The third statute, popularly known as the Sedition Act (reprinted in appendix 5), had two objectives: to define as punishable offenses (1) conspiring with, encouraging, aiding, or advising others in opposing measures or interfering in operations of the national government, or abetting an insurrection, riot, or unlawful assembly; and (2) writing, printing, uttering, or publishing (or procuring or aiding the same) any false, malicious, or scandalous statement against the government of the United States, either house of Congress, or the president with intent to defame or bring into contempt or excite hatred against the same, or with intent to stir up sedition or excite unlawful combinations for opposing the government or for aiding and abetting the hostile designs of any foreign nation. The act also specified (as amended in the House of Representatives) that in any prosecution "for the writing or publishing any libel aforesaid," the defendant could give "in evidence in his defense, the truth of the matter contained in the publication charged as a libel," and that a jury should determine both the facts and the applicable meaning of the statute. The Sedition Act was to expire on the last day of John Adams's current term as president.[20]

The three statutes, especially the third, thrust into the ongoing clamor additional, further inflammatory claims of partisan purpose of the legislation, partiality in its administration, and the unconstitutionality of both. The chief claims of unconstitutionality were not only that the First Amendment allowed Congress to pass "no law ... abridging" speech, press, assembly, or petition but also that the Tenth Amendment had reserved to the states the whole field embraced in the alien-sedition legislation; further, that the federal government had inherited no common-law jurisdiction (and thus no common-law basis of self-defense) among its enumerated powers and that Article III gave the federal courts no jurisdiction over aliens or sedition.

Nearly a decade after adoption of the Bill of Rights, the new nation thus reached a serious examination of how to reconcile vigorous, perhaps unpopular, and for some citizens highly offensive criticism of the character and conduct of public officers with vigorous, perhaps unpopular, and for some citizens highly offensive administration of public policies adopted in keeping with due process of law. The delay may be explained by a startling conclusion of the historian Leonard Levy: we have no evidence that spokesmen for an inviolably free press in the framing of the first constitutions had given searching thought to where the dividing line should fall between the right of citizens to lambaste their government in print and the right of governors to throw up barricades against such assault, or that they intended to alter much if at all the common-law tradition under which "free press" would have simply meant no prior licensing or censorship (but not no subsequent punishment). Referring specifically to the records of the drafting and ratification of the First Amendment to the Constitution, Levy says, "Few among them if any at all clearly understood what they meant by the free-speech-and-press clause, and it is perhaps doubtful that those few agreed except in a generalized way and equally doubtful that they represented a consensus."[21]

Surely, then, the Alien and Sedition Acts would stimulate more deliberate attention to the difficult issues of the limits of liberty—both the limits of expression/publication and the limits of regulation—in particular contexts. So it happened that the first public discussion of the free-speech-and-press clause occurred in conditions of national and partisan excitement, not to say exigency. This discussion began in Congress. (Excerpts from 10 July 1798, the closing, summary day of the long House debate on the Sedition Act, the last of the acts to be passed, are reprinted in appendix 6.)

Response: The Kentucky and Virginia Resolutions

By mid-April 1798 Thomas Jefferson, vice president of the United States, was convinced that the Federalists, who controlled both chambers of Congress, were going to write into the statute books a parcel of legislation

with the announced objective of protecting the government against subversion and sedition—and with the thinly disguised ulterior purpose of
frustrating the campaign then underway to lift Jefferson into the presidency in place of John Adams. A week or more before the Sedition Act
was signed into law, the vice president and his coadjutor, James Madison,
were deep in consultation over the best strategy for rendering the prospective legislation null and void. These conspirators, if indeed they were
conspirators, made no attempt to conceal their activity. They decided to
induce Jefferson's supporters in the Virginia legislature to adopt resolutions declaring the whole alien and sedition package unconstitutional as
invading authority reserved to the states and to induce another state to
follow suit if one with a sympathetic legislative majority could be found.
That state turned out to be Kentucky.

Subsequent events made it apparent that Jefferson laid a heavy hand
on the wording of the resolutions of Kentucky, the first of the two states to
act. James Madison was primary author of the Virginia Resolutions and of
the *Report*, one year later, from a committee of the Virginia House of
Delegates appointed to review both the resolutions and the responses of
other members of the Union to which those resolutions had been sent.

The bellicose resolutions pushed through the legislatures of Kentucky
(in 1798 and 1799) and Virginia (in 1798) in response to the Alien and
Sedition Acts are promontories in American history because they projected
into public attention three questions of supreme importance. First, what
are the bounds of authority conferred upon the national government to
restrain speech and publication aimed at the national government? Second,
what is the locus of authority to mark those bounds and nullify acts of the
national government that transgress them? Third, subsuming these specific questions, what is the fundamental relationship established for three
contending sources of authority: (1) "We the People of the United States,"
(2) the member states that, arguably, brought the Union and the Constitution into existence, and (3) the government of the United States whose
duly enacted statutes are declared by the Constitution to be the supreme
law of the land?[22]

In this plexus of controversy, whose reverberations would be heard
until secession brought on civil war, our account would most appropriately be focused on emerging conceptions of the range and measure of
unrestricted communication required if freedom of speech and press is to
function as a bulwark of liberty and democracy. It must be recorded,
however, that public discussion barely and rarely reached this issue. In

particular, Thomas Jefferson as leader of the opposition at no time left persuasive evidence that he opposed the enactment and vigorous enforcement of such legislation as the Sedition Act, *provided* the enacting body's authority for it *under the Constitution* was indisputable. Jefferson, says Leonard Levy, "never protested against the substantive law of seditious libel, not even during the Sedition Act controversy. His protests at that time were directed against national as opposed to state prosecution for verbal crimes. He accepted without question the dominant view of his generation that government could be criminally assaulted merely by the expression of critical opinions that allegedly tended to subvert it by lowering it in the public's esteem. His consistent recognition of the concept of verbal political crimes throughout the Revolution continued in the period of peace that followed."[23]

Moreover, as Walter Berns has emphasized in a searching review of the controversy, this focus on the federal aspect of the issue, and acceptance of state power to punish seditious speech and publication, characterized virtually all of the opposition to the Alien and Sedition Laws.[24] The argument over the meaning of the First Amendment, that is, was almost solely about the constitutional power of the federal government alone. It rarely reached those larger questions of liberal theory challenging justifications for punishing published opinion, or of democratic theory bearing on the functions of free communication in a republican polity.

James Madison was, as we shall see, at least a partial exception. Madison dissociated himself from promotion of the Kentucky Resolutions—at least after he had read the text that Jefferson transmitted to former Virginia friends and neighbors who had become members of the Kentucky Assembly. Presumably Jefferson's language and that adopted by the Kentucky legislature was too obdurate, offering no promise of yielding to compromise. The assertion that a particular act of Congress, if exceeding delegated authority, "is not law but is altogether void and of no force" raised the prospect that any state, acting unilaterally, might within its own borders obstruct the efforts of the national government to enforce the law. The Kentucky legislators decided not to pursue this course of coercive action when the responses to their first set of resolutions revealed that, of the then sixteen states, only Virginia would join them. Altogether, the Kentucky Resolutions declared that Congress had exceeded the authority delegated to it by the Constitution; that the specifications of crimes and punishments not within the power of Congress to create and define were of no force; and that the states composing the Union had reserved to themselves the power, by a process now to be agreed upon, to render the purported legislation inoperative.

Madison, writing in language he hoped would be agreeable to the Virginia legislators, asserted emphatically that both the Sedition Act and the new laws relating to aliens were not within the power of Congress to enact, but he included no claim that the states had reserved to themselves a power to determine issues of constitutionality, by either individual or collective action. It may be contended, however, that he implied as much when, presuming that other states would agree with the charge that Congress had overstepped its power, he recommended that necessary and proper measures "be taken by each for co-operating with this state in maintaining unimpaired the authorities, rights, and liberties reserved to the states, respectively, or to the people." There are no rules fixing limits for implications. The most Madison would say explicitly in support of Jefferson's appeal for nullification was in section 3 of the Virginia Resolutions: "That this Assembly doth explicitly and peremptorily declare that it views the powers of the Federal Government . . . as no further valid than they are authorized by the grants enumerated in that compact; and that in the case of a deliberate, palpable, and dangerous exercise of other [i.e., assumed] powers not granted by the said compact, the States, who are the parties thereto, have the right and are in duty bound to interpose for arresting the progress of the evil, and for maintaining within their respective limits the authorities, rights, and liberties appertaining to them."[25]

Virginia, like Kentucky, drew a total blank on its request for support from other states. Indeed, most of the state responses at least suggested that consideration by the judicial branch of the federal government, not the states "interposing," was the appropriate mode of decision on the disputed legislation's constitutionality. Most explicit on this score was Rhode Island: "the . . . third article of the Constitution . . . vests in the federal courts, exclusively, and in the Supreme Court of the United States, ultimately, the authority of deciding on the constitutionality of any act or law of the Congress of the United States."[26]

The Virginia House of Delegates then created a committee to review the replies from the states and its action of the previous year. James Madison, newly elected to the House, was named chairman and wrote the committee's elaborate report. If the Virginia Resolutions were more moderate than those of Kentucky—and they were—it may also be said that Madison's *Report* was more emollient than the resolutions it reviewed. "The *Report* of 1800," according to Madison's principal biographer, "first redisplayed and then pulled the teeth of the 1798 resolutions. Had the explanation been offered in the original resolutions, the document would have created not a murmur of alarm."[27]

This may well go too far, but that is a matter of interpretation. For our purposes, Madison's *Report* is notable on four grounds. The first, already implied, is its retreat, when read as a whole, from any counsel of "interposition." The second is its qualified acceptance (in implicit response to the replies from the states) of review by the federal courts as relevant to the Alien and Sedition Laws, although still defending in abstract principle, and as a last resort, determinations by the state parties to the putative constitutional compact of the constitutional validity of acts of the national government, including its courts.

Still more pertinent to our concerns are two further positions in the *Report*. Third, then, is Madison's argument that the First Amendment is an absolute bar to federal government regulation of expression. On this point Madison is adamant, coming at the issue from several directions: classical strict construction of federal powers; rebuttal of every claim in sight that common law passed to the federal government with (or without) the Constitution; and a literal interpretation of the First Amendment's "no law" language, based on his reading of the legislative history of the Bill of Rights. The power to regulate speech and the press, said Madison, was not given to the federal government to begin with, and "the amendment was intended as a positive and absolute reservation of it." It followed, Madison added, that the federal government is indeed "destitute of every authority for restraining the licentiousness of the press, and for shielding itself against the libellous attacks which may be made on those who administer it. . . ."[28] Let us be clear about it, however: this "absolutist" position was primarily a states' rights position, not a civil libertarian position—clearly so in general, arguably so even in Madison's formulation.

Fourth and finally (for our purposes), there remains the question of what free speech and press may mean for those governments (the states) that have some power to regulate it. After all, the common law applies in the states—albeit, Madison argues, not the British common law on speech and the press. Here the argument runs that the American meaning of free speech and press must be different from the British because American political institutions differ from British. American doctrines of freedom of conscience obviously depart from the British. More to the point, location of sovereignty in the people, rather than in Parliament, makes the electoral accountability of legislators as well as "magistrates" more critical in the American setting than in Britain. The function of the press in "freely examining public characters and measures" is therefore more important in America than in Britain. Moreover, because sovereignty resides in the American people, the American constitutions limit both executives and legislatures. The press in America, Madison argues, is therefore necessarily free not only from previous restraints imposed by executive censors but—if the freedom is to be effectual—from subsequent punishments imposed by the law (i.e., by the legislatures).[29] Totally free? Probably not, for Madison's concluding comment on state regulation of the press is: "The committee are not unaware of the difficulty of all general questions, which may turn on the proper boundary between the liberty and licentiousness of the press. They will leave it, therefore, for consideration only, how far the difference between the nature of the British government, and the nature of the American government . . . may show the degree of rigor in the former to be inapplicable to, and not obligatory in, the latter."[30] On the general question, the conclusions are therefore qualified, even ambiguous. But Madison's argument at *this* point is evidently general, not simply federal—referring to American governments and constitutions altogether, not the national government alone. Here, then, in 1800, tucked somewhat obscurely into a document preoccupied with the federal compact and the strict construction of federal powers, we have from Madison the beginnings of an argument about republican freedom of communication.

Probably the third of these four concerns of Madison, the view that the First Amendment prohibits absolutely—rather more a federal than a liberal concern in this context—has had the most attention in modern times, while both the subtlety and ambiguity with which Madison handled state power to regulate expression/communication have been much less noticed.[31] Another of Madison's biographers, Ralph Ketcham, characterizes his treatment of these concerns as his "most important statement of the principles that should guide republican governments in protecting civil liberties during a national crisis," and a few paragraphs later says that the argument "added substantially to the theory of free government he had been evolving for a generation or more."[32]

Ketcham's competence to judge how Madison's later statements extended what he had said on previous occasions is undeniable. Nor shall I deny that there were useful extensions in Madison's *Report*, linking a free press to free elections at an early stage of American democratic theory. Still, taking the Virginia Resolutions and *Report* together as the civil libertarian statement with the strongest claim on our regard as the founding period came to a close, I think we must say that they left us with some serious problems and omissions. One might ask, for example, if the literal, "no-law" reading of the First Amendment was meant to render irrelevant any question whether such regulations as those of the Sedition Act might be imposed in the District of Columbia (to which the federal government moved six months after Madison's *Report* was published and nine months before the Sedition Act expired) or whether such regulations might be found necessary and proper to assembling and maintaining armies and navies and waging wars.

The Lessons and Lapses of the Sedition Law Debate

The Alien and Sedition Laws came late in what is here defined as the founding period, and they did not outlive it. Perversely, the furor they reflected and reciprocally engendered helped to clarify some aspects of the new constitutional regime but also to confuse and unsettle some others. Let us begin with the (partial) clarifications, which had to do with the place of judicial review and common law in the national government.

In general, Federalists supported both judicial review and federal common-law jurisdiction. (That they then controlled the federal courts was not the only reason for this position, though it was no doubt an implicit and material reason for some.) The minority of the Virginia legislature that opposed the Virginia Resolutions, in a statement commonly attributed to John Marshall, thus argued that if the Alien and Sedition Acts were unconstitutional, the federal courts would find them so; it also argued that the acts were not only prudent but constitutional— among other reasons, according to the common law, which "pervades all America" and thus inures to the national government as well as to the states.[33] Thomas Jefferson and many of his supporters, on the other hand, denied the authority of federal courts to invalidate legislation in general on constitutional grounds. Nearly all Jeffersonians denied that common-law authority had passed to the national government as a basis of either judicial action alone or legislation by Congress. If it had, they argued with some cogency, the constitutional enumeration of national powers could soon be negated. Such were the claims of strict separation-of-powers doctrine and strict constitutional construction. The various state responses to the Kentucky and Virginia Resolutions, however, left no room for doubt that judicial review as we know it today was, at least regarding the national government's legislation, broadly accepted in principle among political leaders some five years before John Marshall found an opportunity to begin its establishment in practice.

Nevertheless, the Jeffersonian view of federal common-law jurisdiction, including common-law authority of the federal government to protect itself, did come to prevail in time, with the general assent of political leaders of both parties—oddly enough, in prosecutions of Federalists (for libeling President Jefferson and for illegal trading with the enemy) by Republican administrations.[34] This change of mind occurred notwithstanding that, as Justice Story later reported, "excepting Judge Chase, every Judge that ever sat on the Supreme Court bench from the adoption of the constitution until 1804 . . . held a like opinion" in support of federal common-law criminal jurisdiction.[35] By the end of the War of 1812 it was settled that there could be no federal common law of crimes, including political crimes. Some 110 years later the First Amendment became applicable to state action of this sort.

Various other constitutional issues were in no sense settled by the furor over the Alien and Sedition Acts and the Kentucky and Virginia Resolutions. One of these had to do with the foundations of the Union. According to John Marshall's *Address of the Minority,* "The will of the majority [of the people] produced, ratified, and conducts it"; while, according to James Madison's Virginia Resolutions and *Report,* "the Constitution is a compact to which the states are parties." Marshall also argued that the Constitution is properly amendable through its own procedures, while the Jeffersonian position looked instead down the long road toward the nullification doctrine.

Two closely related issues had to do with the powers and departments of the federal government. In the strict constructionist view of the Kentucky and Virginia Resolutions, federal powers are closely circumscribed; in the familiar Federalist argument of Marshall's Minority Address, the purposes for which the national government was formed are national, not state, and the resulting national powers are sufficient to those purposes—are "whole powers," implicating the means for their implementation and necessarily comprehending measures for preservation of the government, whose exercise of authorized powers of war and peace might otherwise be set at naught by, for example, malicious slander. In the strict constructionist view of the resolutions, presidential authority to deport or sequester aliens "confounds legislative, executive, and judicial powers; it punishes without trial"; and yet, said John Marshall, the legislation really works no differently from other laws in its procedures, while appeal to the courts is contingent in each case and implicit in the legislation.[36]

Most of these issues of federal powers and separation of powers were settled in the next century and a half by civil practice or the Civil War. One further issue—the meaning of the First Amendment, or the limits of speech and the public regulation of speech—is more distinctly modern. The episode of 1798–1801 turned out to be a rehearsal for problems that rose to prominence in the twentieth century (though they surfaced briefly in the War of 1812 and the Civil War). This is the issue that has been our chief concern in this chapter. If the analysis of Leonard Levy considered earlier withstands historical criticism, as I believe it largely has so far—if the "original" meaning of the First Amendment is strictly irretrievable now and was so a decade after its adoption—then those staples of American constitutional debate that were mentioned just a moment ago may be seen to relate directly to perceptions of the First Amendment; to perceptions, that is, of appropriate policies toward fractious free speech about sensitive political matters. In Marshall's argument there is implied power in the federal government to protect itself, its functions, and its responsibilities. In Madison's view that is simply not so; Jeffersonian notions of federalism and the Tenth Amendment support the absolute "no-law" reading of the First Amendment.[37]

There were no doubt hyperbole, extremism, and overanxiety on both sides in this early episode. If Americans tend today, as we long have, to reprobate the Alien and Sedition Laws, can we in equity and candor condone the Kentucky and Virginia Resolutions? How shall we compare the tendencies and effects of both for the young republican polity? I am aware of no careful comparison of this sort in the literature of American history, law, or political science.

What we can say is that the furious debate over the Alien and Sedition Laws largely failed to illuminate usefully the dual issue of appropriate limits of speech, limits of its regulation. This happened chiefly because the absolutist position of the opponents was so procrustean and protective, and because its analytic basis was so much more federal than either philosophical or republican. It thus left us almost no legacy of founding exploration of limits and circumstances, but only the mostly vacuous issue of limits versus no limits at all to political speech at the federal level alone, for *neither* side believed in no limits at all below the federal level. After that episode the issues of freedom of expression in circumstances broadly analogous to it provoked little analysis in American law and politics until well into the twentieth century.

Liberty, Authority, and Limits in the Founding

The Sedition Law of 1798 would almost certainly be unconstitutional today. There is, indeed, dictum of the modern Supreme Court to suggest that it was unconstitutional when passed, though arguably that view is anachronistic.[38] However that may be, the Sedition Law conceivably was ill-advised as public policy in its time, extending federal executive authority too far as against claims of freedom to speak and publish, exceeding any evident justification in the attendant circumstances, and thus lending plausibility to allegations then and historical inferences later that its ulterior purposes were anti-republican and anti-Republican.

Yet the later conclusions—which tend to credit the partisan charges more than the monarchical ones—may be anachronistic also, or partly so. Even the more charitable, less ulterior interpretation that protagonists in the legislation were either authoritarians or overly anxious may suffer from this defect. I believe that it does—that both it and the more sinister interpretations fail to consider sufficiently the deep and troubling uncertainties that must have beset many in responsible positions a bare decade into the American republican experiment.

We can usefully think of it this way: we live today by certain political distinctions—between, in perhaps the most usual language, government, regime, polity, and political community—that are familiar in sophisticated political discourse and probably apparent in a general way to most politically literate citizens. We accept these distinctions as conceptually sensible and as empirically viable in nearly all foreseeable American circumstances— that is, probabilistically, regarding both mass and elite political behavior— because they have prevailed for more than a dozen decades and, with one exception, since the founding. Yet our acceptance of these distinctions reflects long years of experience with the practice of partisan electoral politics and, especially, with the phenomenon of an organized "opposition" party, or faction. We understand pretty well that when, after a strenuous and strident campaign, the opposition wins the election, not only will the regime of republican governing institutions and policies remain intact but certain well-established constraints will tend to govern and contain the new administration's conduct. The bonds of political community that sustain the polity and tend to support the regime have been nourished and tested in these respects for two centuries. We know they once parted sectionally, and we have seen them strained segmentally in recent times; but we also have some confidence in their strength.

Now consider that neither the distinctions nor the experiences that tend to confirm them, still probabilistically, were available in 1798; and consider again the, for all practical purposes, world revolutionary conditions of the time that were noticed in chapter 3 anent the Naturalization Law of that year. (Consider also, if you will, Washington's Farewell Address and Lincoln's First Inaugural.) All things considered, in the context of that time, I think that elected, responsible national officers—especially those most closely associated with "the government"—might not unreasonably have concluded that everything—government, regime, polity, community, in modern terms—was in the balance. They might have so concluded, of course, and still have settled deliberately on policies other than the Sedition Act (and here we are in the most pragmatic realm of all), or they might have settled deliberately on something like the Sedition Act. It verges on the fantastic, however, to assume that the distinctions and relative stabilities of today figured implicitly in the legislation of 1798, even prescinding altogether from its common-law background.

I suggest, therefore, that there are two principal lessons to be drawn here from the episode of the Alien and Sedition Acts—one lesson about the founding, as it still conditions our perceptions of American self-government today, and one about the limits of liberty. As for the founding, the lesson I draw is that it should be clearer to us than it commonly is that the calculations (I use the term broadly) of political leaders had then, as always, to consider the "systemic" effects of governmental actions—but more centrally and uncertainly so then. Public policy and political leadership, this is to say, were more considerably *about* the cultivation of a political community—about the shaping of public perspectives on and convictions about a republican regime. Insofar as this office of political leadership still applies today—as ideally, perhaps, it does—it presumably contends with more settled traditions; and, notwithstanding conceptual ambiguity in the matter, there is far less pragmatic confusion today than there was in the founding period between arguments over the directions of government and those over the premises of the regime. On both sides the controversy over the Alien and Sedition Laws had to do with premises of the regime; also, for supporters of the laws (and perhaps for opponents as well), it implicated issues of the government's responsibility for strengthening the political community and safeguarding the polity. But to state the issues in terms of these modern distinctions is—in a degree not yet seriously estimated, so far as I am aware—to neglect the necessary confusions and uncertainties of 1798. There is just a little more to the lesson: notwithstanding differences already emphasized between then and now, to acknowledge the confusions and uncertainties of 1798 may prompt one also to acknowledge those that cannot be eliminated by knowledge or doctrine today.

What has just been said can also be taken as a lesson in the limits of liberty—that there will normally be some reasonable limit to allowable political communication. Such a limit can be justified if we consider liberty not as the primeval condition of humanity but as (see chapter 6) subsisting in a duly administered republican regime of law. Limits, in this view, will derive (uncertainly and indefinitely) from responsibilities for the welfare of that regime. In times of crisis especially, estimates about the direction in which such responsibility points may depend primarily on judgments about the underlying state of the political community—about the capacities it supports for responsible citizenship. The limits, then, are indefinite and not precisely codifiable, which is the truism with which this chapter began. Beyond that, we are connected here to the concerns in Part 1 with political community and responsible citizenship. The two chapters that follow will expand the dimensions of this concern.

Notes

1. Oscar Handlin and Mary Handlin, *The Dimensions of Liberty* (Cambridge, Mass.: Belknap Press, 1961).

2. *Journals of the Continental Congress* 3 (1775): 280; 4 (1776): 18–20. Summary lists of state legislation are in Claude H. Van Tyne, *The Loyalists in the American Revolution* (1902; New York: Macmillan, 1959), appendixes B, C.

3. Henry J. Young, "Treason and Its Punishment in Revolutionary Pennsylvania," *Pennsylvania Magazine of History and Biography* 90 (1966): 287–313.

4. Leonard J. Levy, *Legacy of Suppression* (Cambridge, Mass.: Harvard University Press, 1960), pp. 182–85; for the Pennsylvania Declaration of Rights, see Francis Newton Thorpe, ed., *The Federal and State Constitutions, Colonial Charters, and Other Organic Laws of the States, Territories, and Colonies Now or Heretofore Forming the United States of America*, vol. 5 (Washington, D.C.: Government Printing Office, 1906), p. 3082.

5. Ibid., vol. 7, pp. 3812ff.

6. Pinckney's proposal (August 20) in Max Farrand, ed., *The Records of the Federal Convention of 1787*, vol. 2 (New Haven, Conn.: Yale University Press, 1937), p. 341; Madison to Jefferson (October 24, 1787), ibid., vol. 3, pp. 135–36.

7. The reports of ratifying conventions are printed in Charles C. Tansill, ed., *The Making of the American Republic: The Great Documents 1774–1789* (New Rochelle, N.Y.: Arlington House, n.d.), pp. 1009–59.

8. *Annals of Congress* 1 (1789–90): 437.

9. John Adams, *Thoughts on Government,* in *American Political Writing during the Founding Era, 1760–1805,* vol. 1, ed. Charles S. Hyneman and Donald S. Lutz (Indianapolis: Liberty Press, 1983), esp. pp. 408–9.

10. Ibid., p. 403.

11. *Annals of Congress* 1 (1789–90): 439.

12. Hamilton is writing here about judicial aggrandizement, or the aggressive practice of judicial review. It is only fair to note, however, that Hamilton's comment in *Federalist No. 78* indicates that he did expect courts to decline to give effect to unconstitutional statutes.

13. See esp. *Cooper v. Aaron,* 358 U.S. 1 (1958). See also Charles S. Hyneman, *The Supreme Court on Trial* (New York: Atherton Press, 1963).

14. Levy, *Legacy of Suppression,* chap. 6.

15. Francis Wharton, ed., *State Trials of the United States during the Administrations of Washington and Adams* (Philadelphia: Carey and Hart, 1849), p. 322.

16. John C. Miller, *Crisis in Freedom: The Alien and Sedition Acts* (Boston: Little, Brown, 1951), pp. 74–75.

17. Charles S. Hyneman, *Popular Government in America* (New York: Atherton Press, 1968), chap. 13.

18. Samuel Eliot Morison, *Harrison Gray Otis: The Urbane Federalist* (Boston: Houghton Mifflin, 1969), pp. 120–21. Still later, Story "abstain[ed] from expressing any opinion" on whether the federal government might constitutionally legislate punishments for licentiousness of the press. Probably he was then acknowledging changes in majority legal opinion as well as certain Supreme Court decisions in the early nineteenth century. Joseph Story, *Commentaries on the Constitution of the United States,* vol. 3 (Boston: Hilliard, Gary, 1833), pp. 743–44.

19. Morison, *Harrison Gray Otis,* p. 121. Morison appears to have changed his mind in reaching this conclusion. Compare his *The Life and Letters of Harrison Gray Otis,* vol. 1 (Boston: Houghton Mifflin, 1913), pp. 115–25.

20. *Statutes at Large of the United States of America,* vol. 1 (Boston: Charles C. Little and James Brown, 1845), pp. 570–72, 577–78, 596–97. For the acts, see also James Morton Smith, *Freedom's Fetters: The Alien and Sedition Laws and American Civil Liberties* (Ithaca, N.Y.: Cornell University Press, 1956), appendix. The 1798 amendment of the Naturalization Act, discussed in chap. 4 above, was commonly included with the three acts by partisan critics who regarded the purpose of extending the naturalization period not only as an oppressive national security measure but also as a Federalist attempt to impair the Republican electorate, to which most immigrants gravitated.

21. Levy, *Legacy of Suppression,* p. 236. See also Walter Berns, *The First*

Amendment and the Future of American Democracy (New York: Basic Books, 1976), chap. 3. For Levy's later, somewhat amended views, see his "The Legacy Reexamined," *Stanford Law Review* 37 (1984): 767, and *Emergence of a Free Press* (New York: Oxford University Press, 1985). As the title of the latter work (a revision of *Legacy*) may imply, Levy's chief revision is an acceptance of the view that, whatever the formal common law on the subject, by 1798 American public policy in the thirteen states had accepted de facto a freedom of the press (not necessarily other speech) that extended beyond prior restraint to ex post punishment. On this point see also David M. Rabban, "The Ahistorical Historian: Leonard Levy on Freedom of Expression in Early American History," *Stanford Law Review* 37 (1984): 795. Otherwise, however, Levy has pretty much reaffirmed and reinforced his 1960 thesis.

22. The Kentucky and Virginia Resolutions are printed in Henry Steele Commager, *Documents of American History* (New York: Appleton-Century-Crofts, various editions), and, with the *Report,* in Jonathan Elliott, ed., *The Debates in the Several State Conventions on the Adoption of the Federal Constitution as Recommended by the General Convention at Philadelphia in 1787,* 2d ed., vol. 4 (Philadelphia: J. B. Lippincott, 1901), pp. 528–80.

23. Leonard W. Levy, *Jefferson and Civil Liberties: The Darker Side* (Cambridge, Mass.: Harvard University Press, 1963), p. 46. For Jefferson's position throughout his presidency, see chap. 3, passim.

24. Berns, *First Amendment and the Future of American Democracy,* chap. 3.

25. Compare Madison in 1789, App. 4, p. 282. On Madison's disinclination to go so far as Jefferson toward "nullification," see Jefferson's letter to Wilson C. Nicholas of 5 September 1799, in Albert Ellery Bergh, ed., *The Writings of Thomas Jefferson,* vol. 10 (Washington, D.C.: Thomas Jefferson Memorial Association, 1905), pp. 130–31.

26. The state responses are in Elliott, *Debates,* vol. 4, pp. 532–39.

27. Irving Brant, *The Fourth President: A Life of James Madison* (Indianapolis: Bobbs-Merrill, 1970), p. 299. Brant says further that Madison "put political objectives ahead of abstract thought. He was trying to knock out the Alien and Sedition Acts by public opinion expressed through state governments.... Whenever [his] argument coincided with his original opinions it was impervious and overwhelming... But when he searched for safeguards against a tyrannous Congress, an arbitrary executive and a persecuting judiciary, anxiety led him farther than reason would let him remain. So came an incongruity— the proposal of joint state action. . . ." Irving Brant, *James Madison: Father of the Constitution, 1787–1800* (Indianapolis: Bobbs-Merrill, 1950), p. 470.

28. Elliott, *Debates,* vol. 4, pp. 572–73.

29. Ibid., pp. 569–73.

30. Ibid., p. 570.

31. We tread on dangerous ground when we credit the author of a state

paper with the presentation of his personal convictions, with precise reporting of events as he saw them, or even with choice of language best suited to persuade others to his view. In both the Virginia Resolutions and the subsequent *Report*, Madison may have modified language to avoid, for example, offending Jefferson or irritating John Taylor, to attract support or pacify opposition, or to interest an audience he thought not yet prepared for nicer distinctions or deeper analysis. See Brant, *James Madison*, chap. 34.

32. Ralph Ketcham, *James Madison: A Biography* (New York: Macmillan, 1971), pp. 399–403.

33. "Address of the Minority to the Citizens of Virginia," *Journal of the Virginia House of Delegates*, 22 January 1799. Marshall's authorship of this document is disputed in William C. Stinchcombe and Charles T. Cullen, eds., *The Papers of John Marshall*, vol. 3 (Chapel Hill: University of North Carolina Press, 1979), pp. 498–99, chiefly on internal evidence but also because Marshall had opposed the Sedition Act, believing it unnecessary because it was already implicit in common-law powers of the national government. Compare, however, Albert J. Beveridge, *The Life of John Marshall*, vol. 2 (Boston and New York: Houghton Mifflin, 1916), pp. 400–410; and Brant, *The Fourth President*, p. 296.

34. *United States v. Hudson and Goodwin*, 7 Cranch 32 (1812); *United States v. Coolidge*, 1 Wheaton 415 (1816). Jefferson, consistently enough, deplored the libel prosecutions and ordered them *nolle prossed* when he learned of them. See Charles Warren, *The Supreme Court in United States History*, vol. 1 (Boston: Little, Brown, 1935), pp. 433–44. See also Charles Warren, "New Light on the History of the Federal Judiciary Act of 1789," *Harvard Law Review* 37 (1923): 49, for evidence that the Judiciary Act of 1789 contemplated that federal district courts would have jurisdiction over common-law crimes (as distinct from common-law civil jurisdiction). Had the Supreme Court consulted the legislative history of the Judiciary Act, says Warren, *Hudson and Goodwin* and *Coolidge* would almost surely have been decided the other way.

35. Quoted in Warren, *The Supreme Court in United States History*, vol. 1, p. 434. This seems probable enough, notwithstanding Justice Story's well-known quest for federal jurisdiction and deep concern over sedition and resistance in New England during the War of 1812.

36. The quoted words are from the *Address to the People* (by Madison) accompanying the Virginia Resolutions. Elliott, *Debates*, vol. 4, pp. 529ff. Jefferson's language in the Kentucky Resolutions is stronger. Marshall's statement is, again, from the *Address from the Minority* (which, by the way, the Virginia legislature refused to publish with Madison's address, though it appears in the legislative record and was printed separately as a pamphlet by its partisans).

37. The *Virginia Address from the Minority* disputes Madison's interpreta-

tion on two related grounds: first, the language "no law respecting . . . religion" is broader and more clearly absolute than the language "no law . . . abridging the freedom of speech . . ."; and, second, punishment of libelous or licentious publication was not a restriction of freedom of the press as currently understood. The Sedition Act thus provided for the punishment of no writing not already punishable as common law.

38. *New York Times v. Sullivan,* 376 U.S. 254 (1964), pp. 273–76. In the view of Justice William Brennan, for the Court, the unconstitutionality of the Alien and Sedition Acts is attested to by the compensatory actions of a (Jeffersonian Republican) Congress in 1802, by the conclusions of Cooley's *Constitutional Limitations,* and by Justice Oliver Wendell Holmes's observation in *Abrams v. U.S.,* 250 U.S. 616 (1919), p. 630. Perhaps so, but one should note the partisan sentiment in that early Congress; and Cooley seems, on a close reading, to leave the constitutional issue in doubt. Thomas Cooley, *Constitutional Limitations,* 7th ed. (Boston: Little, Brown, 1903), pp. 612–13. Justice Holmes's well-known observation is perhaps better characterized as a summary one-liner than as an argument.

8

The Limits of Liberty:
Petition, Protest, and Resistance

IT IS A FAMILIAR CONTENTION in our time that inasmuch as the founders rebelled forcibly against a government long accepted as legitimate, disobedience of law and resistance to government are for Americans appropriate options whenever persons committed to the founding ideals find current public policies and conduct at odds with their vision or version of those ideals. The founders of republican government in America placed a very high value on individual liberty; of that there can be no doubt. The evidence is clear and convincing, however, that they also had no intention of endorsing violation of laws duly enacted or indulging resistance to public officials duly authorized to perform acts found offensive, no matter how deeply the objectors might be committed to cherished constitutional ideals and no matter how certain they might be that those ideals were being disregarded in law or corrupted in official action.

This is so notwithstanding that most of those declarations of rights attached to most of the new state constitutions spoke of the people's collective right and duty to reconstitute government, should the institutions then being established turn out to pervert or subvert the public interest. Even then—in the immediate context of a colonial revolution, and necessarily regarding their constituent measures as somewhat experimental—their statements indicate that they viewed the grounds and the conceivable event of *re*constitution as strictly extraordinary, as nothing like a substitute for ordinary politics in case of strong disagreement over policy. The New Hampshire Constitution of 1784, in one of the most radical of such statements, thus said in Article X:

Government being instituted for the common benefit, protection, and security of the whole community, and not for the private interest of any one man, family, or class of men; therefore, whenever the ends of government are perverted and public liberty manifestly endangered, and all other means of redress are ineffectual, the people may, and of right ought, to reform the old or establish a new government. The doctrine of non-resistance against arbitrary power, and oppression, is absurd, slavish, and destructive of the good and happiness of mankind.[1]

In Maryland's convention of 1787 to consider the proposed new federal Constitution, the following amendment was proposed:

That it be declared, that all persons intrusted with legislative or executive powers of government are the *trustees and servants* of the public, and as such accountable for their conduct. Wherefore, whenever the ends of government are perverted, and public liberty manifestly endangered, and all other means of redress are ineffectual, the people may, and of right ought, to reform the old, or establish a new government; the doctrine of nonresistance against arbitrary power and oppression is absurd, slavish, and destructive of the good and happiness of mankind.[2]

In the end, however, the Maryland convention ratified the federal Constitution unconditionally. This proposal was not among those James Madison presented to Congress in 1788, nor, apparently, was it proposed in the course of congressional consideration of the Bill of Rights.

The original of these pronouncements—together, that is, with language in the contemporaneous Declaration of Independence—appears in the Virginia Declaration of Rights of 1776, omitting the general animadversion on the doctrine of nonresistance (as did all state declarations adopted before 1787 save those of Maryland in 1776 and New Hampshire).[3] Some of these statements made replacement of government a last resort expressly, with reference to petition for redress of grievances. Most of them apparently also drew on the Declaration of Independence.

The Declaration of Independence supports a tightly defined right of resistance. It speaks explicitly and solely to circumstances that justify resistance "whenever any government becomes destructive of these ends [i.e., the securing of certain unalienable rights] . . . when a long train of abuses and usurpations, pursuing invariably the same object, evinces a design to reduce [the people] under absolute despotism." Then it is the people's right, "it is their duty, to throw off such government and to provide new guards for their future security." After cataloging at length the "injuries and usurpations," most of which were regarded as wrongs of *constitutional* dimension, Thomas Jefferson continued, "In every stage of these oppressions we have petitioned for redress in the most humble terms: our repeated petitions have been answered only by repeated injuries."

So John Adams construed this history as well.[4] So, it has been argued in detail, did most delegates to the Continental Congress, premised on English constitutional practice already some four centuries old.[5] For the colonists these traditions were rooted most prominently and recurrently in the English constitutional issues of the seventeenth century, from which republican principles also sprang. Arguably, the colonial recourse to petition was one of those alleged anachronisms connecting the Revolution with pre-Restoration English politics. For colonial conservatives and republicans alike, however, the process of petition for redress of grievances, with resistance strictly limited to noncompliance with the governmental measure(s) on which their grievances were founded, was the appropriate form of response to constitutional default or derogation by government—the form the Continental Congress had followed in 1774 and 1775, before finally voting the Declaration of Independence in 1776.[6]

There was, we know, resort to violence, including rifle fire directed toward troops in the service of His Majesty prior to the Declaration of Independence. More than a few of those who drew blood at Lexington and Concord and the hills known as Bunker and Breed's may have rationalized their behavior as the first stage of a war to oust tyrants from their land. In the main, however, there is reason to believe the leaders, and their followers as well, firing from behind stone fences, hoped the king and his counselors, if taught a lesson, would discontinue the policies his subjects found intolerable. The fighting of 1775 is surely no less interpretable as a response to perceived invasion and as a defense of colonial capacity to resist if necessary than as outright resistance or warfare. On the other hand, there were without doubt individual acts of obstruction and violence in the decade before independence, and the celebrated Boston Tea Party qualified, we may say, as organized protest and resistance beyond constitutional justification. Yet these overmeasures hardly qualify as either acts or policies of the responsible colonial leadership.

Indeed, close scrutiny of any nation's behavior, perhaps especially that of a new nation, will no doubt turn up evidences of contempt for and neglect of approved principles and procedures. Those who conceive that liberty confers a right to do whatever their imagination identifies as in order will readily be receptive to evidence that others have already got away with indulgence of the full range of possibilities.[7] The participants in Shays's Rebellion in 1786 and the Whiskey Rebellion in 1794, all of them members of the founding generation, are plausible witnesses to the effect that some founders and others did believe the regime of liberty to which the New World had committed itself assured persons and communities a right of self-determination with respect to the issues underlying their disputes with those in charge of government. However, they left no accounts of their positions for our perusal and for inclusion with the classics of American political argument.

More in point of the founders' view of the role of organized protest and resistance is the language of the First Amendment. After providing for freedom of religion and freedom of speech and the press, the First Congress ended the First Amendment with provision for freedom "of the people peaceably to assemble, and to petition the Government for a redress of grievances."[8] To assemble and petition was, as we have seen, a venerable practice. It had been honored as a privilege, if not established as a right, in ancient Greece and Rome, and it was familiar to the colonists as, they believed, an established procedure in the British Constitution. The assembly/petition provision of the First Amendment may well be the most direct carryover of constitutional and political tradition, reflecting the least ambiguous founding intention, of any of the statements in this basic article of political liberties.[9] Certainly peaceable assembly and petition for a redress of grievances carried the most direct connection with the Revolution. Clinton Rossiter reported their mention in "hundreds of town and county resolutions" preceding the Revolution and printed one from Middlesex County, Massachusetts, as a "representative statement": "*Resolved, That every people have an absolute right of meeting together to consult upon common grievances, and to petition, remonstrate, and use every legal method for their removal.*"[10] It appears from this history that our constitutional guarantee of these rights was meant to provide for not only a republican forum but a republican decorum as well.[11]

Five of the first round of state constitutions were silent on the subject under consideration here. Maryland and Delaware (1776) guaranteed that "every man hath a right to petition the Legislature, for the redress of grievances, in a peaceable and orderly manner." Not much license there. The other five states were similarly conservative, though they added something. The constitutions of North Carolina and Pennsylvania (1776), Vermont (1777), Massachusetts (1780), and New Hampshire (1784) began the guarantee of right to assemble and petition with the phrase, "that the people have a right" to assemble, consult, petition, and, they all added, "to instruct their representatives."

Here seems to lie plain implication that these five states intended to provide a popular right to interpose contingently in the formulation of public policy. In the three New England states, with their long-established town meetings and legislative representation of towns, this constitutional provision appears to have presupposed that instructions would come from a large proportion, if not a majority, of voters in a civil jurisdiction—probably more often than not regarding the particular concerns of that jurisdiction, as had been the case in colonial Massachusetts.[12] The expectations of North Carolina and Pennsylvania in 1776 are a little less readily interpretable in terms of prerevolutionary practice,[13] but English antecedents may also have figured in these state constitutions. In the reign of Elizabeth I local constituencies began to give instructions to their representatives, mainly on matters of local corporate interest, and the practice grew during the tense first half of the seventeenth century, extending to matters less strictly local (though chiefly those of public policy on religion).[14] Instruction was thus at least loosely coupled with petition in this particular republican tradition to which Americans later recurred. Toward the end of the eighteenth century instruction was frequently attempted again in Britain, and it was recommended by the "radical" movement during the time of the American Revolution and American constitution-writing.[15] It was natural enough for some American constitution-writers to include it, especially in states where (as in Pennsylvania and North Carolina) the revolutionary charters reflected domestic political overturns.[16] The more conservative Pennsylvania Constitution of 1790 thus contained no reference to the right of instruction. Some of the new states carved out of the West, however, were still authorizing instruction as late as 1889, when Idaho became the forty-third state.

Practically considered—at least before party organization and labels developed to help structure electoral accountability—instruction could be regarded as partly (not entirely) a natural extension or an element of petition.[17] By most who proposed it, however, instruction can hardly have been thought to create an unbending obligation to vote legislatively as constituents dictated—save perhaps for local governmental matters. This appears pretty clearly in the congressional debate of 1789 on adding a right of instruction to that of assembly/petition in the Bill of Rights. Representative Thomas Tucker of South Carolina proposed it, and debate on some fundamentals of the theory of representation ensued.[18] Those opposing the addition of instruction tended to emphasize its constraints; those defending it found it less confining and more of an abstract right. Thomas Hartley of Pennsylvania, taking basically a Burkean view, thus argued:

> Representation is the principle of our Government; the people ought to have confidence in the honor and integrity of those they send forward to transact their business; their right to instruct them is a problematical subject. We have seen it attended with bad consequences both in England and America. When the passions of the people are excited, instructions have been resorted to and obtained, to answer party purposes; and although the public opinion is generally respectable, yet at such moments it has been known to be often wrong; and happy is the Government composed of men of firmness and wisdom to discover, and resist popular error.
>
> ... It appears to my mind that the principle of representation is distinct from an agency, which may require written instructions. The great end of meeting is to consult for the common good; but can the common good be discerned without the object is reflected and shown in every light[?] A local or partial view does not necessarily enable any man to comprehend it clearly; this can only result from an inspection into the aggregate. Instructions viewed in this light will be found to embarrass the best and wisest men. And were all the members to take their seats in order to obey instructions, and those instructions were as various as is probable they would be, what possibility would ... exist of so accommodating each to the other as to produce any act whatever? Perhaps a majority of the whole might not be instructed to agree to any one point, and is it thus the people of the United States propose to form a more perfect union, provide for the common defense, and promote the general welfare?[19]

James Madison, also opposing the amendment, argued that free speech and assembly were adequate to secure the people's right to advise their legislators, unless instruction meant "that the people have a right to instruct their representatives in such a sense that the delegate is obliged to conform to those instructions. ... Suppose they instruct a representative, by his vote, to violate the constitution; is he at liberty to obey such instructions?"[20] Michael Stone of Maryland added:

> I think the clause would change the Government entirely; instead of being a Government founded on representation, it would be a democracy of singular properties. I differ from the gentleman from Virginia (Mr. Madison) if he thinks this clause would not bind the representative; in my opinion, it would bind him effectually, and I venture to assert, without diffidence, that any law passed by the Legislature would be of no force, if a majority of the members of this House were instructed to the contrary, provided the amendment became part of the constitution.[21]

On the other hand, Elbridge Gerry of Massachusetts, a prominent Anti-Federalist and probably the chief congressional proponent of instruction, did not consider it so strictly controlling in practical prospect, whatever its theoretical potentiality:

> It has been said that the amendment . . . determines this point, "that the people can bind their representatives to follow their instructions." I do not conceive that this necessarily follows. I think the representative, notwithstanding the insertion of these words [in the proposed constitutional amendment], would be at liberty to act as he pleased; if he declined to pursue such measures as he was directed to attain, the people would have a right to refuse him their suffrages at a future election.
>
> Now, though I do not believe the amendment would bind the representatives . . . yet I think the people have a right both to instruct and to bind them. Do gentlemen conceive that on any occasion instructions would be so general as to proceed from all our constituents? If they do, it is the sovereign will; for gentlemen will not contend that the sovereign will presides in the Legislature . . . [T]o say the sovereignty vests in the people, and that they have not a right to instruct and control their representatives, is absurd. . . . But the amendment does not carry the principle to such an extent, it only declares the right of the people to send instructions; the representative will, if he thinks proper, communicate his instructions to the House, but how far they shall operate on his conduct he will judge for himself.[22]

Behind the debate about a theory of representation—about representatives' discretion versus popular sovereignty—lay an issue of practicality, or so the arguments on both sides seem to suggest. Normally, or at least frequently, constituent opinion would not come close enough to unanimity to render instructions strongly legitimate, and there would thus be room, not to say need, for legislative judgment. In these terms, the arguments seem further to suggest, the issue was largely one of expectations or aspirations regarding the degree of popular involvement in policy-making. Those on the populist side appear to have wanted to encourage popular engagement in policy-making, or interposition in opposition to policy, perhaps assuming a condition of (at least local) community or unanimity that would justify such interposition. Those on the other side believed that constituent divisions—within or between localities—would simply be transferred by instruction to the legislature, setting it at loggerheads and endangering social agreement and the common good.

Neither side—and certainly not the populist or antifederal side— suggested that organized disobedience and resistance should be regarded as a right to be exercised in cases of disagreement over policy by those who had not prevailed in the processes of election, petition, representation, and legislation. It does not appear that the constitutional guarantees of the right to assemble, petition, and (in a few states) instruct representatives afford more than minute support for organized protest and resistance. On the whole they appear to point the other way. Historically, petition was largely an alternative to forcible resistance and was a form of participation in governing, most notably in matters of something like constitutional significance in the English context of primitive electoral-representative institutions. The debate about "instruction," both in Britain and America, looked to the improvement of electoral-representative institutions and the ordering of popular participation in policy-making, not protest and resistance. In modern perspective, instruction may be seen as a supplement to electoral-representative institutions—as facilitating and intensifying popular demands for governmental action and as portending the later "initiative" and other forms of direct legislation. Instruction, however, did not make it into the federal Constitution; nor do we know that it had become anything like common practice (whatever the contingent provision for it) in the states at the end of the founding period or even later.

As for the constitutional rights of assembly and petition, they were simply intrinsic to representative government. So conceived, it can even be argued that their constitutional guarantee was anachronistic or otiose or both. Joseph Story, opining that the assembly/petition clause was probably borrowed from the English Declaration of Rights of 1688, wrote,

"This would seem unnecessary to be expressly provided for in a republican government, since it results from the very nature of its structure and institutions."[23] In this light the provision may largely reflect the inertial persistence of prerevolutionary views of politics based primarily on earlier English republicanism and English constitutional arguments.

However that may be, speech and press, assembly and petition were seen together as central political rights, essential to republican or representative government. They appear to have been as nearly a pair of rights as a group of four: speech and press were connected essentially or functionally, as were assembly and petition; each pair was coupled regularly in eighteenth-century American political discourse, as they were in James Madison's presentation of constitutional amendments to the First Congress, and the commas connecting them were regular eighteenth-century American usage. In thinking about representative government and popular sovereignty, some Americans, reflecting perhaps a commonwealth-republican tradition, leaned more or less sharply toward a populist view, favoring as direct a democracy as possible through opportunity for instruction of representatives. Others opposed instruction, no less for practical and liberal than for "elitist" reasons.

The founding aspiration and expectation, then, was that public policy and statute law would reflect public opinion and participation. Back of this view stood the revolutionary doctrine that in conditions of tyranny and oppression, and failing "redress" through patient recourse to the traditional procedures of representation, the people might alter their regime of governance. Petition and assembly afforded means of changing policy. The community right of revolution or reconstitution afforded means in extremis of altering the institutional conditions of policy; but, critically, this was a *community* right to be exercised by majority rule.[24] Nothing in the American constitutions or, so far as we know, in their surrounding expectations provided rights of resistance to particular policies in response to private judgment. Government was subject to election, petition, and in the last resort to reconstitution. It was not to be subject to incapacitation and could not be so as an instrument of liberty, security, and justice. The people, moreover, had obligations as well as rights; popular government and membership of the public entailed responsibilities on everyone. There was an operative, applicable tradition of thought on this point as well.

The deep concern during the founding period to enlarge the scope of personal freedom or liberty went hand in hand with a determination, perhaps equally pervasive and energetic, to establish in every community

a regime of social discipline. This discipline was considered public, in a
sense, but not primarily governmental in provenance or provision; it was
rather more a supporting condition of responsible republican government.
The determination to establish (or reestablish) it had roots not only in the
republican tradition reaching back to the English civil war but also (and
closely related historically) in the preaching of the churches, especially
those of the Puritan tradition.

In 1750 Jonathan Mayhew, a towering figure in the clerical and intellectual life of Boston, concluded a sermon later celebrated as a challenge to
absolute political authority:

> [L]et us all learn to be *free* and to be *loyal*. . . . Let us prize our
> freedom; but not *use our liberty for a cloak of maliciousness*. . . . There
> are men who strike at *liberty* under the term *licentiousness*. There are
> others who aim at popularity under the disguise of *patriotism*. Beware
> of both. *Extremes* are dangerous. There is at present amongst *us*,
> perhaps, more danger of the *latter*, than of the *former*. For which
> reason I would exhort you to pay all due Regard to the government
> over us; to the KING and all in authority; and to *lead a quiet and
> peaceable life.*[25]

As annoyances with British rule swelled into anger and despair of contri-
tion in London, the Bible was searched and interpreted further for proof
that the power magistrates derive from God is a power only to do good—that
when the consequences of their acts are evil and an abuse of their
authority, the conscientious and thoughtful citizen discovers first a right
and then a duty to disobey.[26] Movement in the direction of independence
infused the justification of disobedience with obligation to overthrow
tyrants.

Stress on the right to resist and rebel had not yet run its full course
when the foundations of republican government were firmly laid, but the
transition from combat to peace and the return of fathers and brothers to
their homes were paralleled by revision of the prevailing doctrine on
reconciling the authority to rule and the right to oppose abuse of power.
By the end of the 1780s virtually all the polemical writings, constitutional
pronouncements, and interpretations of events by those positioned to
exert influence and make decisions testify to the inauguration of a regime
in which a wide range of individual autonomy and freedom of choice
would be presumed, but also a regime in which prevailing community
opinion, rules adopted by majority approval, and decisions of courts and

other authorized officials would combine to assure tranquility, justice, and continuing productivity for Americans.

The conceptions of an exemplary or "true" civil liberty that attained currency while the character of republican government was being shaped were remarkably convergent—remarkably so considering that variance in presumptions about the placement of public authority to act with all the sanctions of law and disagreement about the appropriate scope of governmental authority and desirable limitations on it persisted without prospect of resolution. As for the location of authority, the divergent perspectives of New Englanders focusing on the town, with its decisions by majority vote in town meetings, and of southerners accustomed to substantial control of affairs, even of local officials, from the statehouse was one salient difference among a number—including differences over the role of the new national government in the new federal system. Disagreements about the role of government in general and how to fix its limits probably had a greater influence on the development of doctrine about personal freedom. Here the convictions of men and women largely unnoticed in the annals of history would have carried more weight. Judgments about how family, church, community, and state should share in the socialization, motivation, and education of children—or about how freedom of choice and personal autonomy might be balanced with community standards and social discipline—may well have tended to distinguish Roman Catholic, Mennonite, Puritan, and Jew; or urban dweller, plantation owner, and frontier settler; or those of wealth and cultivated tastes from those who ate at the price of toil and exhaustion.

Common sense suggests that the heirs of the Revolution would arrive at a common position regarding guarantees of free choice and personal autonomy only if they omitted mention of the harshest dilemmas of reconciling liberty with law and order, only if those who proposed terms for such a resolution limited their propositions and exhortations to generalities and indefinite precepts. We can observe this method in the following excerpts of addresses, taken from the second decade of the American Republic, when republican institutions had settled in somewhat but while the controversy over the Alien and Sedition Laws discussed in the preceding chapter was acute. In that controversy, the contingent tensions between liberty and law were often pressed to their limits and to the point of dilemma. The arguments of these by and large conservative thinkers in Federalist territory follow that course but at a high level of generality. They do so to emphasize the perception that civil liberty depends in the last analysis on public order, as responsive law depends on civil liberty, and that both in the end depend on a widely distributed sense of responsibility, social obligation, or civic virtue, on the practice of which they sought consensus.[27]

Israel B. Woodward (Watertown, Connecticut, 1798)

We boast not that every American is *free*—meaning that every villain in America is suffered to act out whatever his wicked heart suggests—This would be to glory in our own shame. Nor do we boast of being a *free people,* when dependent on a *tyrant's will:* This would be glorying in *imaginary freedom.* But when all the principal officers in government are filled by the suffrages of the people,—when law restrains injustice, and encourages virtue and industry,—when learning, and every useful art and science are promoted;—when every man may enjoy all that peace, liberty, and property, which is his just and unalienable right,—when men may serve God according to the dictates of their own conscience, provided they disturb not the public tranquility—Then are a people possessed of all that *liberty,* which the nature of man, and the conditions of this world can well admit; and considering the imperfection of both, perhaps the government of these American States, approaches as near to the zenith of *real liberty,* as it is possible it should.

Noah Webster (New Haven, Connecticut, 1802)

. . . [P]olitical axioms, if not mere empty words, must have reference to a social state. How then, can men, exposed to each others power, and wanting each others aid, be *free* and *independent?* If one member of a society is free and independent, all the members must be equally so. In such a community, no restraint could exist, for this would destroy freedom and independence. But in such a state of things, the will of each individual would be his only rule of action, and his *will* would be supported by his *strength.* Force then would be the ultimate arbiter of right and wrong, and the wills of the weaker must bend to the power of the stronger. . . . Civil liberty, therefore, instead of being derived from *natural freedom and independence,* is the creature of society and government. Man is too feeble to protect himself, and unless he can protect himself, he is not free. But to secure protection, man must submit to the restraints of a sovereign power; subordination, therefore, is the very essence of civil liberty. Yet how often has the abstract, undefined proposition that "all men are by nature free and independent," furnished the motive or the apology for insurrection!

Jeremiah Atwater (Middlebury, Vermont, 1802)

Liberty is a sound dear to all of us; But what do we understand by it? . . . Self-government, as commanded by Christianity, is viewed [by some] as a counter-action of natural freedom, and civil government as an intrusion on natural rights, equally odious. It is [for such persons] the perfection of Rousseau's ordered system, entitled the Social Contract, that "every person while united with all shall obey only himself, and remain as free, as before the union." Such a liberty as this must be pronounced, in the highest degree, detrimental to the interests of mankind. It reduces man back to the very state of barbarism from which government is supposed to have redeemed him. Liberty, if considered as a blessing, must be taken in a qualified sense. The freedom which it implies, must be a limited, not absolute freedom; unless we will pronounce government itself a curse; for the very idea of government always supposes some restraint. But to this restraint the perversity of man's nature has ever been opposed, and vicious men have ever been most loud in favor of unbounded liberty; because such a liberty is no other than the liberty of sinning, the liberty of indulging lawless passion, and of invading a neighbor's rights. It would arm the idle and profligate against the virtuous and industrious, and instead of a rational liberty, would be seen and felt to be the worst of tyrannies; no better than a state of nature, and destitute of the least security for life or property.

Joseph McKeen (Boston, Massachusetts, 1800)

. . . Liberty, like the pleasures of sense, must be enjoyed with temperance and moderation, lest degenerating into licentiousness, it prove destructive. There are none, it may be presumed, who will openly avow that political liberty is, or ought to be, a license for every one to do what is right in his own eyes; yet where the love of liberty is strong, and its nature not distinctly understood, there is too often a disposition to look with an indulgent eye on licentiousness, as only the extreme of a good thing, and therefore pardonable. But the difference between them is greater than some imagine: They are indeed so different, as to be incompatible in society. When one has an excess of liberty, he invades the rights of his neighbor, who is thereby deprived of a portion of the liberty which a free constitution

promises him. Liberty in that case becomes exclusively the possession of the strong, the unprincipled, and the artful, who makes a
prey of the innocent, weak, and unsuspicious. A state of things like
this is a real despotism, and of the worst kind. . . .

To some, who do not distinguish between social and personal
freedom, it may still seem a paradox that restraint should be necessary to the being of liberty. In their view a free government and a
weak government mean the same thing. But scarce any mathematical truth admits of a more conclusive demonstration than this, that
laws wisely framed, impartially administered, and faithfully executed,
are essential to the liberty of a community. Liberty cannot be long
enjoyed under a government that has not sufficient energy to be a
terror to evildoers. The law is not made for the righteous, it is not
made to restrain the honest, peaceable, sober, and industrious members of society, who are a law unto themselves; but it is made for the
lawless and disobedient, murderers, men-stealers, liars, purjured
persons, and others who can be restrained only by the strong arm of
power. That love of liberty, therefore, which prompts men to resist
the laws, and to overturn or weaken the government established for
the common good, is a spurious passion which every well-informed
friend to real liberty will feel himself in duty bound to discountenance.
It is not less necessary that we should understand and practice our
duties, than that we should understand and assert our rights. The
prevalence of sound virtue therefore would afford the best security
to our liberty.

Notes

1. Francis Newton Thorpe, ed., *The Federal and State Constitutions, Colonial Charters, and Other Organic Laws of the States, Territories, and Colonies Now or Heretofore Forming the United States of America*, vol. 4 (Washington, D.C.: Government Printing Office, 1909), p. 2487.

2. Herbert J. Storing, ed., *The Complete Anti-Federalist*, vol. 5 (Chicago: University of Chicago Press, 1981), p. 98.

3. Thorpe, *Federal and State Constitutions*, vol. 7, p. 3813.

4. John Adams, *Novanglus*, nos. 4–6, in *The Works of John Adams*, vol. 4, ed. Charles Francis Adams (Boston: Little, Brown, 1851), esp. pp. 60, 99.

5. Garry Wills, *Inventing America: Jefferson's Declaration of Independence* (1978; New York: Random House Vintage Books, 1979), chap. 4. On English

petitioning in the pre-Restoration seventeenth century, see Derek Hirst, *Authority and Conflict: England 1603–1658* (Cambridge, Mass.: Harvard University Press, 1986), esp. chaps. 8–9. For more than a century after the Restoration, petitioning was restricted by the legislation of 1661 and later parliamentary attitudes, until its revival beginning with the Wilkes controversies. The Act against Tumultuous Petitioning of 1661 is in Carl Stephenson and F. G. Marcham, eds., *Sources of English Constitutional History* (New York: Harper and Brothers, 1937), p. 540 (but compare the unqualified references to petition in the Bill of Rights of 1689, in Stephenson and Marcham, *Sources of English Constitutional History*, pp. 599ff.); for the later period, see Peter Fraser, "Public Petitioning and Parliament before 1832," *History* 46 (1961): 195–211. See also the "Statement of Violations of Rights" and the "Petition to the King" of the Continental Congress, *Journals of the Continental Congress* 1 (1774): 63, 115; the former is also in H. S. Commager, ed., *Documents of American History*, 9th ed. (Englewood Cliffs, N.J.: Prentice-Hall, 1973), p. 82.

6. The relevant declarations of the Continental Congress are in Commager, *Documents*, nos. 61, 62.

7. In point is the familiar story told by John Adams: "I met a Man who had sometimes been my Client. . . . He, though a common Horse Jockey, was sometimes in the right, and I had commonly been successfull in his favour in our Courts of Law. He was always in the Law. . . . As soon as he saw me, he came up to me, and his first Salutation to me was 'Oh! Mr. Adams what great Things have you and your Colleagues done for us! We can never be gratefull enough to you. There are no Courts of Justice now in this Province, and I hope there will never be another!' . . . Is this the Object for which I have been contending? Are these the sentiments of such people? . . . Surely we must guard against this spirit and these Principles or we shall repent of all our Conduct. However, the good Sense and Integrity of the Majority of the great Body of the People, came into my thoughts for my relief, and the last resort was after all in a good Providence." *The Adams Papers: Diary and Autobiography of John Adams*, vol. 3, ed. L. H. Butterfield (Cambridge, Mass.: Harvard University Press, 1961), p. 326.

8. The language originally proposed was, "The freedom of speech and of the press, and the right of the people peaceably to assemble and consult for their common good, and to petition the Government for redress of grievances, shall not be infringed." *Annals of Congress* 1 (1789–90): 759.

9. Compare the language of the Declaration by the Continental Congress, 14 October 1774: "That they have a right peaceably to assemble, consider their grievances, and petition the King. . . ." Commager, *Documents*, p. 83. There is no more discussion of the assembly/petition provision per se reported in the *Annals of Congress* than there is for the speech/press provision of what became the First Amendment—that is, essentially none. (There was only a

little more, and that ambiguous, on the establishment and free-exercise clauses.) The bulk of the debate on the several provisions that became the First Amendment had to do with proposals to add a right to instruct representatives.

10. Clinton Rossiter, *Seedtime of the Republic* (New York: Harcourt, Brace, 1953), p. 386 (emphasis added). Rossiter commented, "The rights of assembly and petition [linked closely, he notes, with those of free speech and press as distinctly political rights] were especially important for the conduct of representative government. These ancient liberties existed primarily for the health of the community rather than for the happiness of the individual."

11. Consider the following specimens from the debates in the states on ratification of the federal constitution, from Storing, *The Complete Anti-Federalist*, vol. 2, p. 262, vol. 5, p. 98 (emphasis added to both). From a listing of "unalienable rights" in the then widely read "Letters from the Federal Farmer" (1787): "The people have a right to assemble *in an orderly manner,* and petition the government for a redress of wrongs." From the amendments proposed by the minority of the Maryland convention: "That every man hath a right to petition the legislature for the redress of grievances *in a peaceable and orderly manner.*" On the then common law of nonpeaceable "unlawful assembly," see, e.g., Glenn Abernathy, *The Right of Assembly and Association* (Columbia: University of South Carolina Press, 1961), chap. 3.

12. J. R. Pole, *Political Representation in England and the Origins of the American Republic* (London: Macmillan, 1966), pp. 70–73. In the Massachusetts Constitution, senators, elected from larger districts, were not subject to instruction. Ibid., p. 231.

13. Ibid., p. 255, reports some resort to instruction in Pennsylvania, beginning in 1763, in the hard contest between the Quaker and Proprietary parties, and on legislative initiative, adding: "The form employed was that of seeking instructions; but of course what was really happening was that the members were going back to inform, in effect to instruct, their electors. Good Old Whig theory was not without its practical applications." Pole also reports at least a little, but apparently not much, use of instruction in late colonial Virginia. Ibid, pp. 162–63.

14. Derek Hirst, *The Representatives of the People?* (Cambridge: Cambridge University Press, 1975), esp. pp. 161–66, 182–85.

15. C. S. Emden, *The People and the Constitution,* 2d ed. (Oxford: Oxford University Press, 1956), chaps. 2–3; and, to the contrary, Edmund Burke's Address to the Electors of Bristol, *The Works of Edmund Burke,* vol. 2 (Oxford: Oxford University Press, 1930), pp. 159–66.

16. Elisha P. Douglass, *Rebels and Democrats* (Chapel Hill: University of North Carolina Press, 1955), chaps. 6–8, 13–14; Pole, *Political Representation,* pt. 3, sec. 2.

17. See, e.g., Emden, *The People and the Constitution.*

18. *Annals of Congress* 1 (1789): 760–77. For excerpts from a congressional debate in 1817 on the doctrine of instruction, see Charles S. Hyneman and George S. Carey, eds., *A Second Federalist* (New York: Appleton-Century-Crofts, 1967), pp. 239ff.

19. *Annals of Congress* 1 (1789–90): 761–62.

20. Ibid., p. 766.

21. Ibid., p. 767.

22. Ibid., p. 765.

23. Joseph Story, *Commentaries on the Constitution of the United States*, vol. 3 (Boston: Hilliard, Gray, 1833), pp. 745–46.

24. Ronald M. Peters, Jr., *The Massachusetts Constitution of 1780: A Social Compact* (Amherst: University of Massachusetts Press, 1978), p. 108 and chap. 3 generally.

25. Jonathan Mayhew, *A Discourse concerning the Unlimited Submission and Non-resistance to the Higher Powers*, reprinted in Jonathan Mayhew, *Sermons* (New York: Arno Press and the New York Times, 1969), quotation from p. 48 of *Discourse*.

26. Thus Mayhew in 1750 had in the Puritan tradition construed the argument of Romans 13 "to conclude only in favor of submission *to such rulers as he himself describes;* i.e., such as rule for the good of society, which is the only end of their institution. Common tyrants, and public oppressors, are not entitled to obedience from their subjects, by virtue of anything here laid down by the inspired apostle." Ibid., p. 28. See generally Richard B. Morris, *The American Revolution Reconsidered* (New York: Harper and Row, 1967), chap. 4; and Alan Heimert, *Religion and the American Mind* (Cambridge, Mass.: Harvard University Press, 1966), chap. 5.

27. Israel B. Woodward, *American Liberty and Independence: A Discourse* (Watertown, Conn.: Printed by T. Collier, 1798), p. 10; Joseph McKeen, *A Sermon* (Massachusetts Election Day) (Boston: Printed by Young and Minns, 1800), pp. 11–13. The statements of Webster and Atwater appear in fuller form in Charles S. Hyneman and Donald S. Lutz, eds., *American Political Writing during the Founding Era, 1760–1805*, vol. 2 (Indianapolis: Liberty Press, 1983), pp. 1228–29, 1172.

9

The Preserver of Liberty: Virtue

THE PREVALENCE OF SOUND VIRTUE would afford the best security to our liberty, said the Reverend Joseph McKeen, addressing the Massachusetts General Court and other newly elected officials in 1800. By then the prevalence of virtue had for a quarter-century and more been the sine qua non for realizing most ideals and goals associated with republican government in the minds of most of those who took to pulpit, platform, or pamphlet on behalf of independence and stable nationhood.

As the new nation moved into the nineteenth century, however, the attainment of virtue as a goal for national endeavor was evidently losing its hold on the American people and those who admonished them. Commitments to republican equality and liberty could survive and flourish as central attributes of independence that made minimal demands on citizens once independence was won. Virtue in the abstract and as the antonym of vice no doubt had similar survival value, but virtue as the republican companion of equality and liberty stood for self-discipline and civic obligation, to some extent instead of social hierarchy and public authority. Moreover, appeals for the development of particular attitudes, qualities, and habits thought to be prerequisites for self-government and a productive society must have prompted premonitions of sacrifice and self-regeneration.

In the religious traditions of the colonial period—especially in the Puritan persuasion—the enduring contest between good and evil and the inconsistencies and inconstancies of the human being in manifesting preferences for one over the other was a central theme of theology and political theory. In both respects the discourse on the choice between good and evil that Americans steadily heard and read emphasized the reciprocal obligations of rulers and subjects: the obligation of rulers to protect and promote the community's well-being and to direct its members into paths of righteousness and reverence; and the obligation of subjects to obey rulers, cultivate rectitude, and worship God. "There is nothing more certain than this," said the Reverend Joseph Baxter in his sermon before the newly elected officials of Massachusetts in 1727, "that the most serious, godly Christians, are the best subjects upon the earth." Those who are in authority over a people ought therefore to improve all the opportunities and advantages they have "to promote Peace and Godliness, and Honesty, among their People." One way of doing this was "by taking care that suitable Persons be employed in Preaching the gospel. . . ."[1]

It would be incorrect to suppose that relations between the people and their governors were a principal preoccupation of the ministry in early America. Moreover, as we shall see, there were other sources and agents of emphasis on virtue in the founding period. Nevertheless, from the initial settlements until the end of the eighteenth century, it was the voice from the pulpit that bore the primary burden of instruction on the indispensability of attitudes, practices, and expectations identified as public virtue. So long as the clergy could profess approval of policies fixed in London and acts of officials performed in colonial capitols, the duty of subjects to comply with the law and respect established authority supplied the theme for occasional sermons. As discontent sharpened into specification of grievances, emphasis shifted to biblical injunctions that rulers are empowered only to do good and to a logical corollary that when protest proves ineffective, subjects may resist commands and thwart the will of governors who abuse their authority.[2] The leap from presumptions of colonial subordination to a resolve to institute regimes of effective popular control, witnessed by the state constitutions promulgated in 1776 or soon thereafter, forced even more striking turns in emphasis. Subject and ruler were then united in the same person; personal and public virtue were then merged; and a regime of virtue came to seem essential.

The Origins and Emergence of Virtue in American Politics

There is a sense in which the history of virtue cannot be written—in which references to virtue in general or to particular virtues simply express the singular moral or characterological priorities of, say, late eighteenth-century American elites with respect to particular concerns—say, self-government and citizenship. In late eighteenth-century America the term *virtue* was also occasionally used to imply moral goodness in general, whatever *that* might mean in the circumstances. The circumstances, however, usually took *their* meanings and implications from moral traditions. Most of the rhetorical and analytic understandings of virtue(s) that figured so largely in the founding period thus referred at least implicitly to given traditions—whether or not these traditions were still vigorous and behaviorally pervasive. In this sense the understandings reflected various traditional ideals, some of them evidencing and extending more general perspectives on self-government and citizenship, even if the reflections were somewhat eclectic.

The reasons for supposing that certain traditional conceptions of virtue, as applied to both public life and politically relevant private endeavor, were figuring in the political discourse of the founding period appear in the terms of the traditions themselves, in what we know about the place of their literatures in the education of American leadership, in what has lately been learned about the American reception of English "republican" doctrine in advance of the Revolution, and in some evident affinities of the pertinent traditions with certain trends of eighteenth-century American religious doctrine, especially in Puritan New England. The history of these traditions cannot be rehearsed appropriately here, but its principal connections with the virtue(s) of the founding period can be indicated, and some conclusions can be drawn about the founding implications of virtue for self-government and citizenship.[3]

To begin with, there is an emphasis on certain virtues, as aspects of character, in classical Athenian ethical theory—in Socrates, Plato, and (most influential of all) Aristotle. For all of these philosophers, wisdom, especially self-knowledge, was central; for Aristotle, the other virtues were largely products of practical wisdom (or prudence) as well. Prominent among the other virtues were justice, courage, and temperance. These four, rendered synoptically as wisdom or prudence, justice, fortitude or courage, and temperance, became, classically, the "cardinal" virtues as codified by Cicero and adopted later in Christian philosophy by Ambrose and Aquinas.[4] For our purposes, moreover, it is significant that *moderation* (and its implication of self-control) was implicitly a virtue for Aristotle, since virtues were identified as means between vices of excess and deficiency. It was not the case, of course, that any of the cardinal (or other) virtues sustained precisely the same meaning as Aristotle's into, say, the sixteenth century; and all serious considerations elaborated on the rubrical cardinal terms at length. There was variation, but there was also similarity enough to make a tradition comprehending the naturalistic analysis, characterological focus, emphasis on self-knowledge and self-control, and a substantial concurrence on the cardinal terms of virtue.[5]

By the sixteenth century in Italy, however—and especially for our purposes by the mid-seventeenth century in England—a distinct, "republican" strand of the tradition is discernible. It emphasizes civic or public virtue, in which citizens put the public welfare or interest ahead of personal welfare or interest, and in which love of country or of the political community is sometimes a central element. Certainly civic virtue was a prominent concern in Plato's *Apology* and *Republic* and Aristotle's *Politics*. The distinctly *republican* tradition or subtradition in its most familiar formulations is, however, best traced from Cicero's identification of a republic or commonwealth as "an affair [the property] of the people [*res publica res populi*]" and of *a people* as reflecting "an agreement with respect to justice and a partnership for the common good," together with the (Aristotelian) view that "faction [*factionis*]" corrupts and voids the commonwealth or republic—that, in the Polybian cycle of regimes, factionalism or loss of commonality is the defining or effective element.[6] As with the cardinal (private) virtues, Cicero's civic virtue is anchored in Aristotle: "for the first cause of such an association [of 'a people'] is not so much the weakness of the individual as a certain social spirit which nature has implanted in man."[7] In all this, as in Aristotle, the ultimate "republican" notion of civic virtue—regard for the public good, including readiness to bear the burdens of governing—is implicit only, not yet quite explicit (though nearly so), and the virtue of the citizen includes various of the "private virtues" as well. After all, "justice" and regard for the public good are close kin, and other attributes of civic responsibility are close to the cardinal virtues. The need for such virtue in those vested with governing powers is explicit enough though; and in general, Cicero provided the Latin vocabulary and the locus classicus of the republican civic-virtue subtradition.[8]

The sixteenth-century Italian city-state renascence of this tradition often lacked its Aristotelian elements; the conceptions of civic virtue were commonly more Spartan and martial than Athenian.[9] It emphasized especially the classical conception of degenerating regimes, of alternating civic virtue and factional corruption. Its reception in seventeenth-century England was not the only route by which classical republicanism arrived there, but it does appear to have contributed a particular emphasis on republican instability and corruption, and thus on the essentiality of public virtue.[10]

In seventeenth-century England Puritanism and republicanism came together consequentially for American ideology a century later, but not particularly for American doctrines in the era of seventeenth-century settlement. English republicanism, as it emerged by the mid-seventeenth century (e.g., in the writings of John Milton or James Harrington) and evolved into eighteenth-century radical Whiggism, was cast largely in the idiom of classical republicanism, often admixed with a "Gothic" myth of Norman expropriation and corruption of Anglo-Saxon equality, community, and simplicity. To the Puritans who established their own societies and polities in New England, preoccupied with love of God, grace, and salvation, the natural virtues were for the most part secondary concerns, save for their roots in self-discipline and their contribution to the covenanted common life and welfare, especially in conditions of scarcity. Indeed, for seventeenth-century Puritans in both England and New England, biblical virtues (humility, simplicity) and utilitarian virtues (diligence and thrift, industry and frugality) effectively rivaled the cardinal virtues, if not the theological virtues; and in England these tended to become republican virtues or values as well.[11] Moreover, Puritanism did endorse the Aristotelian understandings that man was made for society and polity in this world, and that, notwithstanding the stern demands of individual responsibility, governments (and citizens) are charged to give the common good priority.

How, then, from this seventeenth-century setting did a concern with virtue in more worldly terms, including the civic virtue of republicanism and the plural virtues of personal morality, come to figure so prominently in the political discourse of the founding period in America? There is, of course, a familiar argument to the effect that the early American perspectives on certain fundamentals of politics were pretty much defined with reference to late-Tudor, early-Stuart England.[12] The etiology of the late eighteenth-century emphasis on virtue is more complex than this, however. Several historical trajectories seem to have been implicated.

In one of these the Puritan pulpit became the principal locus of concern with the citizenry's virtue(s) in largely traditional terms over the course of a generation or more before the founding period. By the turn of the eighteenth century New England Puritanism was altering both theologically and homiletically in response to a complex of factors, including the altered ecclesiastical circumstances of settlement instanced in its own "half-way covenant," which in 1662 relaxed the original restriction of church (i.e., community) membership to "saints" and their scions; the later

British Act of Toleration (1689); and (probably) some routinization of the faith through the successive generations and changing material conditions of settlement, in which prosperity and economic preoccupations gained ground on the spiritual community. In Perry Miller's magisterial description, election sermons in the early eighteenth century, now enjoined to denominational neutrality by British law, turned to "keynoting," "ancient platitudes," and adjurations to "piety and morality." The common welfare that was the end of government increasingly came to comprehend material as well as spiritual welfare; and religion, no longer authorized to judge government in sectarian terms, increasingly justified itself as conducing to practical piety and social order.[13] Industry, frugality, simplicity, and prudence, as products of self-discipline, and piety as a more outward and inclusive version of grace became prominent homiletic virtues, at least in New England. While in one familiar interpretation Puritanism (in particular within Protestantism in general) encouraged capitalism and individual acquisitiveness, the "economic virtues" of Puritanism might equally have referred to service, self-control, and social welfare.[14]

Puritanism was not, to be sure, monolithic in its eighteenth-century declension; in the "new light" theology of the Great Awakening virtue either was subordinate and inferior to more transcendental concerns or, as in Jonathan Edwards's "true virtue," was instinct in such concerns—in love of God or holiness, as distinct from a more strictly dutiful piety.[15] Still, the progress of "old light" Puritanism in New England may help explain the constitutionally sanctioned place of certain virtues (e.g., industry and frugality) in the American founding—though these particular terms turn up as well in earlier Italian and English republicanism, not to mention Montesquieu.[16] The naturalistic "Scottish Enlightenment" school of moral philosophy also supported attention to particular social virtues as well as to a general benevolence; it was figuring in American higher education by the mid-eighteenth century, and its influence among the American ministry was probably strongest in the Calvinist tradition from which the Scottish school partially sprang.[17] There was evidently more to the development of founding virtue(s) than the evolution of Calvinism, and more than preaching as well, though clearly the pulpit was the signal support of the late eighteenth-century emphasis on virtue in American political discourse.

If we look to what American preachers and political leaders of the founding period learned and read—to their college curricula and general reading—we are likely to find the further sources of their attention to virtue. Clearly, classical literature, especially in Latin, was a source for both particular virtues and regard for a diffuse or generic virtue. The latter usage also figured prominently in English on both sides of the Atlantic pretty much throughout the eighteenth century. Some pertinent illustrations for us appear in *Cato's Letters* (serialized in 1720–23, widely read, and highly regarded in America for the next fifty years or more).[18] There the (private) virtue deemed so dependent on "free government" is equated with moral goodness, though there are also references to certain virtues (e.g., industry, frugality), and to vices that flourish in unfree regimes. "Publick Spirit," on the other hand, exists (classically) in all regimes—vicious in the unfree, virtuous in the free—as a conditioning influence:

> In arbitrary Countries it is Publick Spirit to be blind Slaves to the blind will of the Prince ... but in Protestant free Countries Publick Spirit is another Thing: it is to combat Force and Delusion; it is to reconcile the true Interests of the Governed and Governors; it is to expose Imposters, and to resist Oppressors; it is to maintain the People in Liberty, Plenty, Ease, and Security. ... [I]t is the highest Virtue, and contains in it almost all others. ... It is a Passion to promote universal Good, with personal Pain, Loss, and Peril: It is one Man's care for Many, and the Concern of every Man for All.[19]

Finally, in political theory—republican political theory in particular— Montesquieu's *Spirit of the Laws* (1748; first English translation 1750) probably was as influential for the founding period as any other book, bar none.[20] Among its apparently classical affinities, its emphasis on civic (or public) virtue seemed central:

> It is in a republican government that the whole power of education is required. The fear of despotic governments rises naturally of itself amidst threats and punishments; the honor of monarchies is favoured by the passions, and favours them in its turn: but virtue is a self-renunciation which is always arduous and painful.
>
> This virtue may be defined, as the love of the laws and of our country. As this love requires a constant preference of public to private interest, it is the source of all the particular virtues; for they are nothing more than this preference itself.[21]

Of the particular virtues, prudence, moderation, industry, and frugality got Montesquieu's most explicit attention, especially with respect to republics, of which *democratic* republics were desirably small, unaffluent, simple, and homogeneous.[22] Montesquieu could also be read as the advocate of a more Lockean, liberal, extensive, heterogeneous, commercial society subject to the "mixed" government that was his celebrated separation of powers. In this reading the contributions of virtue and the particular virtues (save perhaps for moderation) might well have seemed less essential, though we know little about how Montesquieu's studied obscurities were understood at the time.[23]

The import of this history is that a long and diverse tradition was available to those most concerned with virtue in the founding period. In some versions it remained classical and naturalistic at its core. In others, even if apparently classical, it probably owed more to a modern impetus toward mastery over nature and a sense of some malleability of human culture (as in Locke and Montesquieu). In still other versions its inspiration was divine. Advocacy of virtue might be premised on either benevolent or selfish interpretations of human nature. Virtue might (and usually did) imply commonality or community, but in certain versions it might be held to flourish in diversity. Similarly, virtue might be (and usually was) advanced in radical republican fashion as a popular necessity for free self-government, but there remained a more classical, aristocratic strand of tradition stressing statesmanship and leadership. Virtue might be considered as intrinsic—even, as it was classically, the end of government—or as largely instrumental: a central condition of free government and perhaps economic development.[24]

Virtue might mean moral goodness in general, its basis ranging from naturalistic to utilitarian to voluntaristic to transcendental.[25] It might refer to specific private virtues (or amount to the sum of these, perhaps plus some penumbra). It might point to *public* virtue, and it might in the same republican vein attach "public" significance to certain virtues deemed private in other connections.

It is far from clear that any certain conception prevailed in the founding period. The Puritan legacy in New England and the Anglicanism of the South probably contributed to some regional variation in virtue, notwithstanding the widely distributed residue of Calvinism shared with areas of Dutch settlement.[26] Views of virtue were probably changing somewhat throughout the founding period, but the usages we are about to explore seem to have had to do mainly with individual responsibility and self-control in both political and social obligation—with attitudes and practices of citizenship conducive to workable self-government and an expanding general welfare. They implied a balancing of individualism with community concerns and a tempering of liberty and equality by the republican elements of virtue they identified.

The Elements and Implications of Virtue

From the Revolution and its preliminaries there ensued a broadening of conceptions of, and a deepening of emphases on, equality, liberty, and virtue—all three. This was certainly not least so for virtue, which came to imply the personal qualities and social behavior thought peculiarly suitable to citizens in the condition of self-government.

As for equality, the chief signification was political: presumptive equality of citizenship, however qualified in practice. This, once established with republicanism early in the founding period, seems to have retained a stable meaning. But emphasis on social equality—on rescission of ascriptive privilege and the mitigation of social distinctions—evidently gained ground, growing not only with the initial impulse of the Revolution but throughout the founding period. In this sense an amplification of *equality* began to spread through much of American life.[27]

Liberty also took on additional meaning and emphasis. Within the white population, liberty reigned in the later decades of colonial America as it did nowhere in Europe; restraints on personal choice thought appropriate at an earlier date had been shaken off as experience with individual enterprise and the availability of unoccupied land whetted appetites for increased autonomy. Then, as annoyance with British policies fattened into specific charges of despotism, ties with the parent country became chains of bondage, and extinction of all vestiges of *foreign* rule became a requisite of liberty. When this condition of self-governance was satisfied by the Declaration of Independence and success in the war it incited, the American goal of a regime of liberty made secure by law was attained.[28]

We have no evidence that *virtue* was subject to concerted redefinition as leaders of thought in the rebelling colonies contemplated the requisites for enlightened rule and responsible citizenship under new republican institutions and conditions. In any case, the leaders of opinion in this new order of things were hardly of one mind about the attributes that would characterize a virtuous citizenry. Nevertheless, in these circumstances of incipient self-government an expansion and reorientation in the understanding of virtue occurred as part of the reception of republican ideology. Perhaps the most notable aspect of this progress was an increasingly common reference to *public* virtue and to the public significance of personal virtues. Carter Braxton of Virginia, for example, remarked on this change right at the outset of the founding period. Addressing the convention charged with writing a constitution for the Old Dominion in 1776, Braxton answered another pamphlet that had advocated a republican or "democratical" government for Virginia as both conducive and responsive to the principle of virtue. The author of this pamphlet, said Braxton,

> seems to have cautiously blended *private* with *public* virtue, as if for the purpose of confounding the two, and thereby recommending his plan under the amiable appearance of courting virtue. It is well known that *private* and *public* virtue are materially different. The happiness and dignity of man I admit consists in the practice of *private* virtues, and to this he is stimulated by the rewards promised to such conduct. In this he acts for himself, and with a view of promoting his own particular welfare. *Public* virtue, on the other hand, means a disinterested attachment to the public good, exclusive and independent of all private and selfish interest, and which, though sometimes possessed by a few individuals, never characterized the mass of the people in any state. And this is said to be the principle of democratic governments, and to influence every subject of it to pursue such measures as conduce to the prosperity of the whole. A man, therefore, to qualify himself for a member of such a community, must divest himself of all interested motives, and engage in no pursuits which do not redound to the benefit of society. He must not, through ambition, desire to be great, because it would destroy that equality on which the security of the government depends; nor ought he to be rich, lest he be tempted to indulge himself in those luxuries, which, though lawful, are not expedient, and might occasion envy and emulation.[29]

In Braxton's more conservative, normally aristocratic view, public virtue and republican government "may be practicable in countries so sterile by nature as to afford a scanty supply of the necessaries, and none of the conveniences, of life; but they can never meet with a favorable reception from a people who inhabit a country to which Providence has been more bountiful." It would therefore be a mistake, he argued, to put all Virginia's eggs in the republican basket. His recommendation was to emulate the English Constitution (except for its hereditary executive) in Virginia—to depend on "mixed government," with strict separation of powers and institutional balances, "to devise the best code of laws, engage their due execution, and secure the liberties of the people."[30]

The constitution that George Mason drafted for Virginia in 1776 was more radically republican than Braxton's recommendations: its central elements were annual elections and legislative supremacy. Braxton also appears to have lost the argument about public virtue, for the Virginia constitutional convention placed in this first-born of American charters the specification of five personal qualities, or principles of individual and civic conduct, declared to be indispensable for the preservation of free government. Pursuant to republican tradition, the Virginia Declaration of Rights thus gave public import to otherwise private virtues.

Of the first state constitutions written before 1787 eight of twelve contained, or were accompanied by, more or less elaborate declarations of rights and priority concerns about the principles and practices essential to the conduct and preservation of free government. (This count includes Vermont's constitution of 1777 and New Hampshire's of 1784, officially the state's second, though its first full-dress effort). These statements were set off distinctly from provisions for the "frame of government"—the structure of public offices and the distribution of public functions among them—and their more hortatory provisions were hardly enforceable in court. Two states—Connecticut and Rhode Island—simply continued into the nineteenth century under their colonial charters, as Massachusetts did until 1780. The remaining four states—South Carolina, Georgia, New Jersey, and New York—wrote new constitutions that chiefly provided for the structural outlines of government. They also identified certain rights of citizens, critical procedures, and civic principles—though much less elaborately and distinctly than those of the first group of states. These were intermingled with the structural provisions, much as James Madison later supposed the items in what became the federal Bill of Rights would be worked into the existing articles of the federal Constitution. For these states, as for Connecticut and Rhode Island, it was pretty much sufficient to settle the most exigent structural issues, for the common law could be assumed to continue in force (some states so stipulated), including its constitutional principles and procedures, except as they were altered specifically.

Of the eight states adopting distinct bills of rights and similar injunctions five identified principles of responsible conduct conducive to public trust and preservation of republican government. Virginia's statement appears to have been the template here: "Sec. 15. That no free government, or the blessings of liberty, can be preserved to any people, but by a firm adherence to justice, moderation, temperance, frugality, and virtue, and by frequent recurrence to fundamental principles."[31] The four states that followed in constitutional provision for this republican palladium—Pennsylvania (1776), Vermont (1777), Massachusetts (1780), and New Hampshire (1784)—all mentioned "frequent recurrence to fundamental principles" as well as a similar list of virtues, or fundamental principles.[32] They departed from Virginia's approach in two marginal respects, however. First, they seem to have sought to give more operative effect to the provision by stating (here the language is Pennsylvania's) that "the people ought therefore to pay particular attention to these points in the choice of officers and representatives. . . ."[33] Second, "virtue" itself was dropped from Virginia's list, perhaps because conceived of as the generic quality and not a traditional reference to "public virtue." It was replaced by "industry." In Massachusetts John Adams added "piety" for a sixth point, though he placed it first.

These state constitutional declarations, together with numerous pertinent sermons from the clergy and the relevant secular literature of the time, form a pattern of public exhortation, lasting a decade and more after the Declaration of Independence, on three closely related concerns for the success of the new American regimes of self-government: (1) the virtuous citizen will cultivate attitudes and habits conducive to both productivity and conservation of goods and services having social value; (2) republican government implies commonality, which implies controlling extreme distinctions of wealth and status, limiting self-indulgence and luxury, and sacrificing personal comfort to prevailing conceptions of the public welfare; (3) free government and the public welfare are proof against the corruptions of faction and the claims of private advantage only when concern for the common good induces widespread readiness to accord it priority over personal interest. Let us consider these concerns.

The commitment of postcolonial leadership to a regime of economic productivity was witnessed in the "fundamental-principles" provision of the four states that followed Virginia in this respect, all of which included *industry,* along with justice, moderation, temperance, and *frugality;* and there is strong evidence of the same concern in Virginia's Declaration of Rights.[34] The agreement that ruled in designating these qualities was probably not matched by an agreement on what constituted an exemplary display of any one of them—though we lack circumstantial contemporaneous accounts of evaluations of behavior in these terms. Such accounts are especially scarce for industry and frugality—arguably the essence of the attitude later known as the Protestant ethic, conceived of as protocapitalistic, self- or salvation-centered virtues or values.[35] But the provenance of these terms, or "virtues," was as much republican as Protestant, insofar as these are separable; and the Puritan derivation, as well as the republican, looked to individual responsibility for collective economic welfare, balancing private property with social obligation. The immediate source for *industry* and *frugality* may well have been Montesquieu, in whose view these virtues helped curb the corruptions of luxury and the amplitude of inequality in small republics and were also associated with economic (commercial) development.[36] Notwithstanding the prominence of these attributes in earlier Puritan doctrine, clerical sponsorship was not a significant factor in the founding period. Only two of several hundred founding-period sermons I have examined referred to industry and frugality as critical to survival of an independent, self-governing state or nation. Zabdiel Adams (in 1782) and Joseph McKeen (in 1800) endorsed the state constitutional injunction to produce and to conserve, but what they offered in the way of explication or justification can excite little interest in our own day.[37] Joseph Lathrop, a Congregationalist minister of western Massachusetts, probably relied on remarks made previously from the pulpit in two series of essays titled *The Censor* and *The Reformer,* published in pamphlet form in 1786. The essays on "Industry" and "Frugality" supply presumptions and reasoning that reflect the republican and public dimensions of those virtues then (see appendix 7).

In the state constitutional specifications, *temperance* (harking back to the cardinal virtues) and *moderation* stood together for self-restraint, if with some redundancy. Certainly temperance implied more than control of physical appetites alone.[38] Moderation, whether or not it was lifted directly from *The Spirit of the Laws,* was the "fundamental principle" of (aristocratic) governance for Montesquieu. Further, it was the distinguishing characteristic, or principle, of *all* nondespotic governments and was particularly associated with "commercial" republics.[39] Recurrence to Montesquieu's consideration of aristocracy may seem out of place in (even) the Virginia Declaration of Rights, but the more general import of mitigating inequality of citizenship and condition seems reasonably clear, and a concern to preserve republicanism and avert despotism is certainly understandable in the circumstances. As composed in the crisis of 1776, the Virginia Declaration of Rights was not a particularly aristocratic document. Commonality, or republican inclusiveness (within Virginia's then indigenous limits), was a serious concern. When temperance and moderation are considered with the rest of its list of virtues, Virginia appears to have disfavored officially excesses of not only civic and social distinction but also leisure and luxury, long associated in republican doctrine with republican corruption in encouraging pursuit of private advantage and discouraging public service.[40]

In the state constitutional listings of fundamental principles *justice* stood first (save in Massachusetts, which gave first place to piety). Justice had traditionally come first among the cardinal virtues; it was also traditionally the link or transition from private to public or civic virtue.[41] We may surmise that such is the direction in which justice points here— toward the common good or public interest and its supportive civic attachments to community, state, or nation; toward republican duty as well as republican inclusiveness. For this reading there was ample precedent in both American Puritanism and European republicanism.[42] More elementally than justice as the public interest, however, public virtue meant public or civic spirit—the preference of public over private interest and the apparently tautological condition of political community.

In distinguishing public from private virtue, Carter Braxton of Virginia, quoted earlier, looked back on a long tradition. But in pressing the distinction, he reckoned without, or rather declined to embrace, republicanism as we have seen it emerge in America from Montesquieu and in its earlier English merger with Puritanism. Various private virtues in addition to conventional public virtue, it developed, had public implications in the new circumstances of full-scale self-government. These implications were not necessarily precise. Even the private virtues were abstract, potentially compound nouns. Further, the language of virtue, perhaps especially in its public applications, was probably more rhetorical (in the best sense of the term) than meticulous. Neither redundancy nor obscure variety within the similar, no doubt imitative state constitutional listings should therefore concern us, for we can identify the general, apparently urgent concerns these listings indicated.

Three such concerns have just been considered briefly. Now a fourth may be mentioned, intimated by the mention of *piety* among the priority virtues for Massachusetts and confirmed repeatedly in sermons (especially in New England) sustaining Puritan doctrine since the first settlement. The fourth concern was that virtues of public relevance find their foundation in the church. To some this implied public support of the foundation reciprocally, while to others such support was coming to seem undesirable, whether or not it was sectarian. A broader, less exceptionable implication, however, was that church, or clergy, and public officials should join hands in the continuing and comprehensive task of civic education and inculcation of virtue, based in the precepts of Christianity. This particular agenda for the invigoration of first principles justifies a somewhat fuller consideration than the first three concerns and is the subject of the following section.

Religion and Virtue

It was in the nature of things that those aspects of virtue that Carter Braxton cast into the category of "private" should have been identified and explicated in religious ceremonies. "What shall I do to be saved?" was the bedrock question to which ministers addressed their remarks when they faced a congregation. The divergent answers to this question largely structured theological debate and provided the basis of division into sects and denominations. Sectarian differences in creed would entail variance in the importance attached to "good works" as a key to salvation. Divided sharply and passionately as they were on the definition and efficacy of good works, ministers of all faiths could agree that emulation of Christ was at the foundation of Christian conduct and demeanor. It followed as a dictate of common sense that the clergy, students of the life and teachings of Jesus, would become authoritative on the context and contours of virtue as exemplified by Christ, by saints who had preceded him in paths of righteousness, and by the apostles who spread his message to the world.

Because they were mostly well-educated men, historically conversant and interested observers of contemporary life, and because they were on hand every sabbath to affirm their convictions, ministers of the Protestant churches could not avoid giving impetus to public contemplation of the fitness of ordinary people to perform creditably the roles assigned them in a self-governing republic. The residue of print that has been brought to our attention supports a conclusion that, generally, the Protestant clergy was as firmly committed to the ascendancy of majority decision over individual preference as Thomas Tudor Tucker revealed himself to be in his uncompromising lecture to the hotheads of South Carolina (quoted in chapter 5 above). Indeed, one finds in the sermons of the Protestant ministers recurring evidence of the conviction that a state tolerable to free citizens could be sustained only if a stern and persistent social discipline repressed idiosyncratic impulses to pursue personal paths to happiness.

The influence attributed here to the Protestant clergy may have had its counterpart among Roman Catholics, Quakers, and Jews. Whether that was the case we have little chance of knowing, for the priest, the rabbi, and opinion leaders among the Society of Friends did not put an equivalent of the Protestant sermon into print.

There remains to be noticed another aspect of the campaign to prepare Americans for the obligations of republican citizenship. This was the controlling assumption, especially prevalent over most of New England, that political and clerical authority must share that task. For example, some fifty years before the bid for independence, the Reverend Joseph Baxter devoted half of the "Massachusetts Election Day Sermon" cited earlier to contending that "Civil Rulers, or those who are in authority over a People, ought to do much to promote Peace and Godliness, and Honesty among their People, [improving] all the Opportunities and Advantages which they have to do it."[43] There is no evidence in the sermon that Baxter feared an undue merging of princely and priestly power; such concern was hardly current then in Massachusetts. By and large, in the colonial America of Baxter's day, religious freedom was understood to mean freedom to choose one's (presumptively Christian) faith and affiliation, including immunity from punishment or harassment in consequence of one's choice. Strict separation—the metaphoric wall—between church and state did not figure then in controversy over the sufficiency of provision for "freedom of conscience" or "religious freedom." Still, by the time of Baxter's 1727 sermon, the English political-religious settlement of 1688 had already undone the Puritans' virtual monopoly in Massachusetts and their exclusive partnership with the state.

Half a century later, as the break with England came about, personal choice in the avowal of religious belief and attachment to a sect or denomination was accorded high priority in formulations of inalienable rights and in the declarations of the new state charters. One topical source of this heightened concern was an apprehension that the parent country, already bent on a course of despotism, was about to "establish" Anglicanism throughout its colonies. The pronounced religious pluralism of most colonies must also have meant that, in such contemplation of independence as occurred before 1776, guarantees of religious liberty would assume not only religious but also political urgency.

As early as 1649 Catholic-dominated Maryland enacted the Toleration Act announcing that "noe person or persons . . . professing to believe in Jesus Christ, shall from henceforth bee any waies troubled, Molested, or discountenanced for or in respect of his or her religion nor in the free exercise thereof within this Province...."[44] This Maryland law, put on the books before the Massachusetts Bay Colony had lived out its second decade and long accorded first honors as a model guarantee of religious freedom for believers in Christ, soon came to have its counterpart in charters issued to other colonies (e.g., Rhode Island in 1663) and in enactments of colonial legislatures. These liberating provisions are too many and too variant to permit summarization. It will be enough, perhaps, to say that in the main the law that took notice of religious beliefs and affiliations allowed no room for doubt that colonial America was Protestant Christian territory. While Roman Catholics, Jews, and infidels of all contrarieties were secure in their homes and immune from authorized harassment, they must have been aware that in most communities they were viewed as second-class citizens.[45]

This would have been the case in the first decades of statehood, as it had been after settlement shook down into stable polities in the final decades of the seventeenth century. Neither during the long stretch of colonial rule nor in the years of fighting for independence did the partisans of liberty argue that enfranchised participation in the forums of political debate and public action should be viewed as everyone's inalienable right. Besides age and sex, qualifications for voting or holding elective office primarily included income or wealth, and religious profession or affiliation, as presumptive tests of the civic probity and responsibility on which public-regarding governance depended.[46]

The history of colonial America included numerous experiences with an established church. Puritans who planted Massachusetts Bay Colony along the Charles River elevated their revisions of English Episcopal dogma and ritual into orthodoxy and modeled their laws on the Mosaic code. This regime was too rigorous to be maintained among a population spreading along a broad frontier. If Massachusetts can be called a theocratic state, it was a theocracy that rapidly disintegrated—first into theocratic communities and finally (as late as 1833) altogether. For generations dissenters in many Massachusetts communities could rightly complain of oppressions attending the legal establishment of a single church. This generalization is applicable to all New England colonies except Rhode Island.

Rhode Island, New Jersey, Pennsylvania, and Delaware had no experience with a denomination declared by law to be the established church of the colony. Outside of these colonies and New England the Church of England represented orthodoxy during most of the colonial period—in

Virginia continuously from the time of earliest settlement until enactment of Thomas Jefferson's Statute of Religious Liberty in 1786. Reviewing the conditions encountered by nonconformists in Anglican territory, a team of eminent historians agreed on this summary statement.

> Despite such demands for uniformity, the Virginia Anglicans planned no campaigns. . . . Puritans and Catholics could remain in the colony, provided they paid taxes to the established Church of England and were reasonably discreet in their public utterances. . . . It was much the same in the other Anglican colonies. Although the Church of England occupied a privileged position and received a small government subsidy, Protestants were generally free to worship as they pleased, outnumbered in every colony.[47]

In Virginia any anxieties over the prospect of a more oppressive establishment in the future must have been relieved by Jefferson's eventual, decisive legislative victory, and by the categorical, perpetual terms of his statute of 1786: "Be it enacted . . . That no man shall be compelled to frequent or support any religious worship, place, or ministry whatsoever. . . . [T]he rights hereby asserted are of the natural rights of mankind, and . . . if any act shall be hereafter passed to repeal the present, or to narrow its operation, such act will be an infringement of natural rights."[48] Still, these assurances can hardly have terminated the concerns of those churches with limited membership that more prestigious or prevalent denominations were advantaged through the goodwill of public officials, community influentials, or the public in general.

When Jefferson's statute was passed, and when the First Amendment to the national Constitution was adopted by Congress, five states (four, by the ratification of the First Amendment in 1791) made constitutional provision for nondiscriminatory public support of (Christian or Protestant) religion, either prescriptively or permissively.[49] John Adams was no friend of religious orthodoxy or oppression. The first article of the Declaration of Rights in the Massachusetts Constitution of 1780 declares certain rights inalienable, and the second article guarantees freedom of conscience in religious worship. Yet Adams appears to have been a vigorous proponent of the provisions for public support of all (Protestant Christian) churches in the third article, which remained in the constitution until 1833:

> As the happiness of a people, and the good order and preservation of civil government, essentially depend upon piety, religion,

and morality; and as these cannot be generally diffused throughout a community, but by the institutions of the public worship of GOD, and of public instructions in piety, religion, and morality: Therefore, to promote their happiness and to secure the good order and preservation of their government, the people of this Commonwealth have a right to invest their legislature with power to authorize and require . . . the several towns, parishes, precincts, and other bodies-politic, or religious societies, to make suitable provision, at their own expense, for the institution of the public worship of GOD, and for the support and maintenance of public protestant teachers of piety, religion, and morality, in all cases where such provision shall not be made voluntarily.

And the people of this Commonwealth have also a right to, and do, invest their legislature with authority to enjoin upon all the subjects an attendance upon the instructions of the public teachers aforesaid, at stated times and seasons, if there be any on whose instructions they can conscientiously and conveniently attend. . . .

And all monies paid by the subjects to the support of public worship, and of the public teachers aforesaid, shall if he require it, be uniformly applied to the support of the public teacher or teachers of his own religious sect of denomination, provided there be any on whose instruction he attends; otherwise it may be paid toward the support of the teacher or teachers of the parish or precinct in which the said monies are raised.

And every denomination of christians, demeaning themselves peaceably and as good subjects of the Commonwealth, shall be equally under the protection of the law; And no subordination of any one sect or denomination to another shall ever be established by law.[50]

Policies like those of Massachusetts prevailed constitutionally in New Hampshire, Connecticut, Maryland, and South Carolina at the time the national Constitution was drafted and ratified (though South Carolina adopted disestablishment in 1790). On the other hand, seven of the other original states (including Virginia) made some provision to the contrary, proscribing the requirement of involuntary tax support of religion, or the legal privileging of a single sect in preference to others, or in some cases both.[51] Disestablishment (either full or nonpreferential) was probably intended also by the notably indefinite language of New York's constitutional article on religious freedom, though it was not uniformly understood to have done so at first.[52]

Thomas Jefferson was, among the founding leadership, more set against religious establishment than most (though not more so than James Madison); yet Jefferson also allowed that considering the mass of the citizenry, the success of republican government probably depended on the support that religious belief and affiliation afforded to private morality and civic virtue. Most of Jefferson's elite contemporaries apparently shared this view, whatever their own spiritual commitments, and were more disposed than he was toward public assistance, financial or otherwise, for religion.[53] It is therefore not evident that the First Congress intended, by the first clause of the First Amendment, to preclude all federal government support of religion or that the various nonestablishment provisions of the states were so intended.[54] Disestablishment in the states did not necessarily mean or lead to strict separation of polity and religion. Finally, even for the apparent minority of public men of the time who favored separation to some extent beyond simple disestablishment, there is little evidence to indicate that freedom of conscience meant, for them, that religious support of values presumptively central to republicanism should be disfavored or that this mission of religion should be discontinued. Still, disestablishment may well have tended to diminish religion's effectiveness in supporting "public" values.

Education and Virtue

As scholars tend to see the second half—the "Federal" phase—of the founding period today, it appears that new conceptions of politics were contending with and partially displacing the old republican or commonwealth notion in which civic virtue and the public good were so crucial. In these new conceptions, acceptance of the pursuit of wealth as an engine of economic development, which was in turn a support of political stability, found a larger place in some people's minds. Similarly—in its acceptance of competition and private interest—a more nearly pluralistic account of politics as the recognition and regulation of endemic interests emerged that, as it took shape in (for example) James Madison's mind, figured together with the more traditional view in the argument of *The Federalist* —notably in the seminal *Federalist No. 10*. The perceptions of Madison's then collaborator, Alexander Hamilton, appear to have departed still more sharply from the traditional view. Probably these perspectives, in any full formulation, did not yet dominate political understanding, even in the "elite" political culture. We can, however, conclude that they were mitigating somewhat the impetus of prescriptions of virtue in both the republican and pulpit traditions, though the prescriptions were continued with vigor.[55]

In the Federal phase of the founding period, however, numerous thinkers began to emphasize another institutional and cultural buttress of civic virtue, namely, education.[56] Concluding his history of education in America from 1607 to 1783, Lawrence Cremin wrote, "However variegated the patterns of provincial education, there were certain larger tendencies that already gave it a characteristic cast by the time of the Revolution. Chief among these was the prevalence of schooling and its accessibility to most segments of the population—the Negroes and Indians, of course, being the leading exceptions."[57] To the exceptions mentioned, which take us back to earlier chapters of this inquiry, Cremin quickly adds that there was little formal schooling in the backcountry. By the conclusion of his account he has dealt also with the tendency for education to be somewhat less generally available in the Middle Atlantic states than in New England and still less so in the South. Nevertheless, the availability of schooling had broadened remarkably in the eighteenth century until its serious disruption and impoverishment in the years of Revolution.[58]

The repair of this impoverishment gradually became a concern of political leadership in the states, both North and South. The republican declaration in John Adams's Massachusetts Constitution of 1780 is often cited as representative of this mission: "Wisdom and knowledge, as well as virtue, diffused generally among the body of the people, being necessary for the preservation of their rights and liberties; and as these depend on spreading the opportunities and advantages of education in the various parts of the country, and among the different orders of the people, it shall be the duty of legislatures and magistrates, in all future periods of this commonwealth, to cherish the interests of literature and the sciences, and all seminaries of them. . . ."[59] Until well beyond the founding period, this republican view of education, including its emphasis on "the different orders of the people," inspired state policy; nearly all the states established funds for common schooling, though these were slow to reach levels affording support of schools generally in any section of the country. Colleges and universities, both public and private, tended to take priority in state provision, partly from republican concern to educate leadership for society.[60] Yet perhaps the most notable of postrevolutionary national initiatives during the Confederation was the principle of land-grant support of general schooling in the western territories, introduced by the well-known words of Article 3 of the Northwest Ordinance of 1787: "Religion, morality, and knowledge being necessary to good government and the happiness of mankind, schools and the means of education shall be encouraged."

The development of something like universal public education was more than a generation in the future when the federal Constitution was adopted, and we cannot attribute much practical educational progress to the founding period. When the American "common school" developed later, it did so in service to states and a nation holding more expressly egalitarian notions and given to less didactic views of religion than had prevailed in the late eighteenth century. We can say that there was a strong and growing conviction among the new nation's well-educated political and professional leadership that there was a vital role for widely available education to play in shaping—"socializing," as we say today—a responsible and productive republican citizenry.[61]

The Decline of Virtue

Gordon Wood concluded his masterly study of the founding period, *The Creation of the American Republic, 1776–1787*, with a chapter entitled "The End of Classical Politics."[62] By the time of the Constitutional Convention, he wrote, the republican conception of politics as the pursuit of *public* (meaning both *common* and *nonprivate*) interests, fatally vulnerable to factional corruption of the public interest and thus dependent on public virtue for the survival of free government, had begun to lose vitality. The contention of unvarnished private or partial interests in politics began to seem expectable if not wholly acceptable. Justice in public policy could be seen to ensue contingently from heterogeneity and competition, as well as from commonality, if problematically so. Political theorists thus began to look to factors and forces other than virtue for the preservation of self-government.

No doubt there was some such shift of perspectives, both in the movement for a new, more national constitution and in the political life resulting from the Constitution. In the midst of the movement for constitutional reform, George Washington, commenting on its prospects to James Madison in the spring of 1787, wrote, "I confess that my opinion of public virtue is so far changed that I have my doubts whether any system without the means of coercion in the Sovereign, will enforce obedience to the Ordinances of a Genl. Government; without which, every thing else fails."[63] So Madison also thought then; perhaps the principal item in his reform program was a national (congressional) "negative *in all cases whatsoever* on the legislative acts of the States, as heretofore exercised by the Kingly prerogative," not only to protect the proposed Genl. Government but to act as arbiter:

> The great desideratum which has not yet been found for Republican Governments, seems to be some disinterested & dispassionate umpire in disputes between different passions & interests in the State. The majority who alone have the right of decision, have frequently an interest real or supposed in abusing it.... Might not the national prerogative here suggested be found sufficiently disinterested for the decision of local questions of policy, while it would itself be sufficiently restrained from the pursuit of interests adverse to those of the whole Society?[64]

Madison was just then formulating the novel, though now familiar, "extend-the-sphere" argument of the *Federalist No. 10* and the end of *No. 51* that the greater heterogeneity of interests in a *large* republic would tend to check one another and thus render majorities benign.[65] The constitutional regime that Madison defended in *The Federalist*, however, lacked the national veto he had proposed as a check on unjust majorities in the less heterogeneous states. Just a month before the *Federalist No. 10* was published, Madison wrote Jefferson a second time that he doubted the new constitution could do the job without this provision.[66] The father of the Constitution had concluded that public virtue had failed in the small American republics. He calculated that, at the national level, a politics of neutralization, moderation, or accommodation among its prospective multiplicity of interests would sustain enlightened, disinterested leadership committed to justice, or the public good. This almost certainly did not anticipate such modern pluralistic notions as coalitional pragmatism and "cross-cutting cleavages" (Madison's explicit language always fell short of these conceptions), but it did break distinctly with "classical" republican politics. Madison, moreover (like Hamilton, his ally as *Publius*), became an organizer of, not simply a participant in, party competition under the Constitution. Surely the many members of Congress who became players in this game late in the founding period must have sensed that public virtue was taking an unexpected turn.

On the other hand, a number of national legislators, Protestant ministers, and other opinion leaders evidently believed as late as 1800 that the success of self-government depended on tempering liberty and equality with virtue. As for virtue, Madison's reliance on it to help approximate the public interest in a scheme of national representation (his well-known "filtration" argument) was a serious theme of *The Federalist,* complementing the heterogeneity argument.[67] The theme was analytic, not just rhetorical. Madison had not given up on disinterested virtue in all circumstances, though he evidently had come to believe that institutional circumstances conditioned virtue, perhaps more than vice versa.

We must conclude from the documentary evidence that virtue as a deontological element in republican politics—that is, virtue as moral obligation, defining political life and the political order—played a large part in the American founding throughout the founding period. Attenuation was setting in by the midpoint of the founding period, yet serious efforts by political leaders to effectuate virtue for republican reasons continued for three decades or more after that, most notably in education but also in state and national politics. No doubt some of the public attention to virtue was just neoclassical, political, and sermonic cant. But the founding was, after all—especially for those Americans who were leaders of action and opinion—primarily and poignantly about the problem of establishing and sustaining full-scale (i.e., autonomous) self-government. In these circumstances, self-government could hardly have seemed self-governing in any systemic sense. The problem of establishing and sustaining it must have seemed ultimately a problem of responsibility—prudence, moderation, community obligation—and of how to motivate responsible civic behavior.

As time passed and experience accumulated, reliance on republican virtue probably declined. The state and national politics of the Confederation were in various respects dispiriting. As we have seen, this experience led some Americans to conclude that virtue was more likely to be found among leaders on a national scale than in local politics and was more likely to be sustained in the population at large through national rather than local institutions. "Federalists" in the controversy over a new national Constitution increasingly inclined toward this conviction, with emphasis on leadership. "Anti-Federalists" saw a direct threat to liberty in a larger, prospectively stronger, "consolidated" government. They further believed that virtue was more likely to prevail in local communities of close and general acquaintance and in the traditional state capitals than in the more remote and contrived national government, which also in their view offered larger and stronger prospects of corruption, especially financial. Many proponents of the new Constitution became Republicans in the party division of the following decade; similarly, many opponents became Federalists. But the divergent positions on the structure of republicanism and the substance and provenance of virtue in the first constitutional division evidently were reflected and further developed in relation to issues of economic and foreign policy in the later party division. National politics under the Constitution gave rise to cleavages no less deep and acrimonious than those in contemporary Britain, but the American Constitution provided no titular sovereign to transcend divisions in the popular sovereign. These divisions may in themselves have tended to invalidate virtue, but we can reserve that topic for the concluding chapter.

Federalists came to emphasize the dangers of popular penetration of government; Republicans stressed the perils of governmental insulation from popular interests. Republican doctrine justified both some Federalists' concerns about popular democratic degradation and Jeffersonian alarm about the alleged corruptions in the administration's closely connected fiscal and foreign policies. The incumbent Federalists apparently perceived themselves as defending public decorum and its presumptively supporting electoral majority, which they believed they represented, against a factional opposition; Jeffersonians saw themselves as patriots protecting the Republic from corruption. Federalists tended to worry about excesses of liberty, Republicans about governmental encroachment on liberty. Among Federalists, virtue seems increasingly to have signified elite qualities of leadership, perhaps rather narrowly distributed, while Republicans (notwithstanding their largely elite southern leadership) extolled such grass-roots virtues as simplicity and frugality, emphasizing their affinities with agriculture and the useful arts as against the corruptions of public debt and politics of commercial development. In the then-modern history of republican doctrine Jeffersonians seem to have harked back to the English "country" opposition tradition, mistrusting public power and insisting on limited, decentralized government, while painting Federalists as monarchists and aristocrats. Federalists, if not exactly a "court" party, were "the administration," which may have had something to do with their perspectives on governing—their more organic constitutionalism as against Jeffersonian strict construction; their regard for effective, national government; and their preference for Hamiltonian executive energy and responsibility over a rigorous separation of powers.[68]

Divergent conceptions of republican government and of public policy were thus linked with divergent perceptions of virtue as time passed and political divisions appeared in the new national arena. On one side, for example, "public" virtue tended to justify nationalization of policy and a substantial public sector; on the other side, emphasis on certain private virtues (of presumptive public relevance) arguably favored local and limited government. On one side, "public" virtue became entangled with the French Revolution and Rousseauism; on the other side, certain personal virtues (e.g., temperance and moderation) were valued as supporting public order. In the severe sectionalism of this first party alignment Federalists probably inherited from Puritanism a regard for responsible leadership, public authority, and obligation to the polity and community; the Cavalier traditions of Virginia probably tended by comparison toward privatism. There was room for divergence within the generic tradition of the virtues and even within the tradition of republican virtue. Competing perspectives had existed in eighteenth-century English politics, not only Whig and Tory but within the Whig-republican tendency. The American revolutionary movement was probably a unifying force in republicanism on this side of the Atlantic, but the subsequent practice of self-government, especially on a national scale across regional subcultures and economic interests, in turn produced divergent perspectives on republican virtue, as did the French Revolution.[69] On each side of the ensuing partisan division virtue had its conservative aspect, and on each side it might support social or political transformation.

Arguably the Republican party ideology, as it developed during the 1790s, looking back to the revolutionary and earlier English Radical Whig traditions, engendered suspicion of public authority and intensified party conflict. It tended to challenge and perhaps to negate those attitudinal elements of virtue that had been advocated by less Radical republicans as civic supports of successful self-government; it argued to the contrary that the principal threat to free government came from the incumbent (elected) governmental leadership.[70] What was lost, at least for a time in the bitter conflicts that ensued over the boundaries of liberty, equality, and authority in the new national system of self-government, was much perceptible relevance of virtue to community or commonality. This lapse, as the next chapter speculates, may well have tended to debilitate virtue still further.

Today, American political scientists disagree about the extent to which the preservation of order, liberty, and justice in republican government (or of republican government itself) depends on shared values and virtues in the population or on enlightened political elites and leadership, or results from such social mechanics as countervailing power and "crosscutting cleavages" or from felicitous constitutional arrangements. We really do not know which of these factors are decisive or whether any of them is dispensable.[71] In this respect, as in many others, we are heirs of *The Federalist,* where the analysis looks to all these factors. For *The Federalist* the coexistence of justice and liberty seems to have depended considerably on institutional provisions that might help effectuate civic virtue in the electorate and the national leadership; but Anti-Federalists also appealed to virtue in 1787–88.

In our much larger, more segmented society the quest for such shared conceptions and intentions may seem simply quixotic. On the other hand, we still have little reason to suppose that self-government is itself self-governing, except as we can govern ourselves as individuals and function in politics with respect for the interests of others and concern for the common welfare. We therefore may still have something to learn from the founding experience and from the founding conviction that liberty, justice, and certain terms of virtue belong together in self-government.

Notes

1. Joseph Baxter, *The Duty of a People to Pray to and Bless God for Their Rulers Who Are to Promote Peace and Godliness and Honesty among Them* (Boston: Printed by B. Green, 1727), pp. 17–20.

2. Two collections of sermons, both drawn entirely from New England, reprint leading clerical productions of the revolutionary period conveniently for present-day readers: John Wingate Thornton, ed., *The Pulpit of the American Revolution* (1860; New York: Da Capo Press, 1970); and Alice M. Baldwin, *The New England Clergy and the American Revolution* (1928; New York: Frederick Ungar, 1965). See also Charles S. Hyneman and Donald S. Lutz, eds., *American Political Writing during the Founding Era, 1760–1805* (Indianapolis: Liberty Press, 1983).

3. For a contemporary philosopher's discussion of some aspects of these traditions, see Alasdair MacIntyre, *After Virtue,* 2d ed. (Notre Dame, Ind.: University of Notre Dame Press, 1984). See also Peter Geach, *The Virtues* (Cambridge: Cambridge University Press, 1977).

4. Aristotle, *Nichomachean Ethics,* esp. bks. II–V; Cicero, *De Officiis,* bk. I, esp. chaps. 15–17; Arthur Cushman McGiffert, *A History of Christian Thought,* vol. 2 (New York: Charles Scribner's Sons, 1933), esp. chaps. 3, 12. See also St. Augustine's *City of God,* XIX.4, rehearsing Cicero's account. For Augustine,

however, no naturalistic ethic suffices even provisionally, and everything depends on motivation—on love of God. This view is of some later importance for Calvinist theology and thus for early American views.

5. As for the naturalistic analysis, there were also, of course, in Christian thought the three "theological virtues"—faith, hope, and charity—accompanying the four cardinal virtues.

6. See, e.g., Cicero, *De Republica,* I.25–36, III.31–35, and *De Legibus,* I.15–20.

7. Cicero, *De Republica,* trans. C. W. Keyes, Loeb Classical Library (New York: G. P. Putnam's Sons, 1928), I.25.

8. This was so even though the manuscripts of his *Republic* and *Laws* were lost in the twelfth century and not recovered (in parts) until the nineteenth, but the formulations were securely lodged in European thought through the copious quotations and paraphrases in Augustine's *City of God,* thus reaching eighteenth-century Protestant preachers. As for the private virtues, *De Officiis* was required reading in the eighteenth century in various American colleges. On the derivative nature of Cicero's writing, see George Sabine [a translator of *De Republica*], *A History of Political Theory,* rev. ed. (New York: Henry Holt, 1950), chap. 9.

9. J. G. Pocock, *The Machiavellian Moment* (Princeton, N.J.: Princeton University Press, 1975), seems to be the basic source here. For Pocock's comment on Athens versus Sparta, see p. 74; and for a remarkable analysis of what the notion of civic virtue entails for Aristotle and thus, at least in part, for the republican tradition, see pp. 66–80.

10. On the English reception, see (besides ibid.), Zera S. Fink, *The Classical Republicans: An Essay in the Recovery of a Pattern of Thought in Seventeenth-century England* (Evanston, Ill.: Northwestern University Press, 1945); Felix Raab, *The English Face of Machiavelli* (London: Routledge and Kegan Paul, 1964); Caroline A. Robbins, *The Eighteenth-century Commonwealthman: Studies in the Transmission, Development, and Circumstances of English Liberal Thought from the Restoration of Charles II until the War with the Thirteen Colonies* (Cambridge, Mass.: Harvard University Press, 1959); and J. G. Pocock, *The Ancient Constitution and the Feudal Law: English Historical Thought in the Seventeenth Century* (Cambridge: Cambridge University Press, 1957). On the later American reception of this tradition, see esp. Bernard Bailyn, *The Ideological Origins of the American Revolution* (Cambridge, Mass.: Harvard University Press, 1967), and *The Origins of American Politics* (New York: Random House Vintage Books, 1967); H. Trevor Colbourn, *The Lamp of Experience* (Chapel Hill: University of North Carolina Press, 1965); Clinton Rossiter, *Seedtime of the Republic* (New York: Harcourt, Brace, 1953); and Gordon S. Wood, *The Creation of the American Republic* (1969; New York: W. W. Norton, 1972), esp. chaps. 2–3, 10–11, 15.

11. See, e.g, Marshall Knappen, *Tudor Puritanism* (Chicago: University of Chicago Press, 1939), bk. 2, for the sixteenth-century foundations; William Haller, *The Rise of Puritanism* (1938; Philadelphia: University of Pennsylvania Press, 1972); Ralph Barton Perry, *Puritanism and Democracy* (New York: Vanguard Press, 1944), chaps. 5, 8–9, 12–13, and passim; and Perry Miller, *The New England Mind: The Seventeenth Century* (1939; Boston: Beacon Press, 1961).

12. Charles H. McIlwain, *The American Revolution: A Constitutional Interpretation* (1923; Ithaca, N.Y.: Cornell University Press, 1958); Samuel P. Huntington, *Political Order in Changing Societies* (New Haven, Conn,: Yale University Press, 1968), chap. 2.

13. Perry Miller, *The New England Mind: From Colony to Province* (Cambridge, Mass.: Harvard University Press, 1967), bks. 3–4, esp. chap. 22.

14. Perry, *Puritanism and Democracy*, chap. 12; Edmund S. Morgan, ed., *Puritan Political Ideas* (Indianapolis: Bobbs-Merrill, 1965), introduction; Edmund S. Morgan, "The Puritan Ethic and the American Revolution," *William and Mary Quarterly*, 3d ser., 24 (1967): 3–43.

15. Jonathan Edwards, "The Nature of True Virtue," in *The Works of Jonathan Edwards*, vol. 8, ed. Paul Ramsey (New Haven, Conn.: Yale University Press, 1989), pp. 539–759. See also Norman Fiering, *Jonathan Edwards's Moral Thought in Its British Context* (Chapel Hill: University of North Carolina Press, 1981), esp. chaps. 6–7. For a later, modified statement, see Ezra Stiles (1783): "True virtue consists in a conformity of heart and of life to the divine law, which is as obligatory upon Christians as if eternal life was suspended on perfect obedience." Election sermon reprinted in Thornton, *Pulpit of the American Revolution*, p. 494.

16. Morgan, "The Puritan Ethic and the American Revolution." On these "virtues" in Italian republicanism, see Pocock, *The Machiavellian Moment*, p. 249; for *industry* (not *frugality*) in Cicero, see *De Republica*, V.6. On *industry* and *frugality* in seventeenth-century and early eighteenth-century English Puritan and republican use, see Pocock, *The Machiavellian Moment*, pp. 429–30, 445–46.

17. For documentation of the probable influence of this school, see Garry Wills, *Inventing America: Jefferson's Declaration of Independence* (1978; New York: Random House Vintage Books, 1979), esp. chaps. 7, 13, 16, 18, and *Explaining America: The Federalist* (Garden City, N.Y.: Doubleday, 1981), esp. chaps. 2, 6, 22.

18. Several of these letters are reprinted in David L. Jacobson, ed., *The English Libertarian Heritage* (Indianapolis: Bobbs-Merrill, 1965). On the popularity and influence in America of these writings, see Bailyn, *Ideological Origins*, and *Origins of American Politics*.

19. *Cato's Letters*, in *English Libertarian Heritage*, ed. Jacobson, p. 89.

20. On Montesquieu's influence, see Wills, *Explaining America*, passim, esp. chap. 22.

21. Quoted here from Montesquieu, *The Spirit of the Laws*, 1st English ed., ed. David Wallace Carrithers (Berkeley: University of California Press, 1977), IV.5 (p. 130). On the French church's censuring of *L'Esprit des Lois*, see ibid, pp. 383–85, and the resulting Avertissement or "Author's Explanatory Notes" in the Hafner Library of Classics edition, ed. Franz Newmann (New York: Hafner Publishing, 1949).

22. See, e.g., Montesquieu, *Spirit of the Laws*, on industry, XIV.9, XVIII.6; on frugality, V.2–6, VII; on moderation, V.8, VIII.1, XII.5; on prudence, XII.5; and on justice, I.1. See notes 30–33 below for a discussion of the probable influence of these passages on statements about virtue in some early state constitutions, especially through George Mason of Virginia.

23. On this interpretation, see esp. Thomas L. Pangle, *Montesquieu's Philosophy of Liberalism* (Chicago: University of Chicago Press, 1973). For commerce and moderation, see Anne M. Cohler, *Montesquieu's Comparative Politics and the Spirit of American Constitutionalism* (Lawrence: University Press of Kansas, 1988).

24. These and other understandings of virtue are emphasized, as is skepticism about the importance of classical republican virtue in the founding, in Thomas L. Pangle, *The Spirit of Modern Republicanism* (Chicago: University of Chicago Press, 1988). See also Richard Vetterli and Gary Bryner, *In Search of the Republic* (Totowa, N.J.: Rowman and Littlefield, 1987).

25. The entry for *virtue* in Samuel Johnson's *A Dictionary of the English Language* (London: Printed by W. Strahan, 1755) gives ten meanings: "1. Moral goodness, 2. A particular moral excellence, 3. Medicinal quality, . . . 5. Efficacy, power, . . . 8. Bravery, valour, 9. Excellence, that which gives excellence. . . ." Perhaps reflecting Johnson's Toryism, civic or public virtue is not included.

26. There *were*, after all, Calvinistic residues in Anglicanism deriving from the sixteenth and early seventeenth centuries. As an example of the close connection between Puritanism and republicanism in colonial thinking, when certain prominent Virginians gathered in Williamsburg in May 1774 to consider an appropriate response to the British Parliament's "Intolerable Acts" against Massachusetts, they "engaged in some searching of archives for forms [of response to arbitrary governmental action] used by the Puritans of England and New England in Cromwell's day. . . ." Helen Hill Miller, *George Mason: Gentleman Revolutionary* (Chapel Hill: University of North Carolina Press, 1975), p. 101.

27. Historians seem to have disagreed about the emphasis on social equality in the founding period since the Progressive historians first emphasized it in the 1920s, but see the recent discussion in Gordon S. Wood, *The Radicalism of the American Revolution* (New York: Alfred A. Knopf, 1992), esp. chap. 13.

28. On the distinction at that time between meanings of *liberty* as individual autonomy and as collective self-government, see Ronald M. Peters, Jr., *The Massachusetts Constitution of 1780: A Social Compact* (Amherst: University of Massachusetts Press, 1978), chap. 1.

29. Hyneman and Lutz, *American Political Writing*, vol. 1, pp. 333–34.

30. Ibid., pp. 336–37. Compare Montesquieu. Some comment on Braxton's pamphlet in the constitutional politics of Virginia appears in Miller, *George Mason*, p. 157.

31. Francis Newton Thorpe, ed., *The Federal and State Constitutions, Colonial Charters, and Other Organic Laws of the States, Territories, and Colonies Now or Heretofore Forming the United States of America*, vol. 7 (Washington, D.C.: Government Printing Office, 1909), p. 3814. North Carolina's constitutional declaration of rights of 1776 (Sec. 21) simply adopted the statement, "That a frequent recurrence to fundamental principles is absolutely necessary to preserve the blessings of liberty," with no list of principles, and this general form was later adopted in the constitutions of, e.g., Illinois and Washington, while West Virginia and Wisconsin took over Virginia's Sec. 15 pretty much verbatim. All these provisions, and those of the five original states, were retained at least to 1984.

32. New Hampshire added to its list "and all the social virtues." Compare the passage in *Cato's Letters*, p. 49: "*Machiavel* tells us, that no Government can long subsist, but by recurring often to its first Principles; but this can never be done while Men live at Ease and in Luxury; for then they cannot be persuaded to see distant Dangers, of which they feel no Part." The reference is evidently to Machiavelli's *Discourses on the First Ten Books of Titus Livius*, trans. Christian E. Detmold, Modern Library Edition (New York: Random House, 1940), III. 1—the chapter titled, "To Insure a Long Existence to Religious Sects or Republics, it is Necessary Frequently to Bring Them Back to Their Original Principles," p. 397ff. As a further likely source of this provision, compare Montesquieu's *Spirit of the Laws*, VIII.1: "The corruption of every government generally begins with that of its principles" (i.e., the particular "principles" of democracies, aristocracies, monarchies, and despotisms): public virtue, moderation, honor, fear. Irving Brant attributes the main influence on Sec. 15 of the Virginia Declaration to Montesquieu, though Brant's highly egalitarian interpretation of the statement seems questionable. Irving Brant, *Life of James Madison*, vol. 1 (Indianapolis: Bobbs-Merrill, 1941), p. 242.

33. Thorpe, *Federal and State Constitutions*, vol. 5, p. 3083.

34. It is clear that Sec. 15 was originally drafted by Mason (see Robert A. Rutland, ed., *The Papers of George Mason*, vol. 1 [Chapel Hill: University of North Carolina Press, 1970], pp. 278–81), and that Mason wrote generally after the model in his Fairfax County Resolves of 1774: "RESOLVED . . . that all Manner of Luxury and Extravagance ought immediately to be laid aside, as

totally inconsistent with the . . . Prospect before us; that it is the indispensable Duty of Gentlemen and Men of Fortune to set Examples of Temperance, Fortitude, Frugality and Industry; and give every Encouragement in their Power . . . to the Improvement of Arts and Manufactures in America. . . ." Ibid, pp. 205–6. On Mason's later attempt to include specific authority for sumptuary legislation in the federal constitution, see Pangle, *Spirit of Modern Republicanism*, pp. 89–94.

35. The issues raised by Max Weber's *The Protestant Ethic and the Spirit of Capitalism* can be passed over here, but see the discussions cited in note 14 above; for a sampling of conflicting views in the subject's large literature, see Robert W. Green, ed., *Protestantism, Capitalism, and Social Science* (Boston: D. C. Heath, 1973). On the attitudes of industry and frugality in the beginnings of English Puritanism, see Knappen, *Tudor Puritanism*, chap. 22.

36. On frugality as a "fundamental principle" of democracy (together with equality and public virtue) in Montesquieu, see *Spirit of the Laws*, V.2–6 and VII; on industry, see ibid., XVIII–XIX. See also Pangle, *Montesquieu's Philosophy of Liberalism*, chaps. 4, 7, on their relation to commerce.

37. Zabdiel Adams's *Massachusetts Election Sermon* (1782) is reprinted in Hyneman and Lutz, *American Political Writing*, vol. 1, p. 539. Joseph McKeen's *Massachusetts Election Sermon* must be read in the original printing as a pamphlet (Boston: Printed by Young and Minns, 1800). For further selections from Lathrop, see Hyneman and Lutz, *American Political Writing*, vol. 1, p. 658. On industry and frugality in earlier Puritanism, see note 14 above.

38. While temperance for Aristotle "must be concerned with bodily pleasures" (*Nichomachean Ethics*, trans. W. D. Ross, III.10, though much less clearly so in the *Politics*), Cicero's classic discussion (*De Officiis*, I.27–43) was far broader, as in general was the tradition of the cardinal virtues. Johnson's *Dictionary* gives both the narrow and broad significations: "1. Moderation; opposed to gluttony and drunkeness. 2. Patience, calmness, sedateness, moderation of passion." Compare the *Oxford English Dictionary* (1971 ed.): "1. The practice or habit of restraining oneself in provocation, passion, desire, etc.; rational self-restraint."

39. Montesquieu, *Spirit of the Laws*, V.8, III.9–10, VIII.8, V.6.

40. See, e.g., ibid, VII.1–2.

41. See, e.g., Cicero, *De Officiis*, I.7, 15–17, which, as mentioned earlier, was widely read in American colleges in the eighteenth century.

42. For Puritan examples (on the duty of rulers to serve the common welfare and of subjects to prefer it) from settlement until well into the eighteenth century, see the selections from sermons reprinted in Perry Miller and Thomas H. Johnson, *The Puritans* (New York: American Book Company, 1938), chap. 2. For republicanism (preference for the public interest), Montesquieu, *Spirit of the Laws*, IV.5 can stand.

43. Baxter, *Duty of a People*.

44. The full text of the Maryland Toleration Act of 1649 can be found in, e.g., Henry S. Commager, ed., *Documents of American History*, 9th ed., vol. 1 (Englewood Cliffs, N.J.: Prentice-Hall, 1973), pp. 31–32.

45. A comprehensive review of provisions for freedom of choice concerning religion finds a compact statement in Robert A. Rutland, *The Birth of the Bill of Rights, 1776–1791* (New York: Collier Books, 1962), chap. 2.

46. See the discussion of suffrage in chap. 1, herein, and the sources cited there.

47. Merle Curti, Richard H. Shryock, Thomas C. Cochran, and Fred H. Harrington, *An American History*, vol. 1 (New York: Harper and Brothers, 1950), pp. 78–79.

48. For the Virginia Statute of Religious Liberty, 1786, see, e.g., Commager, *Documents of American History*, pp. 125–26.

49. For instance, "The Declaration of Rights, &c," in the Constitution of Maryland, 1776: "XXXIII... nor ought any person to be compelled to frequent or maintain, or contribute, unless on contract, to maintain any particular place of worship, or any particular ministry; yet the Legislature may, in their discretion, lay a general and equal tax, for the support of the Christian religion, leaving to each individual the power of appointing the payment over of the money, collected from him, to the support of any particular place of worship or minister...." Thorpe, *Federal and State Constitutions*, vol. 3, p. 1689. In general, see Anson Phelps Stokes, *Church and State in the United States*, vol. 1 (New York: Harper and Brothers, 1950), chap. 5.

50. Massachusetts Constitution of 1780, Art. III, in Thorpe, *Federal and State Constitutions*, vol. 3, pp. 1889–90.

51. As to "both," see the New Jersey Constitution of 1776: "XVIII. That no person ... ever be obliged to pay tithes, taxes, or any other rates ... contrary to what he believes to be right, or has, deliberately and voluntarily engaged himself to perform." "XIX. That there shall be no establishment of any one religious sect in this Province, in preference to another...." Compare the summary statement of Delaware: "There shall be no establishment of any religious sect in this State in preference to another; and no clergyman or preacher shall be capable of holding any civil office in this State...." Thorpe, *American Charters*, vol. 5, p. 2597, and vol. 1, pp. 567–68. For general accounts, see Stokes, *Church and State;* Sanford H. Cobb, *The Rise of Religious Liberty in America* (1902; New York: Cooper Square Publishers, 1968), chaps. 9–10; and R. Freeman Butts, *The American Tradition in Religion and Education* (Boston: Beacon Press, 1950), esp. chap. 3.

52. "XXXVIII... that the free exercise and enjoyment of religious profession and worship, without discrimination or preference, shall forever hereafter

be allowed, within this State, to all mankind. . . ." Thorpe, *Federal and State Constitutions*, vol. 5, pp. 2636–37.

53. There is a good discussion of this point in Walter Berns, *The First Amendment and the Future of American Democracy* (New York: Basic Books, 1976), chap. 1. Compare Stokes, *Church and State*, vol. I, chaps. 4–6.

54. See, e.g., Berns, *The First Amendment*, chap. 1; and Mark DeWolfe Howe, *The Garden and the Wilderness* (Chicago: University of Chicago Press, 1965). For the view that total separation was intended, see Leonard W. Levy, *The Establishment Clause* (New York: Macmillan, 1986).

55. There is considerable difference of opinion about the precise nature and timing of these changes, though. See, e.g., Wood, *Creation of the American Republic;* John P. Diggins, *The Lost Soul of American Politics* (New York: Basic Books, 1984); and Wills, *Explaining America.* Lance Banning, *The Jeffersonian Persuasion: Evolution of a Party Ideology* (Ithaca, N.Y.: Cornell University Press, 1978), pp. 92ff, dissents expressly from Wood's dating of the change in any general sense (arguing for a decade or so later). A particularly useful discussion of the "modernization" of Hamilton's understanding can be found in Gerald Stourzh, *Alexander Hamilton and the Idea of Republican Government* (Stanford, Calif.: Stanford University Press, 1970), chaps. 2–3, esp. pp. 63–75. Two notable studies published since this book was first composed consider the classical republican civic-virtue understanding of politics as substantially defunct by the time of the constitutional convention: Pangle, *Spirit of Modern Republicanism;* Wood, *Radicalism of the American Revolution,* though neither denies either the continuation of a concern for civic virtue among political leaders of the time or the relevance for the American political condition of such concern. On the later survival of virtue, see Banning, *Jeffersonian Persuasion;* and Robert H. Shalhope, "Towards a Republican Synthesis: The Emergence of an Understanding of Republicanism in American Historiography," *William and Mary Quarterly,* 3d ser., 29 (1972): 49.

56. See, e.g., Benjamin Rush, *A Plan for the Establishment of Public Schools and the Diffusion of Knowledge in Pennsylvania; To which Are Added, Thoughts upon the Mode of Education Proper in a Republic,* in *American Political Writing,* vol. 1, ed. Hyneman and Lutz, pp. 675ff.

57. Lawrence Cremin, *American Education: The Colonial Experience, 1607–1783* (New York: Harper and Row, 1970), p. 544.

58. Ibid.; Ellwood P. Cubberly, *Public Education in the United States* (Boston: Houghton Mifflin, 1919), chap. 3.

59. Massachusetts Constitution of 1780, Chapter V, Sec. 2, in Thorpe, *Federal and State Constitutions*, vol. 3, 1907–8.

60. See esp. the discussion in Rush Welter, *Popular Education and Democratic Thought in America* (New York: Columbia University Press, 1962), chap. 2, and sources cited there.

244 Part 2: Republican Government

61. Paul Monroe, *Founding of the American Public School System* (New York: Macmillan, 1940), chaps. 8–10; Lawrence Cremin, *The American Common School: An Historic Conception* (New York: Bureau of Publications, Teachers College, Columbia University, 1951); Welter, *Popular Education and Democratic Thought in America.*

62. Wood, *Creation of the American Republic*, chap. 15, esp. pp. 606ff.

63. Washington to Madison, 31 March 1787, *The Papers of James Madison*, vol. 9, ed. Robert A. Rutland (Chicago: University of Chicago Press, 1975), p. 343.

64. Madison to Washington, 16 April 1787, ibid, p. 384. In the Philadelphia Convention Madison retreated at least partially from his explicit support (p. 385) of a constitutional provision for federal coercive power over the states. See Max Farand, ed., *The Records of the Federal Convention of 1787*, rev. ed., vol. 1 (New Haven, Conn.: Yale University Press, 1937), p. 54.

65. Madison's rehearsals of this argument prior to *The Federalist* appear in his notes on "Vices of the Political System of the United States," *Papers of James Madison*, vol. 9, pp. 345–58; remarks in the Philadelphia Convention are in Farand, *Records*, vol. 1, pp. 134–36, and in his letter to Jefferson cited in note 66. On the probable inspiration of the argument by David Hume, see esp. Trevor Colbourn, ed., *Fame and the Founding Fathers: Essays by Douglas Adair* (New York: W. W. Norton, 1974), chap. 4; and Hume's "That Politics May Be Reduced to a Science" and "Idea of a Perfect Commonwealth" in, e.g., *David Hume's Political Essays*, ed. Charles Hendel (New York: Liberal Arts Press, 1953).

66. Madison to Jefferson, 24 October 1787, *Papers of James Madison*, vol. 10, pp. 212–14.

67. Wills, *Explaining America*, chap. 22, and the introduction to his edition of *The Federalist* (New York: Bantam Books, 1982), pp. xviii-xxiv, makes the case and provides the references on this point, but see esp. the *Federalist No. 55.* The emphasis Wills gives to Madison's reliance on his "filtration theory" of representation, linked to virtue, may not be correct, but Wills's emphasis on Madison's hopes for the role of virtue in national politics under the Constitution seems persuasive.

68. On the different perspectives suggested in this paragraph, see, e.g., Linda Kerber, *Federalists in Dissent: Imagery and Ideology in Jeffersonian America* (Ithaca, N.Y.: Cornell University Press, 1970); Richard Buel, Jr., *Securing the Revolution: Ideology in American Politics, 1789–1815* (Ithaca, N.Y.: Cornell University Press, 1972); Banning, *Jeffersonian Persuasion*; and Robert E. Shalhope, *John Taylor of Caroline: Pastoral Republican* (Columbia: University of South Carolina Press, 1980).

69. For a view of regional subcultures consistent with what has been said here about public versus private concerns tending to distinguish New England

from the regions of Republicanism, see David Hackett Fischer, *Albion's Seed* (New York: Oxford University Press, 1989).

70. As for this interpretation, compare Buel, *Securing the Revolution;* and Banning, *Jeffersonian Persuasion.*

71. Ian A. Budge, *Agreement and the Stability of Democracy* (Chicago: Markham, 1970), considers the first three factors.

Editor's Conclusion

CHARLES E. GILBERT

THE FOUNDING WAS ACCOMPLISHED by many more Americans than the few fathers assembled in Philadelphia whom we customarily celebrate. This had to be so in the free American society of the late eighteenth century. Even if we exclude from active responsibility those who simply went along without comment, and make due allowance for leadership in an allegedly "deferential" politics, responsibility had to be rather broadly diffused in the new political order. The compound polity was new enough, open enough, and dispersed enough in space to require the responsible participation of many.

The many responsible Americans spanned distinct regions and probably distinguishable civic generations, reflected competing economic interests and religious denominations, and stemmed from disparate immigrant stocks, beside inhabiting separate states. They were nevertheless, it was argued in chapter 5, more alike than not in political traditions and capacities and thus appeared likely to compose an effective political community. It was suggested in Part 1 that some aspects of this alikeness were thought to be crucial to a community of civic obligation—and thus to justify the exclusion of numerous other Americans.

The Argument in Outline

The foregoing chapters explored what the responsible Americans established as policies and operative traditions about certain presumptively critical issues, basically two, in republican government. The first of these issues occupied us in Part 1; we can call it one of inclusion/exclusion, or how to delimit the new American political community. This issue has not on the whole (or as a whole) come down to us historically as occasioning notable debate, perhaps because it seemed implicitly problematic at the time, and perhaps because it was settled partly on incidental grounds. It is an issue that might have arisen from avarice, prejudice, chauvinism, or ethnocentrism alone or combined, and might still have been rationalized in republican terms—as presumably occurred to some extent; but there was another side to it as well. The other side was the apparently critical problem of responsible citizenship—the consideration that newly autonomous, fully responsible self-government would require such citizenship. The republican and religious traditions to this effect took on new urgency and substance in the founding period. (There was also a more particular British-American tradition prone to locate republican purity in "Gothic" or Anglo-Saxon provenance, but the effect of this, if any, in restricting American citizenship seems problematical.) Some inhabitants of the American domain, then, might not become citizens of or participants in the American polity if they lacked national loyalty, religious and other ethnocultural attributes conducive to civic responsibility, or histories of participation in and commitment to the traditions of independent republican government. But how were civic responsibility and susceptibility to the appropriate republican traditions to be interpreted? Primarily in terms of *virtue*.

A second founding issue, the subject of Part 2, may be said to have concerned the early working-out of operative understandings of three necessarily connected elements of republicanism—equality, liberty, and virtue. In this study *equality* gets less attention than *liberty* and *virtue*. Not that equality was noncontroversial, for there were more broadly egalitarian tendencies at large in the founding period than those composing the mainstream of more or less elite republican thought on which this work has drawn primarily. In this probably prevalent republican tradition, common citizenship—an approximate equality of responsibility for self-government and an abstract parity of civil status under the law—seems about as near as we can come to the measure of equality in political terms. Yet this measure applied only to those accorded full membership of the political community, and such membership was frequently qualified or denied according to more exclusive social norms.

Both civil and "social" equality gained ground in the founding period, however, through state legislative revocations of privilege and disability. There were other public issues relating to social and economic equality—nationally and perhaps most notably debates between Jeffersonians and Hamiltonians over the direction of economic development, and numerous kindred instances in state politics. As for their political implications, some people saw clearly enough that the distribution of effectively responsible participation in self-government could be conditioned by the direction of economic development; and people disagreed over desirabilities and priorities in this regard. Some questions of governmental structure—for instance, the composition and powers of upper houses and the districting of lower houses—were also questions of equality. On the other hand, various issues bearing on popular control of government, or on popular versus official "power"—for example, about instruction of representatives in legislatures—that we today would tend to consider issues of equality were more likely then to be considered issues of liberty.

Most evident in this study, however (to recur to Part 1), is the close association of *equality* with citizenship and the society's willingness to discriminate between citizens and others. One may find a classic example of this circumscription of equality in Thomas Jefferson's reservations about the free Negro as prospective citizen (see chapter 2), compared with his poignant condemnation of slavery: "I tremble for my country when I reflect that God is just; that his justice cannot sleep forever." Some were more equal than others, we would say today in George Orwell's ambient epigram; and so it was. Citizenship and equality qualified one another; equality was inclusion in full citizenship. Thomas Jefferson thus appears to have believed that both slavery and political authoritarianism violated natural law but also that not everyone had the capacities appropriate to American citizenship. These beliefs were at the very least not unrepresentative. We could say in simple logic that this was so because the founding conceptions of equality were limited, but we might say with greater historical sensitivity that these beliefs were associated with an implicit conception of political community and a more explicit concern for civic virtue.

We cannot, however, easily understand the founding concern with virtue, save in its particular connection with republican liberty. These elements were more central to self-government in the republican tradition than equality was, and they were the central considerations of Part 2 of this study. As for liberty, the growth of rancorous political divisions in the first decade of the new Republic led necessarily then (and consequently in this study) to consideration of the limits of legitimate dissent as a critical problem of republican government. (Indeed, the political divisions had to do largely with contending conceptions of republicanism and virtue.) As for virtue, the problem in this study was to identify its putative attributes and to appreciate its place in the political theory of the founding.

These two inquiries have been closely connected, and we saw at the end of Part 1 that they would be. After all, the founding generations were ready to draw distinctions, pragmatically gross and categorical, concerning eligibility for citizenship. Much of what they had to say about such distinctions pointed to the centrality of virtue in republican citizenship, which we can render today as capacity for "responsible" citizenship. Responsible citizenship required qualities, or virtues, in vocation, civic participation, and official action conducive to the public good or imbued with concern for it. It meant governing the uses of one's liberty and thus the dispositions of "free government" by similar considerations.

Virtue was referred to in the title of chapter 9 as "the preserver of liberty," reflecting an ancient republican understanding. Without a prevalence of virtue—meaning certain private virtues presumptively conducive to the public good, or a commitment of officials and citizens to seek the public good, or both of these—the republican regime would probably falter from corruptions within government or abuses of liberty (likewise corruptions) in the population. Liberty was obviously integral to self-government and apparently problematic.

Republican and Puritan traditions together, however, emphasized a more integral conception of virtue as preserver of liberty—and we tend to forget the extent to which the Church of England as well as other denominations and sects were influenced by the Genevan and English roots of Puritanism. In this conception, as we saw in chapter 6, civil liberty amounts to more than simply individual freedom, and its legitimation entails more than ad hoc, situational weighings of claims between liberty and authority. Civil liberty is instead "a scheme of ordered liberty," to which can be added *well* or *justly* ordered. Liberty, then, takes its meaning in part from the principles of the regime, and in a republican regime these include considerations of justice, along with other virtues. Virtue is involved in the very "ordering," or regulating, of liberty, primarily in its personal and social disciplining of citizenship, secondarily as an attribute of public laws. While a prevalence of virtue in society is favored by a judicious regime and appropriate public policies, it is also reciprocally essential to the preservation of these.

The founding period's emphasis on virtue can thus be seen as a response to the then apparently problematical prospects of full-fledged (and, later, large-scale) self-government. Three major problems or concerns can be identified in the writing and recorded speaking of the time, all of which figured in traditional "republican" literature. One, given impetus by the events of the Revolution, was official corruption, injustice, and abuse of power. A second centered on the constituent problems of interest group particularism, "factional" disagreement or dissension, and declension from public-regarding behavior. A third, especially early in the founding period, reflecting colonial preoccupations as well as republican literature and the special influence of *The Spirit of the Laws,* was economic inadequacy—a failure of societal welfare from lack of individual productivity. Virtue and the particular virtues in point were pretty much the opposites of these three generic concerns, or of aspects of them. Opinion leaders of the time, lay and clerical, evidently hoped to shape an American character appropriate to their (received) analysis of the requirements of self-government by urging virtue. More than merely a utilitarian tactic, however, this was republican praxis, serving visions of a good society.

Virtue was a sort of social discipline, or "social control," in which self-control (individual self-government) was necessary to the effectiveness of collective self-government. It served common or even collective purposes at least incidentally through the private virtues and perhaps constitutively through public virtue. It thus implied political community both because there was a need for general agreement on private virtues and because "public virtue" implied a public good—James Madison's "permanent and aggregate interests of the community." If we take seriously what was said about its substance, however, we must also say that the high regard adjured by virtue for political community was, while qualifying individualism, still much less than communal. Virtue was evidently meant to speak to autonomous persons about the common requirements of "free" self-government and a just, concordant, productive society. It did not spell communitarianism, but it did imply "commonality."[1] There are, however, difficult and perplexing issues in this distinction, to be revisited briefly later.

What Happened to Virtue?

Why was virtue's priority apparently in decline by the end of the founding period? Four related possibilities come to mind, all presumably reflecting the practical experience of self-government, especially full-scale, national self-government in its initial decade: (1) new, more or less fundamental understandings of politics may have ensued from this experience, tending to invalidate classical and radical republican conceptions, and with them republican, even clerical, claims for the role of virtue; (2) perhaps virtue got caught in a cognitive discordance between perceptions of self-seeking as normal in politics and prescriptions approximating self-denial; (3) the party battles that developed in the first dozen years of the Republic may have revealed (and indeed stimulated) divergent conceptions of authentic and workable republicanism, including divergent perspectives on virtue; and (4) the sheer bitterness of these party battles may well have tended to engender pessimism about such presumptively central attributes of virtue as personal moderation and community regard. Let's consider each of these possibilities somewhat further.

As for understandings of politics, Americans in the late eighteenth century faced the consequences of full independence, a new democratic impetus, and economic growth in the states, followed by the essentially novel problems of a *national* politics, with only their limiting *local* experience plus an arguably anachronistic and largely speculative literature for guidance. Perhaps, then, this literature and its diverse traditions of virtue were invalidated by the practical experience of republican government and were at least partly superseded by apparently superior paradigms. According to some historical accounts such a reorientation of political thinking toward a candid understanding of republican politics in terms of competing interests was well underway by the time of the Philadelphia Convention in 1787, based on a decade's experience of state and interstate politics, while other historians have dated it later, mainly after the turn of the century.[2] The famous *Federalist No. 10* was perhaps the most elegant contemporary expression of a new, "pluralist" understanding (the benignity of *numerous* competing interests), though it also looked to the new national constitution for institutional support of appropriately disinterested (i.e., virtuous) national leadership.[3]

These tendencies did not, however, necessarily dictate an abandonment of all reliance on virtue—not the several attributes of virtue that were considered in chapter 9 or other particular virtues; and perhaps not even the simple "public-good" element, which, after all, continued to figure rhetorically in American politics, though traceable more apparently to Locke's *Second Treatise* than to prior republican sources. Both the apprehensions for which virtue was a prescription and the prescription itself were arguably still valid to some extent, with or without the rest of the "republican" understanding of politics. However, while a new understanding of self-government as ineluctably, legitimately, and even advantageously a matter of contending partial or private interests would not *necessarily* have been fatal for virtue, it would necessarily have put virtue in a different position, as more a palliative than a prophylactic; and in this position of degree and discretion it could more easily have been discounted. Apparently it was discounted increasingly as time passed and the nineteenth century progressed.

Virtue was not particularly associated with innocence about "interests" in politics. On the contrary, a prevalent (republican) pessimism about human nature and motivations in politics is commonly reported among Americans of the founding period.[4] If these reports are accurate (their documentation is generally available), then conceivably the quest for virtue stumbled over a contradiction between, on the one hand, expectations of self-interest and, on the other, recommendations of moderation, temperance, and public regard, in which the more "realistic" (or simplistic?) expectations won out. Certainly some early issues of national economic policy—excise taxes and Hamilton's plans for the public debt, for example—manifestly complicated pursuit of the public interest with questions of cui bono.

A tendency to discount virtue could well have been encouraged by the divergent perspectives on virtue—the different virtues that came to be advocated—on opposite sides of the party battles of the 1790s. These differences were considered late in chapter 9. They were in some and probably most cases differences of emphasis only, but there were specifically contending evaluations at least about whose virtue was the more suspect (the government's or its critics' in particular; leaders' or citizens' in general) and the priority of certain virtues (e.g., public economy and republican simplicity). Partisan differences about how virtue applied to the new republic's condition thus could have contributed to skepticism about virtue in general.[5]

It could also be that virtue was imperiled by the rhetorical violence of domestic political conflict during the 1790s. Virtue—that is, the deontological position of virtue—may have fallen victim to the practice of republican politics, as deep cleavages emerged within the national leadership over the directions of national development and international alignment. We now know pretty well that the early "party system" resulting from these cleavages was not extensively organized and that it did not last long. The attitudes of many partisans in the federal period, however, are clear enough in their addresses and letters. There was a remarkable acrimony in this protoparty competition. The issues entailed basic principles; some of the antagonists had known one another well and had earlier worked together for common principles; and the partisanship in which they became engaged was in a sense illicit, a factionalism that was not supposed to happen and was itself something of a fall from virtue. Things reached the point by, say, 1795 that some leaders on each side profoundly mistrusted those on the other side. On each side actions of the other side seemed to threaten republican government. Separation or civil war was occasionally contemplated as a possibility if either opposing party pressed its position far enough, since the (largely sectional) differences seemed so fundamental. These predictions were not simply traditional republican bromides about the effects of factionalism.[6]

Perhaps, then, virtue fell victim to partisan discord. In 1794–95, as we saw in chapter 4, members of Congress from both parties pretty much equally and similarly invoked virtue during the debate on the terms of admission to citizenship. This was shortly before the intensely partisan division of 1795 over the Jay Treaty, which is commonly held by historians of the period to have crystallized party alignments in national politics. By the next debates on naturalization in 1798, and the Alien and Sedition Acts of that year, interpretations of virtue may have seemed all too evidently partisan. Perhaps the argument was so bitter in part because its substance—identification of the critical dangers to self-government—seemed so urgent on both sides.[7] Perhaps national opinion reacted adversely, especially after the Federalist electoral defeat in 1800, to an apparent Federalist attempt to engross virtue—to enlist it (along with much of the clergy) on the Federalist side; or perhaps on both sides virtue lost its virtue in failing to transcend partisanship, notwithstanding its benign appearance in Jefferson's inaugural.[8]

Various other factors, already noticed, probably contributed to a weakening of virtue. American society was undergoing rapid social change. The regional or sectional divisions so prominent in the new national politics evidently reflected not only tangible interests but somewhat different cultural conceptions of virtue. Finally (let us say), the religious impetus for virtue probably was in decline, at least temporarily. Since midcentury or earlier evangelical religion had been gaining ground in the population at large, while rational and skeptical perspectives were doing so among elites. Then "the Revolution . . . disrupted American religion; it scattered congregations, destroyed church buildings, interrupted the training of ministers, and politicized people's thinking. The religious yearning of common people, however, remained strong, stronger than any of the revolutionary leaders recognized."[9] It was not until the early nineteenth century that institutional religion took hold strongly again, which it then did most strongly in evangelical terms. Together these developments may well have loosened religious sympathy and institutional communication between clerical and political leadership, on the one hand, and rank and file, on the other, undercutting both the conviction and persuasiveness of leadership.

Yet the normative decline of virtue, with the gradual dissolution of republican doctrine, did not necessarily depreciate the intrinsic importance of virtue for self-government, as distinct from perceptions of its efficacy. For example, the problem of combining political community and responsible citizenship remained a difficult one in American life, and it was part of the argument of chapter 9 that sustaining such a balance, or combination, was part of the point of virtue in the founding period. If we turn to Tocqueville's portrayal of American society and politics some thirty years after the founding period, we find the author of *Democracy in America* struggling with this issue, projected first as the prospect of a "tyranny of the majority" and then as that of individual(istic) neglect of civic obligation, each threatening to undermine free government and produce despotism.[10] The problem that troubled Tocqueville was that the practice of liberty and equality—in Tocqueville's view, equality in particular —seemed unlikely to be sufficiently informed by something like virtue. Tocqueville's most pessimistic concerns for the future of American self-government have not materialized (perhaps in part because of mitigating factors he also identified), but they have continued to trouble thoughtful observers of American democracy.

The Future of Virtue and Community

Equality and liberty were, we observed earlier, regulated by virtue in the prevalent political theory of the founding. Since the founding, equality and liberty have expanded and altered in conception; virtue has atrophied. Residues of founding virtue surely have continued to figure in American politics but hardly as "fundamental principles" of self-government.

Probably the principal effect of expansions of equality and liberty in American politics has been the extension and diversification, and also the pluralization, of the political community. The more inclusive distribution of full citizenship has almost certainly enhanced equality in nonpolitical aspects of life as well, however far one believes we still have to go. Pluralization (perhaps) aside, this may be the progress of which most contemporary Americans are most proud; it is no part of the argument of this study that things should be otherwise. Implicit in this study, however, is the question of whether broader commonality and more widely shared norms of civic responsibility are possible now *without* compromising the salutary social results of extended equality and liberty and *without* loss of political inclusiveness.

The argument is not that *no* compromise or qualification of equality or (especially) liberty would be entailed in accommodations to virtue. To say that assertions of liberty are appropriately informed by considerations of virtue, or to emphasize the public responsibilities of citizenship, is to qualify liberty—or the conceivable reach of liberty. But a relevant conception of virtue, or of virtue's availability, today would also have to be informed reciprocally by the progress of equality and liberty.

If virtue is not necessarily illiberal respecting its availability, however, it conceivably is illiberal in another sense. Carter Braxton, the very aristocratic eighteenth-century Virginian whom we met in chapter 9, seems to have anticipated another objection to any campaign for a modern American regime of virtue. Is the public order (or, in a republican regime, the majority) to be vested with moral authority—with authority to define not only what is lawful but what is virtuous as well? We probably would not today write virtue, or certain virtues, into the Constitution—but then, the declarations of rights in the early state constitutions were in such provisions mostly hortatory and rhetorical. Each of them in totality tends to deny that the state, though it may assist institutions conducive to virtue, is itself a source of morality. Yet this constitutional history did not preclude extensive state sumptuary legislation, nor was it understood to tend to do so. Perhaps a revival of emphasis on "public virtue" in modern America would provoke issues of this sort—for it appears to be part of the problem of community in American life today that we disagree deeply about the place of the state as custodian of morality regarding numerous regulations, or conceivable regulations, of behavior.

There is, however, a difference between the virtues of old and the prevailing modern views of morality. The virtues we were concerned with in chapter 9 were for the most part considered readily cultivatable and peculiarly suitable to life in society; more traditionally they had been considered "natural." (Temperance seems a good example.) They lacked quite a lot of the imperative and ultimate qualities of much modern "morality" (e.g., temperance as abstinence), and, for the most part, they focused less on what one did politically than on how one did it. In such terms, could we recapture them, virtue might be supportable today, even if still subject to cultural differences.

We also endure inverse disadvantages in a polity unregulated by virtue. One of these is that equality and liberty, untempered by virtue—and not notably more perspicuous conceptually than, say, late eighteenth-century virtue—come to us with their own moral authority, which has not been proof against appropriation by particular interests for partial purposes. Equality and liberty are subject to abuse—they are, that is, if one believes in the utility of community and in justice that includes the general welfare..

Still, the modern tendency is to define self-government as liberal democracy and to define liberal democracy in terms of liberty and equality (assimilating justice largely to equality) to the exclusion of other concerns. In so doing we tend to neglect important normative supports for civic capacity. This study suggests some concern about the American capacity to sustain effective self-government in today's apparent depletion of the moral elements of community or their public forms and commitments. One may rejoin to this concern that, in the author's own account, these elements were attenuating by the turn of the nineteenth century, notwithstanding which the Republic is now the world's longest-functioning liberal democracy; and one may remark that the history of the Alien and Sedition Acts in chapter 7 hardly suggests an effective founding regime of virtue regarding either side of that issue.

Probably the republican formula became too formulaic, at least in the light of modern political understandings. Possibly it tended to overstate the dependence of self-government at all times on particular dispositions and commitments of the population. Perhaps in some versions it bordered on tautology, implicitly equating virtue with popular decorum.

In one view of democratic politics, however, the republican insistence on the essentiality of virtue—of certain virtues—in American self-government seems essentially correct. In this view, a polity in which popular attitudes toward politics and popular habits of political conduct do not matter much can hardly be counted as self-governing. This is a perspective on self-government in which the people, not "the system," are substantially self-governing and in which the people, ultimately if not immanently, are responsible for "the system." It is not the only credible perspective on self-government. Others, more systemic, less voluntaristic or popularly responsible, accord greater weight in the sustaining of self-government to such factors as institutional and coalitional mechanics, constitutional limitations, provisions for official disinterest or distance from popular control, and (or) accretions of Humeian habit and acquiescence in the population as equivalent to republican "consent." The first view, however, is a fuller view of popular government. In it, the people, in some considerable sense and to some considerable extent, make the polity.

In this sense, to this extent, the founding continues so long as the regime continues. In our time liberty and (especially) equality have gained in priority among communicating elites and plain citizens as criteria for public policy. Opportunity for the full participation of all Americans in an expanded political community has become a more urgent objective of public policy. Yet concurrently, and in part consequently, there have developed stronger assertions of particular interest and of subcommunity defined in terms of race or ethnicity, religious conviction, gender, generation, economic status, and traditional or postindustrial culture, inter alia. Immigrant populations from south and west of this nation are expanding especially fast, enhancing apparent diversity—but also perhaps reinforcing conventional virtue. Political communication has been nationalizing faster since the advent of television, and the rhetorical burden may be straining the bonds of political community; we are all in one another's living rooms, aggressively or protectively. A much-enlarged (national) public sector, beginning with the "Great Society" and continuing to grow in the 1970s more insistently than it diminished in the 1980s, has also attracted to *national* policy debate a broader range of disparate and particular interests.

From the standpoint of this study none of these developments is to be regretted per se. Together, however, they implicate republican issues of effective political representation and sufficient political community rather like those raised by the Anti-Federalists against the prospect of national consolidation in the constitutional debates of 1787–88.[11] A national prevalence of such virtues as moderation, temperance, industry, perhaps even frugality, a disinterested concern for justice, and a sense of commonality would probably be helpful in these circumstances, if a national prevalence were possible now, as it may not have been in the founding period.

The point of this study is not to propose a revival of the old-time founding virtue. Just suppose, however, that it were widely proposed to bring back virtue in appropriate contemporary terms, never mind how or in precisely what terms. What responses might we expect?[12] Probably two principal responses, toward the ends of a spectrum. The first is that no revival is desirable, for reasons that have been canvassed already: its implications are variously but fundamentally illiberal; any imaginable prescriptions of virtue would be too parochial for a "great society" or too general to engage the disparate particularisms of modern American life; the polity can probably function systemically and institutionally on automatic pilot without regard to virtue; and perhaps for other reasons as well, none of which seemed to the author of this study to take seriously enough either the promise or the problems of popular government. In the current lexicon of moral and political philosophy the position dictating these responses is commonly styled liberal individualism. A second imaginable response would be positive, and its program would in one philosophical sense be radical, pursuant to two premises: virtue implies moral community, and moral community is inconsistent with liberal individualism.[13] We can call this the communitarian position.

A basic philosophical issue about the nature of community and of the individual, and of course the relation between them, is said to distinguish these two positions. For communitarians, community comes first as attitudes and interactions, shaping perceptions and communications, contributing traditions, governing social intercourse, and pervasively conditioning life's possibilities. Individual morality and opportunity thus derive largely from community and, crucially, are acknowledged to do so. Liberal individualism, on the other hand, has tended to challenge this perspective epistemologically and sociologically and to find in life's source or circumstances more justification of individual autonomy and responsibility than communitarians do. Yet surely this philosophical issue is not just binary; surely most of us understand it, either technically or practically, as a matter of degree and situation, and can hardly understand it otherwise.

According to some accounts, the premises of liberal individualism were well established in America before the founding period; virtue and community were therefore superficial and fated for ephemerality.[14] In some other accounts, the balance of communitarian and individualistic traditions or cultures varied somewhat by region; New England manifested the strongest tradition of moral community, albeit coupled with individual responsibility.[15] In the present work, the diffuse tradition of virtue, subject to regional variation in balance or valence, appealed to both personal responsibility and moral community, each qualifying the other, in the founding period.

The "publick spirit" or regard for public good so much remarked on and admired by modern communitarian commentators was also only one aspect of virtue in the founding period. The prescription of particular, traditional virtues bearing on one's otherwise private conduct was no less important, not least in its implicit stress on individual responsibility and productive individual activity. Virtue, both "private" and "public," implied and reflected political community, but it seems not to have been communitarian in the sense that individual autonomy and responsibility were secondary, any more than the Lockean individualism that some say superseded it was, in *its* Puritan/republican reception, strictly individualistic and lacking in community regard, whatever Locke's esoteric intentions.[16]

Were a modern virtue to evolve to meet the needs of modern American democracy, the perceived needs of the founding would probably still be the pertinent needs. Much of the old virtue, in its ambiguous balance of private and public, would probably be pertinent also; its emphasis on both individual responsibility and political community seems essential to transcending modern particularisms. Of course the operative conception of political community would have to be less parochial than that of the founding. The discipline of citizenship and understanding of justice in a modern American virtue would have to support both inclusiveness and commonality and enable Americans to deal with one another in republican candor.

Yet, while political community need not be narrowly parochial, there probably are limits to its feasible diversities as a locus of effective self-government in the fuller sense suggested above. In the apparently prevailing view of the founding period, a high degree of social homogeneity was requisite to political community and hence to the nourishment of virtue. Whatever the validity of this view may have been then, its practical relevance is much diminished today. Perhaps the critical relationships were overstated in the founding perspective, or have changed, or are subject to change. Perhaps a contemporary reception of virtue (assuming sufficient sources of leadership for it) could itself engender a greater sense of commonality, or political community, and a greater sense of civic discipline, notwithstanding the growth of social heterogeneity, while tempering sundry particularisms and even the several dogmas of the political left and right. Indeed, the chief virtue of virtue might turn out to be, not entirely for the first time in American history, its contribution to reconciling diversity and commonality.

Notes

1. Probably it was not inconsistent with a reception of "Lockean individualism"—not that we are certain there *was* such a reception in the founding period or earlier or that the individualism of the *Second Treatise* was, as written, inconsistent with, say, Puritan conceptions of community. On these issues, see, e.g., John Dunn, "The Politics of Locke in England and America in the Eighteenth Century," in *John Locke: Problems and Perspectives*, ed. John W. Yolton (Cambridge: Cambridge University Press, 1969), pp. 45–80; John Dunn, *The Political Thought of John Locke* (Cambridge: Cambridge University Press, 1969), chaps. 16–18; and Peter Laslett, ed., *John Locke: Two Treatises of Government* (New York: New American Library, 1963), introduction, chap. 5, esp. pp. 120ff; but compare Thomas L. Pangle, *The Spirit of Modern Republicanism* (Chicago: University of Chicago Press, 1988), for a very persuasive contrary interpretation; and John V. Diggins, *The Lost Soul of American Politics* (New York: Basic Books, 1984).

2. On this issue, see chap. 9, note 55, herein.

3. Madison was by then at least skeptical about the republican efficacy of virtue based on experience in the states. See chap. 9, notes 63–67, herein. Compare the *Federalist No. 51* which deals with broadly similar concerns without resorting to virtue in either leaders or electors. Understandably, this paper was long attributed to Hamilton, who apparently had abandoned all hope for an efficatious virtue. See Gerald Stourzh, *Alexander Hamilton and the Idea of Republican Government* (Stanford, Calif.: Stanford University Press, 1970), chaps. 2–3, esp. pp. 63–75.

4. For example: "The optimism of [Americans'] belief in the capacity of men to shape their political institutions was tempered by an almost universally shared conviction of man's ineradicable selfishness. It was assumed that self-interest was the dominant motive of man's political behavior. . . ." Cecelia M. Kenyon, ed., *The Antifederalists* (Indianapolis: Bobbs-Merrill, 1966), p. xxix.

5. The point can be and has been put more strongly: the fundamental and formative division in the "first party system" had to do with competing conceptions of self-government. See, e.g., Richard Buel, Jr., *Securing the Revolution: Ideology in American Politics, 1789–1815* (Ithaca, N.Y.: Cornell University Press, 1972), for an extended statement of this point from what often appears to be a Republican (or Anti-Federalist) perspective; here the competing conceptions have to do with the role of the public or the populace in governing. Compare note 6 below.

6. Some documentation of this point can be found in ibid., pp. 191, 194–95, 197, 210, 219.

7. See, e.g., Marshall Smelser, "The Jacobin Phrenzy: Federalism and the Menace of Liberty, Equality, and Fraternity," *Review of Politics* 13 (1951):

457–82, and "The Jacobin Phrenzy: The Menace of Monarchy, Plutocracy, and Anglophilia," *Review of Politics* 21 (1959): 239–58; and John R. Howe, Jr., "Republican Thought and the Political Violence of the 1790s," *American Quarterly* 19 (1967): 147–65, who argues in particular that the special and progressive vehemence of politics in the 1790s derived from different conceptions of republicanism and the probable threats to it and from the perceived exigency of this issue.

8. On the parenthetical point about the clergy, see Buel, *Securing the Revolution*, pp. 166–75, 231–34.

9. Gordon S. Wood, *The Radicalism of the American Revolution* (New York: Alfred A. Knopf, 1992), p. 329.

10. These two interpretations appear in volumes 1 (chap. 15) and 2 (fourth book), respectively, of *Democracy in America*, which were published some five years apart. See, e.g., Alexis de Tocqueville, *Democracy in America*, ed. Phillips Bradley (New York: Random House Vintage Books, 1945).

11. See, e.g., *Letters from the Federal Farmer*, in *The Complete Anti-Federalist*, vol. 2, ed. Herbert Storing (Chicago: University of Chicago Press, 1981), pp. 230–38; *Letters of Agrippa*, ibid., vol. 4, pp. 75–77; and *What the Anti-Federalists Were For*, ibid., vol. 1, pp. 17–23, 43–45.

12. For one example of such a proposal, albeit in less individualistic terms than the *virtue* of the founding seems to support, by and large, see Robert N. Bellah, Richard Madsen, William M. Sullivan, Ann Swidler, and Steven M. Tipton, *Habits of the Heart: Individualism and Commitment in American Life* (Berkeley: University of California Press, 1981).

13. For this view, see, e.g., Alasdair MacIntyre, *After Virtue*, 2d ed. (Notre Dame, Ind.: University of Notre Dame Press, 1984); and, in part, Benjamin Barber, *Strong Democracy: Participatory Politics for a New Age* (Berkeley: University of California Press, 1984).

14. MacIntyre, *After Virtue*, thus maintains that by the late eighteenth century the philosophical basis of virtue was long gone and that the virtue then in vogue was at most a vestige of the particular Aristotelian tradition he posits and dates as having ended philosophically more than a century earlier. For a somewhat different view, that liberal individualism had pretty much displaced the premises of virtue and community in America by the time of the Philadelphia Constitutional Convention, see Diggins, *Lost Soul of American Politics*; and Pangle, *Spirit of Modern Republicanism*.

15. See esp. David Hackett Fischer, *Albion's Seed* (New York: Oxford University Press, 1989).

16. On Locke's esoteric intentions to communicate a theory of radical individualism, see Pangle, *Spirit of Modern Republicanism*, part 3.

In Praise of Patriotism:
Extracts from Three Addresses

Jonathan Mason, Jr., *An Oration . . . to Commemorate
the Bloody Tragedy of the Fifth of March, 1770*
(Boston: John Gill, 1780), p. 8.

Patriotism is essential to the preservation and well being of every free government. To love one's country has ever been esteemed honorable, and under the influence of this noble passion every social virtue is cultivated, freedom prevails through the whole, and the public good is the object of every one's concern. A constitution built upon such principles, and put in execution by men possessed with the love of virtue and their fellow men, must always ensure happiness to it's members. The industry of the citizen will receive encouragement and magnanimity, heroism and benevolence will be esteemed the admired qualifications of the age. Every the least invasion of the public liberty, is considered as an infringement on that of the subject; and feeling himself roused at the appearance of oppression, with a divine enthusiasm he flies to obey the summons of his country and does she but request with zeal he resigns the life of the individual for the preservation of the whole.

Reverend Israel B. Woodward, *American Liberty and
Independence: A Discourse Delivered . . . on the Fourth of July,
1798* (Litchfield, Conn.: Printed by T. Collier, 1798),
pp. 19–20.

Let it be remembered that the Liberty and Independence of America, has been maintained by the blood of her citizens. This day of remembrance of

Warren at Bunker-hill, of Mercer, on the plains near Princeton; of Worster, and of many other gallant officers from the several places, where it was destined by Heaven, that they should fall—demand a sigh and a tear, the choicest, the most becoming tribute we can pay to their memories.—And when this Town remembers one of her sons to have been instantly severed before the cannon's mouth, and his own brother at another time to have expired by the tortures of the unfeeling Britons,—she will not withhold a sympathetic tear, although in fighting for the common cause of their country, they held but a private station. . . .

Let us then rally round the *standard* of government in defence of our lives, liberties, and properties; in support of our peace, honor, and happiness. Let us keep unfurled the banners of *independence*. Let us now and forever have layed up in our hearts, an offering of attachment to our country, freely to be bestowed in an hour of danger. Let this offering have in it no ingredient of base selfishness, treachery, and cowardice, but let it be the pure offering of love, and a generous magnanimity, that will sacrifice property, repose, and life itself, for the public good.

To effect this patriotic, and truly benevolent purpose, it is indispensably necessary that we be *united, stable, watchful in all our public concerns, and especially careful to maintain public and private virtue.*——*Unanimity* is the strength of a nation:—While it continues one, in sentiment and affection, it has nothing to fear from within; but parties and divisions make a war at home, and bring it into our own houses. If we are united, we have nothing to fear from without; like a bundle of rods, while bound together by the general attachment to government, we shall never be broken.

Reverend Nathaniel Bowen, *An Oration Delivered . . .*
on the Fifth of July, 1802, in Commemoration of American
Independence (Providence: John Carter, 1802), pp. 7, 17–19.

It is the laudable design of this institution, to record in the mind of every American a lasting remembrance of the principles of our revolution, and to induce correspondent sentiments and manners. In conformity to this design, it has been the pleasing task of many, on this occasion, to lay before you a recital, suited to make the heart beat high with mingled emotions of pride and joy. . . . Something more is required of every one, than to dwell on the past glories of his country, or to cherish feelings that may be excited by a review of the scenes through which you passed before those glories were achieved. . . . Look forward and anticipate the time when, quenched by the intoxication of liberty and peace, virtue shall be extinguished in the bosom of Americans. The time may come, when, lost to that true love of country which absorbs every private and unworthy passion, they shall move only at the pleasure of the factious leader's will. . . . The time may come, when, unable to detect the artifices of political deception, or to distinguish between true patriotism and false, Americans will look for true patriotism in those ardent professions of regard for the rights and liberties of the people, which flatter them into confidence, and then make that confidence an instrument of revenge upon political opponents. The time may come, when they shall even mistake for true patriotism that excessive zeal of party animosity, which will deafen men to the common claims of humanity and justice; which will establish heresies in politics, from whose punishment no honesty, no faithfulness, will give exemption; which in the blind pursuit of its gratification, forgetting the public benefit, and national and social security, will fill up the best sources of the one, and throw down every barrier by which the other could be defended. . . .

On this day, then, sacred to the past, swear on that altar of freedom which Heaven has erected for you, that your warmest affections, and your best exertions shall be devoted to the future glory of your country.—Strive to root out from the American mind every germ of dissension, and make that union spring and flourish there, which shall cover our whole land with its shade—and yield the wholesome and delicious fruits of national honour and security—social order, harmony and love.—Think not to effect this by indulging that spirit of party rancour, which by inflammatory invectives would hurl a political adversary from the seat of power. The cause of truth, you know, can derive but little benefit from violence; and your use of irritating measures in its defence, will but produce outrage against it.—Rather expect union and harmony to be the effect of a diffusion among the people of a knowledge of their rights and duties, and of the reasons in which those duties and those rights are founded:—a knowledge that need no where else be sought, than in that school where light shines from above to direct men through the path-way of virtue to happiness and Heaven. The power of true religion can alone give a lasting existence to our republic. Antient popular governments were of short and precarious duration, principally because, wanting true religion, they had not access to the only sources of that virtue which can alone make rulers faithful and their people happy. Let the higher advantages reserved by Heaven for later days, be improved by Americans. Let every *one who loves his country,* strive to spread and strengthen the power of that religion among his fellow-citizens, which by sanctions drawn from eternity enforces *piety, industry, sobriety, moderation, benevolence,* and *peace.*—The people who are distinguished by these virtues cannot be enslaved.

Charles S. Hyneman on
the Declaration of Independence
and Personal Equality

In my opinion it debases the rhetoric and diverts the progression of thought to impose on the Declaration of Independence an intention to assert that all persons or all males are equally endowed by nature with the characteristics and the qualities essential to a successful pursuit of safety and happiness. The reasoning which supports my conclusion was stated carefully in an address at Indiana University in October of 1983. I said:

> The Declaration does indeed assert that "all men are created equal." Moreover, it supplies a list of self-evident truths and the first on the list is just that "all men are created equal." But with that you have heard everything Thomas Jefferson has to say on this occasion that can be construed to mean that God intended every man to be equal to all other men; and if you do construe it that way then you render his remark irrelevant to anything else in the document.
>
> The Declaration was written to inform a skeptical world that the American people were cutting themselves loose from Great Britain, and the statement of why they had decided to do so was introduced by an underlying or foundation principle—a self-evident truth. This was that all men are endowed by their Creator with certain unalienable rights (among them being the right to Life, to Liberty, and to pursue Happiness) and that in this respect (endowment with certain unalienable rights) all

men are created equal. From there we go on to the assertion that the purpose of government is to secure these rights, and when any people find that the government they are living under has proved itself to be destructive of those ends, pursuing a course of action designed to "reduce" that people under absolute despotism, it becomes the right, indeed the duty, of that people to throw off such government, replacing it with a new one they think most likely to effect their safety and happiness. Such has come to be the case with the Americans, so they are now dissolving the bonds which have hitherto connected them to Great Britain and propose to assume among the powers of the earth the separate and equal station to which the laws of Nature and of God entitle them.

Twenty-seven offenses by the King of England which show that his intention is to establish "an absolute Tyranny over these States" are then set forth. Not a one of them drops a hint that the King, or his decrees, or his henchmen had subjected anybody in America to differential treatment or had pursued policies repugnant to equal status among individuals, repugnant to equalness of opportunity, or to equalness in enjoyment of benefits or sufferance of disabilities.

. . . Why, then, did Abraham Lincoln say that the nation was so dedicated when it was brought into being, in 1776, just fourscore and seven years before he spoke at Gettysburg? Why, a full century after that, in the wake of *Brown v. Board of Education* and other race discrimination cases, did a multitude of freedom riders, freedom workers, freedom speakers grasp the same misperception of Thomas Jefferson's intent and install it as the No. 1 exhibit of proof that the United States from the very moment of its first valid claim to be an independent nation had committed itself to a principle that in things legal, in the eyes of the state and its officialdom, one man is to be treated as the equal of every other man or conditions must be altered so that a continuous progression toward equalness of treatment can be assured? The answer must be that they turned to the Declaration of Independence because they could not find the promise they were looking for in the documents where it should have been enthroned—in the Constitution of the United States and the state constitutions which were written during the revolutionary years.

The frailty of constitutional support for a commitment to parity among individuals is too important to allow dismissal of the subject, but limits of space forbid a satisfying summary statement. Ponder the preamble which explains why a new constitution was found necessary less than a decade aftger the first one (the Articles) went effect. To form a more perfect union, of course. But also to establish justice, and to secure the blessings of liberty. Nothing about equality, however. No canon of emphasis or style would have been jeopardized if the final objective of the list of six had read: "and secure the blessings of liberty and equality to ourselves and our posterity. . . . " The word "equal" which appears only four times in the Constitution as originally adopted applies only to procedure in voting for president and dividing senators "as equally as may be" into three classes so that a third of the total may be elected in each even-numbered year. And so it remained with the national Constitution until long after the last survivor of the founding generation had gone to his reward, until ratification of the second of the civil war amendments (1868) that no state may deny to any person within its jurisdiction the equal protection of the laws.26[1]

This reading of the intent back of Jefferson's words, in the view of many distinguished students of the American Revolution, is legalistic, cramped by lack of imagination. The latest to express himself eloquently but cautiously on this point is the English historian J. R. Pole. After noting that some of the language proposed by Jefferson was rejected by his colleagues, Pole says:

> The approved passages are not free from problems of interpretation. Certainly Jefferson himself did not believe that all men had been created with equal endowments of virtue, intelligence, or natural skills. Yet his statement in its clearest sense was undoubtedly universal; it spoke of men as individuals, not as groups or nations. Only in respect of certain rights could they be thought of as equals, and it was no part of the business of a declaration of national independence to enter into a philosophical disquisition on the concept of rights. Rights could be thought of as a sort of invisible essence, as attributes inseparable from the persons to whom they adhered; but while people differed from one another in shape, size, skill, colour, and every conceivable attribute, their rights remained utterly constant, unchanged and unaffected by these differences among the people they lived in.
>
> There were strong contemporary reasons for regarding the Declaration as a universal pronouncement. Ideas of equality among individuals had been common currency for years—as Daniel Leonard had remarked in disapproval. The sheer lack of qualification lent this meaning to Jefferson's language. And yet, although the universal ist interpretation was in many ways the most obvious and easiest to the common mind, and was consonant with much current popular philosophy, its claims

were remarkably bold. It swept away all considerations of time, place, and circumstance. It ignored differences of culture, religion, or morals and presupposed that individual members of different civilisations in different historical periods shared the same values and moral perceptions. Jefferson aimed, as he remarked half a century later, to express "the common sense of the subject." But it was not the only philosophically available common sense. More than a quarter-century had elapsed since the publication of Montesquieu's *De l'esprit des lois*, possibly the most influential work of modern political science known to Jefferson's generation. Both in his book and in his *Lettres persanes*, Montesquieu had diffused among cultivated readers a new kind of moral and cultural relativism, which related laws, customs, and morals to circumstances specific to different civilisations. Alternative views were thus certainly available; and the forms of cultural relativism would soon revive in the new United States of America with the advance of an increasingly ominous differentiation between North and South.

The universalist sense of the Declaration of Independence was the easiest, the most popular, and with the passage of time the only sense in which it was commonly understood. Reformers from that time forth made it their own. From its earliest beginnings in the national period, the antislavery movement adopted the Declaration and held it forth as the definitive American principle, the justification for the independent existence of the United States. The popularity of this interpretation was attested by the fact that when nineteenth-century apologists for slavery attacked the doctrine of human equality, they denied the assertions with which the Declaration began. But they did not as a rule deny that the language carried a universalist and individualist meaning.

A less universal version of the Preamble was available to contemporaries, however. The signers of the Declaration could reasonably have been considered to have committed themselves to nothing more sweeping than the view that one people was the equal of another; and this view had the advantages not only of uniting Americans against Britain without committing them to dangerous innovations at home, but of being consistent with recent American arguments on legislative power. Once British policies had forced Americans to admit that they no longer formed a part of the British people, and that by virtue of their history and their own choice they constituted a people among themselves, it followed that the British could no more make laws for the colonies than the colonies could for Britain—or, to take a popular example, than the Scottish Parliament could have done for England before the Act of Union. There are good reasons for thinking that in spite of its less explicit and more limited implications, this alternative reading of the views that were expected to have practical consequences would have been accepted by Jefferson and his colleagues. Jefferson's own pamphlet, *A Summary View of the Rights of British America,* had recently made this very point; John Adams and James Wilson had independently arrived at the same conclusion. The opening sentences of the Declaration of Independence gave support to this reading by specific reference to the separation of one people from another and to their assumption of a "separate and equal station." That was the practical issue, and it was to justify that step that Congress appealed to "the opinions of mankind."[2]

I must record the fact that I am deeply in debt to Ross M. Lence of the political science faculty of the University of Houston for disciplining my thought on the interpretation of the Declaration of Independence.

Notes

1. Charles S. Hyneman, "The Ideological Foundations of Republican Government," Bicentennial of the U.S. Constitution Lecture Series (Bloomington, Ind.: Poynter Center, Indiana University, October 1983). Used with the permission of The Poynter Center for the Study of Ethics and American Institutions, Indiana University.

2. J. R. Pole, *The Pursuit of Equality in American History* (Berkeley: University of California Press, 1978), pp. 53–55. Used with the permission of Regents of the University of California and the University of California Press.

Robert Coram on Equality

Chapter 4 of a small book entitled *Political Inquiries,*
published in 1791 and reprinted in full in
Charles S. Hyneman and Donald S. Lutz, eds., *American
Political Writing during the Founding Era, 1760–1805,*
vol. 2 (Indianapolis: Liberty Press, 1983), pp. 756–811.

That the system of education should be equal is evident, since the rights given up in the state of nature and for which education is the substitute were equal. But as I know it will be objected by some that the natural inequality of the human intellect will obviate any attempt to diffuse knowledge equally, it seems necessary to make some inquiry concerning the natural equality of men.

That all men are by nature equal was once the fashionable phrase of the times, and men gloried in this equality and really believed it, or else they acted their parts to the life. Latterly, however, this notion is laughed out of countenance, and some very grave personages have not scrupled to assert that as we have copied the English in our form of federal government, we ought to imitate them in the establishment of a nobility also.

For my part, I do believe that if there was any necessity for two distinct hereditary orders of men in a society that men would have been created subordinate to such necessity and would at their birth be possessed of certain characteristic marks by which each class would be distinguished. However, as much has been said of late upon grades and gradations in the human species, I will endeavor to add my mite to the public stock.

In the dark ages of the world it was necessary that the people should believe their rulers to be a superior race of beings to themselves, in order that they should obey the absurd laws of their tyrants without "scrutinizing too nicely into the reasons of making them." As neither the governors nor governed understood any other principle of legislation than that of fear, it was necessary in order that the people should fear their rulers to believe them of a superior race to themselves.

Hence in the Jewish theocracy their rulers came in under a *jure divino* title, consecrated and anointed by the Deity himself. Hence the Mexican emperors were descended in a direct line from the sun, and in order to conduct the farce completely the descendants of the female line only inherited, in order that the blood line of the sun might never be lost. This was a master stroke of policy, perhaps never equalled in the eastern world, but it sufficiently shows that the emperors were apprehensive that if the people suspected an extinction of the blood line that they would conclude they were governed by men like themselves, which would be subversive of the principle of fear on which their government was erected.

But until the light of letters be again extinct, vain will be the attempt to erect a government on the single principle of fear or to introduce a nobility in America. If the Americans could be brought seriously to believe that by giving a few hereditary titles to some of their people, such people would immediately upon their being invested with such titles become metamorphosed into a superior race of beings, an attempt for a nobility might succeed.

But to return to our inquiry—If an elegant silver vase and some ore of the same metal were shown to a person ignorant of metals, it would not require much argument to convince him that the vase could never be produced from the ore. Such is the mode of reasoning upon the inequality of the human species. Effects purely artificial have been ascribed to nature, and the man of letters who from his cradle to his grave has trod the paths of art is compared with the untutored Indian and wretched African in whom slavery has deadened all the springs of the soul.

And the result of this impartial and charitable investigation is that there is an evident gradation in the intellectual faculties of the human species. There are various grades in the human mind[—this] is the fashionable phrase of the times. Scarce a superficial blockhead is to be met with but stuns you with a string of trite commonplace observations upon gradation, and no doubt thinks himself *in primo gradu* or at the top of the ladder.

Nature is always various in different species, and except in cases of *lusus natura*, always uniform in the same species. In all animals, from the most trifling insect to the whale and elephant, there is an evident uniformity and equality through every species. Where this equality is not to be found in the human species it is to be attributed either to climate, habit, or education, or perhaps to all. It must be obvious to every intelligent person the effect which habit alone has upon men. Awkward boobies have been taken from the plough-trail into the Continental army in the late war and after a few campaigns have returned home, to the surprise and admiration of their acquaintances, elegant, ornamental, and dignified characters. Such astonishing metamorphoses have been produced by the army that to habit alone may be ascribed all the inequality to be found in the human species.

If then education alone (for in this sense, the army may be properly called a school) is capable of producing such astonishing effects, what may not be ascribed to it when united with climate? Indeed we have numberless commonplace observations which have been always read as true and which are entirely founded upon this idea of equality in the intellectual faculties of the human race. Take the following—The minds of children are like blank paper, upon which you may write any characters you please. But what tends most to establish this idea of natural equality [is that] we find it always uniform in the savage race.

Now if there was a natural inequality in the human mind, would it not be as conspicuous in the savage as in the civilized state? The contrary of which is evident to every observer acquainted with the American Indians. Among those people all the gifts of Providence are in common. We do not see, as in civilized nations, part of the citizens sent to colleges to learn to cheat the rest of their liberties who are condemned to be hewers of wood and drawers of water. The mode of acquiring information, which is common to one, is common to all; hence we find a striking equality in form, size, and intellectual faculties nowhere to be found in civilized nations.

It is only in civilized nations where extremes are to be found in the human species—it is here where wealthy and dignified mortals roll along the streets in all the parade and trappings of royalty, while the lower class are not half so well fed as the horses of the former. It is this cruel inequality which has given rise to the epithets of nobility, vulgar, mob, canaille, etc. and the degrading, but common observation—Man differs more from man, than man from beast—The difference is purely artificial. Thus do men create an artificial inequality among themselves and then cry out it is all natural.

If we would give ourselves time to consider, we would find an idea of natural intellectual equality everywhere predominant but more particularly in free countries. The trial by jury is a strong proof of this idea in that nation; otherwise would they have suffered the unlettered peasant to decide against lawyers and judges? Is it not here taken for granted that the generality of men, although they are ignorant of the phrases and technical terms of the law, have notwithstanding sufficient mother wit to distinguish between right and wrong, which is all the lawyer with his long string of cases and reports is able to do? From whence also arises our notion of common sense? Is it not from an idea that the bulk of mankind possess what is called common understanding?

This common understanding must be supposed equal, or why should we apply the term common which implies equality? But it will perhaps be objected that the minds of some men are capable of greater improvement than others, which daily experience testifies: to which I answer that there is perhaps as great a variety in the texture of the human mind as in the countenances of men. If this be admitted, the absurdity of judging of the genius of boys by the advances they make in any particular science will be evident. But a variety is by no means inconsistent with an equality in the human intellect. And although there are instances of men who by mere dint of unassisted genius have arose to excellence, while others have been so deficient in mental powers as not to be capable of improvement from the combined efforts of art, yet when we enumerate all the idiots and sublime geniuses in the world, they will be found too few in number when compared with the rest of mankind to invalidate the general rule that all men are by nature equal.

But why should a strict mathematical equality be thought necessary among men, when no such thing is to be found in nature? In the vegetable creation, the generality of plants arrive to perfection, some reach only half way, and some are blights, yet the vegetable creation is perfect. The soil is to plants what government is to man. Different soils will produce the same species of vegetables in different degrees of perfection, but there will be an equality in the perfection of vegetables produced by the same soil in the same degree of cultivation. Thus governments which afford equal rights to the subjects will produce men naturally equal; that is, there will be the same equality in such men as is to be found in all the productions of nature. As one soil, by manuring it in patches, will produce vegetables in different degrees of perfection, so governments, which afford different privileges to different classes of people will produce men as effectually unequal as if the original germ of stamina of production was essentially different.

The notion of a natural inequality among men has been so generally adopted that it has created numerous obstacles to the investigation of their rights and biased the most discerning of modern writers. The Abbe Raynal, whose philanthropy I revere and of whose works I am far from being a willing critic, seems to have adopted this erroneous opinion.

"It has been said," says the Abbe, in his *Revolution in America*, "that we are all born equal; that is not so—that we had all the same rights; I am ignorant of what are rights, where there is an inequality of talents, of strength, and no security or sanction—that nature offered to us all the same dwelling, and the same resources; that is not so—that we were all endowed indiscriminately with the same means of defense; that is not so; and I know not in what sense it can be true that we all enjoy the same qualities of mind and body. There is amongst men an original inequality for which there is no remedy. It must last forever, and all that can be obtained by the best legislation is not to destroy it but to prevent the abuse of it.

"But in making distinctions among her children like a stepmother, in creating some children strong and others weak, has not nature herself formed the germ or principal of tyranny? I do not think it can be denied, especially if we look back to a time anterior to all legislation, a time in which man will be seen as passionate and as void of reason as a brute."

But how is it that we are not all born equal? There may be a difference between a child of a nobleman and that of a peasant, but will there not also be an inequality between the produce of seeds collected from the same plant and sown in different soils? Yes, but the inequality is artificial, not natural. It has been already observed that there is a striking equality in form, size, and intellectual faculties among the American Indians nowhere to be found in what we call civilized nations. Men are equal where they enjoy equal rights. Even a mathematical equality in powers among men would not necessarily secure their rights.

It had escaped the Abbe's reflection that nature, when she formed more men than two, formed the germ or principle of tyranny as effectually as when she created one man of double powers to another, for among three men of equal powers two could as effectually overpower the third as one man of six feet could overcome one of three. But although a mathematical equality among men neither exists nor is necessary, yet the generality of men educated under equal circumstances possess equal powers. This is the equality to be found in all the productions of nature, the equality and the only equality necessary to the happiness of man.

The inhabitants of the United States are more upon an equality in stature and powers of body and mind than the subjects of any government in Europe. And of the United States, the states of New England, whose governments by charter verged nearest to democracies, enjoy the most perfect equality. Those who live ashore are all legislators and politicians and those who follow the sea are all captains and owners; yet their governments are orderly and their ships navigated with as much success as if they were commanded with all the etiquette and subordination of royal navies. But though the constitution of the New England states were democratical, yet their laws were chiefly borrowed from the British code, many of which were unequal, such as vagrant acts, acts which confer rights of residence and citizenship, and the like—hence the equality of the citizens of New England, though striking when compared with any of the European governments, is not strictly natural. But among the American Indians, where no vestige of European absurdity is found interwoven in their laws, where they are governed by the plain and equitable code of nature, here is perfect natural equality.

The Abbe Raynal seems to be mistaken in his opinion concerning the origin of government. Speaking of the miseries to which man is subject in his civilized state, he says, "In this point of view, man appears more miserable and more wicked than a beast. Different species of beasts subsist on different species, but societies of men have never ceased to attack each other. Even in the same society, there is no condition but devours and is devoured, whatever may have been or are the forms of government or artificial equality which have been opposed to the primitive and natural inequality."

Men educated under bad governments, who see nothing but vice and infamy around them, who behold hardened wretches falling victims to the laws daily, are apt to conclude that man is naturally wicked—that in a state of nature, he is a stranger to morality, he is barbarous and savage, the weak always falling a prey to the strong—that government was instituted to protect the weak and to restrain the bold and to bring them more upon an equality.

But this is all a mistake—the man of America is a living proof to the contrary. He is innocent and spotless when compared with the inhabitants of civilized nations. He has not yet learned the art to cheat, although the traders have imposed upon him by every base and dirty fraud which civilized ingenuity could invent, selling him guns which are more likely to kill the person who fires them than the object at which they are presented; and hatchets without a particle of steel—incapable of bearing an edge or answering any use. I have seen whole invoices of goods, to a very considerable amount imported for the Indian trade, in which there was not an article which was not a palpable cheat.

Some excuse indeed seems necessary to those who have brought men under the yoke of cruel and arbitrary governments, and nothing is more easy than to say, it is all their own faults; that is, the faults of the people. They had given themselves up to the full possession of their unruly passions, appetites, and desires, every man tyrannizing over his neighbor. Government, therefore, arose out of necessity. This they will assert with as much confidence and maintain with as much obstinacy as if, forsooth, they had been personally present at the first conventions of men in a state of nature—and although no vestige is to be found of the foundation of any of the governments now existing being laid in any such convention, and although the conduct of individuals in those societies which approach nearest to the state of nature are so very far from supporting this opinion that they rather teach us to believe that men excel in wickedness in proportion to their civilization.

Therefore, instead of supposing with Abbe Raynal a primitive inequality which was found necessary to be lessened by the artificial equality opposed to it in different forms of government, we will suppose a primitive equality, and this equality to be disturbed and broken by an external force, not by members of the same society opposed to each other, but the conquest of one society by another, when the conquering society became the governors and the conquered society the governed.

This is clearly the case in regard to the English government, which we know was founded by conquest, and which Mr. Blackstone, with much eloquence but more sophistry, would fain persuade us had a much more equitable origin. The English, indeed, seem in their theory of the gradation of the human species to have forgotten the state of their ancestors when conquered by the

Romans—a rude and barbarous people, dwelling in caverns, feeding on roots, their only clothing the uncouth representation of the sun, moon and stars, daubed in barbarous characters on their skins; yet the descendants of these wretched savages pretend that there is an evident gradation in the intellectual faculties of the human species. Since, therefore, men are naturally equal, it follows that the mode of education should be equal also.

It is generally observed that most of the American legislatures are composed of lawyers and merchants. What is the reason? Because the farmer has no opportunity of getting his son instructed without sending him to a college, the expense of which is more than the profits of his farm. An equal representation is absolutely necessary to the preservation of liberty. But there can never be an equal representation until there is an equal mode of education for all citizens. For although a rich farmer may, by the credit of his possessions, help himself into the legislature, yet if through a deficiency in his education he is unable to speak with propriety, he may see the dearest interest of his country basely bartered away and be unable to make any effort except his single vote against it. Education, therefore, to be generally useful should be brought to every man's door.

James Madison Proposes a Bill of Rights

Statement in the House of Representatives supporting
proposed amendments to the U.S. Constitution, 8 June
1789. From *Annals of Congress* 1 (1789–90): 436–41.

The first of these amendments [which I have now laid before you, said Mr.
Madison,] relates to what may be called a bill of rights. I will own that I never
considered this provision so essential to the Federal Constitution as to make it
improper to ratify it until such an amendment was added; at the same time, I
always conceived that in a certain form and to a certain extent, such a provision
was neither improper nor altogether useless. I am aware that a great number of
the most respectable friends to the Government and champions for republican liberty have thought such a provision not only unnecessary, but even
improper; nay, I believe some have gone so far as to think it even dangerous.

Some policy has been made use of, perhaps, by gentlemen on both sides of
the question. I acknowledge the ingenuity of those arguments which were
drawn against the Constitution by a comparison with the policy of Great
Britain in establishing a declaration of rights, but there is too great a difference
in the case to warrant the comparison; therefore, the arguments drawn from
that source were in a great measure inapplicable. In the declaration of rights
which that country has established, the truth is, they have gone no farther
than to raise a barrier against the power of the Crown; the power of the
Legislature is left altogether indefinite. Although I know whenever the great
rights, the trial by jury, freedom of the press, or liberty of conscience, come in
question in that body, the invasion of them is resisted by able advocates, yet
their Magna Charta does not contain any one provision for the security of

those rights respecting which the people of America are most alarmed. The freedom of the press and rights of conscience, those choicest privileges of the people, are unguarded in the British Constitution.

But although the case may be widely different, and it may not be thought necessary to provide limits for the legislative power in that country, yet a different opinion prevails in the United States. The people of many States have thought it necessary to raise barriers against power in all forms and departments of Government, and I am inclined to believe, if once bills of rights are established in all the States as well as the Federal Constitution, we shall find that, although some of them are rather unimportant, yet upon the whole they will have a salutary tendency. It may be said, in some instances, they do no more than state the perfect equality of mankind. This, to be sure, is an absolute truth, yet it is not absolutely necessary to be inserted at the head of the Constitution. In other instances, they specify positive rights which may seem to result from the nature of the compact. Trial by jury cannot be considered as a natural right, but a right resulting from a social compact which regulates the action of the community, but is as essential to secure the liberty of the people as any one of the pre-existent rights of nature. In other instances, they lay down dogmatic maxims with respect to the construction of the Government, declaring that the Legislative, Executive, and Judicial branches shall be kept separate and distinct. Perhaps the best way of securing this in practice is, to provide such checks as will prevent the encroachment of the one upon the other.

But, whatever may be the form which the several States have adopted in making declarations in favor of particular rights, the great object in view is to limit and qualify the powers of Government, by excepting out of the grant of power those cases in which the Government ought not to act or to act only in a particular mode. They point these exceptions sometimes against the abuse of the Executive power, sometimes against the Legislative, and in some cases against the community itself, or, in other words, against the majority in favor of the minority.

In our Government it is, perhaps, less necessary to guard against the abuse in the Executive Department than any other, because it is not the stronger branch of the system, but the weaker. It therefore must be levelled against the Legislative, for it is the most powerful and most likely to be abused, because it is under the least control. Hence, so far as a declaration of rights can tend to prevent the exercise of undue power, it cannot be doubted but such declaration is proper. But I confess that I do conceive, that in a Government modified like this of the United States, the great danger lies rather in the abuse of the community than in the Legislative body. The prescriptions in favor of liberty ought to be levelled against that quarter where the greatest danger lies, namely, that which possesses the highest prerogative of power. But this is not found in either the Executive or Legislative departments of Government, but in the body of the people, operative by the majority against the minority.

It may be thought that all paper barriers against the power of the community are too weak to be worthy of attention. I am sensible they are not so strong as to satisfy gentlemen of every description who have seen and examined thoroughly the texture of such a defence; yet, as they have a tendency to impress some degree of respect for them, to establish the public opinion in their favor and rouse the attention of the whole community, it may be one means to control the majority from those acts to which they might be otherwise inclined.

It has been said, by way of objection to a bill of rights, by many respectable gentlemen out of doors, and I find opposition on the same principles likely to be made by gentlemen on this floor, that they are unnecessary articles of a Republican Government, upon the presumption that the people have those rights in their own hands and that is the proper place for them to rest. It would be a sufficient answer to say that this objection lies against such provisions under the State Governments as well as under the General Government, and there are, I believe, but few gentlemen who are inclined to push their theory so far as to say that a declaration of rights in those cases is either ineffectual or improper. It has been said that in the Federal Government they are unnecessary because the powers are enumerated, and it follows that all that are not granted by the Constitution are retained; that the Constitution is a bill of powers, the great residuum being the rights of the people; and therefore, a bill of rights cannot be so necessary as if the residuum was thrown into the hands of the Government. I admit that these arguments are not entirely without foundation; but they are not conclusive to the extent which has been supposed. It is true, the powers of the General Government are circumscribed, they are directed to particular objects. But even if Government keeps within those limits, it has certain discretionary powers with respect to the means which may admit of abuse to a certain extent, in the same manner as the powers of the State Governments under their constitutions may [admit of abuse] to an indefinite extent. [This is so] because in the Constitution of the United States there is a clause granting to Congress the power to make all laws which shall be necessary and proper for carrying into execution all the powers vested in the Government of the United States or in any department or officer thereof. This enables them to fulfill every purpose for which the Government was established. Now, may not laws be considered necessary and proper by Congress (for it is for them to judge of the necessity and propriety to accomplish those special purposes which they may have in contemplation), which laws in themselves are neither necessary nor proper, as well as improper laws could be enacted by the State Legislatures for fulfilling the more extended objects of those Governments?

I will state an instance, which I think in point and proves that this might be the case. The General Government has a right to pass all laws which shall be necessary to collect its revenue; the means for enforcing the collection are within the direction of the Legislature. May not general warrants be considered necessary for this purpose, as well as for some purposes which it was supposed at the framing of their constitutions the State Governments had in view? If there was reason for restraining the State Governments from exercising this power, there is like reason for restraining the Federal Government.

It may be said, indeed it has been said, that a bill of rights is not necessary because the establishment of this Government has not repealed those declarations of rights which are added to the several State constitutions; that those rights of the people which had been established by the most solemn act, could not be annihilated by a subsequent act of that people, who meant and declared at the head of the instrument that they ordained and established a new system for the express purpose of securing to themselves and posterity the liberties they had gained by an arduous conflict.

I admit the force of this observation, but I do not look upon it to be conclusive. In the first place, it is too uncertain ground to leave this provision upon, if a provision is at all necessary to secure rights so important as many of those I have mentioned are conceived to be by the public in general as well as [by] those in particular who opposed the adoption of this Constitution. Besides, some States have no bills of rights. There are others provided with very defective ones. And there are others whose bills of rights are not only defective but absolutely improper; instead of securing some in the full extent which republican principles would require, they limit them too much to agree with the common ideas of liberty.

It has been objected also against a bill of rights that, by enumerating particular exceptions to the grant of power, it would disparage those rights which were not placed in that enumeration; and it might follow by implication, that those rights which were not singled out, were intended to be assigned into the hands of the General Government, and were consequently insecure. This is one of the most plausible arguments I have ever heard urged against the admission of a bill of rights into this system; but, I conceive that it may be guarded against. I have attempted to, as gentlemen may see by turning to the last clause of the fourth resolution.[1]

It has been said that it is unnecessary to load the Constitution with this provision, because it was not found effectual in the constitutions of the particular States. It is true, there are a few particular States in which some of the most valuable articles have not, at one time or other, been violated, but it does not follow but they may have, to a certain degree, a salutary effect, against the abuse of power. If they are incorporated into the Constitution, independent tribunals of justice will consider themselves in a peculiar manner the guardians of those rights. They will be an impenetrable bulwark against every assumption of power in the Legislative or Executive. They will be naturally led to resist every encroachment upon rights expressly stipulated for in the Constitution by the declaration of rights. Besides this security, there is a great probability that such a declaration in the federal system would be enforced. [This is so] because the State Legislatures will jealously and closely watch the operations of this Government, and be able to resist with more effect every assumption of power than any other power on earth can do; and the greatest opponents to a Federal Government admit the State Legislatures to be sure guardians of the people's liberty. I conclude, from this view of the subject, that it will be proper in itself, and highly politic for the tranquility of the public mind and the stability of the Government, that we should offer something in the form I have proposed to be incorporated in the system of Government as a declaration of the rights of the people. . . .

I wish also, in revising the Constitution, we may throw into that section which interdicts the abuse of certain powers in the State Legislatures, some other provisions of equal if not greater importance than those already made. The words, "No State shall pass any bill of attainder, *ex post facto* law," &c., were wise and proper restrictions in the Constitution. I think there is more danger of those powers being abused by the State Governments than by the Government of the United States. The same may be said of other powers which they possess, if not controlled by the general principle that laws are unconstitutional which infringe the rights of the community. I should, therefore, wish to extend this interdiction and add, as I have stated in the 5th resolution, that no State shall violate the equal right of conscience, freedom of the press, or trial by jury in criminal cases; because it is proper that every Government should be disarmed of powers which trench upon those particular rights. I know, in some of the State constitutions, the power of the Government is controlled by such a declaration; but others are not. I cannot see any reason against obtaining even a double security on those points. And nothing can give a more sincere proof of the attachment of those who opposed this Constitution to these great and important rights than to see them join in obtaining the security I have now proposed, because it must be admitted on all hands that the State Governments are as liable to attack these invaluable privileges as the General Government is, and therefore ought to be as cautiously guarded against. . . .

I find from looking into the amendments proposed by the State conventions that several are particularly anxious that it should be declared in the Constitution that the powers not therein delegated should be reserved to the several States. Perhaps other words may define this more precisely than the whole of the instrument now does. I admit they may be deemed unnecessary;

but there can be no harm in making such a declaration, if gentlemen will allow the fact is as stated. I am sure I understand it so, and do therefore propose it.

These are the points on which I wish to see a revision of the Constitution take place. How far they will accord with the sense of this body, I cannot take upon me absolutely to determine; but I believe every gentleman will readily admit that nothing is in contemplation, so far as I have mentioned, that can endanger the beauty of the Government in any one important feature, even in the eyes of its most sanguine admirers. I have proposed nothing that does not appear to me as proper in itself, or eligible as patronised by a respectable number of our fellow-citizens; and if we can make the Constitution better in the opinion of those who are opposed to it, without weakening its frame or abridging its usefulness in the judgment of those who are attached to it, we act the part of wise and liberal men to make such alterations as shall produce that effect.

Note

1. The final paragraph of the fourth resolution reads: "The exceptions here or elsewhere in the Constitution, made in favor of particular rights, shall not be so construed as to diminish the just importance of other rights retained by the people, or as to enlarge the powers delegated by the Constitution; but either as actual limitations of such powers, or as inserted merely for greater caution."

APPENDIX 5

The Sedition Act of 1798

From *The Statutes at Large of the United States of America,*
vol. 1 (Boston: Charles C. Little and James Brown, 1845),
p. 596.

Sec. 1. *Be it enacted . . .* That if any persons shall unlawfully combine or conspire together, with intent to oppose any measure or measures of the government of the United States, which are or shall be directed by proper authority, or to impede the operation of any law of the United States, or to intimidate or prevent any person holding a place or office in or under the government of the United States, from undertaking, performing or executing his trust or duty; and if any person or persons, with intent as aforesaid, shall counsel, advise or attempt to procure any insurrection, riot, unlawful assembly, or combination, whether such conspiracy, threatening, counsel, advice, or attempt shall have the proposed effect or not, he or they shall be deemed guilty of a high misdemeanor and on conviction, before any court of the United States having jurisdiction thereof, shall be punished by a fine not exceeding five thousand dollars, and by imprisonment during a term not less than six months nor exceeding five years; and further, at the discretion of the court may be holden to find sureties for his good behavior in such sum, and for such time, as the said court may direct.

Sec. 2. That if any person shall write, print, utter, or publish or shall cause or procure to be written, printed, uttered or published, or shall knowingly and willingly assist or aid in writing, printing, uttering or publishing any false, scandalous and malicious writing or writings against the government of the United States, or either house of the Congress of the United States, or the President of the United States, with intent to defame the said government, or either house of the said Congress, or the said President, or to bring them, or either of them, into contempt or disrepute; or to excite against them, or either or any of them, the hatred of the good people of the United States or to stir up sedition within the United States, or to excite any unlawful combinations therein, for opposing or resisting any law of the United States, or any act of the President of the United States, done in pursuance of any such law, or of the powers in him vested by the Constitution of the United States, or to resist, oppose, or defeat any such law or act, or to aid, encourage or abet any hostile designs of any foreign nation against the United States, their people or government, then such person, being thereof convicted before any court of the United States having jurisdiction thereof, shall be punished by a fine not exceeding two thousand dollars, and by imprisonment not exceeding two years.

Sec. 3. That if any person shall be prosecuted under this act, for the writing or publishing of any libel aforesaid, it shall be lawful for the defendant, upon the trial of the cause, to give in evidence in his defence, the truth of the matter contained in the publication charged as a libel. And the jury who shall try the cause, shall have a right to determine the law and the fact, under the direction of the court, as in other cases.

Sec. 4. That this act shall continue to be in force until March 3, 1801, and no longer: *Provided*, That the expiration of the act shall not prevent or defeat a prosecution and punishment of any offence against the law, during the time it shall be in force.

Approved July 14, 1798

Excerpts from Debate in the House of Representatives on the Sedition Bill, July 1798

Remarks by John Nicholas of Virginia, Harrison Gray Otis
of Massachusetts, Albert Gallatin of Pennsylvania, and
Robert Goodloe Harper of South Carolina, taken from the
Annals of Congress 8 (1798–99): 2139–42, 2145–48,
2156–57, 2164–65, 2167–68. Nicholas and Gallatin were
Republican leaders in the House; Otis and Harper
were leading Federalists.

Mr. NICHOLAS rose, he said, to ask an explanation of the principles on which this bill is founded. He confessed it was strongly impressed upon his mind, that it was not within the powers of the House to act upon this subject. He looked in vain amongst the enumerated powers given to Congress in the Constitution for an authority to pass a law like the present; but he found what he considered an express prohibition against passing it. He found that, in order to quiet the alarms of the people of the United States with respect to the silence of the Constitution as to the liberty of the press . . . that one of the first acts of this Government was to propose certain amendments to the Constitution. . . . It is now expressly declared by that instrument "that the powers not delegated to the United States by the Constitution nor prohibited by it to the States, are reserved to the States respectively or to the people;" and also, "that Congress shall make no law abridging the freedom of speech, or of the press." . . .

Gentlemen have said that this bill is not to restrict the liberty of the press but its licentiousness. He wished gentlemen to inform him where they drew the line between this liberty and licentiousness of which they speak. . . . Will they say the one is truth and the other falsehood! Gentlemen cannot believe for a moment that such a definition will satisfy the inquiry. The great difficulty which has existed in all free Governments would, long since, have been done away, if it could have been effected by a simple declaration of this kind. It has been the object of all regulations with respect to the press, to destroy the only means by which the people can examine and become acquainted with the conduct of persons employed in their Government. If there could be safety in adopting the principle, that no man should publish what is false, there certainly could be no objection to it. But it was not the intention of the people of this country to place any power of this kind in the hands of the General Government—for this plain reason, the persons who would have to preside at trials of this sort, would themselves be parties, or at least they would be so far interested in the issue that the truth or falsehood of the matter would not be safe in their hands . . . Gentlemen exclaim, what! can anyone be found to advocate the publication of lies and calumny? He would make no answer to inquiries of this sort, because he did not believe he could be suspected of being an advocate for either. But, in his opinion, this was a most serious subject; it is not lying that will be suppressed, but the truth. If this bill be passed into a law, the people will be deprived of that information on public measures, which they have a right to receive, and which is the life and support of a free Government; for, if printers are to be subject to prosecution for every paragraph which appears in their papers, that the eye of a jealous Government can torture into an offence against this law, and to the heavy penalties here provided, it cannot be expected that they will exercise that freedom and spirit which it is desirable should actuate them; especially when they would have to be tried by judges appointed by the President, and by juries selected by the Marshal, who also receives his appointment from the President, all whose feelings would, of course, be inclined to commit the offender if possible. . . .

Mr. N. hoped there was no necessity for examining the opinions of the gentleman from South Carolina [Robert Goodloe Harper] as to the common law being part of the law of the United States. He should be glad to know where gentlemen found an account of their having so adopted it. Do gentlemen suppose that, in adopting the Constitution, the United States adopted the common law of all the States, which is so various that he would venture to say no man perfectly knew it at the time. . . . The common law of England has undergone various improvements and modifications in the several States, which it would not be supposed would be rejected by the Convention, who formed the Constitution, in silence. . . . If the common law was not adopted by the Constitution, and does not form a part of it, where is the rule by which to ascertain where the liberty of the press ends, and its licentiousness begins? If gentlemen say it is adopted by the Constitution, it must remain unchangeable, and there could be no authority for passing this law. . . .

Mr. OTIS said the professions of attachment to the Constitution, made by the gentleman from Virginia, are certainly honorable to him; and he could not believe that an attachment so deeply engrafted, as he states his to be, would be shaken by this bill. The gentleman had caught an alarm from the first suggestion of a sedition bill, which had not yet subsided; and though the present bill is perfectly harmless, and contains no provision which is not practised upon under the laws of the several States in which gentlemen had been educated, and from which they had drawn most of their ideas of jurisprudence, yet the gentleman continues to be dissatisfied with it.

The objections of the gentleman from Virginia, he believed, might be reduced to two inquiries: In the first place, had the Constitution given Congress cognizance over the offences described in the bill prior to the adoption of the amendments . . . ? and, if Congress had that cognizance before that time, have those amendments taken it away? With respect to the first question, it must be allowed that every independent Government has a right to preserve and defend itself against injuries and outrages which endanger its existence; for, unless it has this power, it is unworthy of the name of a free Government, and must either fall or be subordinate to some other protection. Now some of the offences delineated in the bill are of this description. Unlawful combinations to oppose the measures of Government, to intimidate its officers, and to excite insurrections, are acts which tend directly to the destruction of the Constitution, and there could be no doubt that the guardians of that Constitution are bound to provide against them. And if gentlemen would agree that these were acts of a criminal nature, it follows that all means calculated to produce these effects, whether by speaking, writing, or printing, were also criminal. From the nature of things, therefore, the national government is invested with a power to protect itself against outrages of this kind. . . . This essential right resulting from the spirit of the Constitution, was still more evident in the language of that instrument. The people of the individual States brought with them as a birthright into this country the common law of England, upon which all of them have founded their statute law. If it were not for this common law, many crimes which are committed in the United States would go unpunished. No State has enacted statutes for the punishment of all crimes which may be committed; yet in every State he presumed there was a Superior Court which claimed cognizance of all offences against good morals, and which restrained misdemeanors and opposition to the constituted authorities, under the sanction merely of the common law. When the people of the United States convened for the purpose of framing a federal compact, they were all habituated to this common law, to its usages, its maxims, and its definitions. It had been more or less explicitly recognized in the Constitution of every State, and in that of Maryland was declared to be the law of the land.

If, then, we find in an instrument digested by men who were all familiarized to the common law, not only that the distribution of power and the great objects to be provided for are congenial to that law, but that the terms and definitions by which those powers are described, have an evident allusion to it, and must otherwise be quite inexplicable, or at best of a very uncertain meaning, it will be natural to conclude that, in forming the Constitution, they kept in view the model of the common law, and that a safe recourse may be had to it in all cases that would otherwise be doubtful. Thus we shall find that one great end of this compact, as appears in the preamble, is the establishment of justice, and for this purpose a Judicial department is erected, whose powers are declared to "extend to all cases in law and equity, arising under the Constitution, the laws of the United States," &c. Justice, if the common law ideas of it are rejected, is susceptible of various constructions, but agreeably to the principles of that law, it affords redress for every injury, and provides a punishment for every crime that threatens to disturb the lawful operations of Government. Again, what is intended by "cases at law and equity arising under the Constitution," as distinguished from cases "arising under the laws of the United States?" What other law can be contemplated but common law; what sort of equity but that legal discretion which has been exercised in England from time immemorial, and is to be learnt in the books and reports of this country? . . .

Mr. OTIS contended that this construction of the Constitution was abundantly supported by the Act for establishing the Judicial Courts. That act, in describing certain powers of the District Court, contains this remarkable expression: "saving to suitors in all cases the right of a common law remedy, where the common law was competent to give it." . . .

It was, therefore, most evident to his mind, that the Constitution of the United States, prior to the amendments that have been added to it, secured to the National Government the cognizance of all the crimes enumerated in the bill, and it only remained to be considered whether those amendments divested it of this power. . . . The terms "freedom of speech and of the press," he supposed, were a phraseology perfectly familiar in the jurisprudence of every State, and of a certain and technical meaning. It was a mode of expression which we had borrowed from the only country in which it had been tolerated. . . . This freedom, said Mr. O., is nothing more than the liberty of writing, publishing, and speaking one's thoughts, under the condition of being answerable to the injured party, whether it be the Government or an individual, for false, malicious, and seditious expressions, whether spoken or written; and the liberty of the press is merely an exemption from all previous restraints. In support of this doctrine he quoted *Blackstone's Commentaries*, under the head of libels, and read an extract to prove that in England, formerly, the press was subject to a licenser; and that this restraint was afterward removed, by which means the freedom of the press was established. He would not, however, dwell upon the law of England, the authority of which it might suit the convenience of gentlemen to question; but he would demonstrate that although, in several of the State constitutions, the liberty of speech and of the press were guarded by the most express and unequivocal language, the Legislatures and Judicial departments of those States had adopted the definitions of the English law, and provided for the punishment of defamatory and seditious libels. [There follows a lengthy review of such state legislation.] ...

Mr. GALLATIN observed that the ... gentleman from Massachusetts (Mr. OTIS) had attempted to prove the constitutionality of the bill by asserting, in the first place, that the power to punish libels was originally vested in Congress by the Constitution, and, in the next place, that the [first] amendment to the Constitution ... had not deprived them of the power originally given. In order to establish his first position the gentleman had thought it sufficient to insist that the jurisdiction of the Courts of the United States extended to the punishment of offences at common law, that is to say, of offences not arising under the statutes and or laws of the Union—an assertion unfounded in itself, and which, if proven, would not support the point he endeavors to establish. That assertion was unfounded; for the judicial authority of those courts is, by the Constitution, declared to extend to cases of Admiralty, or affecting public Ministers; to suits between States, citizens of different States, or foreigners, and cases arising under the Constitution, laws, and treaties, *made* under the authority of that Constitution; excluding, therefore, cases not arising under either—cases arising under the common law. It was preposterous to suppose, with the gentleman from Massachusetts, that, in cases arising under the Constitution, were included offences at common law; for the cases meant were only, either such as might arise from any doubtful construction of the Constitution—for instance the constitutionality of a law—or those arising immediately under any specific power given or prohibition enjoined by the Constitution; such, for instance, as declaring a retrospective law of any State to be null and void. Nor was that gentleman more fortunate in his choice of arguments, when he thought he could derive any proofs in support of the supposed jurisdiction of the Federal Courts from the number of technical expressions in the Constitution ... which, as he supposed, recognized the common law. He had there confounded two very distinct ideas—the principles of the common law, and the jurisdiction of cases arising under it. That those principles were recognized in the cases where the court had jurisdiction was not denied; but such a jurisdiction could by no means extend the jurisdiction beyond the specific cases defined by the Constitution. But, had that gentleman succeeded in proving the existence of the jurisdiction of the Federal Courts over offences at common law, and more particularly over libels, he would thereby have adduced the strongest argument against the passing of this bill; for, if the jurisdiction did exist, where was the necessity of now giving it? ...

Mr. HARPER said that he should hardly expect, at so late an hour, to be indulged by the House in a detailed answer to the objections urged against this bill, even if he thought it necessary. He did not, however, think it necessary...; some few only, which he thought it important to controvert, had remained unanswered....

In the first place, gentlemen who oppose the bill had said that hitherto the Government of the United States had existed and prospered without a law of this kind, and then exultantly asked: "What change has now taken place to render such a law necessary?"... The change, in his opinion, consisted in this: that heretofore we had been at peace, and were now on the point of being driven into a war with a nation which openly boasts of its party among us, and its "diplomatic skill," as the most effectual means of bringing us to its own terms. Of the operations of this skill among us, by means of corrupt partisans and hired presses, he had no doubt; he was every day furnished with stronger reasons for believing in its existence, and saw stronger evidence of its systematic exertion. We knew its effects in other countries, where it had aided the progress of France, much more effectually than by force of her arms. He knew no reason why we should not (sic) harbor traitors in our bosom as well as other nations; and he did most firmly believe that France had a party in this country, small, indeed, and sure to be disgraced and destroyed as soon as its designs should become generally known, but active, artful, and determined, and capable, if it could remain concealed, of effecting infinite mischief....

The gentleman from Pennsyvania (Mr. GALLATIN) had gone a step further, Mr. H. said, in his opposition to this bill than the rest of its opposers. They had contended that it was contrary to the [first] amendment.... The gentleman from Pennsylvania had discovered that, independently of that amendment, Congress had no power to pass a law against sedition and libels none such being expressly given by the Constitution. But can there, said Mr. H., be so great an absurdity... as a Government which has no power to protect itself against sedition and libels? Has not the Constitution said that "Congress shall have power to make all laws which shall be necessary, or proper, for carrying into execution the foregoing powers, and all other powers vested by this Constitution in the Government of the United States, or in any department or officer thereof;" can the powers of a Government be carried into execution, if sedition for opposing its laws, and libels against its officers, itself, and its proceedings, are to pass unpunished?...

In the other objection, he admitted there was more plausibility; the objection founded on [the First Amendment]. He held this to be one of the most sacred parts of the Constitution, and one by which he would stand the longest and defend with the greatest zeal. But to what, he asked, did this clause amount? Did this liberty of the press include sedition and licentiousness? Did it authorize persons to throw, with impunity, the most violent abuse upon the

President and both Houses of Congress? . . . Every man possessed the liberty
of action; but if he used this liberty to the detriment of others, by attacking
their persons or destroying their property, he became liable to punishment for
this licentious abuse of his liberty. The liberty of the press stood on precisely
the same footing. Every man might publish what he pleased; but if he abused
this liberty so as to publish slanders against his neighbor, or false, scandalous,
and malicious libels against the magistrates, or the Government, he became
liable to punishment. What did the law provide? That if . . . any person should
publish any false, scandalous, and malicious libel against the President or
Congress, or either House of Congress, with intent to stir up sedition, or to
produce any other of the mischievous and wicked effects particularly described
in the bill, he should, on conviction before a jury, be liable to fine and
imprisonment. A jury is to try the offence, and they must determine from the
evidence and the circumstances of the case, first that the publication is *false*,
secondly that it is *scandalous*, thirdly that it is *malicious*, and fourthly that it
was made with the *intent* to do some one of the things particularly described in
the bill. If in any one of these points the proof should fail, the man must be
acquitted; and it is expressly provided that he may give the *truth* of the
publication in evidence as a justification. Such is the substance of this law. . . .

APPENDIX 7

The Reverend Joseph Lathrop on Industry and Frugality as Elements of a Virtuous Society

Two essays in a series titled *The Censor,* originally pub-
lished in 1786 and reprinted in Charles S. Hyneman and
Donald S. Lutz, eds., *American Political Writing during the
Founding Era, 1760–1805,* vol. 1 (Indianapolis: Liberty Press,
1983), pp. 661–64. Used with permission of Liberty
Fund, Inc., Indianapolis, Indiana.

The Censor, Number 3: Industry

But what are the virtues of immediate use to society, and of chief importance at the present day? *Industry* is undoubtedly one. This is a country which
affords all the means not only of subsistence, but of wealth. But means must
be applied or the end is not attained. Greater industry may be necessary here,
than in some other climes; but this is no unhappiness. A people that grow rich
suddenly and without much labour, soon become luxurious and effeminate.
They presently sink again into poverty, or their wealth is confined to a few.
They lose their strength and vigour and the spirit of liberty, and fall an easy
prey to the first powerful invader or ambitious usurper. A habit of industry is
first acquired by necessity, and, once acquired, it may continue for a while,
after the necessity abates, unless their circumstances alter too suddenly. It
strengthens the body, braces the mind, aids other virtues; it gives patience in
adversity, courage in danger, and perseverance in difficulty. No people ever
maintained their liberty long, after they ceased to be industrious, and became
dissolute and luxurious. Agriculture ought to be one main object of industry

in such a country, and at such a time as this. Our lands are our chief source of wealth; but lands uncultivated are like gold sleeping in the mines. It is culture only that makes them useful. Too great attention to commerce will soon introduce idleness and luxury; and though it may enrich a few particular persons, it will impoverish the country.

Our husbandry ought to be directed into such a channel, that after supplying our own necessary consumption, the surplus may bring us not merely luxuries, but such foreign articles as will be really useful, and a sufficiency of silver and gold for a medium. Grain of various kinds, flax, sheep, pork, beef, butter, and cheese are commodities that may be turned to much better advantage, than those cargoes of horses and lumber, which are shipped for the West-Indies, only to bring in upon us a flood of ardent spirits, to drown our vitals and our morals.

To agriculture we must join the necessary arts of life, and the more useful and important branches of manufacture. We may purchase many articles cheaper, than we can manufacture them: but if we purchase them, they must be paid for: if we make them they are our own. Manufactures will promote industry, and industry contributes to health, virtue, riches and population. If we purchase our cloathing one half of our women must be idle, or only trifling: how then will those young women who depend on their labour, procure the next suit when they have worn out the present? If we manufacture, our men will be employed in procuring and preparing the materials; and our women will not be under a necessity of spending five afternoons in a week in giving and receiving visits, and chatting round the tea-table. What they do is so much added to the wealth of the country. When industry becomes reputable among ladies in higher life, it will of course take place among all ranks. And the rosy cheek, the ruby lip, and the sparkling eye will then be deemed more beautiful, than the pale, sickly countenance. Vivacity, strength and activity will not then be thought too indelicate, coarse and masculine for a fine lady, nor will affected timidity, artificial faintings and laboured shrieks and startings be supposed to have charms.

The Censor, Number 4: Frugality

Industry and *frugality* are kindred virtues and similar in their principles and effects. They ought always to accompany each other and go hand in hand, for neither without the other can be a virtue, or answer any valuable purpose to the individual or to society. He that is laborious only that he may have the means of extravagance and profuseness; and he that is parsimonious only that he may live in laziness and indolence, are alike remote from virtue. Each is governed by his strongest passion, and enslaved to his predominant vice. To live sparingly for the sake of amassing a useless heap, is not *frugality*, but *sordidness*. To live within the bonds of nature, that we may enjoy better health and may be more free from worldly embarrassments, is *prudence*. To live frugally, that we may be just to all men; may do more good to the indigent, and may be more useful to society is *virtuous*. *Decency* and *propriety* ordinarily require, that we live according to our rank and ability. But there are times, when *patriotism* calls upon those in affluence and high life, to fall a little below the usual mark, that their example may encourage moderation among others. As private oeconomy enriches the individual, so the prevalence of it would enrich the community. A country so deeply in debt, and subjected to so great expences, as this country now is, should consider frugality as a cardinal virtue. Let it begin with particular persons and spread through the community; let it take place in families, nor be over looked in government; let it not be confined to the poorest, or the middle ranks; but appear among the rich and great. While the poor are frugal from *necessity,* and the common farmers and mechanics are frugal from *prudence,* let the opulent be frugal from *patriotism:* and if they would make their patriotism a still more excellent virtue, let the savings of extraordinary frugality be applied to some charitable purpose. For the rich no certain rules can be prescribed; their frugality must be voluntary and discretionary. People of moderate fortunes, and moderate incomes should aim at a regular conduct. Excuse a few hints, even though they may appear too trifling to be observed. If they appear worthy of notice, let them be carried into practice.

Spend not your money before you have earned it, nor promise it before you are sure of it. Promises made on other men's credit, or on mere contingencies are liable to fail. If you disappoint your neighbour often, you lose your credit, and his confidence, and perhaps provoke a suit, which breaks friendship, disturbs your peace, augments your expence, and throws your money into the hands of those, whom you chiefly envy. Estimate your probable incomes, making some allowance for disappointments, and let your expences fall so much short, that something may be left at the year's end. He that daily consumes the fruits of daily labour is unprepared for the day of misfortune. Most men, if they will live within the bounds of nature, may by moderate industry, provide for themselves and their families. It is always reputable to live moderately, when we have not the means of living splendidly. Compute the needless consumption of ardent spirits for one year, and will it not make a sum worth saving? The example of others is not the standard by which we are to judge of extravagance, but our own circumstances and abilities. That may be extravagance in one, that would be parsimony in another. Enter not into too close connections with those of superior fortunes, if they are disposed to live faster, than you can follow. Never make a vain ostentation of wealth, which you don't possess, nor live at other men's expence, so long as you can live at your own. Waste not in indulgence, that time which you owe to the duties of life, the culture of your mind, and the support and education of your family. Consume not in luxury the money, which you owe to your creditor or to the publick, or by which you might relieve your family from distress. When you see another grow rich, or *seem* to grow rich in any calling, conclude not that you could do the same, nor quit your own profession for one which you don't understand and have not the means of pursuing. Many have fallen by reaching at things too high for them. Lay out for yourself business to fill up your time, but not more than you can manage well. Be not in too great haste to be rich: The moderate profits of your own proper business are the surest, and the honest gains of industry and frugality are the most sweet, reputable and durable.

Index

CHARLES S. HYNEMAN was born in southern Indiana in 1900, educated at Indiana University (A.B.), the University of Illinois (Ph.D.), and the University of Pennsylvania. He taught at Syracuse University, the University of Illinois, Louisiana State University, Northwestern University, and Indiana University, where he was Distinguished Service Professor of Government. He held various executive positions in the federal government during World War II and was president of the American Political Science Association, 1961–62. He was author, coauthor, or coeditor of *Bureaucracy in a Democracy* (1950), *The Study of Politics* (1959), *The Supreme Court on Trial* (1963), *A Second Federalist* (1967), *Popular Government in America* (1968), and *American Political Writing during the Founding Era* (1983), among other books and articles. He died in 1985.

CHARLES E. GILBERT is professor emeritus of political science at Swarthmore College and author of books and articles on American politics, including *Governing the Suburbs* (1968).